Historic Goose Creek, South Carolina, 1670-1980

By

Michael J. Heitzler

Edited by

Richard N. Côté

Southern Historical Press, Inc.
Greenville, South Carolina

Copyright 1983
By: Southern Historical Press, Inc.

All rights reserved. No part of this publication may be reproduced, stored in a retrieval system, transmitted in any form, posted on to the web in any form or by any means without the prior written permission of the publisher.

Please direct all correspondence and orders to:

www.southernhistoricalpress.com
or
**SOUTHERN HISTORICAL PRESS, Inc.
PO BOX 1267
Greenville, SC   29601
southernhistoricalpress@gmail.com**

ISBN #0-89308-274-0

Printed in the United States of America

Raising my eyes ever and anon to look down that dark and silent Goose Creek avenue, my thoughts would run ever upon olden stories . . . .

from Elizabeth A. Poyas,
The Olden Time in South Carolina.

Miniature etching by Elizabeth O'Neill Verner

*To my mother and father,
Gentry Virginia
and
Joseph S. Heitzler,
who gave me a home,
and to the people
of Goose Creek
for the same reason.*

TABLE OF CONTENTS

Chapter		Page
	Introduction	ix
I.	Goose Creek: The Name and the Place	1
II.	The Early Goose Creek Settlers	10
III.	The Goose Creek Indians	22
IV.	Goose Creek as a Carolina Frontier	29
V.	Goose Creek Under Proprietary Government	49
VI.	Goose Creek as a Plantation Society	67
VII.	The Goose Creek Plantation Community	83
VIII.	The Political History of Goose Creek, 1719-1783	121
IX.	The Political History of Goose Creek, 1783-1900	141
X.	Early Education and Schools	160
XI.	St. James' Church, Goose Creek	177
XII.	Goose Creek Ghosts and Legends	202
XIII.	Goose Creek in the Twentieth Century	215
	Appendices	239
	References	251
	Bibliography	277
	Index	285

CREDITS

The author would like to acknowledge the kindness of the following for permission to reproduce the following illustrations: St. James' Church, Goose Creek, an etching by Elizabeth O'Neill Verner, used by permission of the Tradd Street Press, Charleston; plantation photographs from Harriette Leiding's *Historic Houses of South Carolina* (Philadelphia: J.B. Lippincott, copyright 1921), by permission of Harper & Row, Publishers, Inc.; the South Carolina Historical Society; Duke University Press and the University of South Carolina Press.

INTRODUCTION

This work records the cultural development of the Goose Creek community. More importantly, it is the historical rediscovery of Goose Creek in the sense that there is no previously compiled record and its rich local history has been generally inaccessible.

Prior to this work a little of Goose Creek's past could be found in piecemeal fashion in the historical publications on Charleston and other local communities. Most of the historical data was scattered among the records in the historical societies, libraries and archives of South Carolina. The absence of a compiled history has been an injustice to the frontiersmen and women, the planters, missionaries, soldiers, housewives and the white, red, and black builders of past and contemporary Goose Creek.

Although this history is intended to rectify this injustice, the historical rediscovery of Goose Creek was not undertaken in search of local heroes to rival those of better-known places. It was written to enhance community self-concept, to make the history accessible, to instill a rightful and deserved community pride and to pay tribute to past and present Goose Creekers.

Typical readers often are too preoccupied to read history carefully. Consequently, they fail to crystallize local historical events and give them their proper place in the forming of national institutions. For the same reason the importance of local events is often underestimated, partially because many of the events are common to numerous other communities. In the most part, the history of Goose Creek is the story of common people thinking common thoughts about common things. Although many of the every-day events of Goose Creek parallel those of numerous other communities, it is from these events that the real "American" element of this nation evolved. There are many periods in history when important changes have been brought about not by heroic leaders or political reformers but by the people who live their lives unaware that their day-to-day activities are causing far-reaching changes.

The trials of the frontier, the dilemma of slavery, the poverty and prosperity of a developing economy and the evolution of political thought are all recorded in the historical accounts of Goose Creek. In this sense, Goose Creek has many, many heroes. One early minister, the Reverend Francis

LeJau of St. James' Church, led a life of true heroism for over ten years. His letters to his missionary society are a major source of historical Goose Creek record from 1706 to 1717. They record the varying attitudes of the Goose Creek planters toward the Negro slaves. They reflect on the importance of the local Indians to the life of the community. The letters reveal many of the causes of the developing discontent with distant British rule, and memorialize the hardships and trials of the early Goose Creekers.

Captain George Chicken was another Goose Creek hero. He led the Goose Creek militia and prevented the Yemassee Indians and their allies from over-running the community. Other Goose Creek notables are men like Alexander Garden, doctor and botanist; Ralph Izard, the Revolutionary patriot, and Gideon Dupont, planter-inventor. Contemporary Goose Creek has produced its share of note-worthy personalities, two of which are S.E. "Speedy" Felkel and the controversial Mayor, Malvin Mann.

Pirates, Indians and land policies were some of the controversial issues of colonial Goose Creek. During the most recent decades of this century, public works, zoning, taxation and community development issues have entered the political arena with much the same fervor that characterized the turbulent Colonial era. It was the "Goose Creek Men" who led the dissent in South Carolina during much of the Colonial era. Although these men were often despised by the Lords Proprietors and ill-revered by their colonial opponents, the Goose Creek people had considerable impact on the politics of that day. Three chapters of this work are entitled in part "Those Goose Creek Men" because those words appeared so often in the correspondence of the Lords Proprietors; correspondence which in most cases, provided instructions on how to deal with the trouble-makers in Goose Creek.

Goose Creek changed considerably as the colony matured: first as a frontier ruled by distant Proprietors, secondly as a plantation society ruled by the British Parliament, thirdly, after the Great Revolution, as a new state in the Republic and lastly as an active community in the old and new South. The political history of Goose Creek is generally one of dissent. The earliest protests were levelled against the Lords Proprietors, who formulated frontier policies from far-away England. Quarrels between the Lords Proprietors and the "Goose Creek Men" led to 22 changes in the Governor's office during 50 years of Goose Creek dominance.

Largely as a result of the refusal of the Goose Creek people to support the Lords Proprietors, the colony became a Royal colony under the direct tutelage of the British Parliament. Decades later, the turbulence of the American Revolution received sympathy and support in Goose Creek. The Goose Creek people again dissented from the distant control of their home affairs. The Revolution meant victory, but it brought economic crisis to the Goose Creek planters. Recovery was slow and arduous, but the last decades of the 18th century witnessed the partial renewal of the once-rich planter community.

The Goose Creek prosperity waned and rapidly declined until it finally totally collapsed due to the loss of the Civil War. The ruin of the slave-dependent planter society and the trials of Reconstruction resulted in bitter political quarrels until the dawning of the 20th century.

The "Goose Creek Men" earned a reputation for unity, prowess, and political clout. They had dynamic impact on the history of South Carolina and left their special mark on Goose Creek as a proud and dynamic community. Most communities are born, develop and sometimes die, based upon their ability to support or not support their people. Seldom does a community settle, thrive for 200 years, disappear and then reappear 100 years later. The Goose Creek community is unusual in this and in many other ways. The influence of the local Indians, the missionaries, malaria, rice production, war, Reconstruction, southern politics, 20th century suburbanization and the water of the creek itself blends to compose a local history that contains a unique identity for the residents of the 1980's.

Not too many parallels can be drawn between the Goose Creek of the 18th and 19th century and the Goose Creek of today. It is better to think of two separate Goose Creeks. The first was the local society built by colonists enduring the trials of the wilderness. This Goose Creek is best exemplified by their splendid plantations. The second was born in the Atomic Age, burdened by population explosions and the trials of rapid industrial and commercial development. If there are any parallels, the reader is left to find his own and to draw his own conclusions on the existence of any historical threads that bind Goose Creek's 300 years.

This rediscovery is an accounting of history, observations, and an occasional inference from data. It is an attempt to give the people of Goose Creek a grip on their past and a better opportunity to march into the last twenty years of this century with confidence, pride and better hindsight.

This is a labor of love.

Michael J. Heitzler

Goose Creek, South Carolina
January 10, 1982

CHAPTER I

GOOSE CREEK: THE NAME AND THE PLACE

The name "Goose Creek" is not only one of the oldest place names in South Carolina, but is also unique in that it is shared with no other city or town. According to the 1977-78 National Zip Code Directory there are nearly 800,000 places in the United States having a zip code. Among these is only one city or town with the unusual name of Goose Creek. The 17,000 inhabitants of this small city share the distinction of living in a city with a name they share with no others. "Just a little bit and you're in the country," said Goose Creek resident A.L. Collier during an interview with the *Charleston Evening Post* in 1978.[1] The residents greatly enjoy the semi-rural character of the Goose Creek community and are not overly enthusiastic about the impending urbanization which has encroached upon the area during the last 20 years.

The city of Goose Creek is a suburban community located in the southernmost section of Berkeley County, South Carolina among vast acreages of undeveloped swamp, forests and crop land. This gives it a semi-rural character but also the developmental resources to accommodate the rapid population growth of the greater Charleston area. Since 1960, Goose Creek was one of the fastest growing municipalities in South Carolina.[2] The area's growth has been due, to a large extent, to the spread of urbanization and new industrial growth radiating from Charleston. This development has greatly affected the city and the greater Goose Creek area. In addition to this, population increases have been due to the preference of many to live in a suburban or semi-rural environment. According to a population and economic survey conducted in 1975 by the Berkeley, Charleston and Dorchester Regional Planning Council, Goose Creek can expect additional increases in population in the future as the urbanization process continues.

The name "Goose Creek" is unusual. Much to the credit of the name itself, the community often is referred to as a country town despite its dynamic growth. Although the people of Goose Creek do not share their city's name with any other United States cities or towns, there are 24 locations with similar names.[3] The origin of the name has been unfortunately lost. The search for the original name of the creek and the source of its present name discovered no origins which could be substantiated or documented. There are theories as to the origin and many interesting speculations, but no proof. Thus the name has some mystery about it.

Names of towns and cities are of interest to geographers and historians. Not only can they provide a background or introduction to regional investigations but can also provide insights into the history of settlements, migration patterns, cultural heritage and landscape elements. South Carolina place names such as DeKalb, Marion and Sumter have originated from personalities in the State's history. Names such as Ten Mile, Great Falls, Little Mountain and Myrtle Beach indicate type of terrain or location. The name "Goose Creek" provides little indication of the community history except the physical location of the creek, which meanders through the area until it reaches the Cooper River.[4] Besides Goose Creek there are two other similar names in South Carolina. Near the Society Hill bridge along the Pee Dee River there is a section named Goose Mash.[5] There is also a Gooseplatter Creek located near the Aiken County line.[6]

There are a number of place names in the Goose Creek area which are interesting. Daisey Swamp is located about three miles northwest of the City of Goose Creek just north of the junction of U.S. Highway 176 and State Highway 45. It is reportedly named after the Deas (dĕz) family who owned the land in that area during the Colonial Period. "Daisey" is simply the corruption of the name Deas.[7]

Groomsville is another location just north of the City of Goose Creek. It is one of the oldest known communities in Berkeley County with a surname as its designation. Reference was made to this community in Joseph I. Waring's history of St. James' church. The vestry of that church established a school there in 1828. Groomsville is located near the junction of State Highways 9 and 375 about five miles southeast of Oakley. The name is derived from the Grooms family who lived in the area. Groomsville Road is the local name given to State Highway 9, between U.S. Highway 52 and 17-A.[8]

Strawberry appears to have begun as a station on the Atlantic Coastline Railroad. In 1940 it had a railroad station, a post office, a saw mill, two stores and five houses. The saw mill went out of business in the 1940's. The post office and the railroad station went out of business shortly thereafter. Strawberry takes its name from the old Strawberry Planta-

THE NAME AND THE PLACE

tion nearby. It is located where State Highway 9 crosses the Atlantic Coastline Railroad just north of the City of Goose Creek.[9] Mount Holly takes its name from the old Mount Holly Plantation. It is likely that this village began as a railroad stop. It has a post office even today and a number of houses, but the store is no longer in use. Mount Holly borders on the incorporated line of the City of Goose Creek, and is located at the intersection of State Highway 45 and U.S. Highway 52.[10] Casey Hill was the largest of three black communities located in that area. The name comes from the Casey school, Casey Assembly Hall and Casey Church; the latter being the last of the remaining structures. It unfortunately burned to the ground in 1978. Casey was, according to some sources, a former slave who started a small religious assembly which eventually developed into a well populated settlement.

In St. James' Parish, Goose Creek there are a number of names which have been important to or were connected with outstanding personalities in Goose Creek's history. Wassamassaw Swamp, the site of one of the St. James, Goose Creek vestry schools, was named for the Indian tribe of that name. The Indian meaning of the word Wassamassaw is "connecting water."[11] Villeponteaux Branch is a small body of water named for Zachariah Villeponteaux, a wealthy Huguenot vestryman of St. James' Church. He became well known for the grey brick which he made at his Parnassus Plantation on Back River. He supplied the brick for the now famous Pompion Chapel.[12] Chicken Creek is another body of water in the Goose Creek area well known by local fishermen. It was probably named for the Chicken family, prominent among whom was George Chicken. He was the captain of the Goose Creek Militia and Commissioner of the Indian Trade during the early Colonial Period.[13]

The names of the various neighborhoods in contemporary Goose Creek are of interest. Some are merely advertising phrases such as Boulder Bluff, Beverly Hills, Forest Lawn and Greenview Acres. Other names can reasonably be traced to some origin. The Oaks was named after the old Middleton plantation on which it is situated. Menriv Park is a blend, or port-mon-teau word formed from the name of U.S. Representative L. Mendel Rivers. Sedgefield may have been named after a field of sedge (coarse grass). There is also Pineview

Terrace. No terrace exists, but the pine trees do. Camelot Village is named after King Arthur's legendary castle.[14] The origin of the name "Goose Creek" is not as easy to ascertain.

The Etiwan, Seewee and Wando Indians most certainly had one or more names for the creek. Just what the local Indians called Goose Creek has never been satisfactorily determined. The early white settlers ignored most of the Indian place names and immediately supplanted them with English ones. Some early place names were borrowed from influential leaders at home or abroad. Goose Creek had its Indian name supplanted almost immediately after the first European settlement, making it necessary to arrive at the original name through analogy.

There is only one instance where an Indian name is given directly to any part of Goose Creek. At a meeting of the Grand Council on December 28, 1678, just eight years after the earliest Charles Towne settlement, it was resolved that Mr. Edward Middleton would take up:

> His great lott of land on the upper part of Adthan Creek his whole breadth and not the one-fifth part there of upon that part of the aforesaid creeke where is soe settled such upper part being not naviagable nor capable to be so made.[15]

The word "Adthan" was investigated by Judge Henry A.M. Smith, a noted local historian. Judge Smith examined the original manuscript and interpreted the spelling as being not "Adthan" but "Adthau."[16] Words ending with a consonant referring to water are very rare among coastal Indian names. The endings "ee," "e," "au" and "aw" could be the original intention when recorded in the Grand Council journal. Judge Smith believed the name was really "Adshau."

The suffix "e" or "ee" among the coastal Indian languages indicated a river or body of water. The rivers Pee Dee, Combahee, Santee, Congaree and Wateree are examples of some consistency to this.[17] The creek flowing near Goose Creek now known as Foster Creek, named after an early settler, John Foster, was called Appeebee by the local Indians. A number of early land grants in the Goose Creek area refer to it. One such warrant, dated October 20, 1699 was to Col. Robert Gibbes. It was for "five hundred acres of land lying upon Appeebee being part of a great parcel formerly laid out for John Foster."[18]

THE NAME AND THE PLACE

Judge Smith's appraisal may be correctly interpreted as "Adthan" or "Adthau" if the original name was of the Muskhogean language. The common "ee" ending was not common to Indians speaking this language. It was different from the Siouen language from which the Pee Dee and Combahee was named. Goose Creek's original name may have been Adthau.

Another Indian name for Goose Creek may be found in the land warrants for Yeshoe, now called Otranto Plantation. Arthur Middleton came to Carolina with his brother Edward in 1678.[19] On September 7, 1678, the brothers were issued a warrant for 1,780 acres of land. This land was granted to them on September 6, 1679, and was located at the head of Yeaman's Creek, now called Goose Creek. On May 20, 1680, Edward conveyed to his brother Arthur all of his estate "in ye plantation scituate [situated] upon the South side of Goose Creek alias Yeamans Creeke in this province."[20] In 1682 Arthur Middleton married Mary Smith, widow of John Smith, the owner of Booshooe Plantation on the Ashley River. By the marriage settlement dated December 7, 1682, Arthur Middleton conveyed in trust to his intended wife:

> Mrs. Mary Smith late wife of John Smith of Booshooe in Ashley River in this Provence, Esq. decd. and for her joynture the Plant'n on wch ye sd Arthur Middleton now lives nigh Goose Creek in ye province afsd called Yeshoe containing 1780 acres ... with ten negroes.....[21]

The name Yeshoe, like Booshooe is obviously an Indian name. The "e" suffix indicates a reference to water, but whether it referred to the creek or the locality cannot be accurately determined.

Thus it is found that there are two Indian names, one or both of which may have been the original name(s) for Goose Creek. The translation of these Indian names is nearly impossible to determine. There is no vocabulary of the coastal Indians left, but due to the efforts of a Confederate soldier, Oscar Lieber, there is a compilation of a vocabulary of the Catawba tribe.

While Lieber worked as a geologist for the State of South Carolina in 1856, his camp servant was a Catawba Indian. From his servant he compiled a vocabulary list of the Catawba language. The Catawbas spoke a language that was Siouen.[22] They were closely allied with the coastal Indians, adding to the possibility of some commonality of language and place names. Judge H.A.M. Smith, delivering an address on the history of St. James' Church, Goose Creek suggested that the name "Goose Creek" referred to as Yeshoe or Yeowee by the coastal Indians, could be translated to mean "green water" from the Catawba word "ya-hah." Smith relied on the vocabulary compiled by Oscar Lieber.[23] Although it was a mere supposition, this translation is not devoid of plausibility. Using the same analogy, it is also possible that Yeshoe meant snake creek, from the Catawba word "yah," meaning snake. This could have referred to the snake-shape bends and curves of the creek's course. There is no Catawba word in Lieber's vocabulary even resembling the name "Adshan" found in the early grant to Edward Middleton. Adshan may well have been an Etiwan or Wando Indian word having no connection with the Catawba language.

What the Indians named the creek may never be satisfactorily determined. The original Indian name was replaced by one given by the settlers at an early date. In the early grants the creek is known as Yeamans' Creek, the name of the second Proprietary Governor, Sir John Yeamans. Yeamans' estate lay along Goose Creek near its junction with the Cooper River. On September 5, 1674 a warrant was issued to Lady Margaret Yeamans for 1,070 acres for herself and servants arriving in 1671 and 1672. This acreage was granted in February 1674/75, described as bounding upon "Yeamans his Creeke in Ittawan River."[24] Thus it appears that the Indian name was replaced immediately by Sir John Yeamans. Upon this site was built a plantation house and estate known as "Old Goose Creek."[25] The house was built shortly after 1691, not far from where the creek takes a goose-neck turn in its course.[26] "Old Goose Creek" was used to refer to the mansion house and the estate until well into the nineteenth century. Mrs. Elizabeth Poyas wrote in her book, *Olden Time in Carolina*, published in 1855, that Leize F.B. Lockwood married the house owner, George Henry Smith in 1850. She had much work done on the old house and renamed it Yeamans' Hall. Prior to this time it was referred to as Old Goose Creek.

Mrs. St. Julien Ravenel in her book, *Charleston: the Place and the People,* credits the source of the name to the winding course and goose-neck turns in the creek. This is

THE NAME AND THE PLACE

reasonable, but there is no documentation for this claim. Another such unsubstantiated claim is based on the possible presence of Canadian geese which may have abounded on the creek. It appears, however, that at the time the area was given its present name geese were not conspicuous. The lists of foods comprising the native diet in the Goose Creek area did not include geese and they were not listed by the early white settlers as being an important part of their diet.

Another very untenable explanation for the name source relies on an early probate court record. The Reverend Robert Wilson, writing in 1922, stated that the source of the name came from "Goes" Creek, which he found in records describing a transfer of land on a creek called Goes Creek.[27] Reverend Wilson reasoned that the Dutch pronunciation of Goes Creek would be "Goose" Creek and hence the name. It is most likely that the word "Goes" in the record was simply a misspelling of the word "Goose." A look at almost any early document reveals that there were multiple spellings for most words, depending on the writer's command of the language. One can easily find multiple spellings of "Goose Creek" in the early records. Misspellings include Goes Creek, Goose Creeke, Goose Crick, Goos Creek and Goosegrick. In the will of Anthoine Prudhomme dated 20 July 1695, a French spelling was applied: "L'Eglise Francoise qui assemble sur Gouscrick." To further weaken Reverend Wilson's argument there were no probate courts in South Carolina in the 1670's when Goose Creek was given its present name. Also there were few German or Dutch settlers in Carolina until much later.

The original name and the source of its present name may never be satisfactorily determined. Even territory was vague at first. By 1706 all the lands on both sides of the creek as far north as Back River and Foster's Creek and even to the headwaters of Goose Creek within five miles of the present town of Summerville were settled.[28] In 1706 this entire area was generally referred to as Goose Creek, and the settlers as the Goose Creek man or Goose Creek people.

The Church Act of 1706 more clearly defined the territory of Goose Creek. The act divided the settled coastal region of South Carolina into nine parishes. The parish of St. James, Goose Creek was one of them.[29] Like the parishes of the established Church of England, the divisions were political as well as ecclesiastical. The area was commonly referred to as the Parish of Goose Creek, but it was properly known as the Parish of St. James, Goose Creek. The name Goose Creek was used to distinguish it from another parish of St. James created the same year, St. James', Santee.

The parish of St. James, Goose Creek, as defined in the Church Act of 1706 included part of Charleston Neck, which today is North Charleston and Hanahan. The parish was bounded on the east by the Cooper River and extended north to Back River. From the point where Back River branches from the Cooper, the parish line follows Back River to its source. The line then runs west, from south of Pimlico, Fairlawn Barony, to the unsettled Carolina frontier. The southern boundary at the Charleston Neck runs west-northwest parallel to the west-northwest parish boundary to the frontier. The Church Act did not define the western boundary — it extended the parish indefinitely into the frontier.

In 1768 the province of South Carolina was divided into seven judicial districts.[30] This act made Berkeley County a part of Charles Town District. This arrangement lasted until 1799 when the state was divided into districts, counties and parishes in accordance with another act, passed by the General Assembly on December 21, 1798.[31] Under the provisions of this act, Charleston District was divided into the parishes of St. Michael; St. Philip; Christ Church; St. Thomas and St. Dennis; St. James, Santee; St. Stephen; St. John's, Berkeley; St. James, Goose Creek; St. Andrew and St. John's, Colleton. By this act the parishes, including St. James, Goose Creek were independent units, regulating themselves under district law and sending representatives to the state legislature. The new state constitution enacted following the Civil War abolished the parish electoral system. In January, 1882, the act creating Berkeley County included part of St. James', Goose Creek.[32] This new political division left parts of the old parish in Berkeley and Charleston counties. In 1896, the area of Berkeley County was reduced in size by cutting off a small part of the former parish of St. James, Goose Creek.[33] This placed all of the town of Summerville in Dorchester County. By the same act, Orangeburg County acquired large sections of the undefined western parts of the parish of St. James, Goose Creek.[34]

THE NAME AND THE PLACE

Old St. James' parish was again divided politically on February 28, 1921.[35] At this time another section of Berkeley County was lost to Charleston. This area lay between Dorchester County and the Atlantic Coast Line Railroad, south and west of a line from the head of Goose Creek to Ladson.

Today (1981) the name of Goose Creek is usually used in reference to the small city. As a city it is a young one, and was chartered in 1961. Now the corporate limits take in a much greater amount of land than did the original incorporation. Further annexation is expected with an increase in the population. Goose Creek's population was estimated at 4,298 in 1970, increasing to 8,000 in 1978,[36] and 17,000· in 1980.[37] The present city occupies a very small section of St. James' parish, and incorporates lands bounding only on the northernmost reaches of the creek. "Goose Creek" can historically be used in reference to the creek, the lands bounding the creek, the parish or the city.

Identity is often a crucial ingredient in the healthy existence of a community. In regard to the Goose Creek community this identity cannot be substantiated by the name itself, but the community is dynamic. Despite the lost origin of the name, the people of contemporary Goose Creek are quick to confirm that they know exactly who they are and have a fix on where they are going.

CHAPTER II

THE EARLY GOOSE CREEK SETTLERS

As is so often the case, the natural forces of economics and geography have more influence on historical events than the best made plans of men. This was the case in the 17th century when Barbadian islanders left their plantations to come to Carolina and to settle on and near the waters of Goose Creek. They were forced from their home island of Barbados in the West Indies by adverse economic conditions. Once in Carolina, they used their colonial experience to transplant a plantation system to Goose Creek where the water, soil and the climate were ideal for plantations, slaves and a landed gentry.

The people from Barbados were soon joined in Goose Creek by others. These additional arrivals were primarily from England, but also included French Huguenot immigrants. Most had come to stay with a vision and a hope for a better life in the Carolina frontier. For many decades the struggle for survival here was a battle between man and his natural enemies. The struggles also included battles between man and his fellow man: white, black, and red; and battles with their own personal frailties. Old St. James' Church still stands today as a symbol of the success of these early settlers. It survived Indian wars, slave insurrections, British invasions, cyclones, earthquakes and the great Civil War.[1]

The forces of racial and cultural conflicts were coupled with religious and political motivations, all of which influenced the development of the Goose Creek community. These forces were, however, secondary to the dominant impact of the natural laws of economics and geography which influenced the social, political and economic order of colonial Goose Creek. The introduction of sugar production on the British islands of the West Indies, combined with the summer heat and low swampy fertile soils of Goose Creek favored the establishment of a landed gentry supported by a plantation slave system. This basic order dominated the affairs of Goose Creek until the Civil War.

The first two decades of the 17th century were a period of English experimentation in colonization. The English colonial management plans proved successful in establishing new colonies in Virginia, Newfoundland, New England, South

EARLY SETTLERS

America and on islands in the West Indies. An island in the West Indies was the origin of the Goose Creek settlement: Barbados. It is located in the Caribbean Sea just north of Trinidad. Between 1620 and 1640 the population of this small island swelled to 18,000.[2]

Theoretically, Barbados and all the British islands in the Caribbean were the feudal possession of one man, the Earl of Carlisle. Under the proprietary form of colonial government, the powers of local government exceeded even those of the King. The Proprietor could govern as he saw fit, although a representative parliamentary government evolved later to compel the practical administration of these colonies by their proprietors. The legislative Assemblies on these small islands were composed of men elected by all the landowners in all their parishes. This idea was progressively democratic and was later to be transplanted to Carolina by the independent-minded Goose Creek people.

Tobacco was the first profitable crop to be cultivated in Barbados. As it became more difficult to compete with the better-smoking Virginia tobacco, other crops were sought for experimental planting. In 1640, Pieter Brower, a Dutchman, introduced sugar cane to Barbados.[3] His experiments proved successful and by 1660 sugar cane had replaced tobacco as the staple crop.

The cultivation of sugar cane forced many Barbadians to seek homes elsewhere and caused many to venture to Carolina. Sugar cane planting brought significant changes to the island's economy. The business of raising sugar cane required large capital investments and large plantations. In addition, sugar production required large amounts of labor. This labor could best be managed with black slaves. These business necessities forced the small farmers out of Barbados. The colony was quickly rearranged by economic forces from an island of small tobacco farms to a community composed of large sugar cane plantations.[4]

An actual decline in white population resulted as these small farmers left in search of opportunity elsewhere.[5] By 1670 the number of white inhabitants had declined to about 20,000, with approximately 40,000 slaves on a 166 square mile island.[6] A contemporary estimate placed the number of farms and plantations at 11,200 in 1645. By 1667 only 745 plantations were in operation.[7] In addition to these economic pressures on the small farms, many plantation owners became discouraged and began to leave due to unexpected declines in sugar prices.

The Barbadians experienced even more pressures. Enforcement of the British *Navigation Acts* raised the cost of manufactured goods and thus the cost of living. Political crises, floods, crop damage and other natural catastrophes added to the plight of the Barbadians in the 1660's. Many of them listened to the promises of opportunity in Carolina and left for that new adventure with hope for a better life.

In February, 1671, the infant English colony at Charles Towne welcomed 106 new settlers from Barbados. Many of these Barbadians ventured up the Cooper River to the Goose Creek area. Until about 1696, practically every ship entering Charles Towne harbor brought persons seeking new homes in Carolina.[8] The Cooper River was navigable for more than 30 miles and attracted many of the new arrivals. By the year 1700, small settlements, farms and plantations were on both sides of the river, as well as along the Wando and Ashley rivers and Goose Creek.[9]

The desire to settle land along these rivers and their lesser creeks was a formative influence upon Goose Creek's development. Some of the best lands were found on the banks of Goose Creek and, being navigable from the Cooper to near what is today the town of Summerville, it was ideal for transporting people and products.

The newcomers from Barbados brought with them and implanted in Goose Creek their Barbadian customs. They brought the parish electoral and the slave systems,[10] the established Anglican Church, a class of landed gentry and a sense of staunch independence. The Barbadians differed from the "plain people," who were mostly dissenters from the Church of England, and a sense of rivalry resulted.[11] Writing to Lord Ashley on March 21, 1671, Governor West observed that "wee find that one of our servants brought out of England is worth 2 of ye Barbadians, for they are soe much addicted to Rum, that they will doe little whilst the bottle is at their nose. . . ."[12] Lord Ashley most likely shared the Proprietary view that the self-supporting Barbadians could provide colonial expertise, money and leadership during the first difficult years and that they were valuable to the colony. He disagreed with the Governor and wrote, "The poorer settlers serve only

EARLY SETTLERS

to fill up numbers and live upon us."[13]

The Goose Creek Barbadians had much in common and quickly became allied politically. The Barbadian settlers were generally of a higher class, were wealthy, members of the Anglican Church, shared similar political views and had prior colonial experiences. The people of Goose Creek became increasingly allied against the Lords Proprietors and looked down upon the other settlers, whom they considered poor novices from England.[14] Many other Carolinians thought the Goose Creek men to be arrogant, overbearing and not nearly as valuable to the colony as they themselves.[15]

The summer heat caused the Barbadians to believe that they had resettled in the tropics. During the summer months the average temperatures on the South Carolina coast are in fact equal to those in Barbados during the same period.[16] The demands of the climate were believed to make slavery unavoidable and that institution was established when the settlement began. As the settlement developed staple crops, the demand for inexpensive labor increased. Most believed that the hot, humid climate and low coastal lands were too oppressive for white laborers. The Barbadians had long depended on slave labor in the West Indies and easily implanted this system in Goose Creek. This social order, based on slave labor and a landed gentry, persisted in Goose Creek for nearly 150 years. It was accepted during the Colonial Period, survived the American Revolution and remained a distinct and influential political force in South Carolina until 1865.[17]

The early immigrants to Goose Creek were not limited to just the Barbadians. To escape religious persecution, many French Huguenots [Protestants] took refuge in England in the latter part of the 17th century. In 1680, the ship *Richmond* arrived at Charles Towne with 45 of these refugees.[18] Peter Girard compiled a list in 1689 showing that 31 French people were located in Goose Creek in that year.[19] Other immigrants had come directly from England to Charles Town, many of whom eventually found their way up the Cooper River to Goose Creek.

It is difficult to accurately account for all of the Goose Creek people during the early Colonial Period. As noted, the majority of the earliest settlers were from Barbados. Others had immigrated from other islands of the West Indies. There was a sizeable settlement of French Huguenots, a small number of Anabaptists and others coming directly from England. These white settlers shared Goose Creek with an increasing number of black African slaves and a rapidly decreasing number of local Indians.

The lands along Goose Creek began to be settled by white Europeans as early as 1672 and 1673. According to a careful and competent investigator, all the lands along both sides of the creek, as far as Back River and Foster's Creek were occupied by 1680.[20] The settlement of the Goose Creek lands went counter to the wishes of the Lords Proprietors. They had planned for the province to be developed contiguously, both for safety and order. It was the Barbadians who defied these plans and sought out the rich lands of Goose Creek.

The Lords Proprietors of Carolina issued instructions for granting land in 1669. For 40 years these instruction were revised and reformed but remained basically the same. The settlers appeared before the Governor and Council to request land. The governor issued a warrant to the settler and the Surveyor General made a plat. When the warrant was properly certified, signed and recorded the settler became a land owner.[21] A new form of nobility was established in Carolina and Goose Creek through the Carolina land grants.

The identities of many of the early settlers in the Goose Creek area are recorded in *Warrants for Lands in South Carolina, 1672-1711,* edited by A.S. Salley, Jr. These records account for the date, size and number of warrants, the grantee and recipient, location and in some cases other information as to need for the land or reason for the request. One such grant was to Sir John Yeamans, who arrived in Carolina in 1671. His warrant appears to be one of the earliest in the Goose Creek area. Although he never lived in Goose Creek, a warrant was issued upon his death in 1674 in favor of his widow, Lady Margaret Yeamans, for 1,070 acres for her and her servants when she arrived in 1671 and 1672.[22] The grant for this land was issued February 9, 1675, and described it as being upon "Yeamans his Creek in Ittiwan River."[23]

George Cantey came from Barbados in 1670 with the first expedition. He was the son of Tiege Cantey, who came to Carolina in 1672, and later became a vestryman of the parish church of St. James, Goose Creek. Cantey received a warrant for 300 acres of land situated between the Ashley River

EARLY SETTLERS

and Goose Creek on the 5th of October, 1704. He was a member of the Commons House of Assembly for Berkeley in 1703 and 1704. His son George Cantey was a captain in the militia and participated in several Indian campaigns. In 1712-1713 he was in the second expedition against the Tuscarora Indians under Col. Moore, and in 1715-16 he was with Captain George Chicken of Goose Creek in the Yemassee Indian War.[24]

Bordering the Yeamans grant was another tract granted to Mr. William Murele, who was among the first settlers in the Province and arrived about 1671. He received 400 acres in his first grant. On July 12, 1679 a warrant was issued to lay out 920 acres of land for William Perryman.[25] On March 1, 1681 he received a grant for 574 acres on Yeamans Creek. On January 10, 1694/95 a grant was made to Samuel Hartley for 400 acres on the south side of Goose Creek.[26] On August 17, 1704 another was made to John Sanders for 300 acres on the south side of Goose Creek adjoining the aforementioned 400 acres.[27] On November 11, 1704 a warrant was issued for 500 acres of land to Lewis Lansac.[28] According to later deeds, a grant was made on May 14, 1707 to Lansac for 600 acres on the south side of Goose Creek, adjacent to the 400 acre grant to Samuel Hartley, owner of the grant called "Bigelowe's."[29]

Arthur Middleton, a former London merchant, together with his brother, Edward, came to Carolina in 1678. On September 7, 1678 a warrant was issued to lay out 1,780 acres of land for Edward Middleton and Arthur Middleton.[30] This warrant was followed by a grant to them dated September 6, 1679 of 1,780 acres at the head of Yeamans Creek, since called Goose Creek. These were the original grants of the famous Otranto Plantation, originally referred to as Yeshoe.

Just west of and adjoining Otranto was the plantation and the original home of the Parker family of lower South Carolina. John Parker emigrated from Jamaica, and on January 3, 1694/95 warrants were issued to Thomas Barker, the husband of John Parker's widow.[31] He received 500 acres of land. John Parker, the son, was the original owner of the "Hayes" plantation.

Brick House or Maritindale's was the original plantation settlement of the Barkers. A 1,200 acre grant was made to

Thomas Barker in 1704. West of Brick House was a plantation which was formed by an accumulation of smaller tracts. The only name that appeared on the deeds was that of Thomas Mell.[32]

The original settlement of the Izard family in South Carolina was situated just northwest of Otranto and northeast of Hayes and Woodstock. Ralph Izard, the immigrant, arrived in the province on October 3, 1682.[33] Ralph Izard the son devised a collection of grants and conveyances to form the beautiful Elms plantation which he owned until his death.

At a meeting of the Grand Council December 28, 1678 it was resolved that Mr. Edward Middleton might take up "his greate lott of land" on "the upper part of Adthan Creek [Goose Creek]."[34] On February 23, 1679 a warrant was issued to lay out acreage for Middleton and on November 14, 1680 an additional formal grant was issued to him for 1,000 acres at the head of Goose Creek. This plantation was originally called Bloomfield or Broom Hall.[35]

The plantation known as Fredericks was originally composed of the land granted to Thomas Moore between the lines of Thorogood, Berringer, Stevens and Mallock, and on September 20, 1683 Captain James Moore was granted 2,400 acres formerly known by the Indian name of Boo-chaw-a and Wapensaw.[36] Captain Moore was afterward known as the Honorable James Moore and acted as Governor of the Province.

Job Howe of famous Howe Hall received a number of land grants dating as early as April 4, 1683.[37] He, like Ralph Izard and others, applied for and received several grants and finally amassed a large estate.[38] Some early arrivals eventually assembled thousands of acres. A warrant dated October 12, 1692 granted 2,100 acres, part of the 12,000 acres granted to John D'Arsens Seigneaur de Wernhant by the Lords Proprietors.[39] This tract came to be known as Medway Plantation and is still a historical landmark in Goose Creek. Medway, on Back River, is said to be the oldest house in South Carolina. It was built of brick in 1688 by Jan Van Arrsens, who arrived in the colony as the leader of a small group from Holland. Van Arrsens died soon after his arrival to Carolina, and his widow married Thomas Smith, who subsequently became a landgrave and governor. Van Arrsens died in 1694

EARLY SETTLERS

and is buried at Medway.

Goose Creek lands were also granted to Edward Middleton. This land became known as "Crowfield," long considered the best landscaped plantation in the province. Another grant to him was the "Oaks," which still can be recognized today by its stately avenue near old St. James' Church.

A perusal of the *Abstracts of the Wills of the State of South Carolina*, 1670-1740 and 1740-1760 revealed the names of many of the planters in the Goose Creek community during the Colonial Period. Some of the names recorded were:

> Nathaniel Snow, John Foster, Robert Gibbes, John Emporer, Peter Lamb, David Davis, Thomas Barker, Anthoine Prudhomme, John Goodby, John Sanders, Daniel Mackdaniel, John Bauyly, Benjamin Marion, Wilson Sanders, James Goodbee, Moses Wilson, John Bagbee, John McKay, Philip Herbert (son of Col. John Herbert), James Lucas, Edward Keating, James Rochford (from Ireland), Matthew Beaird, Peter Taylor, John Jacob Bruck, Peter Hurne, Hugh Grange, Benjamin Godin, Maurice Keating, William Allen, Richard Singleton, William Wood, Francis Kirk, James Withers and Thomas Mell.[40]

The Edict of Nantes, which granted religious toleration to Protestants in France was revoked by King Louis XIV in 1685. Before the revocation, the Huguenots there had been allowed to live free from abuses and restrictions. After the revocation, religious and civil persecution was inflicted on the Protestants by the Catholic majority. Soldiers were stationed in their houses, children taken from parents, and thousands of French Protestants were tortured and killed. Emigration from France was prohibited by law, but many escaped to Holland and from there came to England. It was from England that the emigrant Huguenots to Goose Creek sailed for the new world.[41] In 1680 King Charles IV of England gave free passage to some Huguenot families on the ship *Richmond*. It was hoped that these French would introduce the successful cultivation of vines for wine and the production of olive oil and silk.[42] The Lords Proprietors promised free land to the Protestant refugees. Those Huguenots who came to South Carolina were mostly tradesmen, farmers and mechanics, and were very valuable additions to the struggling young colony. Evidence of French Huguenot families settling in Goose Creek is found in the correspondence of Anglican missionaries during the first three decades of the 18th century and in early newspaper accounts.

Land in the vicinity of Goose Creek was granted to Huguenots as early as 1680. The George Gouden (Gourdin) grant of 300 acres is dated November 15, 1680 and records that he was already in possession of the land.[43] Among the French families prominent in Goose Creek during this time were the families of:

> Antoine Prudhomme, Abraham Dupont, John Goble, Peter Bacot, Henry Bruneau, Pierre Dasseu, Isaac Fleury (alias De France), Gideon Faucheraud, Elias Prioleau, Anthony Bonneau, Charles Franchomme, Francis Guerin, Benjamin Marion, John Postell, Dr. Isaac Porcher, J. Du Gue, Philip Trouillort, Paul Mazyck, Isaac Perronneau, Ann Le Brasseur, Elie Horry, and Zachariah Villeponteaux.[44]

Gideon Faucheraud settled on Goose Creek in 1707 and amassed an estate of more than 3,300 acres, according to the *South Carolina Gazette*, February 12, 1737. According to the same source, by 1734 Benjamin Godin was a Charles Town merchant who lived at Goose Creek, but prior to 1748 he returned to his Goose Creek country home. On April 27, 1748 the *South Carolina Gazette* paid a memorial tribute to Benjamin Godin as being "A gentleman of unblemished character for Integrity, Benevolance and every Moral Virtue." The issue of February 2, 1733/34 showed that Paul Mazyck was a Goose Creek plantation owner of 900 acres. He built a fine eight room house, with coach houses, stock barns, sheep pens and slave quarters.

Two brothers by the name of Fleury were French Huguenot immigrants to Carolina after the revocation of the Edict of Nantes. Abrahm Fleury Sieur de la Plaine settled on the headwaters of Goose Creek with his daughter, Marianne in 1680. On November 1st, 1683 a warrant was issued to lay out "unto Monsier de la Plaine three hundred and fifty acres of land being for himself and four servants arriving upon his account in April 1680." On November 7, 1683 another warrant was issued to him for 140 acres of land.[45] Isaac Fleury, brother of Abraham, appeared to have been granted land in Goose Creek as early as 1694.[46]

The exact arrival of John Boisseau in Goose Creek does not appear on record. He received his first grant for 210 acres on Dec. 1, 1696, at the head of Yeamans Creek and

EARLY SETTLERS

adjoining the land of Abraham de la Plaine. His widow Mary Boisseau married James Gignilliat. It may have been Mr. Gignilliat who served as the only minister of the Goose Creek Huguenot Church.[47] Dr. Isaac Porcher, the ancestor of the South Carolina Porcher family, obtained a grant for 150 acres adjoining Fleury.[48] Porcher later obtained a large grant near the Cypress Swamp not far from where the Southern Railway crosses it. He continued to increase his holdings until he eventually gathered an estate of over 4,400 acres. This tract remained in the family until 1848.[49] Another Frenchman, Benjamin Marion, the grandfather of Francis Marion, settled near the Fleurys.[50]

The French comprised an important part of the early Goose Creek population. According to an incomplete enumeration preserved in *The Olden Time of Carolina*, the following were taxpayers of Goose Creek in 1694. The abundance of French names is obvious:

> As assessment of the inhabitants of the Parish of St. James' Goose Creek, for January 1694, which states that Landgrave Thomas Smith, of Back River place, "has property at Goose Creek to the amount of 2,773 pounds. Edward Hyrene . . . had 212 pounds. Thomas Smith, (son of the Landgrave, then twenty-four years of age), had 604 pounds. Colonel James Moore, 361 pounds. Madam Maurice Moore, 167 pounds. John Owen, David Webster, Thomas Flud, Nicholas Bennett, Mordica Nathan, Edward Webb, Daniel Dean, a wheelwright; John Redwood, overseer; Stephen Monck, a cooper; J. Eldress, Villeponteau, Moses Mereau, Richard Singleberry, William Weston, a weaver; Thomas Baker, Jr., a blacksmith; James Brown, James Bernard, overseer; William Norman, Thos. Baker, Senr., Humphrey Hawkins, Samuel Bisco, James Baker, John Rattone, Robert Stevens, Esqr., Mrs. Ann Cravon, Roger Goffe, James Lawson, Richard Baker, Joseph Garrat, Bryan Realy, Captain George Chicken, 1,820 pounds, (Forty-six years after this date, in 1740, his widow became Mrs. Elias Ball, of Kensington, St. John's Parish). James Ogilby, overseer, 218 pounds. James Winlock, 2,419 pounds. Captain Arthur Middleton 4,003 pounds. Captain David Davis 3,328 pounds. Captain Benjamin Schencking, 1,332 pounds. Col. Grange's estate 1,643 pounds. Robert Howe, Madame Elizabeth Gillard, 2,234 pounds. Mrs. Willoughby and sons, 1,233 pounds. Benjamin Gibbes and Brothers, 1,089. Dr. Nathaniel Snow 1,382 pounds. James and Jacob Snow, Jonathon Goodby, Sr., John June, John Roberts, Peter Lamb, Benjamin Dennis, Madame Emperor, 339 pounds,

John Feare, Mrs. Frost at David Deas, 156 pounds. James Dealton, John Herbert, Mr. Gill, Shepard and Bullins, 1,042 pounds. Peter St. Julien, for Mr. Louis Pasquereau, 350 pounds. Robert Chambers, John Saunders, Richard Edgehill, Francis and Peter Guerin, Abraham Le Plaine, Gideon Fisherau, (Faucheraud) (his son Charles married Jane Smith), John Stone, J. Beard Madera Allen's plantation; Mr. Pople, Jonathon Fitz, Benjamin Marion, the Huguenot emigrant (Dr. Geddings' Elm plantation now takes in his land), John Parker, Mr. Floree, 80 pounds. Ben Wood, David Galloway, 44 pounds. John Pight, Sarah Barker, John Filbien, 540 pounds; Thomas Barker.... John Wright, John Brown, Mr. Ashe, a blacksmith; Captain James Saunders, William White, a carpenter; Dr. Christian Cooper, Joseph Mead, Benjamin Godin, Mr. Mazyck, Henroyda Inglish, John Hasford, Captain John Newe, Edward Weekly. Landgrave Smith again, 1,662 pounds.[51]

The names of the early Goose Creek English and French settlers can be found in the records of land grants, wills, correspondence and newspaper accounts of births, deaths and marriages. It is far more difficult to identify the names of the Indians and Africans who comprised a large measure of the early Goose Creek population. Although the Etiwans were the principal tribe in Goose Creek, the records seldom refer to them by individual names. King Robin and Crowley were two Etiwans in Goose Creek.[52] The Etiwan tribe numbered about 300 at the time of the arrival of the British and French. Their numbers quickly diminished, leaving hardly a trace. The identity of the newly arrived Africans is as difficult to ascertain as that of the Indians. Their African identities, tribal and individual, were suppressed here. Many of the Negroes were brought from the West Indian islands where they had already been given new names by their island masters. Many fresh from Africa had their identities eradicated by the abrupt departure from Africa, the perilous voyage and their implantation in the new world.

Generally, the cargoes of slaves were advertised as "very prime Congo slaves," "prime Mandingo Africans," or "choice Gold Coast negroes" or "prime Windward Coast Africans."[53] There are few records of the actual origin of the newly arrived black Americans. Truth in advertising was questionable, and even if a slave had been brought back from the Congo or a similar location his tribal identity was lost, and an "American" identity bestowed upon him. In Goose Creek, as in most

EARLY SETTLERS

plantation communities, the slave's identity was that of his owner. A slave would be known as the property of Mr. Deas or Mr. Izard. At best, the slave was given a first name or a nickname.

The blacks quickly outnumbered the whites in Goose Creek and in South Carolina. In 1720 there were approximately 1,500 slaves in Goose Creek with approximately 80 white families.[54] The population figures reveal the important role played by the black laborers in Goose Creek. One historian wrote that "America was saved by Africa."[55] Written records about the Goose Creek Negroes were made by white men who were unable to interpret the multitude of African languages and cultures. Early records evidence the high intelligence of many of these slaves. Many were quick to learn to read and write English, but most of their rich African culture was lost in the process of Americanization. The important role of the African and the Indian in the frontier drama of colonial Goose Creek was critical to the survival of the English and the French. The English, the French, the Indians and the Africans formed the unusual population makeup of early Goose Creek.

The earliest European settlers found in Goose Creek dynamic challenges that would test their ability to survive. Survive they did, and in the early decades of the 18th century, they developed a progressive and independent community. They were true pioneers in a wilderness far different from any they had experienced. These Europeans were not the first inhabitants of the Goose Creek lands, of course. They were greeted by small bands of natives who had travelled to these lands centuries earlier and had learned the secrets of survival. The Barbadians, the French Huguenots and other settlers were grateful to learn their frontier survival skills from the native Indians. The Goose Creek Indians were to be important participants in the colonial drama for that part of the frontier.

CHAPTER III

THE INDIANS OF GOOSE CREEK

Long before the arrival of the first white settlers, bands of Indians hunted and planted along the rivers and creeks of coastal Carolina. The Cusabo, a small group of less than a dozen tribes, occupied the Carolina low country from the Savannah to the Wando River. They were the first to greet the English settlers at Old Town, the original location of the Charles Town settlement. Although much smaller and weaker than the powerful tribes of the interior, the Cusabo assisted the newly arrived English colonists and were important to the survival of the infant colony.

As the English settlers followed the rivers and creeks from the sea coast, they found the Etiwan and Sewee tribes in the area which is today Berkeley County.[1] These Indians dwelled along the banks of the Cooper River and its tributaries. The Sewees inhabited the lands near the headwaters of the Cooper River and their territory extended to the Santee River. The Sewees were of Siouan stock with a language and culture different from the Etiwan.[2] The Etiwan were of Mushkogean stock and occupied what is today southern Berkeley County. The exact number and composition of the Indian tribes in the low country prior to the arrival of the British isn't known, but it is known that the Etiwan and Sewee were semi-nomads of Goose Creek and the area east and north of it when the English began to settle there.[3] The Etiwan, a rather weak and dwindling tribe, were the principal native inhabitants to live among the early white planters of colonial Goose Creek, and the Sewees were their nearby neighbors. The Etiwans and the Sewees did not leave conspicuous reminders of their past. Their culture was either destroyed by or merged with that of the invading white race, and the existance of these Indians as a race and distinct culture was threatened from the very outset by the white settlement. By 1715, just 38 years after the first settlement on Goose Creek, one Etiwan village of 240 inhabitants remained. One village of 57 Sewees could be accounted for the same year.[4] Their numbers dwindled rapidly and these Indians were eventually overwhelmed by the invading European culture, which was more dynamic and advanced than theirs.

THE INDIANS

Before their disappearance, the Goose Creek Indians played a significant role in colonial life. They lent many of their cultural traits to the Goose Creek settlers, as did the tribes near other European settlements. Important modifications in English food, housing, methods of travel and warfare are attributed to the contributions of the local Indians.

At the time of the first English settlements, the native culture in Goose Creek was based upon the planting and harvesting of corn, as it was in most parts of the Southeast.[5] Hunting, fishing and gathering gave the Indians their nomadic character, but the dependence on corn production caused strong territoriality and the appearance of village life. In addition to the products of hunting and fishing, other foods included wild fruits, peaches, melons, squashes, pumpkins and beans. The Etiwan relied primarily on agriculture and secondarily on hunting. They lived in semi-permanent houses in small villages.

Recorded descriptions of Cusabo towns indicate that the Etiwan villages of Goose Creek had fields of Indian corn and numerous family huts.[6] A cleared field would be maintained in front of a central "state house" or meeting place. The field was often used for assemblies, religious ceremonies and games of sport.[7] One game of skill was called chunkey. It was an Indian game in which a stone was bowled onto the field while contestants threw long thin poles. The objective was to spear the pole close to the final resting place of the stone. Many accounts of the game recorded its popularity among Cusabo tribes.

The Etiwan activity field was used for ceremonial purposes in addition to gaming. An English missionary in Goose Creek during the early colonial years recorded the following account of an Etiwan ceremony:

> In October last, I went to see how our Ittiwan [Etiwan] Indians kept one of their solemn festivals. I saw about fourty trimed, painted and dressed in fineries coming from the woods near a little hut supported upon pillars all painted and adorned. There was a pause and a speech. Three young men holding one another under the arms began a dance followed by the rest in a long train and serpenting about several times with pretty motion steps and figures they had rattles for their music and sang after a pause only four notes, singing the same again.[8]

Early accounts recorded several types of ceremonies and festivals on the field, which was surrounded by domed huts used as family residences. They were small, warm and tight, and well suited to protect against the weather. Made of branches and bark, they were simple and easy to construct and well adapted to the needs of the semi-nomadic tribes.[9]

Near the huts were family vegetable gardens in which several varieties of beans, peas, melons, and squashes, as well as roasting corn were grown. These gardens were common, but the staple crop, corn, was probably planted in communal fields. The tribal culture was based on corn production and a cooperative effort was needed to ensure success. A Goose Creek observer recorded the following account:

> At the dawn of it, one by order goes aloft and whoops to them with shrill calls 'that the new year is far advanced — that he who expects to eat must work — and that he who will not work must expect to pay the fine according to old custom, or leave the town, as they will not sweat themselves for an healthy idle waster. At such times may be seen many war-chieftains working in common with the people.... About an hour after sun-rise they enter the field agreed on by lot, and fall to work with great cheerfulness....[10]

The Etiwan women were charged with the duty of guarding the unfenced corn crop against wild birds, animals, and their own domestic stock.[11] This allowed the men to return to the hunt after cultivation and planting. It appeared that a democratic use of labor, including the war chiefs and women, was common among many Carolina tribes. This democracy extended to women, refuting the popular idea that the Indian women were reduced to a role of inferior servitude. A certain equality of the sexes is also evident among the Cusabo tribes. An ancient treaty between the Cusabo Indians and the early settlers at Charles Town contained the marks of 14 "women captains" who held positions of authority within the tribe.[12]

Among the Siouan river tribes, the position of the Indian women was much closer to the popular conception. The Seewee were a neighboring tribe to the Goose Creek Etiwan; of Siouan stock and much more primitive than other Indians of this area. Their women were held as distinctly inferior to men, and a Seewee woman could be sold by her husband or traded for another wife at his will.[13] Polygamy was also com-

THE INDIANS

mon among this tribe. The Seewee men excelled at hunting and were famed for their endurance on the war path.[14]

The Goose Creek area was the meeting place of two divergent Indian cultures. The Seewees were related to the plains Indians of the west. The Etiwan were Muskogean, with a different origin and language. The white settlers of Goose Creek were aware of the cultural differences of the neighboring tribes, but this probably had little influence on their interaction with them. The settlers were primarily concerned with survival, and were therefore willing to adopt the Indians' survival secrets, including methods of travel, hunting and farming, in order to secure a foothold on the Goose Creek frontier. The desire to acquire land on the banks of the fertile rivers and creeks was a chief formative influence on South Carolina's economic development. This brought the early settlers in contact with the Etiwan and Seewee shortly after the original Charles Town settling. The rivers and creeks also provided the easiest means of travel, and many accounts indicate the adoption by the settlers of Indian canoes and other shallow boats for local travel.[15]

Indian contributions helped the early settlers avoid starvation. Indian corn became an important food crop in Goose Creek. According to an early chronicle, Indian corn, beans, pumpkins, squash, melons, peas, peaches, figs and even tobacco were acquired by the white settlers through trade.[16] Many of these crops were later grown by the Goose Creek settlers to provide themselves with a reliable food supply. The whites also learned from the natives how to preserve the harvest for winter and to use and look to nature's untended fruits for food. Berries and nuts were a welcome variety to the limited diet of the Goose Creek colonists.

To some extent the Indians had even prepared the land for the Europeans. They had made clearings in the almost complete forest cover by burning the vegetation and trees. This facilitated the hunting of deer and other wild game. Unless prepared for cultivation, burned forest lands quickly cover with grasses. This becomes a natural place for game to graze, and here the game could be easily stalked. These fields were taken over by the whites and tilled as their first corn fields.[17] It is very likely that the Goose Creek settlers also adopted Indian hunting and fishing techniques. In an era when guns had limited range and effectiveness, it was necessary to hunt the deer and other game that abounded near the shores of Goose Creek as the local Indians did.[18]

The early Goose Creek settlers also relied to a large extent on Indian survival methods. This important interaction extended into a significant business relationship. Barter with the Indians constituted the first commerce in the province and the single most important business for many years: the Indian trade.[19]

Indians exerted many influences in the areas of commerce, agriculture, education, slavery and war, yet the full impact of their contributions was never well recorded. The impact of the white culture on the Indians, however, was clearly evidenced. The destruction of the Indian culture is well recorded by early settlers, and the rapid reduction of the Indian population is also recorded in early census reports. Contacts with the white settlers produced an economic, social and cultural revolution that made the local Indians dependent on the whites for mere existence. This dependence evolved into helpless submittal to the dominant white culture and finally into the complete disappearance of the native race. An Indian census taken in 1715 found the following relating to the Goose Creek Indians: "Mixt with ye English, Itwans [Etiwan], villages 1, men 80, women and children, 160, total souls, 240."[20] A report from Governor Robert Johnson of South Carolina in August, 1716 claimed the complete elimination of the Sewees along with some other tribes.[21] Although the accuracy of Governor Johnson's report has since been challenged, it was not too many more years before the Sewees and the Etiwans had disappeared as identifiable tribes.

The weakening of the Indian culture was apparent from the start of white settlement. Upon their arrival in the 1670's, the English colonials found only remnants of once powerful tribes. The coastal Indians, including the Etiwan and the Sewee, had been reduced to small bands by disease and Indian wars. European diseases had been contracted through earlier Spanish and French contacts. The English further weakened the Indians by contributing smallpox and alcohol. As reported by a Goose Creek missionary,

> The Indians were peculiarly subject to all the diseases that struck down the whites. Whether small pox, for instance, struck the English or French first it always had a devastating effect on the Indian population.[22]

THE INDIANS

The English also found that the Indian culture had been contaminated prior to their arrival. The prior Spanish and French explorers had introduced horses, Christianity, European languages and other cultural features. Accounts of an early Goose Creek missionary offer several religious interpretations of Etiwan ceremonies. One centered around a symbol of a ship and involved three Indian participants. It was interpreted as a reenactment of Noah, his three sons and the ark.[23] Other interpretations involved the origin of man, Adam and Eve and animal sacrifice to a divine spirit.[24] Such reporting indicates the strong possibility of Christian influence prior to the arrival of the English. One cannot discount the Christian frame of reference by the missionary observer and reporter of these ceremonies, however.

The European influence prior to English arrival did not seem to discourage the friendly reception of the English by the Indians. Dispite nearly a century and a half of contact with other Europeans, the coastal Indians were hospitable, peaceable and friendly to them.[25] They welcomed the English colonists as protectors against the more powerful inland tribes, especially the much dreaded Westos. The Indians reported the Westos to be ferocious warriors and cannibals.[26] The mutual reliance of the Indians and colonists on each other helped merge the tribal cultures with that of the whites.

An economic and social revolution resulted from the Indian contact with the whites. The stone ax was replaced by metal ones and firearms were soon necessary for protection. Alcohol was introduced and abused, and discriminatory and grossly unfair colonial Indian laws were enacted.[27] An Indian tribute and slavery system was introduced to support white-controlled commercial agreements.[28] The Indian became economically dependent and found it impossible to retain a native culture anywhere near a European settlement. A letter from a Goose Creek missionary to his superiors in London explains:

> . . . I discoursed lately with some of our free Indians . . . . They have forgotten most of their traditions since the establishment of this colony, they keep their festivals and can tell but little of the reasons; their old men are dead; many are gone further up in the country through bad usage they received from some of our people and daily complaints

come of cruelty and injustice of our Indian traders, no longer than three months ago one of those traders caused a poor Indian woman as slave of his to be scalped within two miles of my house. She lived two or three days in this miserable condition and was found dead in the woods . . . .[29]

In addition to pressures on the native culture, the virtual annihilation of the Sewee tribe resulted from an ill-fated commercial expedition. According to a story told by an Indian trader, the Sewee were not content with the rate of barter current among the Carolinians, and they decided to deal directly with England. Having observed that all the ships came from one direction, they thought they knew the way to England. They believed that since so many ships came, England could not be too far away. The Sewees then assembled a fleet of gigantic canoes filled with skins. "The affair was carried out with a great deal of Secrecy and Expedition, so as in a small time they had gotten a Navy, Loading, Provisions and hands ready to set sail, leaving only the old, impotent and minors at Home, 'till their successful return . . . ."[30] The canoes with mat sails were tossed by storm until all but a few were drowned. The survivors were picked up at sea by commercial shops and sold into slavery.

The tragedy of the Sewees is matched by the immoral and illegal methods used by Indian traders to incite Indian wars and sell the captives into slavery.[31] Goose Creek was situated near an important Indian trade route and at a point where two Indian cultures converged.[32] The Goose Creek settlers were witnesses to the Indian struggle, and the native culture was contaminated and finally destroyed. Disease, alcohol and increase of the Caucasian genetic influence finally resulted in the virtual elimination of the Indians. The brief blending of cultures greatly improved the likelihood of white survival. This cultural borrowing improved the white settlers' life style and provided important business and agricultural opportunities during the first several decades of European settlement. The result was the survival of the white culture at the expense of the Indian.[33]

CHAPTER IV

GOOSE CREEK AS A CAROLINA FRONTIER

Goose Creek was a frontier wilderness during the earliest years of settlement. The challenges of the wilderness were confronted on equal terms by the well-to-do Barbadians, the persecuted French Huguenots, the Englishmen seeking a parcel of land, and the Indian traders. The records show years of frontier trials before the marsh and pine lands were shaped into prosperous plantations. What remains today of the records, chronicles and correspondence of the Goose Creek frontiersmen reveals the hardships faced by all. There is mention of the "starving period," "wild Indians," "pestilence," "witches" and superstitions. Yet despite all obstacles, the frontier was conquered, plantations were established and Goose Creek became an important community in colonial South Carolina.

The lands along Goose Creek were rich and began to be occupied shortly after the first English arrivals at Charles Town. Maurice Mathews, an early Goose Creek politician and Indian trader, left a written description of the province in 1680. He commented that contiguous settlement extended from new Charles Town up the Cooper River to the head of Goose Creek, and that along this route 115 men had started plantations. He also described Back River as being settled.[1]

Goose Creek was a frontier in every sense of the word. The creek's marshland and pine forests had never before been settled by white men. Starvation was the most immediate problem, with secondary needs such as basic shelter and security from the occasionally hostile Indians. In addition to the already forbidding circumstances were the constant threats of Spanish invasion and the almost complete absence of community protection. Safety was available to the extent to which a man could provide for himself and his family. The Goose Creek frontier offered the English settlers a stark change from their former homeland environment. The overpowering isolation from friends, family and in many cases from other white settlers caused a severe hardship and forced upon them a strong sense of independence. The slowness of communication, the difficulties of travel, inflation, shortages of essentials and the absence of everyday necessities were endured by the Goose Creek people, as they were by their frontier counterparts in other American settlements. Crop failures, minor injuries and illness, coupled with lack of effective medicine, could easily mean death. A man without resourcefulness was doomed to failure in an environment where survival was a daily trial. The pioneer was hardy, but the ravages of illness always kept the population within close sight of death.

The Goose Creek people were to become leaders in the political development of South Carolina during the Colonial Period. Their previous experience as planters in Barbados, coupled with the strengths acquired as frontiersmen, were to influence their political thinking and, in turn, the politics of South Carolina. Frederick Jackson Turner, trained at John Hopkins University, produced a brilliant paper entitled "The Significance of the Frontier in American History" (1893).[2] His essay relates as closely to the Goose Creek frontier as it did to most other American pioneer settlements. The conquest of the American frontier, in his opinion, was an evolutionary process. American democracy, he contended, originated in the American forests, be it those of Goose Creek or the back woods of Tennessee.[3] The European settlers in Goose Creek eventually conquered the wilderness, but during their long struggle they were transformed by their swamp and pineland environment. They were stripped of much of their European civilization and forced to adapt or to perish. Turner wrote:

> The advance of the frontier has meant a steady movement away from the influence of Europe, a steady growth of independence on American lines. And to study this advance, the men who grew up under these conditions, and the political, economic, and social results of it, is to study the really American part of our history.[4]

The frontier had dynamic impact on the settlers. The Barbadians, the English, the French and the black Africans were to become Americanized on the Goose Creek frontier.

In an attempt to obtain the most fertile lands, the Goose Creek settlers made their homes along the branches of the Cooper River. This was interfering with the plans of the Lords Proprietors, who desired the province to be developed contiguously for safety and orderly settlement. As frontiersmen settling considerable distance from Charles Town, the Goose Creek people struggled for a hand-to-mouth existence.

A CAROLINA FRONTIER

They turned to immediate sources of food, and forest products were exported for livelihood. Later, the frontier period passed and the fine rice and indigo plantations developed. By this time the Goose Creek people had already defied the Proprietors and had weakened their control. The Proprietors never realized a true return on their investment, due largely to their ignorance of the frontier influence and the independence of the frontiersman.

It was not difficult for an early settler to acquire land. The Proprietors of Carolina issued their first instructions for granting land in 1669, before the first settlement at Charles Town.[5] Although later arguments were to ensue in the Colonial Assembly about land granting procedures, the process was relatively simple, and for most Goose Creek settlers the land was there for the taking. Land was the prize for which colonists endured such hardships, and it was the scarcity of land in Europe and Barbados which was the single most important force luring the Europeans to Carolina. But before the profits of land holdings could be realized, the Goose Creek frontiersmen had to survive the initial "starving period" during the first years after their arrival in the new world.

Despite the hardships, the Goose Creek colonists had many advantages over their counterparts in other colonies, and even some advantages over their Charles Town neighbors. In 1682, Thomas Newe, a Goose Creek landowner wrote that the first Charles Town settlers were "tradesmen, poor and wholly ignorant of husbandry . . . so that their whole business was to clear a little ground to get bread for their families . . . ."[6] At least the majority of the Goose Creek settlers had farming experience, most having newly arrived from their Barbadian plantations. Other advantages were found upon meeting the coastal Indians. The Goose Creek settlers made their homes in the midst of scattered Indian villages, one of which was located quite near the present site of St. James' Church. The Indians were willing to trade food for European goods and taught the settlers valuable hunting and fishing techniques.

The weather surprised the settlers. The Goose Creek Barbadians expected to enjoy the same tropical climate they were accustomed to in Barbados. Despite the severity of the first winters, the weather was not nearly as severe as the killing winters suffered by the English at the Massachusetts settlements 50 years earlier. To survive the "starving period" and the winters, the people of Goose Creek relied on their Indian neighbors. They began planting immediately and relied on hunting, fishing and gathering to provide their diet. The lessons learned from the neighboring Indians were invaluable.

Despite the desires of the Proprietors to establish plantations of staple crops, success was minimal. It was quickly found that the local soil and climate was not suitable for many European grains. At first the settlers did not realize the importance of Indian maize, but its many uses soon caused it to be widely cultivated on virtually all Goose Creek farms. The search for a staple crop was prolonged and the settlers kept herds of cattle and hogs which ran free and foraged on natural vegetation. Barrels of salted beef and pork were marketed in the West Indies. The forest and climate was most suitable for raising livestock, and the forests abounded in deer. Venison was an immediate resource, and deer skins soon became a major export for the developing economy.[7]

The forest also provided other natural resources for export. The low swampy, fertile soils produced many varieties of woods, including live oak, cypress and pine. Pine trees were not common in western Europe, and were likely a strange sight to the Goose Creek frontiersmen. The soft and hard wood became important as building materials for domestic use and for export. Besides lumber, naval stores from the pine forests, including tar, pitch, turpentine and resin offered good export opportunities, but the difficulty of producing these products due to lack of tools and equipment prevented much actual production at this time. Naval stores were not an important export during the frontier period.[8]

Immediate survival and learning to grow food were only the first steps in settling the Goose Creek frontier. There was still a need for a commercial crop. The people had little to barter with for their needs, and had only the money they brought with them to apply against their personal debts and to pay for imports. This notwithstanding, from 1675 to 1690 there appears to have been some improvement in the standard of living. Trade and commerce developed through Charles Town. Sugar, wine, rum, and other foods were being imported. Indian corn remained the most important source of flour. Despite some improvement in the standard of living, extreme problems existed in Goose Creek even after the turn of the 18th century. A Goose Creek missionary during that decade complained of extreme food shortages. He wrote to his missionary society:

> We hardly have a joint of fresh meat once a week, Indian corn bread and water is the common food and drink for my children with a little milk.[9]

Starvation was not the only threat to life in Goose Creek: disease and illness also took a deadly toll. As mentioned earlier, the Goose Creek pioneers had many advantages not enjoyed by others and, when comparing their circumstances with their European kinsmen, the outlook was not entirely bleak. After the initial "starving period," the living conditions for the average Goose Creek colonist were in most respects superior to those in Europe. Land was cheaper and more abundant. Even food became plentiful after the lands were cultivated. The people were generally self-sufficient. The relatively better life did not protect them from the ravages of disease, however. Sickness was common in Goose Creek, and was often blamed on the water and the mud of the creek itself. Samuel Thomas lived for 34 years in Goose Creek before he died from "pestilential fever." It appears quite likely that he was a victim of malaria.[10]

Throughout the 17th and 18th centuries, medical science was still a primitive art in Europe and America. Only a few trained physicians had come to America, and only a few of these had medical degrees. There were doctors in Goose Creek during most periods prior to the Civil War, but there is much evidence that they could do little to lessen the effects of many illnesses. The Reverend Robert Stone wrote on March 6, 1750, that: "... in Goose Creek ... health was so bad that forty five was considered the common age of man."[11] By the time he wrote this, Goose Creek was already a well-established community. All indications are that disease and illness during the first decades of the frontier settlement were even more severe.

Malaria was a serious problem in Goose Creek and had very negative effect on the development of the community. An authority who had traced the early history of malaria in South Carolina concluded that it persisted as a problem because of the "oak lands."[12] The best lands along the rivers and creeks were also the areas heavily infested with disease-carrying mosquitoes, as was the case in Goose Creek. The same fertile land that produced the rice, indigo and other agricultural goods also made malaria a constant problem for the people. Though modern medical experts have difficulty classifying some diseases based on symptoms described by early observers, there were many malarial symptoms reported in Goose Creek. Other diseases which infected the inhabitants were scarlet fever, diphtheria, smallpox, measles, typhoid, tuberculosis and perhaps typhus.[13] Dysentary affected nearly everyone at some time. Commonly called "the flux," it was not always fatal but frequently caused disability for months or years and left the victim weak and susceptible to other diseases.[14]

Epidemics were also common. The Reverend Francis LeJau reported that "distemper" had killed large numbers of people in Goose Creek. Large numbers of white people and 400 slaves died during a four-month period.[15] The settlers had only their own resources to rely on to restore health after illness or injury. It is likely that they adopted native cures which frequently had little or no medicinal value. There was one instance when an old man in Goose Creek was bitten on the thumb by a rattlesnake. He had enough courage to pull the snake from a hole and take it to a nearby house. There he reportedly survived the bite by eating the boiled liver of the snake and by sipping a broth made with the snake's flesh.[16] Such superstititious cures were believed to be effective by many during this period, including the learned Reverend LeJau.[17]

Goose Creek had a number of doctors serving the community beginning as early as 1678. Some Charles Town doctors remained in the city only until they earned enough funds to equip a plantation and move to the country. Country doctors like Peter Bodett, who was settled on Goose Creek by 1678, supplemented his income with Indian trade.[18] Robert Adams arrived in Charles Town in 1680 with four servants.[19] He moved to a plantation near the head of Goose Creek, and was one of the earliest Goose Creek doctors. Dr. Isaac Porcher came to Carolina in 1696; a Huguenot refugee who lived first at the Santee settlement. He later moved to his property at Goose Creek and became a prominent citizen.[20] Dr. Nathaniel Snow owned property in Goose Creek as early as 1694.[21] Dr. Bernard Christian Cooper was at Goose Creek and died there

A CAROLINA FRONTIER

in 1718/19.[22] Thomas Rose of Thame in Oxfordshire, England practiced medicine in Charles Town and possibly also in Goose Creek.[23] In 1716, he was one of a very few who recovered from being scalped by the Yemassee Indians, and Rose lived until 1733.

In 1709 there were approximately 90 families living in the Goose Creek area with a total population of about 1,000. Reports of the Goose Creek frontiersmen tell of extreme hardship. One reported:

> We had nothing but storms four four months, many persons are ill of strange distempers whereby they lose the use of their limbs and suffer intolerable pains.[24]

If it wasn't the storms that are common to coastal Carolina, the summer heat brought its toll of hardships. Another report recorded, "the great heat has thrown many into fevers."[25] Yet despite the many hardships there remained an ironic optimism as revealed in a letter from a Goose Creek missionary: "This is truly a charming country when we are blessed with health. Rumors of death has kept our neighbors of supplying us with necessities as flower, wine, sugar. Indian corn itself is very rare. No salt for four months."[26] On another occasion the same chronicler recorded: "The climate and soil are admirable, produces asparagus, roses, and woods full of flowers very fine and unknown to Europe. Green peas and beans, greens all year, fish and fowls."[27] "We have all manner of grains, fruits, herbs and flowers. Fruitful soil where anything grows without much trouble."[28]

The starvation period passed, and Goose Creek developed into a thriving plantation society. Despite many hardships there were at least some frontiersmen who recognized the beauty and the richness in the land they had traveled so far to settle.

The activities of the Society for the Propagation of the Gospel in Foreign Parts (the S.P.G.) were important to the frontier history of Goose Creek. Much of the S.P.G. history in Goose Creek is recorded in the account of St. James' church in another chapter of this work. The mission of the S.P.G. was to christianize the "pagan Indians" and African slaves. In addition to catechizing the Indians and slaves, the S.P.G. missionaries reported being appalled by the ignorance of the white people. They immediately set about to improve the situation by providing religious guidance to the planters.

HISTORIC GOOSE CREEK

The early missionaries in Goose Creek were not only confronted with ethnic complexities but also with non-religious or dissenting groups such as the atheists and Anabaptists. The latter were much despised by the Anglican missionaries. In 1715 and 1716 the Anglican priest Dr. LeJau of St. James' church was remarrying persons who had been married by Dissenting ministers on the grounds that these were not legitimate marriages. This same Goose Creek minister wrote:

> I must observe that the last sedition was begun while the Judge was examining evidences relating to the accused witch that is still in our prison. It don't belong to me to judge but she had many friends here. It is a dismal sight to perceive how powerful the spirit of the Devil contrary to that of Christ is here.[29]

The S.P.G. in London received several letters concerning Mr. Atkin Williamson who was supposed to have christened a bear in Goose Creek.[30] This was certainly not a common occurrence, but Reverend LeJau of St. James' church was requested to investigate.

The early missionaries instructed the Indians and slaves in Christianity, preparing them for baptism and teaching some to read and write. Despite the good intentions of the missionaries and their many efforts to prevent cruelty to the Indians and slaves, they were not successful in altering the impending fate of the Indians. They were eventually eliminated through disease and abuse, and the slaves lived a rather miserable existence in bondage until their emancipation during the Civil War.

There were apparently no instances when the Etiwans rebelled against the local whites, but other Indian revolts were not uncommon in the province. This caused constant distrust of the Indians and their intentions. It was not long after the arrival of the whites that the Indian children began to speak English and adopt much of the white culture. The Goose Creek missionaries encouraged acculturization of the Indians to facilitate their goals of christianization. Reverend LeJau made favorable reports in regard to the Goose Creek Indians: "The Indian children of our neighborhood speak English, there is hope that in process of time they may be instructed amidst their wild ways of living we may perceive a great deal of patience, sobriety, justice and modesty."[31] On another occasion he reported, "I take notice that the young Indians born since we inhabited these parts . . . speak good English . . . some lads are free enough to discourse with us, I encouarge them as much as I can."[32]

Indians were enslaved in many parts of the province, but it does not appear that the Goose Creek planters used Indian slaves locally. It was reported that Indians did not make good slaves and those who were captured were frequently sent to the Caribbean Islands. It was not a common practice to enslave the Goose Creek Etiwans, although there was a common practice among the low country planters of "keeping an Indian." For a small fee, an Indian would supply a household of many people with an ample quantity of game, venison, turkeys, ducks and more. This custom lasted until the American Revolution and in some cases even longer.[33]

It appears that the most notable achievement of the S.P.G. missionaries in Goose Creek was their work among the white inhabitants. The church, the church school, and the predominance of Anglicanism in Goose Creek was substantially the result of the S.P.G. activities in the area. The early missionaries started a long history of christian leadership which united the community more than any other institutional factor. Despite the S.P.G.'s good works, a conflict developed between its designs and those of the Goose Creek planters. The conflict centered on the fear of slave rebellion. The masters feared that the missionaries might cause rebellions by educating and christianizing the African slaves. This fear never materialized in Goose Creek, but slave revolts were not uncommon in the province. It was not considered immoral to own slaves, and several of the ministers of St. James' Church did. At least one slave was a gift to the rector from the church vestry. The Reverend Ellington of St. James' Church owned as many as ten slaves at one time, yet the S.P.G. made christianization of slaves an active aim. All but a few Goose Creek masters opposed religious instruction, fearing it to be the first move toward liberation. Reverend Samuel Thomas began teaching the slaves at Goose Creek in 1695, and was so successful that ten years later he identified 20 Negro communicants as able to read and write.[34]

The concerns of the planters were voiced to the ministers and to the S.P.G. They argued that religion injured the slave as laborer, involved danger of insurrection by encouraging assemblies, and could lead to conflicts with laws in South Carolina which prevented slaves from owning property, carrying arms or moving about without permission.[35]

As the missionaries continued with their efforts, the concerns of the planters intensified. The S.P.G. position was that christianization was not emancipation, but that a christian slave who could read and write would be a better slave. This position did not ease the planter's fears. The first rector of St. James' Church reported to the missionary society that he was reassuring the Goose Creek planters by making the slaves swear allegiance to their master before he would baptize them.[36]

Shortly after this correspondence, the Reverend LeJau recorded that a rumor had spread throughout the community about an intended Negro conspiracy. He was told that the plot had been formed in Goose Creek where there were a good number of fine slaves. LeJau reported to London that 12 to 15 Negroes living on the north side of the Cooper River had been apprehended. It appeared that a Negro from Martinique had been found to be of "stubborn temper." He had enticed some slaves to join with him that they might get their liberty by force, but he had been caught and was finally put to death. Two more had been severely punished for following him, but there was not sufficient proof to take their lives. The others denied the crime and were acquitted. Reverend LeJau reported that there had not been any Goose Creek Negroes accused of having knowledge of the plot. He also reported that one of the "most sensible" of the slaves had said that if he ever heard of any ill designs of the slaves he would report it to the Reverend.[37]

The problems resulting from slavery in the Goose Creek community were aggravated by the cruelty of many white planters and their belief that Negroes were little more than beasts. Reverend LeJau reported that a poor slave woman was barbarously burnt alive near the priest's home. She was accused of burning the master's house and punished without proof. She proclaimed her innocence to Rev. LeJau until she finally died.[38] LeJau protested the belief that Negroes and Indians were no more than beasts and should not be used as such.

A CAROLINA FRONTIER

The early slave code was brutal. Criminal law was typically harsh all over the world, as the planter saw a need to impose special cruelty to rule the "savages" from Africa.[39] Heinous slave crimes in South Carolina were punished by burning the offender alive, and until well into the 18th century slaves were branded for identification. Both actions were legal and in accordance with the slave code.

Despite many "good masters" who cared for their slaves well, there were numerous reports of atrocities to slaves in Goose Creek. Under one former law, a runaway slave, if a man, was to have his testicles amputated; and if a woman, her ears.[40] Reverend LeJau protested against the law and found some support among the planters. Another report by LeJau regarded a man who punished his slaves for small faults by crushing them. The guilty slave was laid in a coffin where he was crushed with a weighted lid. His feet were chained and he was left in that state for 24 hours.

Reverend Lejau reported that his investigations revealed that overwork and want of food and rest were the causes of runaways. One Negro man who was baptised by this priest had been punished for spilling a parcel of rice. The master locked the slave in a "coffin like" box for several days, during which he was scourged twice a day and not allowed to eat. After much punishment he asked one of his children for a knife. While manacled, he stabbed himself to death. This was the fifth slave the master had destroyed through cruelty within several years.[41] LeJau reported that the majority of the planters were "good natured" and treated their slaves well, but reported that others "... hamstring, mame, unlimb those poor creatures for small faults."[42] He also reported at the same time that a planter had a very fine Negro slave baptized and other masters would come on their own accord to have their slaves baptized.

In 1690, special courts were provided by law in South Carolina for the trial of slaves. Trials were without jury, and punishment consisted of whipping, branding, amputation of the ears or death, depending on the offense. The situation was also complicated by the many cultural differences between the planter and the African slaves. One of the most scandalous and common crimes in Goose Creek, according to the Reverend LeJau, was the matrimonial practices of many slaves. He complained that the slaves frequently changed their wives and husbands, which often caused great confusion. He instructed the slaves that Christianity did not allow plural marriages or any changing of wives. In the baptismal proceedings, he would have a slave profess to keep his wife until death.[43] He also felt need to instruct the slaves not to make merriment on the Lord's Day, and threatened to keep them from communion if they did not comply. But the moral crimes of the slaves seem insignificant when compared to the reported brutality of some Goose Creek planters. Despite the many reported atrocities, however, Reverend LeJau believed that the slaves in Goose Creek were treated much better than in the English sugar islands.

Starvation, disease, slave uprisings and numerous other dangers were ever-present in the Goose Creek frontier. There was one instance when it appeared that the entire Goose Creek community was in danger of annihilation. This threat came at the hands of the Yemassee Indians, who in 1715 set out to destroy the white civilization in Carolina and came quite close to accomplishing it. This war resulted from the unfortunate and unfair relationships that developed between the Indians and the European settlers.

Most of the Goose Creek planters in the early days were merchants as well as planters, and the Indian trade was too lucrative a business to ignore. Goose Creek was but a trading extension of Charles Town. "Charles Town trades for one thousand miles into the continent," said one writer, and the Goose Creek planters became greatly involved in this trade.[44] Before rice became a profitable staple crop, the products of the Indian trade were almost the only exports of the young colony. This trade provided several valuable commodities for export, the most important ones being Indian slaves, deer skins, and fur. Goose Creek was ideally situated to take advantage of this lucrative business. An old map shows the Indian trading path running from Charles Town through Goose Creek on to the ford of the Edisto or Colleton River and further westward to the "Indian Town" and trader's fort.[45] Goose Creek's location on the trading path and the close proximity of the Sewee and Etiwan tribes thrust the Goose Creek planters into the business of trading with them. A letter from Maurice Mathews to Lord Ashley on August 30, 1671, not even a year after the first settlement, commented on the trade with the Etiwan (Ituan) and Sewees.[46]

A CAROLINA FRONTIER

Trade with the Indians, though mutually beneficial, worked mainly to the advantage of the white man. Small amounts of European goods could be exchanged for valuable skins and furs. This exchange was eagerly sought by both the Indians and whites.[47] Over the years, Indian trade underwent several stages of development. The earliest was simple swapping of European goods for food necessary to survive the first months at Charles Town. Constant skirmishes with Indians over land rights, destruction of crops or cattle provided excuses to capture the offenders and sell them into slavery, often to the West Indies.[48] From an early date, the exportation of Indian slaves was favored as sound public policy. They made poor slaves, however, as they were always running off, and in the frontier settlements there was always a fear of conspiracies by enemy Indians. In Charles Town an Indian would sell for £18 or 20 in South Carolina currency, compared to nearly twice that sum for an African.[49] The Indian trade eventually became formalized, regulated and conducted almost exclusively by professional traders who would go into the back country as representatives of Charles Town merchants.

The unregulated Indian trade deteriorated to a grossly unfair business. Some of the traders were accused of enslaving friendly Indians in addition to other unfair trading practices.[50] A commission was appointed by the Lords Proprietors consisting of Joseph West, Andrew Percival, Maurice Mathews, William Fuller, John Smith, Jonathon Fitch and John Boone.[51] The purpose of the commission was to intervene in disputes between "Christians and the Indians." In appointing this commission on May 17, 1680, the Proprietors cited instances of injustice and declared that "peace and a friendly correspondence with the Indians that are our neighbors . . . cannot be expected long to continue without due care be taken for the equal Administration of Justice to them and to preserve them from being wronged or oppressed."[52] The commissioners were to settle differences with the local Indians and to protect all friendly Indians living within 200 miles of Charles Town from being enslaved.

The practice of enslaving Indians did not stop, however. At first, the friendly Cusabo and several neighboring Siouan tribes brought in slaves, supposedly captured from nations hostile to the English. Eventually, stronger tribes became involved in the traffic. The Indians began preying upon each other for the purpose of capturing and selling slaves for profit.

A fixed price was placed on every Indian the settlers could take prisoner and bring to Charles Town. The captives were sold to traders, who would in turn send them to the West Indies as slaves. The English rationalized this arrangement by claiming a humanitarian motive. Indians, they claimed, were in the habit of torturing captives of warfare. They could not now suppress this time-honored custom and threaten the friendship of the Indian allies. The life of a slave in the tropical West Indies was better than a death by torture, they reasoned. Absudly enough, the captives' consent had to be obtained before he was transported to the islands. There is at least one recorded example of slaves consenting to be transported. The Sewees, on one occasion, had captured and delivered slaves to the English. The captured Indians were enemies of the Sewees and the English, and gave their consent to work in the colony or to be taken elsewhere.[53]

The Lords Proprietors honestly tried to suppress the slave traffic, but without success. Greedy slave dealers, eager for more merchandise, were instrumental in bringing on both the Westo and Winyah Wars.[54] The alleged excuse for the Westo War was that these Indians had outraged the friendly Cusabo. This argument would have been more reasonable had it been the habit of the English of treating the Cusabo with fairness.[55] The Proprietors upbraided the settlers for buying friendly Indians, inciting wars and for doing "all these horrid wicked things to get slaves."[56] After two years, the Proprietors declared the powers of the commission null and void. They believed that the commission "Rather to be obtained for the oppression than the protection of ye Indians . . . ."[57]

The inequitable relations between the Indians and Europeans was preserved by legislation. An act was passed in 1695 during Governor Archdale's administration providing especially for the offence of stealing or setting a boat or canoe adrift. Whereas white persons violating the law were only fined, Indians received 39 lashes on their bare backs for the first offense and suffered the amputation of an ear for the second.[58] The same year the colonial legislature reduced the local Indians to a state of serfdom.

The Goose Creek area Indians, the Etiwans and the Sewees, were included in a list of Indian nations who would be obligated to pay tribute. The law explained that the Indians freely volunteered and consented to be obligated to kill and to bring animal tribute levied by the colonial Assembly. Each year the Indians were obligated to bring in one wolf's skin, one tiger's (panther's) skin, one bear skin or two cat skins.[59] The law required every Indian bowman capable of killing a deer to bring the required number of skins. Indians failing to meet this obligation were to be severely whipped on their bare backs in sight of the inhabitants of the town.[60] Any Indian nation refusing to obey the law would, in addition to the punishment of their hunters, be denied protection and benefits of the English government.[61]

It was further enacted that "all and every Indian who shall bring and deliver to the Receiver or receivers as aforesaid, more than one skin of any of the beasts, aforesaid, shall have and receive from the said Receiver, for every such [additional skin . . .] one pound of good powder and thirty bullets."[62] Additional legislation was passed eight years later to encourage the killing of predatory animals which constituted a real problem to the white community. Every white person bringing in the skin of a bear, wolf, or tiger (panther) would receive ten shillings. An Indian would receive only half this bounty.[63]

In general, the weak Cusabo tribes, including the Goose Creek Etiwans, received little harassment from the colonial government as long as they brought in the required tribute of skins and obeyed the Governor's orders. Many Indians were employed as canoe men and as hunters for plantations. Governor Archdale recorded that "Those that live in the Country Plantations procure of them the whole Deer's flesh and will bring it many miles for the value of about six pence, and a wild turkey of 40 Pound for the value of two Pence."[64]

Fair and harmonious business relations were marred by fraudulent transactions in buying skins and slaves, which were sometimes accomplished by making the Indians drunk. Abuse of the rum trade forced many Indians into dependent poverty whereby their property would be sized for debts. In addition, the common practice of instigating Indian wars to stimulate Indian slave trade and unfair legislation is recorded as an unfortunate part of the history of colonial Carolina and Goose Creek.

One of the purposes of the 1711 Indian Acts which licensed traders was to end many of the trade abuses, but this was not the result. The Board was limited in power, and the whims of the Governor and the Commons House of Assembly controlled many Indian matters. Traders charged with trade and Indian abuses were often excused with either light penalties or none at all.[65]

The cause of the Yemassee War of 1715 may be summarized as being the result of Indian resentment toward the many years of abuses suffered at the hands of the traders and settlers. The destruction wrought upon the Goose Creek settlers took years from which to recover. The war left South Carolina impoverished, with the parishes of St. Helena, St. Bartholomew, St. John and St. Andrew almost totally desolated. It is not likely that there has ever been an Indian uprising in the Carolinas which exceeded this war in geographic scope or number of Indians involved.[66]

In 1715 when the war began, there were 240 Etiwans in Goose Creek.[67] This was no small number, considering that the white population was not more than a few hundred during the same year. The Etiwans presented no threat to the people of Goose Creek. In the words of Reverend Francis LeJau, "the poor Itwans settled among us are few in number and bad soldiers."[68] The conspiracy involved the Yemassees, who in the 1680's moved from Georgia to South Carolina, locating between the Combahee and Savannah rivers. According to the Colonial Assembly, the struggle involved as many as 15 Indian nations extending from the coast to Alabama.[69] The Etiwans of Goose Creek and the Sewees nearby remained friendly during the war. Some effort was made to insure justice, punish Indian crimes and investigate transgressions involving Indians in Goose Creek. A letter to an Indian chief from James Glen, Indian commissioner, recorded:

> I am glad your People had no hand in killing the Pedees in Goose Creek or in carrying [off] these two children. However when they are brought back we are more likely to have all that affair cleared up.[70]

Lewis Jones, the Pedees chief, went to Goose Creek to investigate the murder and kidnapping of his people in Goose Creek. A free Indian named Prince who lived at Goose Creek told him that the mischief was done by five Cherokees and one Notchee.⁷¹ It appears that the whites and Indians were cooperatively seeking justice in regard to at least this one instance in Goose Creek. Many men of conscience were sensitive to the abuses and lack of justice in some cases. From September of 1710 to April of 1715, two dozen complaints were officially made against traders in the journals of South Carolina Commissioners of Indian Trade.⁷² Dr. Francis LeJau, rector at Goose Creek, had seen the impending trouble as early as 1708. That year he wrote: "The Indians are very cruel to one another . . . but it is not to be feared some white men living or trading among them do forment and increase that Bloody Inclination in order to get slaves."⁷³ Three years later he wrote: "I hear that our Confederate Indians are now sent to War by our traders to get slaves."⁷⁴ On February 20, 1711/1712 he wrote: "It is evident that our traders have promoted Bloody Wars this last year to get slaves and one of them bought lately 100 of these poor souls."⁷⁵ Soon he reported that the Indians were murdering their traders.⁷⁶

William Andrews was an Anglican missionary to the Mohawks. In July of 1715 he wrote to the S.P.G. that:

> The Indians have lately done a great deale of mischief in South Carolina having cut off a great many inhabitants but as we are very well informed, it is what they have brought upon themselves by abusing the Indians with drink and then cheat them in trading with them stealing even their children away and carrying them to other places and selling them for slaves.⁷⁷

Andrews said that he had gotten his information from a French minister in New York who had gotten the information from a French minister in South Carolina.⁷⁸ The South Carolina minister may well have been Dr. JeJau, who was a perceptive observer of the racial problems of his day.

In 1712, Captain Cantey of Goose Creek and 41 Catawba Indians were sent with other Carolinians to engage the Carees, Tuscaroras and other hostile tribes of North Carolina.⁷⁹ The troubles in North Carolina were soon to be shared by the South Carolinians upon the outbreak of the Yemassee War in 1715. The Indian war strategy was first to kill the traders and then attack the settlements. The Commissioner of Indian Trade sent trader Samuel Warner to the

HISTORIC GOOSE CREEK

Yemassees, Appalachicolas and the Creeks to set up a meeting and hear their protests. Agent Thomas Nairne and John Cockraw were to represent the Governor until Warner arrived. John Wright, a Goose Creek planter, accompanied Captain Nairn and Mr. Cockran in April of 1715 to interview the chiefs of the Yemassee and prevent the threatened outbreak. On April 15, 1715, the council house where he and the other agents were lodged was attacked, and he and the others were massacred.[80]

John Fraser lived on a 545 acre plantation between the public road and Goose Creek. He was an Indian trader who had gained the friendship of Sanute, one of the chiefs. Sanute warned Fraser of the threat, allowing him to escape the massacre and take refuge in Charles Town.[81] By June of 1715, about 90 of the approximately 100 traders in the province had been killed. John Fraser's warning made him one of the lucky few to escape death.

The war went heavily in favor of the Indians at first. At daybreak April 13, 1715, the Yemassee attacked Pocotaligo and neighboring plantations, killing over 90 persons.[82] Governor Craven was able to meet this group near Combahee River and halted their advance temporarily.[83] Martial law was imposed on the colony and all available troops were mobilized. Thomas Smith of Yeaman's Hall sent his family to Charleston and took command of the Goose Creek company. Part of his company consisted of William Bull, James Alfrod, William June, William Scott, John Woorams, John Moore, John Dickson, Charles Hastings, Maurice Moore, George ʾChicken and John Herbert.[84]

Captain George Chicken, who resided at Groomsville, about four miles north of the Goose Creek parish church, commanded the Goose Creek militia.[85] Despite some success by Colonel Macky at routing the Indians, about 400 still crossed the Santee River and started towards Goose Creek. A party of 70 Cherokees reached the plantation of Mr. John Herne, 30 miles from Goose Creek. They asked for dinner and inferred that they wanted to make peace. After they had eaten they attacked their host and destroyed his plantation.[86] Upon hearing the news, Captain Thomas Barker of Goose Creek collected a force of 90 mounted men and went north to meet them. Most of Barker's men were from Goose Creek. His force was ambushed after being betrayed by an

Indian guide and he and 26 of his men were killed.[87] Goose Creek was then exposed to the Indian advance with no formidable defense between them and the invaders. People fled from Goose Creek to Charles Town, depopulating the entire countryside. Men, women and children with cart-loads of goods hurried down the road to the safety of the city.[88] The Indians were virtually unopposed, and could have easily taken all of the parish's plantations. About 70 white and 40 black defenders behind fortifications staved off the Indian offense. The Indians were not able to overcome the small Goose Creek stronghold, so sent proposals of peace which the defenders foolishly accepted. The Indians took advantage, rushed inside and killed nearly all.[89]

The Indian advance on Charles Town was stopped by the Goose Creek militia under the command of Captain George Chicken. He marched from the Ponds with 120 men, dividing his force into three parties and attempted to surround the invading Indians about eight miles north of St. James' church. Before he could carry out his plan, he was forced to shoot two Indian scouts, which revealed his position. He was then forced to attack his foes immediately. The Goose Creek militia killed about 40 Indians, wounded some more, took two prisoners and released four white prisoners. Dr. LeJau gave this report:

> June 13 [1715] the Captain of our Goose Creek Company, one Mr. G. Chicken with 70 White and 40 Blacks or Indians, Surpriz'd that Body of Northern Indians being a mixture of Catabas, Sarraws, Waterees &c. to the Number of three or 400 and fought them from four in the Afternoon 'till it was Dark and Killed above 60 among whom my Son believes there was some Women & Children whom the Indians did Endeavor to Secure, they fled at last in the Woods and Marshes leaving behind Arms, Ammunition, Provisions, and Plunder they had got from Our poor People whom they had Massacreed in all parts of the Province from the beginning. Since this Blow the Northern parts of this Province have been pretty quiet....[90]

Fortunately, the local Indian tribes provided assistance during the crisis. Numerous instances are recorded of friendly local Indians taking Yemassee scalps for bounty. On August 9, 1715, coats were ordered to be made for King Robin and Crowley, two Goose Creek Etiwans, for their service during the war.[91] The Etiwans continued to provide deer skins during the war, and in 1716, the Goose Creek Indians helped defend the province against the Santee and Congaree Indians, who were still hostile.

Soon after the war had begun, the Governor had requested aid from the Lords Proprietors and from the Governors of North Carolina and Virginia. During the Fall and Winter of 1716, the North Carolina and Virginia troops and the Goose Creek militia remained stationed at Wassamassaw in St. James' parish to protect the frontier.[92] Captain John Herbert of Goose Creek was well experienced in Indian affairs and reportedly lent a great deal of aid to the commanders of the North Carolina and Virginia troops.[93]

Despite the recent successes of the colonial troops, there was still a great deal of fear, and most all of the Goose Creek inhabitants remained in Charles Town. In December of 1716, the assembled troops at Wassamassaw finally drove the Indians from the colony and across the Savannah River.[94] The people were then able to return to their homes in the country parishes.

The hardships of the Indian war, coupled with numerous other complaints, were to be the final protests of the Goose Creek people against the Lords Proprietors, who offered little assistance against the hostile Indians. South Carolina was soon to become a royal colony, and the frontier period in Goose Creek's history was coming to an end. A great plantation economic and social system was becoming entrenched, founded upon rice, indigo, foodstuffs and slavery. The Goose Creek low country frontier was being replaced by a frontier in the Piedmont sections. Settlers there would later have to confront many of the same frontier trials as had the Goose Creek planters. The Goose Creek people faced the starving period, disease, slave revolts, Indian wars, the many trials of fear and personal tragedy. But they had, nevertheless, survived.

CHAPTER V

GOOSE CREEK UNDER
PROPRIETARY GOVERNMENT,
1670 - 1719

Many of the original Goose Creek settlers were from the West Indian island of Barbados. These immigrants were comparatively homogeneous, and soon unified to become the dominating political force in South Carolina during the first 50 years of settlement. The Barbadians were the largest group of immigrants into the colony during its first decade. They were members of the Church of England and opposed the religious dissenters who had come to Carolina for religious freedom. During the period of Proprietary rule from 1670 to 1719, government policy changed dramatically, but the political animosity between the people of Goose Creek and the Dissenters remained constant. Although the politicians from Goose Creek became known as the "Goose Creek men," it was all the Goose Creek people who unified to present a solid political bloc during the early period. Even the Goose Creek women were politically active then. One Goose Creek chronicler recorded that "the women of the town [Goose Creek] are turned politicians also and have a club where they meet weekly."[1] This was very progressive for that early period.

Throughout the 17th century the people of Goose Creek opposed Proprietary policy. They did not like the Fundamental Constitutions designed by John Locke for the colony. They did not agree with religious toleration. They refused to settle as the Proprietors directed. They became relatively wealthy and independent. The Goose Creek men also engaged in illegal business activities including the Indian slave trade and trading with the pirates.

The Lords Proprietors repeatedly tried to fill the political offices with loyal Dissenters and other Proprietary supporters, but these attempts only made matters worse. The Goose Creek men remained in control and were eventually able to force the Lords Proprietors to compromise. After 1700 the Proprietors amended their position on religious toleration, and to compromise with the Goose Creek men they established the Church of England as the state church of South Carolina in 1706.

Political turmoil was commonplace during the period of Proprietary rule. The Goose Creek men debated land policies, quit-rents, currency problems, representation and in most cases seemed to be primarily interested in making their own fortunes, which was usually counter to the management plans of the Lords Proprietors. The political history of Goose Creek during Proprietary rule was one of protest, dissent and political chicanery.

The first settlers in Charles Town arrived in 1670. Under the leadership of Governor Sayle they were faced with starvation, Spanish attacks, hostile Indians, and indebtedness. The Proprietors, who owned Carolina, were immediately challenged with the colony's inability to produce enough food to feed itself. In addition, the Governor repeatedly complained of low moral standards and desertion. The latter caused them to pass laws to discourage colonists from leaving. Although the situation was grave, trade with the Indians and the use of slave labor provided some economic relief during the early years. The colony grew slowly at first, and in 1683, 13 years after the first arrivals, there were only 1,000 immigrants in the colony.[2]

On his deathbed, Governor Sayle picked Joseph West to succeed him until the Lords Proprietors selected another. It was at this early stage that the Barbadians began to organize as a political faction. They were ambitious, experienced, and occasionally unscrupulous. At first they did little but complain about incompetent colonial leadership. In 1671 Sir John Yeamans arrived with 50 new Barbadian immigrants and immediately became the leader of the faction. He began to organize the "Barbados Party" with the help of Maurice Mathews, a Goose Creek settler. About this time, John Yeamans was appointed Governor by the Lords Proprietors, but was not popular. In 1674 he summoned the people to assemble, and had the Fundamental Constitutions read into law. Without submitting it to the people for a vote, he declared it to be the law of the land.[3]

The Fundamental Constitutions were the cause of many problems. After some earlier misadventures with American settlement, Anthony Cooper assumed the leadership of the Carolina Proprietors. He and his friend, the distinguished philosopher John Locke, formulated a new political design

THE PROPRIETARY PERIOD

for the colony known as the Fundamental Constitutions.[4] It was noted for its expression in regard to society and government in the frontier. The design proposed by Locke provided for an aristocratic society based on land ownership. He believed that land ownership was the best foundation for a social order since, in his words, "all power and dominion is most naturally founded on property."[5]

As provided by the constitution, two fifths of the lands of the colony were to be assigned to the nobility, with three fifths assigned to the manorial lords and commoners. The highest level in this governmental and social hierarchy was the eight Carolina proprietors. The governor was to be assisted by a single legislative house, the Assembly, and a Grand Council of 50. The Council was expected to propose laws to the Assembly for acceptance or rejection. The constitution also stated that the province was to be divided into counties of 480,000 acres, each with one landgrave. Landgrave Thomas Smith of Goose Creek was such a person. There were also to be two caciques in each county, which was divided into 40 squares of 12,000 acres each. Each landgrave was entitled to four squares, and the caciques were each entitled to one square. The Lords Proprietors were granted one square each in the original charter. These squares were called "baronies" if owned by a landgrave or a cacique and "seigniories" if owned by a Proprietor.

The constitution was very liberal for the times, especially in relation to religion. It required only that the people believe in God, but had no other restrictions. The Assembly was to be composed of the Governor, eight deputies of the proprietors, all the landgraves and caciques of the province, and the elected deputies of the freemen.

The Fundamental Constitutions, though elaborately planned, never worked well in the colony. The Goose Creek planters were ardently opposed to its provisions. They were living in a frontier society and would not accept a government that restricted them from sharing in its management.

Dissatisfied with Governor Yeaman's administration, the Proprietors replaced him with Joseph West in 1674. For nearly ten years thereafter, West remained relatively undisturbed as governor. As more and more of the Barbadians settled in Goose Creek, they increased their domination of the Council and the legislature.[6]

HISTORIC GOOSE CREEK

The relatively harmonious decade from 1674 to 1682 during Governor West's administration was not satisfactory to the Lords Proprietors. The governor and the Barbadians worked well together, but at the expense of the Proprietor's plans. The colonists refused to pay the governor's salary in a manner which satisfied the Proprietors. They agreed to pay not in money, but in commodities. They could never agree, however, on the market value of those commodities.[7] Another area of Proprietary dissatisfaction was inefficiency in land distribution. It was not done according to their instructions. The settlers were also disgruntled, due to their inability to get clear title to their land. During the first decade the Proprietors invested almost £10,000 in Carolina, but by 1682 they had realized no return on any of it.[8] They were confronted with a dilemma: either they must send new instructions for management reform or they would continue to lose their investment.

Confronted with the problem of an unprofitable colony, the Proprietors began to attempt reforms in the 1680's. During this period they embarked upon a recruiting campaign to bring hundreds of new families to Carolina. Most of these families were Dissenters. The new immigrants and the new reforms were met with heavy opposition from the Goose Creek men. By the 1680's, Goose Creek was in a large extent controlled by the Goose Creek party. A decade of political chaos ensued.

The Proprietors lost faith in the ability of Governor West to lead the colony efficiently. West became involved in illegal Indian slave trade and was influenced by the Goose Creek party.[9] In 1682 he was dismissed and replaced by Governor Joseph Morton, a leader among the newly arrived English Dissenters. The Lords Proprietors repeatedly attempted to make the Fundamental Constitutions work successfully in the frontier colony through instructions to the Governor. What followed during the 1680's and 1690's was a series of instructions which made matters worse. The earliest ones resulted in controversies over land policies, centering on the mechanics of granting the land. There had been much discretion left to local officials, which resulted in annoying inefficiency. A source of greater irritation was the insistence that the settlers live in adjoining settlements to advance commerce and facilitate defense. The fact that

THE PROPRIETARY PERIOD

the Goose Creek people settled along the creek and miles from Charleston was in defiance of Proprietary directives.

The shortage of currency made the payment of land rents (quit-rents) burdensome. The Fundamental Constitutions, the Proprietary instructions and the so-called Agrarian Laws required the settlers to pay an annual rent of one penny (or the value thereof) per acre. In 1682 the Proprietors struck the words "or the value thereof" from the law. This meant that only cash could be used to pay the rent. In 1683 a provision was added providing that that land could be confiscated by the Proprietors if rent became six months in arrears. The settlers were also required to sign an indenture which contracted them to the quit-rent provisions. Coin and other currency was so scarce in Goose Creek as well as the rest of the province that it was unreasonable to ask for payment in currency. The colonists much preferred to pay in commodities or country produce.[10]

In addition to the shortage of currency, many of the settlers had never received conveyance for the land they already occupied. The Proprietors granted land not for profit from land sales, but for annual and perpetual rent. The Goose Creek people regarded the quit-rents as a burdensome obligation and paid only grudgingly. To the Proprietors it was a permanent endowment of considerable worth, considering the millions of acres they held.[11]

The Proprietors would not accede to the settlers' plea to be permitted to pay the quit-rents in salable produce. Many settlers refused to sign the new indentures that bound them to pay the rents. Some refused to pay any rent at all, on the grounds that the deeds were not signed or sealed by all the Proprietors. In 1685 the Lords Proprietors responded by stopping the issuance of warrants for land until the indenture was signed by the grantee.[12] The Proprietors ordered the grantee to sign or leave the colony. The inefficient methods of land distribution, the rent and the indenture requirements were problems that were not to be easily solved. What resulted was an overall change in policy. The Proprietors were persuaded to cease requiring the rent payment only in cash. Paul Grimball, Receiver of Rents, was empowered to collect rent in various currencies or country produce. The Proprietary instructions read:

> ... where the person is to pay hath not English money to receive the same in Spanish money, or in cotton, silk, indigo at such rates as they will clear in England, the freight customs and all other charges deducted and that you take care that you receive that is good of each specie.[13]

Governor Joseph Morton became well aware of the bitter factionalism between the Proprietary and anti-Proprietary parties. The leaders of the Goose Creek men were Maurice Mathews and James Moore. They were despised by the Proprietary supporters who were mostly religious dissenters. John Stewart, a Dissenter, called Maurice Mathews "Mine Heer Mauritius" and his "Welch Highness." He claimed that Mathews was "Hel itself for malice, a Jesuit for Designe politick." He labeled James Moore "the heating moore" and "the next Jehu of the party."[14] Mathews was one of the leading dealers in the illegal slave trade. Moore was also invovled in the trade and did a lucrative business with pirates. He later became Governor with his Goose Creek support. This James Moore was supposed to be the son of Roger Moore, one of the leaders of the Irish Rebellion in 1641. James supposedly inherited his father's rebellious nature.[15] He married the daughter of John Yeamans and became one of the most notorious of the Goose Creek men.

Other "Goose Creek Men" were Landgrave Thomas Smith, Provincial Governor; Peter St. Julien; Thomas Smith, Jr.; Captain George Chicken, of the Goose Creek militia; Benjamin Schenickingh; John Newe; Benjamin Godin; Henroyda Inglish; Major Robert Daniel; Arthur Middleton, Provincial Governor; Ralph Izard, statesman; Robert Gibbes; Edward Hyrne; and Benjamin Mazyck.[16] A common background bound these leaders together. They were mostly experienced Barbadian planters. They were relatively well educated, had some investment capital and were Anglican. They shared Barbadian social customs, and in addition had a ready communication line along the easily-traveled waters of Goose Creek. They unified in opposition to the Proprietors, and were eventually able to establish both slavery and the parish electoral system in South Carolina. This organized political activism left a lasting impression.[17]

Governor Morton was powerless at the hands of the Goose Creek men due to their control of the Assembly. The Proprietors attempted to regain control by removing Goose Creek men from office and replacing them with supporters

THE PROPRIETARY PERIOD

of the Proprietors. The Proprietors removed Maurice Mathews and James Moore from the Assembly by declaring them to be outlaws, but this had little effect.[18] The Goose Creek men had a great deal of popular support. They opposed land reforms in order to protect their own claims; opposed the quit-rent payments in specie, and opposed the Proprietors' instructions against Indian slave trade and trade with pirates; all to protect their own profits. Lastly, they resented the new Dissenter arrivals whom the Proprietors were putting in high places. Despite a list of questionable motives, their popularity increased.

Currency shortage was one of the most frustrating problems for the colonists. A temporary solution was found by doing business with the coastal pirates. The Goose Creek men became very active in the pirate trade, which was lucrative and provided much needed currency in South Carolina. Long before Charles Town was settled, the bay and the coastal islands were used by pirates as a safe retreat. After English settlement, the pirates came to recognize Charleston as a favorite resting place. Henry Morgan, Richard Worley, Captain Kidd, Stede Bonnet, Captain Flood and others frequented the protected waters of Charles Town Bay. Many of the Goose Creek planters found advantage in trading and dealing with them. The pirates would purchase goods from the colonists for silver coin, which provided a quick and easy market and source of currency.[19] The Barbadians of Goose Creek saw little harm in such trade, as dealing with pirates had been a common practice in Barbados. They found mutual advantage in the business and did not recognize it as any threat.

Pirates were not much of a bother to the colonists at first. They were just a struggling lot, hardly worth the pirate's bother. In fact, the pirates provided some protection for the colonists by their sporadic fighting with the Spanish. On many occasions the British government encouraged pirate plundering of Spanish ships. As long as the hostilities were directed against the Spanish, the colonists were tolerant of the swaggering pirates on Charleston's streets who spent their stolen silver freely. Smuggling was a common and profitable business for the pirates and colonists alike.

This mutually benefitial arrangement was short-lived. The Proprietors began to object to the pirate trade. It gave a semblance of independence to the colonists who had already rejected some of the Proprietors' plans. Despite some obvious advantages to the colonists, the Proprietors moved to stop the pirate trade by declaring it illegal.

The removal of Maurice Mathews and James Moore from office had little positive effect on the Proprietors' situation. They next appointed an Irish Governor, Sir Richard Kyrle in 1684. He died soon after his arrival and was succeeded by Robert Quary. Governor Quary joined the ranks of the Goose Creek men and was dismissed for trading with the pirates himself.[20] Others began to join the increasingly popular Goose Creekers, including Ralph Izard, Benjamin Waring, Job Howe, James Stanyarne and many of the newly arrived French Huguenots. Governor Joseph West followed Robert Quary as Governor, but left the colony altogether shortly thereafter.

Joseph Morton returned to the governorship in 1685. He was again confronted with an Assembly controlled by the Goose Creek men. They had such an unrelinquishing hold on it that the returning governor ceased his struggle against them. He stopped enforcing the laws against the Indian slave and pirate trade, and openly began trading with the pirates himself. This situation made Charles Town a welcome port to the pirates, who moved in town unmolested. This brought occasional protests from the Charlestonians, but provided a source of silver coin, commodities like silk, and armed security against the Spanish for a short time.

James Colleton followed Joseph Morton as Governor. He conscientiously followed Proprietary instruction and attempted to end the outlawed trade. He had some short-lived success controlling the Indian slave and pirate trades, but like his predecessors, he was out-maneuvered by the Goose Creek politicians. He had been warned by the Proprietors before he took office to beware of the Goose Creek men. He was especially told that Nathaniel Johnson was one of the worst of them.[21]

Colleton was no match for Goose Creek. The Goose Creek-controlled Assembly magnaniously offered to raise the governor's salary by levying a tax on liquor and sugar. Governor Colleton, as was expected, supported the proposal and even convinced some Proprietary supporters to vote for it. The bill passed the Grand Council, and it was then that the

THE PROPRIETARY PERIOD

Goose Creekers made their attack. They accused the Governor of being a tyrant, and opposed the proposal in the Assembly. They argued that the tax bill would place such a high price on commodities that the governor would get rich at the people's expense.[22] The maneuver placed the governor in an embarassing position. The tax levy bill was defeated, and the Goose Creek men became more firmly entrenched — at the governor's expense.

Colleton also lost much political support when he attempted to solve problems resulting from the Fundamental Constitutions. Goose Creeker Ralph Izard supported its adoption as did the majority of the Goose Creek people. There were, however, a number of Proprietary men who were opposed to it. The Goose Creek faction even challenged the legality of the governor's authority. Goose Creeker Maurice Mathews issued a resolution declaring that the only legal constitution was the Royal Charter.[23] His resolution also declared that all laws passed under the new Fundamental Constitutions were null and void. Another Goose Creek planter, Job Howe, had the charter resolution passed through the Assembly, but the Council rejected it. The Goose Creek men's attempt to pass the bill and the subsequent rejection of it by the governor and Council caused many colonists to believe that the Proprietors were forcing an illegal government upon them. Opposition was strong. In retaliation, Governor Colleton refused to reconvene the Assembly. He lost popular support and continued to do so until his eventual ouster. The Goose Creek men steadily strengthened their political ranks, and former Governor Morton and a number of other Dissenters joined with Goose Creek. One was Sir Nathaniel Johnson, a man of wealth and prestige, who was a powerful addition to the Goose Creek alliance.

Despite his weakening political position, the Governor continued to carry out the instructions of the Proprietors to the best of his ability. Additional restrictions were placed on Indian trade and land owners were re-ordered to pay their land rents. It appeared that compromise was beyond political possibility when Goose Creek leaders James Moore and Maurice Mathews defied the new orders and openly sent an expedition to trade with the Cherokee Indians.[24] Political tensions mounted, and it appeared that Goose Creek might even resort to violence. It was about this time that news of the "Glorious Revolution" and the impending war with France reached the colony. In response, Governor Colleton declared martial law. In lieu of resorting to violence during this time, the Goose Creek men gathered 500 signatures on a petition to have Seth Sothel appointed as a new governor. Sothel allied with the Goose Creek-dominated Assembly and ousted Colleton from office.

It was at this time that an unrealistic fear of the French settlers began to spread. The impending war with France led the legislature to distrust and disenfranchise the Huguenots. The absence of the French dissenters' votes further strengthened the political power of the Goose Creek men in the legislature. Their political prowess led to their virtual control of the colony.

Governor Sothel did not pursue the reforms of his predecessor. He allowed the powerful Goose Creekers to pursue their illicit pirate trade and sought a personal fortune by collecting a tax on the Indian trade.[25] Seth Sothel and his compatriots quickly moved to consolidate their political victory. Paul Grimball was put into jail for refusing to relinquish the Great Seal of the colony, and Sothel dismissed many Proprietary supporters. He sent Maurice Mathews to England to present the grievances of the Goose Creek men to the Proprietors and to get their support. During this time of internal colonial revolution Governor Colleton and four Proprietary supporters were barred from political office for life and were banished from South Carolina.

As news of the increasing number of irregularities during Governor Sothel's administration reached England, the Proprietors became increasingly alarmed. They suspended Sothel from office, and appointed Governor Philip Ludwell as the new governor in 1691. During Governor Ludwell's administration the Proprietors attempted to make some concessions. They sent a letter to Governor Ludwell granting a general pardon for all offenses committed against them or the constitution prior to Ludwell's administration. Not included on the pardon list were Col. James Moore, Maurice Mathews, Arthur Middleton and a few other Goose Creekers.

The Proprietors wrote some very explicit instructions to Governor Ludwell: ". . . as the Goose Creek men are resolved to oppose us right or wrong you will take care not to encour-

THE PROPRIETARY PERIOD

age or employ them — keep a watchful eye upon Sir Nathaneil Johnson."[26] In 1693 they wrote: ". . . beware of the Goose Creek men, reconcile yourself to our deputies, don't expect to carry on the government with all parties . . . ."[27] Despite these warnings, Governor Ludwell had no success with Goose Creek.

The currency, pirate and quit-rent problems were not the only ones raised by the Goose Creek people during the first two decades of the colony. Political representation was another heated issue. When the colony was established, it was ordered that representatives from each county compose a parliament. The Goose Creek planters had protested this arrangement so adamantly in 1685 that the Proprietors sent a written response:

> . . . you say the people of Berkeley will not submit to have ten members chosen out of each county. Pray are you to govern the people or the people you? — these things go by the place and not the proportion of people.[28]

The debate over political representation continued until 1691. At that time new instructions were sent to Governor Ludwell. The parliament of 20 was to be comprised of five members from each of the four counties of Albemarle, Craven, Berkeley, and Colleton. Because of the great distance from Albemarle, now in North Carolina, the Proprietors directed that seven delegates be sent from Berkeley and Colleton and six from Craven. Governor Ludwell called for an election in accordance with these instructions. Berkeley County sent Major Benjamin Waring, Colonel James Moore, Ralph Izard, John Ladson, Jonathon Amory, John Powis and Joseph Pendarvis. The people of Goose Creek resented having only equal representation with Colleton County. They especially resented the six representatives from Craven, because that county was sparsely populated and most were French. They argued, "Shall the Frenchmen who cannot speak our language make our laws?"[29] This ethnic controversy continued for many years, with the French often appealing to the Proprietors for assistance. This hostility finally subsided. The French regained their citizenship, and during Governor Blake's administration, he was able to assure the Proprietors that the French, "have a long time lived together as if they were one nation, their former animosities being quite forgotten."[30]

HISTORIC GOOSE CREEK

Ludwell was replaced as governor in 1693 by Landgrave Thomas Smith, a wealthy Goose Creek planter. Smith had some successes. James Moore, who had refused to pay his land rents, came forth with payment. The governor was able to suppress the pirate trade and the Indian slave trade. Shortly before his death in 1694, he reported to the Proprietors that the colony was finally progressing in the right direction. He was correct to be optimistic. During the reign of his successor, Governor John Archdale, Carolina enjoyed new prosperity based on a new rice culture and expanded Indian trade with the Cherokees, Creeks, Choctaws and Chickasaws.[31] During this time the landed gentry became a more distinct class. Goose Creek planters built beautiful creek-side plantations using slave labor. A man's wealth began to be measured by the number of his slaves and the size of his plantations. Much of this progress can be credited to able leadership of Governor John Archdale, who began his duties in 1695. Archdale had been given full authority to "do anything that can reasonably be thought to advance peace and prosperity."[32]

At the turn of the century the colonial government remained in the hands of the Goose Creekers. 19 men can be identified as legislative leaders in the period from 1692 to 1703.[33] All religious and political factions were represented, although most of the leaders associated with the Goose Creek faction were Anglican. The Assembly was dominated by Goose Creekers like Job Howe, Ralph Izard and Robert Stevens.

Under pressure from the Goose Creek faction, Governor Archdale insittuted a liberal quit-rent law. It remitted rents for three years for all who held land by grant, and for four years for those who held land by survey. Simpler laws for conveying land were prescribed and grants were to be made without delay. All former grants or purchases from authorized agents were confirmed and new settlers were exempt from rent for five years.[34] The long and bitter controversy over quit-rents ended with the enactment of this law. It also alleviated much of the confusion caused by the previous land distribution methods.

Despite the reforms, the Fundamental Constitutions were not accepted by the people. Major Robert Daniel was one of the Goose Creek men not included in the general pardon of

THE PROPRIETARY PERIOD

1693. In 1698 he was in England, where he and Edmund Bellinger were helping the Lords Proprietors revise their often-rejected Fundamental Constitutions. It was at this time that the "nobility of Carolina" was put on the market. The title of landgrave could be purchased for £100, and that of cacique for £50. Major Daniel was created a landgrave without cost and was authorized to sell six titles of landgrave and eight of cacique.[35] Daniel brought this plan and a revised constitution back to Carolina for approval, where it was again promptly rejected by the people. This was the last attempt to enforce the adoption of the constitution. Ironically, it was a Goose Creek man who brought the final revision back to the colony and it was the Goose Creek people who most adamantly opposed it.

The Fundamental Constitutions did not prohibit the purchase of land, but had arranged for the land to be distributed from the Proprietors on a rental basis, ensuring perpetual Proprietary control. By 1695, many Goose Creek people were purchasing large quantities of land outright. The money from quit-rents was used to pay the salaries of the appointed officials, but receipts from land sales went directly to the Proprietors. By the beginning of the 18th century the Proprietors were finally realizing an actual return on their colonial investment through land sales.[36] These sales, however, were reducing the colonists' dependence on the Proprietors and in many cases the land was being purchased with money earned from illegal pirate trade, Indian trade and Indian slave trade.

Governor Archdale had been successful in compromising many long-standing political differences. He settled the land question through a liberal quit-rent law. When his successor Governor Joseph Blake took office, South Carolina had most of its political problems settled and was enjoying a new prosperity. During Blake's administration the British Parliament created the Board of Trade to oversee the enforcement of the shipping and trade laws of the empire. The colonies had been guilty of flagrant disregard for these laws. Three quarters of a century later these same laws were to be the basis for the grievances of the American patriots which eventually led to revolution.

Although the Goose Creek men were staunch Anglicans and resented the various religious dissenters, religious rivalry was not of primary importance and took second place to more pressing issues during the first 30 years of settlement. At the turn of the 18th century some of these issues had been solved and religious conflicts came to the surface. Upon the death of Governor Blake in 1700, an Anglican (Church of England member) became Governor over a leading Dissenter. James Moore, the fierce Goose Creek activist, was supported for Governor by the Palatine of Carolina, an aggressive Anglican. The elevation of James Moore over the Dissenter, Joseph Morton, was the catalyst for a bitter religious rivalry between the Anglicans and the Dissenters. It was at this time that the Society for the Propagation of the Gospel in Foreign Parts became active in South Carolina. The Goose Creek men, along with other Anglicans, moved to establish the Anglican Church as the official state church.

At the same time that the church establishment issue was being battled, the issue of Indian trade became equally important. The magnitude of the unfair Indian trade practices and the strong possibilities of Indian uprisings caused the Goose Creek men to unify in opposition to the Dissenters to gain control of the Indian trade and to reform trade practices. The Huguenots aligned with the Goose Creek men in controlling the Indian trade. The Goose Creek leaders, including James Moore, now Governor; Sir Nathaniel Johnson, a wealthy slave owner; Ralph Izard, planter; Job Howe, planter; and Robert Daniel were, as Anglicans, the center of the Indian trade reform movement.

Moore was the first governor to regulate Indian trade with agents. He was in debt when he took office and used his high position to profit from the Indian trade. He tried to have a bill passed that would have given him a monopoly, but the bill was defeated. In retaliation, he ordered the Assembly dissolved and called for new elections. He hoped to gain control of it through the new elections, but failed. Governor Moore was replaced in 1702 by an ally of the Goose Creek men, Nathaniel Johnson. After his replacement, Colonel James Moore simultaneously held the offices of Receiver General, Attorney General and Judge of the Admiralty, and was also a member of the Grand Council. The Goose Creek men maintained their political stronghold.

Robert Stevens, a former leader of the Commons House of Assembly and an Anglican communicant at St. James'

THE PROPRIETARY PERIOD

Church, became a spokesman for the Anglicans and the establishment of the Anglican Church.[37] In 1706 the Church of England was established under Governor Johnson as the state church.[38] The colony was divided into parishes, which were named after the parishes of Barbados.

The Goose Creek minister Reverend Francis LeJau wrote the S.P.G. in regard to the political hostilities between the Anglicans and the Dissenters,

> . . . I have known some Dissenters in Europe & have had a great respect for their interior Disposition of Soul which I found to be really Sober, humble, patient, poor in Spirit, & of great Charity but it is quite another thing here among the Leaders of the Party: for some of their meanest sort of people seem to be better disposed.[39]

The bitterness which resulted between the Anglicans and the Dissenters carried over to the regulation of Indian trade. The ususal factionalism occurred, but in 1707 an Indian trade act was passed establishing agents and trade regulations.[40] Shortly after the establishment of the official church (1706) and the Indian trade act (1707), a series of events led to the revolution which changed South Carolina from a Proprietary to a Royal colony. The Proprietors, in their attempt to make a profit, were poor managers and neglected some of the colonists' most urgent needs. South Carolina was tenuously located in a region where the threat from the French, Spanish and the Indians required constant protection. The Proprietors would not pay for it. As soon as the colony was wealthy enough to be worth the bother, the pirates preyed upon it without Proprietary protection. A large number of colonial ships were attacked along the coast, and it became impossible to take a voyage without being in danger. The Proprietors had declared pirate trade to be illegal but never invested in the protection of the colony from it.

The abuse by the Indian traders caused the colonists to seriously fear a potential Indian war. That war came in 1715; the culmination of years of Indian complaints. It brought havoc to South Carolina and was especially destructive to the plantations around Goose Creek. This was to be the final provocation of the Goose Creek people.

The Yemassee Indians were friendly to the English settlers at first, but became angry at dishonest traders. Encouraged by the Spanish in Florida, they decided to push the English out of Carolina. At day-break on Good Friday, April 15, 1715, the Indians attacked and massacred over 90 people at Pocotaligo, near Beaufort and neighboring plantations. Martial law was declared, and all of the troops were put under the command of Colonel James Moore of Goose Creek, Colonel John Barnwell and Lt. Colonel Alex Mackey. The Goose Creek militia was put under the command of Captain George Chicken.[41] Over 400 people were killed in the short war.

While the colonial Assembly was struggling with the aftermath of the Indian wars and the break down in Indian trade, a revival of an old grievance returned to the political areana. Pirates still roamed the Atlantic Ocean and some had established a base of operations on the Cape Fear River in North Carolina. The pirates were a formidable problem for the colonists. To make matters worse, the Proprietors repeatedly disallowed laws passed by the colonial Assembly for defense. They refused to allow the colonists to issue paper money or raise money for their own defense. This presented an alarming dilemma for the colonists. Increasingly richer cargoes of imports, coupled with weak defenses, made South Carolina a prime target for pirates.

The notorious pirate Blackbeard terrorized Charleston harbor. Others followed him to Charleston, and for half a year the city was paralyzed. The colonists appealed to the Proprietors for help but they did not respond. The coolonists then attacked the problem themselves. A Virginia fleet killed Blackbeard, while a South Carolina fleet led by William Rhett captured Stede Bonnet and his crew.[42] Under the personal command of Governor Johnson, the colonists broke up a pirate blockade of the port of Charles Town. The captured pirates were tried and most were hanged. Although the pirates were driven off, the colonists were not soon to forget the lack of Proprietary help.

The Yemassee Indian war and pirate problems led the Assembly to appeal to the British government to be made a Royal colony and to receive the protection of the Crown. Not only did the Proprietors fail to provide adequate protection, but they hampered the efforts of the colonists to protect themselves. According to the instructions of the Proprietors, the colony was to have elections from time to time.

THE PROPRIETARY PERIOD

The representatives were chosen by the people from each county.

It had become customary to choose the members of the Assembly at Charles Town. By establishing parishes and appropriating duties to the wardens of each, the control of the elections was decentralized from Charleston to the various parishes. St. James' parish, Goose Creek was allocated three representatives. The first election under the new law occurred in April of 1717. The people were pleased with the greater freedom of procedure in balloting in the parishes. There were no drunken riots and confusion at the elections, as there had been in Charles Town.[43] The Proprietors objected, however, and ordered the governor to void the new parish election law and dissolve the Assembly. They called for a new election in accordance with the old election law and declared all laws passed by the dissolved Assembly to be repealed.[44] This repeal was dangerous to the colony because the laws regulated trade and raised the taxes for defense. After the election, the new members protested the orders of the Proprietors and formed themselves into a convention. The infuriated conventioners announced their intention to cast out the Proprietors and seek the protection of the King of England.

Governor Robert Johnson was very popular among the Goose Creek men. He was asked to continue as governor in the King's name. He refused, declaring his loyalty to those who appointed him. The political turmoil was further complicated by a threat of a Spanish invasion, giving the governor the excuse to mobilize the militia. He hoped that the Spanish threat would keep the colonists' minds off political issues, but this maneuver failed. The militia, once mobilized, became a formidable force, and it almost unanimously supported the move to reject Proprietary rule. The colonial Assembly refused to recognize the Proprietary vetoes, and when Governor Johnson refused to align with the Assembly, the convention chose James Moore II. He was the son of the former governor, James Moore, a Goose Creek man. The threat of militia violence was at hand and Governor Johnson, despite a number of attempts to restore Proprietory rule, succumbed to the revolution. James Moore II was installed as the new governor and served in that capacity until the first Royal governor arrived in 1721. The first revolution was complete, and South Carolina became a Royal colony.

During the first 50 years of the colony, the settlers of Goose Creek were remarkable people. They were energetic, ambitious, resourceful and independent-minded. With each passing year they, as products of the frontier, became more apt and able to resist oversea authority. The Goose Creek people had rich land to develop and had an impressive history of pioneer accomplishments. They were not to be content until they enjoyed a large measure of their political destiny. To achieve that end, the people of Goose Creek battled aggressively not only to survive in the Carolina frontier, but to impose their political philosophy on the British colony. The political arena was harsh during the years of Proprietary rule. It was a rough frontier society where violence was commonplace and where a man's worth was measured by his strength and cunning.

The transition from Proprietary to Royal government did not alleviate all of the problems which so troubled the Goose Creek men. There were still the heated issues of currency, political representation and taxation left unsettled. These issues would be argued and debated and finally lead to an even more significant revolution for independence. 50 years after the rejection of the Proprietors, the sons of the same men who praised the King as the new ruler were rejecting the King's ministers in the great revolution of 1776.

CHAPTER VI

GOOSE CREEK AS A PLANTATION SOCIETY

The revolution which freed the settlers from the negligent rule of the Proprietors is much easier to place in historical chronology than the passing of the Goose Creek frontier. The frontier had dynamic impact but it was as transient as Proprietary rule. By 1719, South Carolina had become a Royal colony, plantations were well established, and the beautiful parish church was being filled to capacity with worshipers. By this time the people of Goose Creek had also earned a reputation for political strength and prowess. The frontier times had passed and Goose Creeek had entered into one of its most exciting historical periods.

A fine description of the gentleman frontiersmen who became the Goose Creek landed gentry is provided by Mrs. St. Julien Ravenel in her book, *Charleston, The Place and The People*. She wrote:

> ... many rich planters from Barbadoes and other West Indian Islands came to the province, bringing their negroes with them. They settled themselves chiefly on a small affluent branch of the Cooper, called, from the fancied resemblance of its winding course to the curving neck of the goose, "Goosecreek..." Thus began — and not from the fanciful nobility — that untitled class of landed gentry which, perfectly well understood and accepted during the colonial period, survived the Revolution and formed a distinct and influential element of Charleston society down to 1865.[1]

These gentlemen had the nerve, the energy and the know-how to tame the frontier and pave the way for the subsequent settling of other tradesmen.

According to Alexander S. Salley, State Historian, an advertisement appeared in the *South Carolina Gazette* in 1732 designed to encourage tradesmen to settle "contiguously in the Parish of St. James on Goose Creek."

> John Lloyd, Esq. will grant building leases of 64 acres of land, viz., 8 Lotts consisting of 8 acres each Lott, all fronting the Broad Path, from the Brow of the Hill Mr. Rich. Walker now lives on, to the Fence joining Mr. Humes' Land on the North West side of the Broad Path. The land is all cleared, and very proper for either Pasture, Corn, or Rice, within 20 miles of Charleston, and four of Goose

> Creek Bridge; and the Trades thought most proper to settle on it are, a Smith, Carpenter, Wheel-wright, Bricklayer, Butcher, Taylor, Shoemaker and a Tanner.[2]

By the time this article appeared in the Charleston newspaper, the frontier period had passed. Proprietary rule had been replaced by that of the English Parliament. The pirates had been cleared from the waters and the hostile Yemassee Indians were only memories in the minds of aging militiamen. The plantations were now in need of craftsmen and tradesmen, and Goose Creek had become a plantation society in the truest sense of the word.

The lives of the Goose Creek people during the years of the plantation society have little in common with ours of the 20th century. The carriage ride from the avenue of the Oaks plantation to the old church was elegant. The rice, indigo and silk society of old Goose Creek produced prosperous and exciting times, and a wedding cake receipe of that time began with 20 pounds of butter and 200 eggs.[3]

Tidewater Virginia, Maryland and northeastern North Carolina were colonies of English extraction. In these areas the economy was based on tobacco. Under the political leadership of an elite group of large landed proprietors they kept close ties with the mother country and adopted the manners of the English aristocracy. Powerful families, especially the Carters, Lees, Byrds and Randolphs of Virginia and the Carrolls, Dulanys and Galloways of Maryland became politically and financially dominant in their respective areas. The Carolina low country was settled later than Virginia, Maryland and North Carolina and differed from the colonies of Maryland and Virginia in its ethnic composition, its economy and its culture.

The origin of the Carolina landed gentry, so prominent in colonial Goose Creek, was in the Fundamental Constitutions devised by the renowned philosopher, John Locke. Large grants of land were awarded to settlers in accordance with Locke's Fundamental Constitutions and upon these grants was founded the aristocracy of the low country.[4]

The Goose Creek land grants were large due to the nature of the land and the methods of agriculture. The quality of a land grant could be judged by the type of trees growing upon it. Goose Creek had good quality lands containing oak, cypress and some hickory but frequent soil exhaustion

THE PLANTATION SOCIETY

was caused by ignorance about the use of fertilizers. Manuring and crop rotation were not practiced during the Colonial Period. As one field was exhausted, another had to be prepared for planting. The large amount of swamp and the need for vast amounts of fertile lands account for the need for large Goose Creek estates.

To manage the vast acreage and the large amounts of slave labor, the Goose Creek planter had to be a "jack-of-all-trades," including being a farmer, a lumberman, a cattle raiser and a merchant. He relied heavily on the waterways for inexpensive transportation, and provided the country produce which made the waters of the Cooper River and its tributaries the life-blood to the cultural center of the colony, Charleston.

Colonial Charleston was supplied by a great highway of trade along the Ashley and the Cooper Rivers. The Cooper was navigable for 20 miles from Charleston and its many tributaries, Goose Creek included, reached into the pinewoods and forests of the low country. The water of the Cooper was busy with traffic during the Colonial Period. Governor Glen wrote in 1751,

> Not withstanding we have a few ships of our own. Cooper river appears sometimes a kind of floating market and we have numbers of Canoes, Boats, and Pettygues that ply incessantly, bringing down the Country Produce to Town and returning with necessarys as are wanted by the Planters.[5]

Life for the Goose Creek people on their great plantations was generally not the lonely and isolated existence of their frontier forefathers. The Goose Creek community was a mosaic of business, and plantations were close enough for easy social intercourse. The creek and rivers provided the easiest means of transportation, but various designs of fine carriages were used and superb riding horses were available.

The colonists borrowed the production of maize from the Indians, and by 1739 it had become a valuable article of export. Near the end of the 17th century rice started to become an important product of the province. It was first cultivated on dry lands, but by the early decades of the 18th century, swamp lands beyond the reach of high tide (salt water kills rice) were put to use. This was ideal for the Goose Creek planter. In 1783 Gideon Dupont, Jr. of Goose Creek sought compensation from the state for inventing the method of water cultivation.[6] He developed the system of flooding the fields by river water, which was backed up by and later drained off by the tides. Water cultivation not only promoted the growth of rice but also killed grasses and weeds, which formerly had to be removed by hand and hoe. Slaves would have to stand bent over for endless hours removing the weeds prior to Dupont's water method. Until long after the American Revolution great amounts of slave labor were used to clear fields and erect networks of dikes and sluice gates for the production of water-cultivated rice. This method became widely used on Goose Creek and Cooper River plantations, enabling rice production to become an important money crop. This was especially important to Goose Creek during the difficult economic period after the American Revolution.

Silk production was also tried here. England was importing silk from the Far East but desired to decrease the amount brought in from non-English territories. Many entries in the journals of the Commons House of Assembly record low country interests in silk production. On January 19, 1738 a Mr. Morris offered 100 acres in Goose Creek for the production of silk. He also requested that the Assembly appeal to the Parliament of Great Britain to reduce the duty on silk. Despite much effort, the experiment in Carolina failed. Silk production died out about the same time as the Indian trade but not before hundreds of mulberry bushes were planted on the Goose Creek plantations to provide food for the productive silk worms.

Indigo culture was almost abandoned at first, but was later revived in the 1740's. It became an important crop in Goose Creek. So much attention was given to rice in the Goose Creek area that the production of indigo was at first virtually ignored. Indigo cultivation increased rapidly when the British Parliament placed a bounty on it, which was paid until the Revolution. The Lords Proprietors also encouraged the production of cotton. Some was planted at an early date but the process of removing the seeds made it unprofitable. It wasn't until the invention of the cotton gin in 1794 that cotton became a leading industry in South Carolina. Cotton was never produced extensively around Goose Creek.

THE PLANTATION SOCIETY

Livestock was brought to the colony at an early date and was soon to be raised on every plantation in Goose Creek. The cattle were not susceptible to disease, and because of the mild winters, they thrived and multiplied with little attention. Within a few years beef was an important article of export.[7] Cattle became so numerous that in 1695 an act was passed calling for the destruction of wild cattle. In addition, hogs were of great advantage to the poor or small farmer. They could be raised with little trouble and soon became another valuable export.

Horses were also imported and bred well. Soon many plantation owners bred them for racing as well as for general use. Several race courses were established in Berkeley County and many fine racers were bred on the plantation. Many of these were descendants of imported English thoroughbreds. Horsemanship was one of the necessities of the gentleman planter, not only for plantation management but for deer and fox hunting and the lavish competitive tournaments.[8] Two of the greatest race horses were owned by Goose Creek planters. Col. Singleton's plantation on Goose Creek was the home of "Shadow," the winner of the first great race in South Carolina between a native and an imported horse. "Shadow" remained at Singleton's until 1771. A popular race course was built at the estate of Goose Creek planter Robert Hume.[9] "Tartar," an imported horse belonging to Hume, ran several seasons at Goose Creek and lived until 1767. By the end of the 17th century the colonists were prospering, but doing so contrary to the designs of the Proprietors. They wanted a colony of planters, not stock raisers.

The rich plantation society which characterized Goose Creek prior to the Civil War produced a number of natural and medical scientific endeavors. The frontier doctor who earlier risked being scalped while supplementing his medical practice with Indian trade was more likely to devote his full energies to the practice of medicine during the plantation era. One of the early physicians in Berkeley County was a Frenchman named Lewis Mottet. He lived at Stone Landing and attended some of the plantations in St. James Goose Creek. In the spring of 1761 he moved to Goose Creek to continue his medical practice.[10] Dr. Mottet was a native of France and a very educated and talented physician. Dr. Joseph Johnson recorded some very humorous stories about

HISTORIC GOOSE CREEK

Dr. Mottet in his book entitled *Traditions and Reminiscences, Chiefly of the American Revolution in the South,* published in 1851. The following is one of them:

Dr. Mottet during some of his visits would tell the family that if a good fat calf was butchered he would extract from it something especially beneficial to his patient. He also would profess that a bit of veal or a good calf's head soup would strengthen his nerves and provide for him better insight into the patient's disease. When properly fed, he professed, he made a better diagnosis. On one occassion the country doctor sent a bill to a gentleman who objected to the charges. He refused to pay the bill. Mottet made no protest and waited patiently until the gentleman again needed his medical help. The gentleman was in great pain. The doctor paid a visit, made diagnosis and then deliberately took a seat in the chamber. The man pleaded for assistance but the good doctor did nothing. After great deliberation the doctor finally consented to provide relief only if the man paid his past bill immediately. The man promptly paid and in turn was relieved of his ailment.

Doctor Johnson also retold an incident leading to a lawsuit against Doctor Mottet. It seems as if a young gentleman sick with fever had failed to abide by the doctor's instructions and went into a relapse. The good doctor upon finding his patient weak with the fever and nearly delerious stripped off the bed clothes and soundly thrashed the young man with a twig-whip. He then carefully covered up the patient and left him raging with fever and pain. A profuse perspiration followed and the young man soon recovered. Although the young man was cured of his fever he had no relief for his wounded pride. The man sued the doctor for assault and battery. Dr. Mottet requested permission to defend his own case. He was granted this right and proceeded to defend himself in such a manner that turned the case into something ridiculous and had the penalty laughingly dismissed. He assured the court that he had only acted professionally. It was his duty both to prescribe and administer for the relief of his patient. He recounted that the man had refused to comply with his instructions and prescriptions. Having failed to comply and having experienced a relapse the doctor had arrived at a crucial time of need. He proclaimed that he could not spare the time for other remedies such as blister, mustard plasters and potions. He was obliged to administer a radical stimulant to the extremities of his patient. The whipping was an application that caused instantaneous results. No other treatment, said he, could have had more immediate effects. He then appealed to the patient and the court to an acknowledgement that the disease was cured. Dr. Mottet

THE PLANTATION SOCIETY

was French and in this case he exaggerated his accent and pretended to misunderstand the meaning or words. He very gravely assured the court that the charge of "salt and batter" was altogether unfounded. He said it was for a cook to use salt and batter, he was a physician and was indignant at the imputation. The court became convulsed with laughter and the doctor was released with one shillings damages.

Having triumphed in court, Dr. Mottet sent the young man the bill for his radical treatment. The man paid instead of facing the doctor in court a second time. Doctor Mottet was a comical addition to a long list of Goose Creek doctors during the days of plantation life.

Among other physicians, Dr. Stephen St. John is recorded as dying in Goose Creek in 1805[11] and a Dr. Poyas was also in Goose Creek in 1790. The tombstone of Dr. Robert Brown (1714-1757), a surgeon, could once be found at the Goose Creek Chapel of Ease.[12] Dr. John Martini retired to Goose Creek, and Dr. John Hendrick Swint resided in Goose Creek in 1763. Dr. John Watson, Jr. served as a Goose Creek representative in 1805. Dr. Richard Boddin was in Goose Creek in 1742, as well as Dr. A. Brown (Broun?). Dr. Peter Hurne (Hyrne?) was there 1740, and Dr. George Smith 1751.[13] It appears as if there were always a number of physicians in Goose Creek during the plantation society period until the Civil War. Although the Goose Creek economy slowly declined during the 19th century, there were five Goose Creek doctors as late as 1860. In 1850, Thomas L. Gilson and Tamil H. Hamilton were Goose Creek physicians.[14] In 1860 Doctors I.B. Varner, L.B. Gilmore, H.J. Abbott, L. Fitzsimons and O.C. Rhame were all living in St. James Parish, Goose Creek.[15]

The most noteworthy Goose Creek practitioner during the plantation years was Dr. Alexander Garden. He resided at Otranto plantation on Goose Creek and was the most important scientific figure in colonial Carolina. His eminence was in botany and natural science, but he was also a renowned personality in Charles Town's medical circles from 1752 until after the American Revolution.[16] Dr. Garden did not make major contributions to medicine except as a practitioner. His only published writings connected with medicine were *An Account of the Medical Properties of the Virginia Pinkroot* and *The Effects of Ashes of Tobacco in the Cure of Dropsy*.[17] His contributions to natural science were

73

far more numerous and noteworthy.

There appears to have been little advancement made in treating illness and disease in Goose Creek after the frontier period. There were many cases of yellow fever, malaria and pleurisies (chest and lung disorders).[18] In 1751 "quinsis" (throat problems) and "fluxes" (fluid discharges) were serious problems, and in 1752 whooping cough was common.[19] Measles, smallpox, and the like would frequently cause death and were virtually incurable by medical science in those days.

The most critical issue in Goose Creek during the plantation period was created by slavery. From an early date the number of black slaves in Goose Creek began to outnumber the whites. In 1709, 80 families owned 450 slaves.[20] By 1790 there were more than five slaves for every white inhabitant in the parish. In 1737, Lieutenant Governor Broughton warned that "our negroes are very numerous and more dreadful to our safety than any Spanish invasion."[21] Yet despite the constant fear of rebellion, the planters in Goose Creek became economically dependent on large amounts of slave labor. The 2,333 slaves in Goose Creek in 1790 were owned by just 116 families. This number was likely less than were present prior to the Revolutionary War because many slaves had been taken from Goose Creek by the British troops.[22] There were only 20 families which owned no slaves, and there were five families in Goose Creek which owned nearly one third of all the slaves in the area. John Deas, Senior had 208 slaves; John Deas, Junior had 170; Joseph Glover had 123 and Ralph Izard owned 105 slaves on his Goose Creek estate. In 1790 he owned 594 slaves on his eight plantations in three parishes, and was the second largest slave owner in South Carolina. He and Benjamin Mazyck (with 100 slaves) were the largest slave owners in Goose Creek.[23] Despite the widespread use of water culture to eliminate the rice weeds, the demand for slaves remained, whether to produce rice, indigo, other foodstuffs or tend to the livestock.

The number of slaves depended upon the amount of swamp land on the plantation. These lands required a vast amount of human toil in unhealthy environs before they were useable for rice cultivation. The thick forest growth of the swamp had to be cleared away, ditches dug, embankments constructed and water reservoirs prepared for the irrigation

THE PLANTATION SOCIETY

process. Their tools were of the kind that had been used for centuries. The hoe was the principle implement used in the cultivation of rice, indigo, corn and other crops before the Revolution. Harvesting was done with sickle and scythe. Timothy Ford wrote in his diary in 1784:

> The number of slaves supply the almost total want of instruments of husbandry; & the dint of muscular force the want of invention and improvement.[24]

The Reverend Richard Ludlam, who officiated at St. James' church from 1723 to 1728 was a keen observer of local social and economic conditions during the early years of the plantation society. His travels through the parish brought him into contact with the great plantations and the small farms. His letters to the S.P.G. mentioned the importance of rice as the staple crop in South Carolina. The warm climate, the low Goose Creek swamps, the port at Charleston and the proximity to the West Indian slave trade all were factors contributing to rice production. Rice became more of an "institution than a cereal."[25] In 1725, Reverend Ludlam wrote:

> ... As matters stand with us we make use of a wile for our present security to make the Indians and negros a check upon each other lest by their vastly superior numbers we should be crushed by one or the other. This I imagine one cause that intimidates the planters from being willing that their sensible slaves should be converted to Christianity lest as they allege they should make such an ill use of meeting to do their duty to God as to take the opportunity at such times of seizing and destroying their owners.[26]

In his Fundamental Constitutions, John Locke stated that "every freeman of Carolina shall have absolute power and authority over his negro slaves, of what opinion or religion soever." Slavery was sanctioned and its existence was protected against any presumed jeopardy. In no other colony did slavery begin more auspiciously nor was there any greater prospect for its success.[27] Many South Carolinians were concerned about the large importations of blacks, and in 1686 the colonial legislature passed laws to insure the domination of the white master over the slave as promised by the Fundamental Constitutions. Slaves were not allowed to engage in business or trade or leave the plantation at night without written permission.

The slave code was strengthened in 1722. It forbade slaves to possess weapons and provided severe penalties for offenses. Murder, burglary, robbery, arson and running away were capital offenses. Lesser crimes such as stealing hogs and chickens were treated by branding the slave with an "R." Chronic offenders were to be put to death.

Runaway slaves and slave rebellions were not uncommon. On March 8, 1742, the following entry appeared in the journal of the Commons House of Assembly:

> No. 56. A Certificate of Jeju Grange, Captain of Goose Creek Company, in Favour of Mr. James Barrie, dated the 12th Day of September, 1739, for a Beef killed for the Use of the said Company in the Time of the Negro Insurrection amounting to the Sum of £6:00:00.

Slaves were the property of the white master. Runaway slaves were frequently advertised for and even branded. Thomas Monck owned a Goose Creek plantation during the 18th century. In September of 1736, Monck offered a reward of 40 shillings each for the return of three Gambia Negroes.[28] He was one of the few slave owners who branded his slaves. In an advertisement in the *South Carolina Gazette* of March 12, 1737, he offered a reward of £5 local currency for the return of an Angola Negro named Cudja. He described him as being 'branded on his right breast 'T Monck.' "[29] In January of that year he advertised for the return of a slave named Sampson "to me at my plantation in Goose Creek."[30] A slave was a costly investment which could not be allowed to depreciate. No idleness was permitted and the slaves' year had few holidays. From Spring until September the slaves cultivated rice, indigo and other crop lands. In the Fall the slaves beat out rice in crude hand mills, cleared land, sawed lumber, split rails, made staves and shingles and coopered barrels.

Building and maintaining roads and bridges was done by slaves under the supervision of road commissioners. All male slaves from 16 to 60 years of age were required to perform road duty. Road commissioners from St. James Goose Creek named in the 1721 road act were Thomas Smith, Capt. Benjamin Schenekingh, Capt. Roger Moore, Capt. William Dry, Capt. Edward Hyrne, John Stone and John Parker.[31] The maintenance of roads, bridges and ferries was a constant problem in Goose Creek. The marsh and pinelands were traveled via roads which were seldom more than wagon trails or horse paths. The many low creek and river inlets made bridges and ferries necessary. The journals of the Commons House of As-

THE PLANTATION SOCIETY

sembly contain a number of petitions from Goose Creek people desiring bridge or road repair. This was done with slave labor.

The slave's working day was monotonous and demanding. A British officer described the working day as lasting from daybreak to late in the evening. At night he said, "they sleep on a bench, or on the ground, with an old scanty blanket, which serves them at once for bed and covering." Attempts have been made to glorify the singing Negro as he toiled in the field, and to portray him as a content, "happy-go-lucky" carefree inhabitant of semi-tropical Carolina. His singing was not always indicative of his jovial mood, however. The endless hours in the fields were made less monotonous with song. The rhythm maintained a steady working motion and commands or orders could be relayed. Songs were a conspicuous characteristic of the African slave. As the plantations varied so did the characteristics of the slaves. Their songs, their stories, even their spirituals changed from plantation to plantation. It was noted that a more singing speech and a lifting of the tone on the last syllable was common on the plantations settled by the Huguenots. The slaves of different plantations had different songs.[32]

Not all slaves toiled endless hours in the fields. Some were house servants who performed the majority of the daily chores. One such so-called "domestic" of the older times was a slave named Bob. He is recorded as being one of that respectable class of grey-headed family servants who "a native and to the manor born, never passes without involuntarily removing his hat." Bob began his career as a postillion "boy." His old "maussa" would ride behind him and four horses to the parish church. He was promoted to the position of driving his "old Misses" when she would attend a sale at the Ten Mile Hill house. Bob remained at his home at Goose Creek plantation (now Yeamans' Hall) until his death.[33]

There was some concern for the education of the slaves in Goose Creek. Despite much opposition from the planters, the Goose Creek S.P.G. missionaries had remarkable success compared to other parishes. One planter wrote:

> I humbly take the freedom to acquaint you that whereas I have not known or, heard of any care generally taken in Carolina by masters or owners of slaves to instruct or cause them to be instructed ... only in or near Goose Creek. The case of these poor people ... is much to be pitied.[34]

77

HISTORIC GOOSE CREEK

Some Goose Creek planters cooperated with the missionaries and were zealous in encouraging the instruction of their slaves. Lady Moore, Captain David Deas, Mrs. Sarah Barker and several others encouraged slave instruction.[35]

The missionaries generally worked to gain the confidence of the slave masters so the slaves could be educated and baptized. Reverend Le Jau of Goose Creek was especially successful at this. He also worked to abolish the harsh slave laws. Even the skillful Le Jau had problems maintaining the confidence of the Goose Creek slave owners and was not confident that all slaves should be educated. He wrote:

> We want a schoolmaster in my parish for our white peoples children, but as for the negroes or Indians with all submission I would desire that such a thing should be taken into consideration as the importance of the matter and the consequences which may follow do deserve. The best scholar of all the negroes in my parish and a very sober and honest liver, through his learning was like to create some confusion among all the negroes in this country. He had a book wherein he read some description of the several judgments that chastise men because of their sins in these latter days, that description made an impression upon his spirit, and he told his master abruptly there would be a dismal time and the moon would be turned into blood, and there would be dearth of darkness and went away. When I heard of that I sent for the negro who ingeniously told me he had read so in a book. I advised him and charged him not to put his own constructions upon his reading after that manner, and to be cautious not to speak so, which he promised to me but yet would never show me the book; but when he spoke those few words to his master, some negro overheard a part, and it was publicly blazed abroad that an angel came and spake to the man. He had seen a hand that gave him a book; he had heard voices, seen fires, etc. As I had opportunities I took care to undeceive those who asked me about it; now it is over, I fear that those men have not judgment enough to make good use of their learning and I have thought most convenient not to urge too far that Indians and negroes should be indifferently admitted to learn to read, but I leave it to the discretion of their masters . . . .[36]

Despite the good intentions of some Goose Creekers, slavery remained a hideous institution until the Civil War, and dominated the social and cultural development of the Goose Creek community.

The Goose Creek planters retained an independent spirit longer than Americans of some other parts of the nation.

THE PLANTATION SOCIETY

They, their families and their businesses were isolated in large, relatively self-contained domains. They ruled over not only vast estates but also over dozens or even hundreds of laboring subjects as part of the Carolina nobility. The women were also independent free-thinkers. Their duty was to provide supplementary services to the plantation including food, clothing, medical treatment, education and discipline. The plantation system resulted in an almost complete absence of a town or community center. The establishment which most resembled one was St. James' Church. It was not only a place of worship, but was a very popular meeting place for the community. An opportunity to visit friends and neighbors was afforded before or after church services. The large majority of English residents were Anglicans, and the relatively large settlement of French Huguenots also eventually became members of the Anglican St. James' Church.

There were also other social clubs which provided for social camaraderie and a place to exchange news. The Goose Creek Friendly or River Club often met at Edward Keating's place. He had for many years a social hall at the Twenty-three mile house. According to the notes of Motte Alston Read, a membership list was found among the papers of the Rev. Melivard Pogson. The following list of members of the Goose Creek Friendly Society was recorded by Mr. Benjamin Mazyck, who noted that the club met every last Saturday of the month at Mr. Edward Keating's. The original members of the club were:

> The honorable James Kinloch, William Middleton, Isaac Childs, Zacher. Villeponteaux, Benjamin Mazyck, James McKelphin, Peter Taylor, Thomas Wright, Thomas Middleton, John Morton, Richard Shingleton, William Allen, Nathaniel Broughton, Andrew Broughton, Richard Gough, John Gough, Peter Hume and Robert Boddin.[37]

There were a number of Baptists in the Goose Creek community beginning with the earliest settlers. Samuel Thomas found on Goose Creek two families of Anabaptists.[38] The Baptist congregation appears to have grown steadily but slowly during the 18th century. Shortly after the American Revolution, Richard Furman engaged in missionary efforts in the areas around Charleston. He, with the help of Mrs. Hepzibah Townsend, was able to expand the Baptist congregation in Goose Creek and established a church there. During the early years of the 19th century, Rev. Mathew McAllsers served at Wassamassaw Baptist Church in St. James' parish. He was later the pastor of the Goose Creek Baptist Church.[39]

The early Goose Creek settlers found profit in lumber, rice, pitch, tar, turpentine, cattle, hogs, deer and other skins. These items formed the economic foundation of the low country, but the Goose Creek economy began to suffer in the midst of a flourishing plantation culture. The progress being made in England in retaining or restoring fertility by using manure did not spread to South Carolina until long after the Revolution. The loose, light soil of the low country soon began to show signs of exhaustion. As early as 1736 the S.P.G. reported a migration of some people from the eastern to the western section of the parish and some leaving the parish entirely.[40]

Rev. Robert Stone wrote on March 6, 1750, that the lands in Goose Creek parish were worn out. He said that many inhabitants were dead and that many were "running away" to new settlements. In 1741, nine families and 202 slaves moved from the Parish. This general movement of people from Goose Creek received a temporary reprieve as a result of the war with the Cherokees. Rev. Harrison of St. James' church wrote in 1759 that his congregation had increased. The S.P.G. recorded in 1750 that people were returning from the frontier because of the war.[41]

The Revolutionary War was a victory for the Americans but it also meant an end to the bounty on indigo. Shortly after the war and during the early decades of the 19th century the Goose Creek inhabitants continued to move out of the community, and the habits of many large planters gradually changed. They had built their homes along the river and creek to provide for convenient cultivation of the rice and indigo, but the wet swamp lands were blamed for bad health. It appeared to them that during the hot summer months a fever with chills was caused by a gas which they called "miasma" which rose from the mud and stagnant water. The planters began to spend their summers in Charleston, returning to their plantations after the first frost. The slaves remained in Goose Creek year around with their overseers. By 1768 the blacks far outnumbered the whites in attendance at St. James' Church. Reverend Harrison commented that attendance was good that year for about two months in the

THE PLANTATION SOCIETY

Spring with about 30 or 40 white people and about 100 blacks.

Shortly after the Revolutionary War, planters began to build summer homes in the pine woods of upper Berkeley County. Small settlements like Pinopolis and Pineville began to develop. The high, well-drained pine lands did not foster the mosquitoes and the malaria that plagued Goose Creek. The plantations continued to be worked for a profit by absentee landowners until the emancipation of the slaves during the Civil War. This act shattered the Goose Creek economy. Blacks comprised the bulk of the population in Goose Creek until the second half of the 20th century. Their freedom caused an abrupt and radical change in the character of the Goose Creek community. The term "planter" is usually used for the holder of at least ten slaves. Using this definition, most heads of households in 1790 in Goose Creek were planters. Nineteen families in Goose Creek in 1790 had 40 or more slaves and 42 families were small planters owning 10 or less slaves. There was even a Goose Creek free black woman named Binah who owned two servants. Besides Binah, there were no other free blacks who owned slaves out of 15 free blacks in Goose Creek in 1790.[42]

This trend is generally followed well into the 19th century. In 1840 there were 14 professionals according to the census, including doctors, lawyers and teachers. Another 14 residents were engaged in navigation and trade, and 338 made their living by agriculture. In 1850 most all adult white males were listed as planters.[43] Other white adult occupations were listed as midwife, blacksmith, surveyor, wheelwright, wood cutter, capitalist, tollgate keeper, pump mender and many listed as laborers. Other occupations were reported as brickmakers, overseers, coachmakers, watch makers, coal burners and turpentine makers. There were two physicians and three school teachers.[44] In 1850 there were 1,857 free inhabitants in St. James' Parish, with 370 families living in 295 houses.

Perhaps the most significant comparison of census reports indicates the radical change which occurred in Goose Creek between 1860 and 1870. According to the 1860 census report made just prior to the Civil War, there were 357 families in St. James' Parish Goose Creek, including four physicians and four school teachers. The 1870 census showed a complete absence of professionals or skilled laborers.[45]

HISTORIC GOOSE CREEK

Most occupations listed in 1870 were phosphate laborers, small farmers and farm laborers. The report differs widely from the 1860 reports. Most were small black farmers and nearly all were illiterate. This trend continued, according to the 1880 census report. In that year almost all inhabitants were small farmers, farm laborers, phosphate workers or railroad laborers. Almost all inhabitants were black, with few reported as literate and no professional occupations listed.[46] The enslaved bodies and minds of so many Goose Creek blacks resulted, after emancipation, in a freedom which many were unprepared to take advantage of.

The Emancipation Proclamation put an immediate end to slavery, but the culture of the Goose Creek blacks took many more decades to blend with the white society. Remnants of the black slave culture survived well into the 20th century, and even today many black families retain the names of the masters of their ancestors. Middleton, Singleton and Mazyck are still common names among the remaining black families of Goose Creek — the names of antebellum Goose Creek planters.

A writer during the last decades of the 19th century gives a good account of Goose Creek during the prosperous days compared to its desolation of the latter years.

> This Parish so stripped, so denuded of inhabitants, once swarmed with a thickly settled and increasing population. Here at this chancel once knelt more communicants than could be found at Old St. Philip's on Easter Day. These fields and swamps, which nature has long since reclaimed and where solitude now reigns, save where broken by the shriek of the water fowl, or the hunter's horn, once resounded with the hum of busy industry and bear upon their faces even now, the mark of old time enterprise, energy and skill. Those lawns and pleasure grounds; those elaborate terraces and artificial lakelets; those walks once beautiful with imported gravel from Holland but now thickly matted with the pine and the oak and the myrtle; were once the resorts of refinement and elegance and beauty. Here along the roads once galloped those gay parties of which family tradition tells us, and here before these doors with its rich liveried attendants, drew up in no stinted numbers, as I saw it in my ancestral home across the Ashley, the old English coach with its massive panels of unbroken gilt.[47]

CHAPTER VII

THE GOOSE CREEK PLANTATION COMMUNITY

The Goose Creek community was accessible from Charleston by a road called "The Path" at first and later referred to as the "New Broad Path." Proceeding north along it from the Charleston neck, a traveler came upon a number of taverns named in accordance with the tavern's distance from Charleston. Thus, ten miles from Charleston and within the southern boundary of St. James' parish was the Ten Mile House Tavern. Located nearby was Andre Michaux's French Garden. Michaux was sent by the Royal French Government to study American flora, and here he conducted many botanical experiments. Adjoining French Garden was Cyprian Bigelowe's and Peter Manigault's tracts. Manigault called his plantation Steepbrook, and it bordered on the waters of Goose Creek, west of Yeamans Hall. Dozens of interesting stories are connected with Yeamans Hall, once known as Old Goose Creek Plantation. Next to it and at the point where Goose Creek flowed into the Cooper River was the estate known as Palmettos. North of Peter Manigault's Steepbrook was the large estate of Benjamin Godin known as Fountainbleau. This estate contained 3,847 acres with a large frontage on Goose Creek. This merchant-planter was one of the wealthiest low country land owners.

The New Broad Path proceeded past Fountainbleau and along the estate called The Hayes, once owned by John Parker. Next to The Hayes and Fountainbleau was the renowned Otranto estate. This early Middleton property was later the home of the renowned botanist Alexander Garden. West of Otranto and the Hayes was Martindale's, Thomas Mell's and Windsor Hill, the home of the famous Moultrie family. Bordering to the north of The Hayes was John Barker's estate. Also here was Woodstock, a large house with lofty columns supporting the roof of the portico. Also nearby was The Elms, the country home of the Honorable Ralph Izard, renowned statesman. There at The Elms the New Broad Path came to a fork. The western branch ran parallel to The Elms for several miles until it intersected the Dorchester Road. Approximately four miles from that intersection was the village of Dorchester; St. George's Church, Dorchester; and Fort Dorchester, once defended by Francis Marion.

The eastern branch of the New Broad Path came through the center of the Goose Creek community. The road crossed the Goose Creek bridge and passed the Goose Creek tavern. Here was the beautiful avenue of live oaks, the main entrance to the Middleton estate known as The Oaks. Near here was Red Bank Road, which passed near St. James' Church and the church school house. The road proceeded approximately five miles west to Red Bank Landing on the Cooper River. Located here was Red Bank Plantation, which was for a long time the property of Mr. John F. Poppenheim of an old Goose Creek family. He resided at the dwelling house of Marrington plantation on the northern part of his tract. There was formerly an extensive pottery for the manufacture of tile at Red Bank.

About three miles north of Foster Creek on Back River Road was Mount Pleasant plantation. This was once the home of William Wither, who died there in 1778. The property deteriorated during and after the American Revolution and was later acquired by Mr. John Poppenheim who sold it to the Orangeburg Hunting Club. The eastern branch of the road from the Broad Path was known as the State Road. After it crossed the Goose Creek bridge and passed the tavern and The Oaks estate it turned northwest. At this turn a road branched east to Ararat Plantation on Foster Creek, the home of Mrs. Horry of Santee. She so named the location after having been driven there by disastrous floods in the Santee country. Nearby was Howe Hall, settled by Job Howe, the speaker of the Commons House of Assembly in 1704. Nearby were Liberty Hall, Brick Hope, Parnassus and The Cottage plantations.

In 1883 Liberty Hall was the property of Dr. Bachman and later became the home of Charles Desel. In the 1930's it was part of the estate of Calin McKay Grant and was leased as a hunting club. Liberty Hall adjoined the small Brick Hope plantation, formerly the home of Charles Groves. Today Liberty Hall and Brick Hope are part of the Naval Weapons Station.

Intersecting the State Road was the Back River Lower Road and the Back River Upper Road, both of which led to

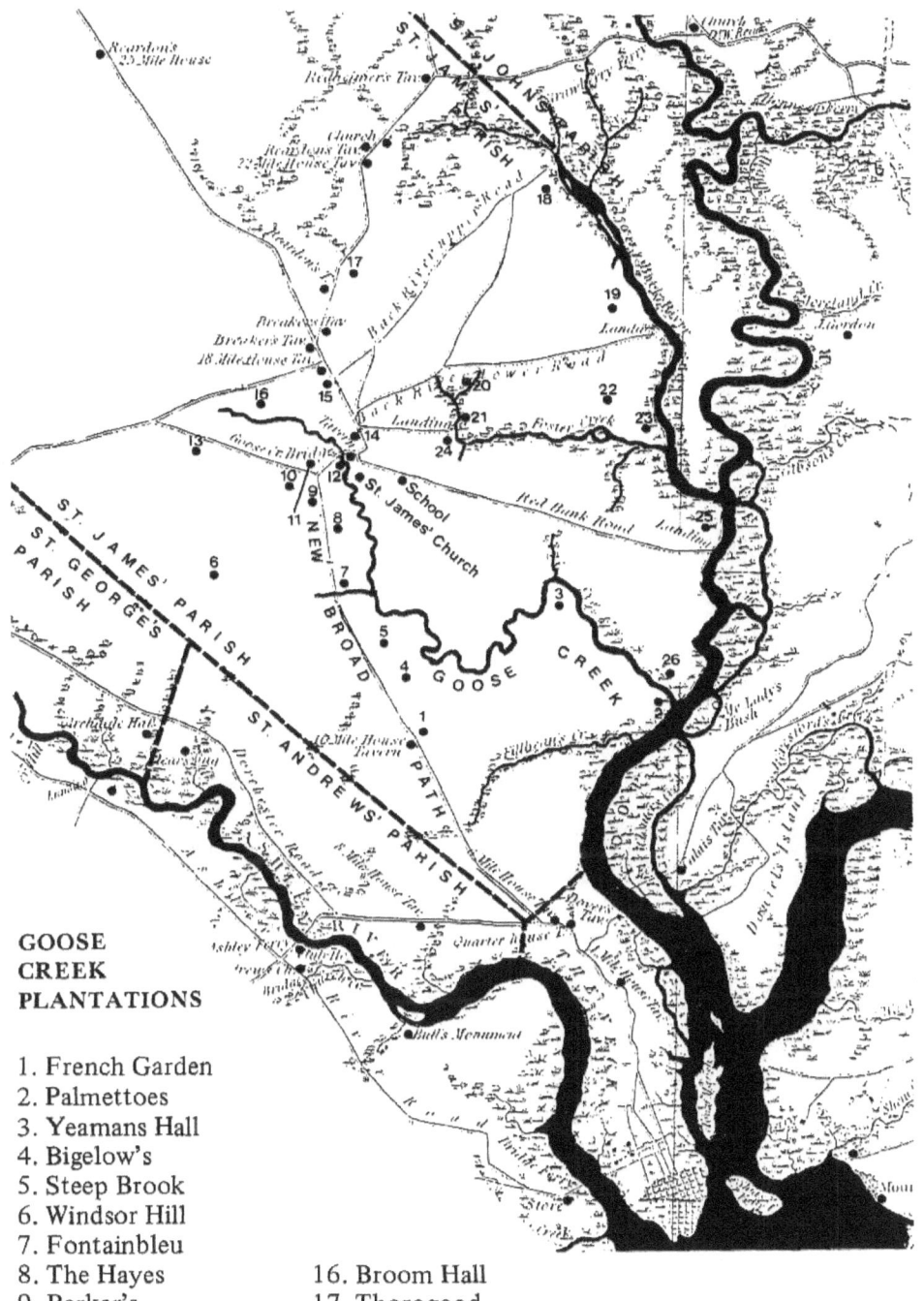

GOOSE CREEK PLANTATIONS

1. French Garden
2. Palmettoes
3. Yeamans Hall
4. Bigelow's
5. Steep Brook
6. Windsor Hill
7. Fontainbleu
8. The Hayes
9. Barker's
10. Woodstock
11. The Elms
12. Otranto
13. Martindales
14. The Oaks
15. Crowfield
16. Broom Hall
17. Thorogood
18. Medway
19. Parnassus
20. Liberty Hall
21. Howe Hall
22. Mount Pleasant
23. Brick Hope
24. Ararat
25. Red Bank
26. White House

THE PLANTATION COMMUNITY

landings on Back River. On Back River in old St. James' parish can be found the remains of Cotebas and Parnassus plantations.

Just north of the Back River Upper Road at the Eighteen Mile House Tavern, the State Road was intersected by the Dorchester Road. Less than one half mile from the Eighteen Mile House was Breaker's Tavern. Here a road branched north toward Moncks Corner. This road proceeded north past Reardon's Tavern before it entered the Parish of St. John's, Berkeley. At Breaker's Tavern the State Road proceeded west toward Wassamassaw Swamp. This road, known as the Wassamassaw Road, became part of the "Mountain to the Sea Highway" which was built according to an act of 1818, and was the continuation of the State Road. The taverns along the colonial highways were used not only for rest and recreation but frequently served as general stores and livestock trading centers.

The Wassamassaw Road led to the western reaches of St. James' parish. It passed Reardon's Twenty Five Mile House; Tares' and Wilson's estates and then crossed the Wassamassaw Causeway over the Cypress Swamp. The road proceeded west to Holly Hill, Four Hole Swamp and eventually the Columbia area. Wassamassaw was a small settlement in St. James' parish. There was a chapel there and a small settlement of families. Reverend Millechamp of St. James' Church reported in 1736 that he administered the sacraments at the Wassamassaw Chapel because the village was too distant for the people to attend the Goose Creek church. In 1759 Rev. Harrison reported:

> ... about sixteen miles from the Church, at ... Wassamasaw, are eight families settled in a Neighborhood of a Chapel, where I officiate five or six times a year.[1]

Dr. John B. Irving in his book, *A Day On Cooper River*, gives brief descriptions of many Goose Creek plantations. Judge Henry A.M. Smith, past member and president of the South Carolina Historical Society, is credited with tracing the warrants, grants, and deeds of many of the Goose Creek land owners.[2] The findings of these two men are combined with several other sources to provide a brief description of the Goose Creek plantations.

HISTORIC GOOSE CREEK

MEDWAY PLANTATION

Sometime near the year 1687, the Signeur D'Arssens arrived in South Carolina.[3] He was likely related to Franciscus von Aarsens or Aarssens born at The Hague, who negotiated the marriage of The Prince of Orange and Mary, daughter of Charles I of England. This van Aarsens died in 1641. His relative arrived in Carolina to settle on a 21,000 acre tract in Goose Creek.[4] The Lords Proprietors issued the following instructions to Governor Colleton:

> Mr. John D'Arsens seigneur of Wernhaut being a Person of Quality and the First of his Nation that hath undertaken to Plant in our Province of Carolina ... Have thought fitt And doe hereby Require you to order the Surveyor Generall to admeasure out such Quantity of Land for the said Mr. D'Arsens as he shall desire not exceeding Twelve Thousand Acres ... And alsoe We will That (when he shall desire it) The Lands he erected into a Manor with all the Priviledges of a Barony.[5]

Upon this land Signeur D'Arssens built a house which is still standing today and is one of the oldest houses in South Carolina. The estate was known as Medway. Upon his death, his widow, Sabina De Vignou, appealed to Governor Colleton for administration of the vast estate. In 1687, Mr. William Dunlopp was, "Lycensed to joine together in the holy Estate of matrimony ... Thomas Smith Esq. and Sabina de Vignou Dowager Van Wernhaut provided there be no lawfull Lett shewne to you to the centrary."[6] Mrs. E.A. Poyas in her book, *The Olden Time of Carolina,* wrote:

> Happily they settled down upon a plantation on Back River, and caused to be built the first brick house in the province, beyond the precincts of the town. (It is now the property of Mr. P.G. Stoney.) There they engaged in that art of arts, agriculture, without which man would be a savage to the end of time, and the world a desert ever. In twenty-three years from their arrival to the period of his death, in 1694, they had amassed a splendid estate by industry and good conduct.[7]

Sabina was quite a profitable marriage for Thomas Smith. The marriage made him one of the wealthiest men in Carolina. Mrs. Poyas wrote:

> We see that drink was served to guests in goblets of pure silver in 1692. Yes, the Blakes, Boones, and many other

THE PLANTATION COMMUNITY

> gentlemen were asked into the Back river parlor to drink beer, smoke a pipe, and take a sly chew from the landgrave's "Tobacco Box."[8]

Sabina Smith died in 1689 and was buried near the Medway house in the presence of a number of Goose Creek gentlemen who evidenced the fact.[9] Thomas Smith was the sole owner of the 12,000 acre tract with a stately house and outbuildings. He was appointed governor, granted an additional 48,000 acres and was made a landgrave.[10] During his term as governor he was faced with controversies in regard to tenure of lands, payment of quit rents, naturalization of the French Huguenots and other issues with the Proprietors.

At the age of 46, Landgrave Thomas Smith died. He was at that time the Governor of the Province. His children buried him beside his wife, Sabina. A slab was laid over his grave, the inscription of which can still be read today. Sabina had no stone, as all grave stones had to be imported at great expense, and she had no children to do this for her. Governor Archdale described Thomas Smith as "a wise sober and moderate well-living man." The Proprietors, writing to Governor Archdale on January 10, 1695, stated:

> We forward copies of letters written by Colonel Smith not long before his death, that you may enjoy with us his satisfactory account of the growing condition of the province and of the peace and union to which he had brought it. He appears to us to have been a man not only of great parts, integrity and honesty but of a generous temper and a nobleness of spirit as to the public good as is scarcely to be met withal in this age.[11]

The plantation house and lands have been altered somewhat during the past 300 years. The original structure was built with handmade bricks and styled by Jean de' Arrsens as a typical one-story stuccoed Dutch house. After the death of Landgrave Smith, the house and plantation had many owners. Thomas Drayton once owned the estate and sold it to John Bee Holmes. It was purchased from him in 1797 by Theodore Samuel Marion, son of Job Marion and the nephew of General Francis Marion.[12] Theodore Marion died in 1827 leaving his estate to his grandson, Theodore Samuel Dubose, who married Jane Porcher. She is responsible for planting the large oaks and ornamental trees in a pattern around the house. A second story was added, retaining the stepped gable style.

HISTORIC GOOSE CREEK

Peter Gaillard Stoney, whose wife was Anna Maria Porcher, bought Medway in 1833.[13] He added an unsymmetrical wing in 1855 but blended the new with the old Dutch style.

Mud along the Cooper River banks made brick-making profitable. Brick was made on Medway from an early date but Peter Gaillard Stoney is credited with improving the quality. Fort Sumter was built with the "Carolina grey" brick produced at Medway.[14] Peter Stoney was a very successful planter, whose plantation was most suitable for rice production. He also raised thoroughbred horses there and an old race track can still be traced on the grounds. Medway was the largest of several Back River plantations. Pine Grove, Parnassus Brick Hope and Liberty Hall neighbor on Medway. When deer were in season, they were hunted twice a week from one of these plantations after these lands were fenced in as hunting parks.

Peter Gaillard Stoney and his six sons all fought for the Confederacy. Captain William Edmund Stoney was severely wounded and Isaac Dwight Stoney was promoted from a private to a lieutenant for bravery. The second son, Thomas Porcher came back from San Francisco to volunteer. Another son, Thomas Porcher Stoney, was born at Medway and served two terms as mayor of Charleston. Two other grandsons of P.G. Stoney, Arthur Jervey Stoney and Pierre Gaillard Stoney, fought in the Charleston Light Dragoons, the headquarters troop of the 30th Division, when it successfully penetrated the Hindenburg Line in World War I.[15]

In 1906 Medway plantation was sold to Samuel Gaillard Stoney.[16] After 1905 his wife Louisa Cheves Stoney restored the old gardens and planted additional ones. The fifth generation of the Stoneys gave way in 1930 when Medway was sold to Mr. and Mrs. Sidney Legendre of New Orleans.[17] The Legendres added extensively to the outbuildings and improved the interior of the old home. Following World War II, the celebrated "Medway Plan" (named after the Goose Creek plantation) was adopted for the rehabilitation of Europe. American cities adopted French cities and sponsored rehabilitation.

Today much of the old splendor of Medway remains. Rice is no longer planted, but one of the old tracts is still referred to as Smithfield, named after the landgrave. Thoroughbreds are no longer raised there, but the old racetrack can still be traced and the deer drives, beautiful gardens and the

THE PLANTATION COMMUNITY

timeless pride of the old grey brick house are memorials to the Goose Creek plantation society. Mr. Legendre is now buried on the grounds just a few dozen yards from Landgrave Thomas Smith and his wife, Sabina. Medway is still the winter home of Mrs. Sidney J. Legendre.

The grave markers can be found near the ancient dwelling. Within a brick wall may be found a stone slab with the inscription:

> Here Lieth Ye Body of the Right Honble Thomas Smith Esq.
> one of Ye Landgraves of Carolina who Departed This Life
> Ye 16th of November. 1694.
> Governor of the Province of Carolina in Ye 46 year of his age.

Enclosed by a metal railing nearby is another marker:

> Sidney Hennings Legendre
> November 1, 1903 March 8, 1948
> The Lord is my Shepard
> I shall not want.

The graves are very close to the old house, which is now shaded by giant oaks and climbing ivy. Many ghosts are said to walk inside the low-ceiling rooms with the large fireplaces and narrow windows. At one of the windows, it is said, one can see the shadowy image of a lady who sits and waits for the return of her husband. Some have claimed to see an old gentleman seated in front of the fireplace smoking his pipe in another room.

In an old walled cemetery on a part of the original tract is a marble marker over the remains of Reverend Elias Prioleau.[18] He was a native of Poms and Saintonge, France, and one of the Huguenot emigrants. According to the mural tablet erected to his memory in the Huguenot Church in Charleston, he became a minister of that faith. The Medway marker states that his family was one of the Doges of Venice. Miss M. Elise Langley of Charleston has in her possession some documents of Antoine Prioleau who died in Venice in 1623. It is from him that the Carolina Prioleau family came. The Reverend Elias Prioleau died at his plantation on Back River near Medway in 1699. Samuel, son of Elias Prioleau, was born in 1690, and married Mary Magdolen Gendron. An interesting memorial to Mary and her four sisters was made by the planting of five live oaks. The trees were known for many years as the five sisters.[19] The trees survived many fires, but in 1918 a timber company damaged them badly, and only one tree remains today. Samuel Prioleau was a member of His Majesty's Council, and in 1732 was an officer in His Majesty's Horse Guards. The Horse Guards were the military forerunner of the Charleston Light Dragoons.[20]

The son of Samuel Prioleau was also named Samuel. Samuel inherited the plantation and increased the acreage by purchasing surrounding tracts. The Prioleau family continued to expand the estate until 1796, by which time the plantation had increased to approximately 1,200 acres. The land was sold to Peter Gaillard Stoney in 1834. In 1853 this tract was purchased by Mrs. Mary S. Stevens, sister of Dr. Charles Tennant of Parnassas. Her son, Norman Stevens, Jr., was an invalid and a little cottage house with high, sharp gables was built for him. Norman Stevens and his wife lived there, and the plantation came to be known as "The Cottage."[21] "The Cottage" was later owned by a German named Lousi, who was accused of killing his neighbor's cattle and of killing a short avenue of oaks by "ringing" them.

PARNASSUS

Parnassus was once called Mount Parnassus and was once the home of Zachariah Villepontoux, a wealthy Huguenot and a vestryman of St. James' Church.[22] He was said to have furnished the brick for St. Michael's Church in Charleston from his Parnassus plantation. In 1842 the plantation was the property of Dr. Charles Tennent and remained so until Reconstruction.

Dr. John B. Irving visited Parnassus in the 1960's. He found little remaining save a giant oak and the remains of an avenue which led for nearly a mile toward Goose Creek. A few magnolias, rose vines and other garden flowers still remain. Parnassus had not been affected by the Civil War until late 1865, but the war had forced all except Mrs. Tennent and her daughters to abandon the plantation. A band of marauding Negro troops invaded the house and demanded dinner, which caused the Tennents to leave the next day. This left the house to be ransacked and vandalized. Shortly thereafter, smallpox drove the marauders from the plantation, but not before the home was ruined.

After the war Parnassus was sold by the Tennent family. One group of owners further damaged the place. They cut the walk of cedar trees and looted the brick from the house and graveyard. Today there remain only remnants of the grave markers. On the Negro burying ground is reportedly a stone which marks the grave of a nurse of the Tennent family. The inscription reads, "Bella, a faithful servant."[23]

THOROGOOD

Mr. John Deas owned Thorogood plantation, located on the Old Moncks Corner Road. It was first granted to Joseph Thorogood who sold it in 1684 to James Moore.[24]

Thorogood, much of which is presently occupied by Boulder Bluff subdivision, was an expansive and beautiful country home. Dr. Alexander Garden of Otranto and John Bartram, a botanist, visited Thorogood to inspect the gardens and agricultural methods. Bartram and Benjamin Franklin had been the co-founders of the American Philosophical Society. One visit is quoted here from Edmund and Dorothy Smith Berkeley's book, *Dr. Alexander Garden of Charles Town:*

> Early in the morning, Deas and his two guests rode over to one of his "quarters" to view his fields of indigo. They were unusual as he had planted rows of corn ten feet apart, with the indigo planted between. The latter was about ready to cut and it intrigued Bartram to learn that it might be cut twice again if the favorable weather of plentiful rain continued. He was impressed with how well the corn had grown....
>
> When they returned to "Thorogood," after breakfast, Bartram had time to inspect the kitchen garden, redolent with ripening grapes and the pond in front of the house. It had been constructed from a worn-out rice field and its romantic beauty was enhanced by the gannets and white herons. With regret, Garden and Bartram took their leave of Deas at three in the afternoon, arriving in Charles Town by nightfall.

This account provides a pleasant description of the property. A very fine miniature of John Deas was painted by Pierre Henri, and is in the collection of Eugenia C. Frost.[25] Doctor Joseph Johnson tells a comical story of Mr. John Deas. He recalled:

> Preceeding downwards, we reached the rice plantation of Mr. John Deas, called Thoroughgood, about twenty-two miles from Charleston, on the Moncks Corner road, and

were there kindly entertained several days, while my father went down on Goose Creek Neck, about twelve miles, to inquire after his farm and negroes on Red Bank. It was the lowest settlements in that neighborhood, and was called the White House, about thirteen miles, by water, from Charleston. Mr. Deas was at that time with the younger part of his family, spending their holidays in the country. The intimacy thus formed has continued to this day among the survivors.

The gentlemanly deportment and cordiality of Mr. Deas was singularly agreeable with him was no formality, parade or constraint his courtesy and urbanity was never surpassed, if equalled, in any one that I ever met with. Mrs. Deas was with her daughter and elder sons, in Charleston, taking care of the property there. A gentleman, who frequently travelled on the Goose Creek road, fell once into conversation with Mr. Deas, and, on hearing his name, observed that there must be a large family of that name, as he scarcely ever passed along that road without meeting with one of them. Dr. Deas said yes, he had nine sons, and each son had a sister. The gentleman, with astonishment, supposed that there were eighteen children, but my readers will perceive that his only daughter (Mrs. Brown) was a cherished sister to each of his sons.[26]

YEAMANS HALL

Yeamans Hall, as the plantation has been known since 1827, lies on a high sandy section overlooking Goose Creek. On September 5, 1674, a warrant was issued to Lady Margaret Yeamans for 1070 acres for herself and her servants arriving in 1671 and 1672.[27] The grant was issued some time later for acreage bounding upon "Yeamans his Creeke in Ittawan River."[28] Yeamans Creek is known today as Goose Creek and the old plantation built there was for many years known as the Old Goose Creek Plantation. Sir John Yeamans, Lady Margaret Yeamans' husband, died prior to the date of the land grant and never resided at Goose Creek. In 1677 the proprietor of Yeamans' estate was James Moore, who later became the Governor of the Province in 1700. James Moore married Margaret Berringer, the daughter of Lady Yeamans by a former husband. The plantation consisting of 1,070 acres was passed to Thomas Smith, the son of the first Landgrave Smith.[29] His descendant, Mrs. Poyas, known as the "Ancient Lady," stated that Thomas Smith took possession of the estate in 1694. When Smith died, he devised to his eld-

THE PLANTATION COMMUNITY

est son, Henry, as stated in his will, "My brick house or family mansion at Goose Creek together with 500 acres of land joining on my brother, Dr. George Smith." The 1738 will of Landgrave Thomas Smith divided the land among his children, which split Yeamans Hall estate into a number of tracts. His son Henry received the house and some adjoining land.

The brick house referred to in the will is the large brick house built about 1693, known as the mansion on Goose Creek. It was constructed for defense against the Indians when the Goose Creek territory was still a frontier. The house had portholes for defense and a well under the house for water supply during Indian attacks. It supposedly had a subterranean passage from the cellar to the graveyard which continued to the creek where boats were tied. This was an escape passage in case of prolonged Indian attacks, but historian Henry A.M. Smith expressed skepticism that there was actually such an escape passage. The land was situated such to make a passage most impractical. Mrs. E.A. Poyas, in her 1855 book, *The Olden Time of Carolina,* wrote:

> A well near the house 100 feet deep, fixed with a chain and a bucket, had been, until lately (1842), in common use. The spring that flowed into the well, also filled a spacious pond below the hill, which was generally well stocked with fish ... About a mile from the house there is a stream of such sparkling aspect, and so clear, as to have acquired the appellation of "the silver spring"; this the water company offered to purchase, to supply the City with water, and plenty of it.[30]

Edward McCrady recorded that there was a secret chamber in the old house, consisting of a small space between two walls with a sliding panel leading into it. It was used to hide valuables during the turbulent period of Proprietory rule and was also used to hide the family silver during the American Revolution.

Upon the death of Thomas Smith, his son, Henry Smith, became the owner, who passed the land to his son, Thomas Smith. From him the land descended to Thomas' son, George Henry Smith. From George Henry Smith the land was passed to his son, Thomas Henry Smith, whose representatives retained ownership into the 20th century.[31]

The first mention of the property under the name of Yeamans Hall was found by Judge Smith in Mrs. Poyas' book,

Olden Time in Carolina. Judge Smith considers it possible that the name had been used even earlier. Leize F.B. Lockwood gives credit for the name to her grandmother Eliza F. Lockwood, who married George Henry Smith in 1850. She was supposed to have had the old portholes cut into windows and named it Yeamans Hall.[32] The house is two stories high with stuccoed walls and old-fashioned panels. The piazza or gallery on the front face was reportedly a late addition. Piazzas, so common in the South, were not generally introduced until the end of the 19th century.[33]

Since 1927 Yeamans Hall has been a country club. Groups of corporation-owned cottages and private homes were built around the white brick club house. The grounds extended to the Cooper River where boat landings provided for members' yachts and boats, and there is also an 18 hole golf course. Buried on the grounds are Thomas Smith, second Landgrave, and his Dutch wife, Anna Cornelie Myddagh.[34]

BROOM HALL, BROOMVILLE OR BROOMFIELD

Perhaps the only instance of an Indian name being recorded as the name of Goose Creek is contained in the journal of the Grand Council for December 28, 1678. At the meeting of that date it was resolved that Mr. Edward Middleton was to acquire "his greate Lott of Land" on "the upper part of Adthan Creek."[35] The word "Adthan" written by the editor of the printed warrants could be a misspelling of the word "Anchaw" or "Anchau," likely an Indian word referring to water. This property was granted on November 14, 1680, to Edward Middleton as 1,000 acres at the head of Goose Creek. On January 16, 1684, Edward Middleton conveyed the 1,000 acres to Robert Mallock, a merchant. The land descended to Robert Mallock's son and through the son's lawyer to Moses Medina for £200. The estate passed from Moses Medina to Benjamin Gibbes, who made Broom Hall his home. The Gibbes family genealogy mentions that a Gibbes ancestor came from Brome or Broom house in the parish of Backham, Kent in England. This is probably the origin of the name of the Goose Creek estate.[36] Benjamin Gibbes had married Jane Elliott in Barbados. She died on August 19, 1717, and a tablet to their memory can be found today at St. James' Church. The coat of arms on this tablet is the same as that on the tablet of Col. John Gibbes, which shows a relationship.

Benjamin Gibbes married Amarinthia Smith after the death of his first wife, Jane, and had one daughter by Amarinthia. He died in 1722, leaving the estate to his wife and daughter.[37] Amarinthia then married Captain Peter Taylor. There is also a tablet to the memory of Peter Taylor in St. James' Church. Buried with him are his wife, Amarinthia, and their son, Joseph. Mr. Peter Taylor gave the vestry of St. James' Church £100 sterling to be paid after his death for the building of a school house for the Goose Creek children.[38]

In the will of Peter Taylor dated July 1, 1765, his Broom Hall plantation was devised to Thomas Smith, who died in 1790. His son, Peter Smith, married Mary Middleton of The Oaks.[39] Peter Smith died in 1811 and he directed in his will that his plantation, then called "Bloomville," be sold. The proceeds were to be divided between his son and daughter. Peter Smith's son Henry Middleton Smith seems to have resided on the estate until his death.[40] Henry married Elizabeth Sully, a sister of the noted portrait painter. She survived her husband and in 1853 conveyed the estate to Arthur S. Gibbes, describing it as Bloom, Bloom Hall, Bloomville, and Fredericks.

It appears that the name of the plantation was originally Broom Hall, which in process of time was corrupted to Bloom Hall, Bloom and Bloomville. It was finally known as Bloomfield.[41] Broom Hall had a large brick house with several brick outbuildings, a dairy and stable. The house remained well preserved until after 1865 when it was destroyed by a fire caused by some careless deer hunters who occupied the house for a night. The remaining walls were shaken down by the 1886 earthquake. The old house was approached by two oak-lined avenues. Judge Henry A.M. Smith visited the site in 1883 and found considerable evidence of gardens and ornamental grounds. He also reported there "one of the finest springs for furnishing water."[42]

FRENCH GARDENS

French Garden plantation is remembered because of the extensive botanical nursery which was developed and nurtured there. French Garden was originally a grant to Robert Wood on March 12, 1716/17.[43] It originally consisted of 220 acres located southwest of the Live Oak Hill adjoining Yeamans Hall. The land passed by conveyance to Andre' Michaux in 1786. Michaux was the celebrated botanist who was sent to the United States by the Royal Government of France to explore its trees, shrubs and other plants for possible use in France.[44] His journals were published by the American Philosophical Society in 1888.[45] He lost his first two volumes when he was shipwrecked on his return voyage in 1796, and the printed journals begin only in April 1787.

Michaux left France and arrived in New York in 1785, accompanied by his son, and there established a nursery for his seeds and plants. Andre' Michaux had a residence at French Garden, which he called "la plantation" and "L'habitation." This residence was probably the old one built by Robert Wood. It was used as his headquarters while he made botanical and collecting expeditions throughout the eastern States from Florida to Canada, including the Appalachian and Allegheny mountain regions and as far west as the Mississippi River. His journals are a careful record of his explorations and his successful botanical experimentation. He used his Goose Creek plantation as his nursery and propagating ground. In Goose Creek he planted the seeds and plants he gathered, after which he sent seeds and seedlings back to France.

Michaux is credited with the introduction of many plants to Carolina. The beautiful *Camellia japonica* is reported to have been introduced by him, as was the *Salisburia adiantifolia* or Ginkgo tree and the *Stillingia sebifera* or Candleberry tree.[46]

Michaux left Charleston to return to France in August 1796. He was shipwrecked off the coast of Holland, but, having fastened himself to a plank, was washed ashore unconscious. He lost his baggage and some of his journals, but most of his packages of plants and seeds were salvaged. In 1800 he sailed to Madagascar on a new botanical expedition. While preparing his nursery there, he was taken ill with fever and died in November 1802.[47] The French Garden Plantation, although conveyed to Michaux, had been purchased with government funds and was the property of the French Government. On April 27, 1802, his son F. Andre' Michaux sold the

THE PLANTATION COMMUNITY

property on behalf of the French Government to J.J. Himley. This property was later conveyed to the Agricultural Society of South Carolina which held it until 1820. The land was then conveyed to John Carwile in 1820 and subsequently changed hands many times.[48]

BIGELOW'S OR INGLESBY'S

Dr. John Moultrie was an immigrant to Carolina and the ancestor of the famous Moultrie family. He came prior to 1729 and made his home in Goose Creek. The original grant was made January 10, 1694/5 to Samuel Hartley, for 400 acres on the south side of Goose Creek.[49] Dr. Moultrie married Lucretia Cooper from the neighboring "Cripps" or "Langstaffes" plantation, which also lay on Goose Creek.[50] By Lucretia Cooper, Dr. Moultrie had four sons. His son John became Lieutenant Governor of East Florida under the Royal Government and supported the British government during the Revolution. The second son, William, became a Major General in the Continental army during the Revolution and afterwards the Governor of the new State of South Carolina. James became the Chief Justice of East Florida, and Thomas became a captain in the regiment of his brother, William. Thomas was killed April 24, 1780, at the seige of Charles Town.

Dr. Moultrie later married Elizabeth Mathewes, by whom he had one son, Alexander Moultrie. In 1776, Alexander became the Attorney General for South Carolina. All of Dr. Moultrie's sons attained prominent positions of public service. Dr. John Moultrie died in 1771, leaving his estate to his four sons John, William, Thomas and Alexander. The sons conveyed the land to William Gickie "late mariner but now of St. James Goose Creek, Gentleman."[51] Gickie held the property about seven years, and eventually divided it into halves, selling the northern half to Dr. Charles Drayton and the southern half to John Fisher, "cabinet maker." The land changed ownership many times until it was conveyed to William Inglesby who immediately conveyed it away. Some maps refer to this plantation as Bigelow's, after Cyprian Bigelow, the owner in 1793, and also as "Inglesby's."[52]

HISTORIC GOOSE CREEK

WIGTON

Charles Fraser, the celebrated portrait painter and author of *Reminiscences of Charleston,* was the youngest child of Alexander Fraser of Goose Creek. Alexander had received his Goose Creek plantation from his father, John Fraser, who had emigrated from Wigton, County Galloway, Scotland.[53] The plantation was referred to as "Wigton" after his home country, and was originally a grant to Captain John Sanders in 1702.[54] The property was eventually sold in 1834 to Robert Y. Hayne, sometime Governor of and senator from South Carolina.[55] Hayne, a Goose Creek land owner, was the opponent of Daniel Webster whom he debated fervently in the United States Senate during the nullification crisis.

THE ELMS

Northwest of Otranto and northeast of Hayes and Woodstock was the original settlement of the Izard family. Ralph Izard immigrated to Carolina in 1682. It was on January 10, 1604/5 that John Francis Gignilliat received a grant for 250 acres which he in time conveyed to Ralph Izard. This was the beginning of the Izard plantation.[56] It was willed by Ralph Izard to his eldest son Ralph. The second Ralph Izard added additional acreage to his estate, and by the time of his death in 1743, the Elms contained 1,696 acres. His son Henry Izard acquired the Elms and resided there until his death in 1748/9. His estate was willed to his only son Ralph. Ralph Izard, the son, acquired additional lands from the neighboring estate of the late Benjamin Marion.[57]

In 1801 The Elms consisted of more than 2,000 acres according to surveyor Joseph Purcell. In addition to the Elms, more adjoining land was added until Ralph Izard's Goose Creek holdings totaled more than 4,000 acres.[58]

Ralph Izard was one of the most outstanding men of Goose Creek. He served his country in many ways and was generally referred to as the Honorable Ralph Izard. Izard was educated at Cambridge University, England, and lived for a short time in London. There he became the friend of Edmund Burke, the great English statesman, who had advocated conciliation in the dispute with the American colonies.

THE PLANTATION COMMUNITY

Ralph Izard, Benjamin Franklin and Arthur Lee met in London for the purpose of presenting petitions to the Parliament and the King opposing unfavorable British laws in America.[59] While Izard was in London, the American Congress appointed him commissioner to the Grand Duke of Tuscany. After he returned to America in 1780 he again resided at his Goose Creek plantation. In a letter to Thomas Jefferson of April 27, 1784 he wrote, "I am settled upon an agreeable spot about 18 miles from Charles Town. A plantation long neglected but pleasantly situated and capable of improvement. This I am attempting; and my inclination would lead me never to enter again into public life."[60] In 1795 he was visited at the Elms by the Duke de la Rochefoucault-Liancourt, who spent some time at the Elms and who reported that the name "The Elms" was conferred upon the property because of the "fine plantation of Elms planted by Mr. Izard." He recorded:

> His slaves amount to five hundred. His mansion is, properly speaking, only a country house, built by his great grandfather, who arrived from England at the time, when the first settlements were founded in this country . . . This settlement which Mr. Izard has named Elms, from a fine plantation of Elm trees, which he planted himself contains about 1400 acres. He cultivates only three hundred and keeps on his estate from twenty-five to thirty negroes.[66]

Ralph Izard planted about 100 acres of rice and 300 acres of Indian corn, potatoes and barley at The Elms. While Izard and his wife Anne de Lancey of New York were in Rome in 1775, their portrait was painted by Copley, the celebrated American artist.[62]

Mr. Izard entertained the French General La Fayette very lavishly when he made his tour of the country. One of the octagonal wings of The Elms house was renovated into an elegant entertainment hall, where La Fayette spent the night. Afterwards that part of the house was known as La Fayette Lodge. Ralph Izard died in 1804 at the age of 62, and his eldest son Henry acquired the house and most of the estate.[63]

Henry Izard, the son, resided at the Elms until his death in December 1826, after which The Elms was sold to Jacob Barrett in June, 1831.[64] The other brother, George Izard, had acquired a portion of the Elms after his father's death. George was an officer in the regular Army of the United States, was made a Major General during the war of 1812 and was afterward Governor of the Territory of Arkansas, where he died at Little Rock in 1828. It appears that he resided not at his plantation, but in Pennsylvania while not engaged in his official duties. George Izard's section of the original Elms eventually passed in 1858 to Lewis Cannon.[65]

The Izard family enjoyed their country homes, living in good houses with fine gardens and grounds of taste and beauty. The house of General George Izard was built in 1718. The family arms were embossed in plaster on various parts of the exterior. He says in his autobiographical sketch that the house at the camp, "Which I will remember when I was a boy was burned before the year 1789, it had been some years the residence of the overseer."[66] "The venerable edifice at the Elms underwent the same tale about twenty years afterwards and has been replaced by one of more modern construction by my brother Henry within a few years."[67]

Almost all the evidence of the beauty and luxury of the Elms had disappeared by the dawn of the 20th century. Dr. Joseph Ioor Waring recorded that all that remained of the old house near the end of the 19th century was "a single tall column of the lofty porch, standing like a monument over its departed glory."[68] Dr. Waring continued, "It is difficult now to find even a path leading to the old house. Around the ruins, the spring of the year, amongst wild grasses and weeds, bulbs and garden plants still grow, marking the site of the flower gardens."[69]

By the turn of this century the house had crumbled to a mass of brick amidst a tangle of trees and vines. A few shrubs and ornamental trees remained on the garden terraces. The botanist Andre' Michaux made visits to the Elms. Judge H.A.M. Smith, during an investigatory search of the plantation near the close of the 19th century, found a nutmeg hickory tree. Andre Michaux had recorded many years earlier:

> I am acquainted with the Nutmeg Hickory only by a handful of nuts given me at Charleston in the fall of 1802, by the gardner of Mr. H. Izard, which he had gathered in a swamp on his master's plantation of the Elms, in the parish of Goose Creek.[70]

This species of hickory, according to Smith, had not been found anywhere else. Judge Smith wondered, during his investigation of the site, if the tree he had found was the

THE PLANTATION COMMUNITY

same tree sampled by the botanist Michaux or a lone survivor of what was then the extravagant shrubbery of the beautiful Elms.

The Izard family, like the Elms, has nearly vanished. In the Museum of Fine Arts in Boston hangs a large double portrait of Mr. and Mrs. Ralph Izard painted by the artist Copley. The Izard family intermarried with the family of the last Royal Governor, Campbell, among others. Before that time the will of Ralph Izard bequeathed: "All that my tract of land situate, lying and being on or near the south side of Goose Creek in the County of Berkeley."[71] A memorial tablet and his hatchment may be seen on the walls of St. James' Church, Goose Creek. The remains of Ralph Izard are interred in the cemetery outside. Part of the northern portion of the Elms on the Izard estate finally came into the possession of Dr. Eli Geddings, a famous physician of Charleston. The rest is owned by the Commissioners of Public Works of Charleston. The city residence of the Izard family is still standing in Charleston; a square brick building on the north side of Broad Street, one door west of King.[72]

STEEPBROOK

The Honorable Peter Manigault, Esquire, a Speaker of the Commons House of Assembly, owned 1,300 acres of land with a large frontage on Goose Creek.[73] Peter was the son of Gabriel Manigault who, upon his return from England, purchased a country home for rest and recreation.

This land was originally a 600 acre grant to Lewis Lansac on May 14, 1707 on the south side of Goose Creek next to Bigelow's plantation.[74] The land was passed down through conveyances and wills until on June 14, 1757, John Wilson conveyed to Peter Manigault all his part northeast of the road. On December 15 Moses Wilson conveyed his part southwest of the road to Peter Manigault. The property amounted to 633 acres at that time. Manigault also acquired the adjoining plantation when on December 27, 1757 the owner, Mr. Isaac Godin, conveyed to Peter Manigault, "Barrister at Law," all that part of the plantation lying on the east side of the public road between the public road and Goose Creek. Additional land was conveyed to Peter Manigault by Isaac Godin until the Manigault estate amounted to 1,300 acres.

HISTORIC GOOSE CREEK

Steepbrook was one of the many estates owned by the Manigaults, and was used as a weekend retreat. Mrs. Anne Manigault's diary constantly notes visits of her family to Goose Creek in the 1760's and 1770's.[75]

Peter Manigault spent a great deal of his time at his Goose Creek plantation. The following notice appeared in the *South Carolina Gazette* on November 10, 1766:

> Wednesday last being the Anniversary of the Glorious Revolution, by the landing of King William and the Nation's happy deliverance from the horrid Popist Plot, the same was observed here with suitable demonstration of joy. The hon. Peter Manigault, Esq., speaker of the Commons House of Assembly, gave upon this occasion, an elegant entertainment to the Light Infantry Company, at his seat at Goose Creek, 14 miles from Charles Town where the Company arrived at 7 o'clock in the morning, Spent the day most agreeably, and returned before 9 at night.[76]

Peter Manigault referred to his Goose Creek residence as Steepbrook. This name was most likely derived from the fact that the property is crossed by a stream leading to Goose Creek. It cuts through the high land on the bank of Goose Creek, forming a slight ravine. It was near this ravine that the house was built.

Allen Ramsey of London, renowned portrait painter, made a portrait of Peter Manigault which is now in a London collection. Peter Manigault was also sketched in ink by George Roupel. The picture was of him at a dinner party at his Goose Creek estate.[77]

OTRANTO

Arthur Middleton, a former merchant in London, came with his brother to Carolina in 1678. A grant dated September 6, 1679 for 1,780 acres was made to Arthur and his brother Edward Middleton at the head of Yeaman's Creek (Goose Creek).[78] Edward Middleton lived at the Oaks plantation and conveyed his share of the original grant to his brother Arthur in 1680. Arthur Middleton's estate was referred to as "Yeshoe" during the early years and is referred to by this name in his marriage settlement to Mary Smith. "Yeshoe" appears to have been an Indian name. It has not been clearly ascertained whether the Indian name was in

THE PLANTATION COMMUNITY

reference to the location or the creek on which the plantation was located. Under the terms of his deed and will, the property passed to Arthur's widow, Mary Middleton.[79]

Mary Middleton married Ralph Izard, the immigrant and ancestor of the South Carolina Izard family. Upon Mary's death, Ralph Izard acquired all of this Goose Creek land. In 1696 he sold 1,649 acres to Jacob Allen, retaining 131 acres adjacent to The Oaks plantation, which was owned by Edward Middleton.[80]

The land obtained by Allen from Ralph Izard was passed to his son and in 1721 conveyed to Benjamin Godin, a wealthy Charles Town merchant. He retained the property, until his death when it passed to his son, David. Although Benjamin Godin owned this land he never resided there, but made his residence on the adjoining property known as Fountainbleu. The original Arthur Middleton land, minus the 131 acres, passed to his wife Mary, to her husband Ralph, to Jacob Allen, Benjamin Godin to his son and grandson until on January 18, 1758 the (now) 1,689 acres was conveyed to the Honorable John Moultrie. This John Moultrie was the son of Dr. John Moultrie mentioned in the account of "Bigelow's." John Moultrie was Lieutenant Governor of East Florida under the Royal Governor. He probably resided here until he moved to East Florida. He conveyed this land in 1771 to Dr. Alexander Garden.

Alexander Garden was a noted medical practitioner in Charles Town for many years and was renowned for his skill. He was well known as an excellent botanist and a correspondent of the renowned Linnaeus.[81] Linnaeus named the genus of plants called gardenia after Alexander Garden which includes the *Gardenia florida*, commonly called the cape jessamine. This flower is not a jessamine and does not come from the Cape of Good Hope, but from China, which makes it difficult to ascertain the derivation of the name.[82] In Dr. Johnson's book, *Traditions and Reminiscences, Chiefly of the American Revolution in the South*, he tells a delightful story of another Goose Creek doctor who named a flower. Dr. Mottett (mentioned in another section of this book) had a remarkable sense of humor. Dr. Johnson wrote:

> Mottet was jealous of the well-merited celebrity of Dr. Alexander Garden, and having been told that the doctor

had been complimented by Linnaeus, in calling a very beautiful plant "Gardenia," he said that was nothing; that he had discovered a very beautiful native plant, and had named it "Lucia," after his cook "Lucy." He did not advert to the difference between Mottet and Linnaeus.[83]

Dr. Garden was an excellent scholar, corresponded with Linnaeus in Latin, and was one of the most outstanding Carolina naturalists. He recorded his work in his correspondence with John Ellis of England, Linnaeus in Sweden, John Bartram in Philadelphia and other famed naturalists. His discoveries included the Congo snake, the mud eel, and the medicinal qualities of the pink root. In 1764, Dr. Garden published a botanical account of the Virginia Pink-Root or *Spegelia merilondecia*, an herb indigenous to South Carolina.[84] As a Doctor of Medicine he introduced the method of isolation and vaccine for small pox,[85] and was elected vice president of the Royal Society in 1782.[86]

He was most interested in raising experimental plants for healing, but he published and read a paper on "The Electric Eel" to the Royal Society of London. His account of the male and female cochineal insects was read before the Society in 1762. His "Account of Amphibious bipes" was published in 1766 and later his "Account of two new Tortoises" in May 1771. His "Account of the Gymnotus electricus" was published February 24, 1778. He was elected a member of the Royal Society in 1773.[87]

Dr. Garden often expressed concern about the dependence on slave labor for the cultivation and threshing of rice. His letter to William Shipley expresses this concern and gives a good description of the process:

> Our Staple Commodity for some years has been Rice and Tilling, Planting, Hoeing, Reaping, threshing, Pounding have all been done by the poor Slaves here, Labour and the loss of many of their lives testified the Fatigue they Underwent in Satiating the Inexpressible Avarice of their Masters, You may easily guess what a Tedious, Laborious, and slow Method it is of Cultivating Lands to Till it all by the Hand, but the worst comes last for after the Rice is threshed, they beat it all in the hand in large Wooden Mortars to clean it from the Husk, which is a very hard and severe operation as each Slave is tasked at Seven Mortars for One Day, and each Mortar Contains three pecks of Rice. Some task their Slaves at more, but often pay dear for their Barbarity, by the loss of many so . . . Valuable Negroes,

THE PLANTATION COMMUNITY

>and how can it well be otherwise, the poor wretches are Obliged to Labour Hard to Compleat their Task, and often overheat themselves then Exposing themselves to the bad Air, or Drinking Cold Water, are immediately . . . Seized with dangerous Pleurisies and peripneumonies of which soon rid them of Cruel Masters, of more Cruel Overseers, and End their Wretched Being here.[88]

To relieve this condition, Dr. Garden advocated the improvement of horse-powered threshing machines. He continually sought ways to improve the living conditions in the low country.

Dr. Garden became ill and returned to Europe where he died. He had one son by his wife Elizabeth Perronneau of Charles Town. He conveyed his 1,689 acre plantation to his son Alexander before he left for Europe. Alexander, the son, was born in 1757 and received his education in England. He was admitted to Lincoln's Inn as a barrister at law. The son returned to Carolina to assist in the struggle for independence. He served in Lee's Legion and later as aide-de-camp on the staff of General Nathaniel Greene with the rank of major.[89] It is said that his father, Dr. Alexander Garden, was a most ardent Loyalist and that he never forgave his son for supporting the American cause. The son married Mary Anna Gibbes after the Revolutionary War and was author of *Anecdotes of the Revolutionary War in America,* published in 1822. He also wrote *Anecdotes of the American Revolution*, which was published in 1828.[90]

Major Alexander Garden died without children in 1829. On January 4, 1785 he had conveyed to Ralph Izard, Jr., 339 acres between the public road and the road to the Goose Creek bridge. Ralph Izard incorporated this acreage into his estate. It was in this deed that the plantation was referred to as Otranto. When the name Yeshoe was changed to Otranto is not certain, but in 1798 Major Garden conveyed the remainder of the plantation to Robert Reeve Gibbs under the name Otranto.[91] The estate passed through several hands and was divided into smaller holdings. It was about this time that the Reverend Mr. Pogson of St. James' church resided there. The original parsonage deteriorated, and Rev. Pogson occupied the little house at Otranto in 1796. A 400 acre parcel with the dwelling and out-building passed through several hands until 1851, when it was conveyed to Philip Porcher, who named the place Goslington.[92] Goslington, meaning little goose, was a name said to have been bestowed upon the location by Honorable James L. Petigue on the occasion of a dinner party given in the ancient building, now the club house.[93] It was Mr. Porcher's daughter Marion who watched Brigadier General R.B. Potter's troops ransack the family home during the Civil War. It was this same woman who later married Arthur Peronneau Ford and moved to Aiken. When asked to visit some new members of the Episcopal Church, she refused to visit one of the officers who had ravaged the Otranto home. She said, "I will ... with pleasure when they return my silver!"[94]

After Mr. Porcher's death the property was sold in 1872 to trustees of the Otranto Club, which was formed that year.[95] The club restored the name Otranto which it has retained to this day. The name was originally derived from Horace Walpole's gothic novel, *The Castle of Otranto*, published in 1764. From 1801 to 1804 Otranto was owned by John Stanyarne Brisbane. It was reported that when John Brisbane's father was banished from Charleston in 1782, John hid under the seat of a small passenger boat and returned to shore instead of boarding the ship bound for England. In 1795 John Brisbane married Maria Hall, daughter of the Honorable George Abbott Hall and Lois Mathews.

Mr. Joseph Ioor Waring, during the last decade of the 19th century, stated that:

> The place now known as "Crovatts" was the original Otranto, and was owned by the Hamiltons, who constructed a private race track, which started in front of the house and ran in a circle for one mile, in order that guests could sit on the piazza and have a full view of the course and races.[96]

The southern part of the Otranto tract was at one time owned by Thomas R. Waring. His executor conveyed the southern portion to Dr. George Prince as trustee for Theodore F. Crovat, together with the 350 acres of the northern half formerly owned by Milward Pogson, to Thomas Gadsden.[97] The Otranto club held the property longer than any previous owner. The old dwelling was used as a club house. It is not certain when the dwelling was built, but it was most likely prior to the American Revolution. According to some historians, the original edifice was built by Arthur Middleton in the 1670's.[98] Additions were later made by the

THE PLANTATION COMMUNITY

Garden family in medieval style. The 1672 Culpepper map of Charles Town shows remarkable similarities to the basic structure as proof of the earlier origin. There is a three-sided fireplace to heat the living room, study and kitchen, and the house is characterized by a colonnade.[99] The slave-built columns are of Italian design, and a wide veranda extends around three sides of the house to provide shade during the hot Carolina summers. It is probably located on the site of Arthur Middleton's original home. The charming little house is now surrounded by homes and condominiums. The ancient live oaks, the avenue of which tradition says was planted by Captain John Cantey, remind contemporary visitors of the grandeur of such a place.[100] On February 17, 1977 the house was named to the National Register of Historic Places.[101]

Also located there are the remains of two old indigo vats, two of the few brick ones constructed in Carolina.[102] Indigo became an important cash crop when a war with France in 1763 caused the halt in trade of dye imports. Indigo is relatively easy to grow, but the process of extracting dye from the plant is a long, tedious procedure. According to Samuel Gaillard Stoney, "the quality and price of the manufactured dye varied widely and took a split-second judgement (as) just when to stop the steeping or the beating of the liquor, and when to let in the lime water that precipitated the 'mud,' as each step might settle the question whether you got something that remained truly better than mud, or the fine purple more desired."

Brick pillars and an iron gate mark the entrance to six acres of the old Otranto property not yet developed in 20th century style. The two brick indigo vats are located here. They are approximately six feet square, one higher in elevation than the other to allow the fluids to flow from the upper to the lower vats. This undeveloped section of old Otranto abounds in natural beauty reminiscent of the expansive landscaped gardens of bygone days. Magnolia, dogwood, and numerous hardwood trees provide a dense covering for the old site.

Plats of the Otranto estate are in the possession of the Charleston Museum. They show that the public road from Charleston to Goose Creek ran through the eastern quarter of the estate. At the northern border of the estate the road forked. To the west, the road served as a boundary between

Otranto's western sections and Ralph Izard's "The Elms," after which the road proceeded west to Dorchester. To the east the road served as a boundary between Otranto and The Elms until it crossed the Goose Creek bridge. Otranto was bordered on the west and south by John Parker's "The Hayes" plantation. Part of the western property line bordered Woodstock plantation. Near the public road entrance to the Otranto property was what appears to be a circular entrance drive with a central fountain. The drive continued from this to a collection of buildings known as the Otranto settlement. A plat of the property showed sections for rice production, cleared lands for producing provisions, various sections of hard and soft woods, and uncleared forest.

DE LA PLAINE'S OR PARKER'S

Two brothers by the name of Fleury were among the French Huguenot immigrants to Goose Creek. Abraham Fleury arrived in the Province in 1680.[103] He received a number of warrants for land totalling 1,390 acres by 1704. It was on Abraham Fleury's plantation that the early French Protestant Church was built.[104] There was a large congregation of Huguenots in Goose Creek, but records of the church have been lost.

The plantation passed through family lines until George Parker acquired the estate. He and his brother William were not descendants of Abraham Fleury and were not related to the Parkers of "The Hayes" Plantation. They were Charleston merchants. This plantation stayed in the Parker family until 1837 when it was sold to William Washington Ancrum. It changed hands in 1849, and on January 11, 1858, it was purchased by Lamb Stevens, a free black.[105] This man was described as being "nearly coal black," and of having unusual capacity and integrity. He had purchased his freedom from his master and became owner of the old Parker estate and the Bacot's "Cherry Hill" estate adjoining it. He was a successful planter who amassed considerable personal property including a number of slaves.[106] He was said to have the respect and consideration of his white neighbors. Like all the land-holding class in South Carolina, he lost all but his land as a result of the Civil War. Upon his death, he left his land to his children.

Historian H.A.M. Smith visited the site in the early years of this century and reported that the old house of Abraham

THE PLANTATION COMMUNITY

Fleury and the Parkers is marked only by a few remaining broken bricks. The old French church site was surrounded by land owned by the Colored Orphan Aid Society at the beginning of the 20th century. The land upon which the old church rested was conveyed from the Colored Orphan Aid Society to the Huguenot Society, which owns it today.[107]

FONTAINBLEU

A wealthy Charleston merchant named Benjamin Godin was the owner of a large amount of land on Goose Creek. His plantation, named Fontainbleu, consisted of 2,158 acres adjoining Otranto.[108] He was at one time the owner of Otranto, which when added to his neighboring Fontainbleu estate, made a total of 3,847 acres with a large frontage on Goose Creek. This was an excellent location and made him one of the wealthiest low country land owners.

The beginning of the collection of tracts which eventually formed Fontainbleu was a conveyance on August 18, 1707, by William Sanders and his wife to Benjamin Godin, consisting of 500 acres on the southwest side of Goose Creek.[109] Upon his death he left to his son Isaac Godin his plantation in Goose Creek consisting of 2,158 acres.[110] The plantation passed to his wife, who on September 18, 1784, conveyed it to Benjamin Guerard. Guerard was one-time governor of South Carolina during the early years of the republic from December 1783 to December 1785, and died in 1789.[111] One of his executors was his first cousin, Major Charles Fining. Major Fining purchased and became the owner of Fontainbleu. He remained in ownership until his death in August 1813, after which the property was divided and sold in tracts.

The beautiful old brick house has long ago crumbled. H.A.M. Smith described the remains as evidence of a good size house with a number of outbuildings. Smith found little of the garden in the early 20th century, but it is likely that the wealthy Godin and his well-to-do successors maintained a well-built and ornamented plantation as a typical country seat of the period.[112] The old family cemetery is near the plantation house and enclosed by a brick wall.

THE HAYES OR INGLESIDES

Adjoining Otranto and Fontainbleu lay "Hayes," a beautiful plantation which was the home of the Parker family.[113] John Parker came to Carolina from the island of Jamaica and died, leaving his widow, Sarah Parker, and a son, John Parker. The grandson of John and Sarah Parker was also named John Parker. The latter made the Hayes plantation his home and added an additional 146 acres of adjoining land in 1755. The Honorable John Parker was born in 1749, was a member of Congress from 1774 to 1789, and married Miss Susannah Middleton. At the time of the Revolution, Mrs. Parker was shot at by a group of British marauders. The musket ball missed Mrs. Parker but struck the wall. The bullet hole could be seen in the wall for many years thereafter.

John Parker died in 1822 and the Hayes plantation passed down through the family until 1871, when it was conveyed to Professor Francis S. Holmes.[114] From the first grants in 1702 until the sale in 1871 to Professor Holmes, the Hayes estate had remained in the same family for a total of 169 years.

Francis Simmons Holmes obtained the friendship of the leading geologist of the State, Professor Agassiz. A similar friendship was also formed with Count Poutales, an engineer who arrived in America about the same time as Agassiz. Agassiz and Pourtales spent considerable time with Professor Holmes researching and collecting fossils. Professor Holmes is credited with the discovery of the commercial value of South Carolina phosphate rock, and phosphate became a valuable agricultural fertilizer. He also served as a professor at the College of Charleston until the Civil War. During the war he was appointed as officer in connection with coastal defense and became Chief of the Nitre and Mining Bureau in South Carolina and Georgia. The commercial prosperity of Charleston in the fertilizer industry is credited to the achievements of Professor Holmes.[115] After his retirement from the College of Charleston, he bequeathed his entire collection of fossils to the Charleston Museum.

Mrs. John Deas, another Goose Creek resident, described the country home at Hayes as "situated on the crest of a gentle elevation; a square hip-roofed brick dwelling having two stories, an attic and was sufficiently high from the ground to admit of rooms beneath." The front door opened directly

THE PLANTATION COMMUNITY

from the large front porch into a large parlor room. Each floor had four rooms which were wainscoted halfway up and had deep, low window seats. The back door of the house was extremely thick and heavy, being built, so tradition says, to resist Indian attacks during the colonial days.[116] From the front door could be seen a wide expanse of lawn. Near the lawn extreme was the Parker burial plot, which was marked by a marble shaft. The markers have all been moved to the cemetery at St. James' Church, Goose Creek.

From the back of the house the land sloped to the lake, which served as a reservoir for irrigating the rice field. Near the lake was a giant oak named "Marion's Oak." Tradition marks this spot as a meeting place of Francis Marion.[117] There is much doubt that Francis Marion assembled under all of the oak trees so reported, which are much like the hundreds of beds in which George Washington is supposed to have slept.

This plantation was located on a Goose Creek swamp which formed one of the headwaters of the creek. It was planted in rice during the ownership of Professor Holmes, when historian H.A.M. Smith saw rice growing there in 1875. By the turn of the century the plantation began to fall into ill repair, as did the large brick mansion building, which had a great deal of ornamental hand-carved woodwork. It was from this mansion home that Mr. John Parker fired on a party of deserters from the British army, killing one of them.[118]

The house eventually burned, and today the spacious old gardens cannot be discerned from the surrounding terrain. During Professor Holmes' occupation (starting 1871) the Hayes plantation was called "Ingleside," by which name it is generally referred to today.[119]

CROWFIELD

The beautiful Crowfield Plantation of Goose Creek was, in the opinion of some historians, one of the most extensive plantations of colonial Carolina. It was built on the Ashley River and was second only to Middleton Place in its beauty and expansiveness. Crowfield was also an early Middleton plantation. It could boast landscaped gardens, ponds, and a fine brick mansion long before Middleton Place was built. Judge Henry A.M. Smith recorded his visit to the plantation site sometime in the 1880's and left a record of his impression:

> The walls of the "Capital Brick Mansion" were still standing intact to the eaves of the old roof. The roof of course was gone and so were all the floors and all the staircases, but the old walls both exterior and interior were in such condition that the beams and floors and roof could have been replaced so as to practically present the honor as it originally stood. Very considerable remains of the old gardens and ground remains...[120]

Judge Smith also found extensive remains of the mounds and earth work enclosing the pond. A small island centered the pond where he found the remnants of the old "Grotto" or summer house. He accused the local people of having cut the pond's dam to get at the fish.[121]

The house was destroyed even more by the earthquake in 1886, leaving only portions of the first story wall intact. A plan for the Crowfield gardens drawn in 1938 by T.S. Stoney showed rectangular landscaped gardens, and also showed the main house with a large secondary house on either side.

The original 1,800 acre grant for the property later known as "Crowfield" was made May 17, 1701, to John Berringer. It appears that Berringer had emigrated from Barbados, but did not inhabit his estate for very long. He accompanied his relative, Col. James Moore, on a military expedition against the Appalachian Indians in 1703-4 as a captain and was killed.[122] His sister, Mary, received the estate. Mary Berringer resided in Barbados, and with her husband, Robert Bishop, conveyed the South Carolina property to Col. John Gibbes. Col. Gibbes was a man of some prestige in Barbados, having several times been elected a member of the Assembly. John Gibbes moved to South Carolina and probably resided on his newly acquired Goose Creek estate. He died in 1711 and was buried in St. James' Church, Goose Creek. A tablet was placed in the church in his memory, along with his coat of arms, but the arms were destroyed by the 1886 earthquake.[123]

After the death of Col. John Gibbes, the property was inherited by his son, John Gibbes. The second John Gibbes married Anne Broughton, the daughter of Thomas Broughton of Mulberry Plantation on the Cooper River. He held the property until 1722, when he divided and conveyed it in sections to several people. One thousand four hundred and forty acres were conveyed to Arthur Middleton, later President of the Council and Commander in Chief of the Province. This land passed from Arthur Middleton to his eldest son

THE PLANTATION COMMUNITY

William Middleton. William Middleton resided there and built the fine "Capital Brick Mansion." He surrounded the house and grounds with beautiful gardens.

Eliza Lucas visited the gardens in 1740 and wrote an elaborate description to a Mrs. Bartlett:

> The house stands a mile from but in sight of the road, and makes a very handsome appearance; as you draw nearer new beauties discover themselves; first the beautiful vine mantling the wall, laden with delicious cluster, next the large pond in the midst of a spacious green presents itself as you enter the gate. The house is well furnished, the rooms well contrived and elegantly furnished. From the back door is a wide walk a thousand feet long, each side of which nearest the house is a grass plat ornamented in a serpentine manner with flowers; next to that on the right hand is what immediately struck my rural taste, a thicket of young, tall live oaks, where a variety of airy choristers poured forth their melody — and my darling the mocking bird joined in the concert, enchanted me with his harmony. Opposite on the left hand is a large square bowling green, sunk a little below the level of the rest of the garden, with a walk quite round bordered by a double row of fine large flowering Laurel and Caralpas — which afford both shade and beauty. My letter will be of unreasonable length if I don't pass over the amounts, wilderness, etc., and come to the boundary of this charming spot, where is a large fish pond with a mount rising out of the middle the top of which each side are other large fish ponds properly disposed which form a fine prospect of water from the house beyond this are the smiling fields dressed in vivid green.[124]

William Middleton, the builder of the Crowfield mansion, was the son of Arthur Middleton of "The Oaks," and was also the older brother of Henry Middleton of Middleton Place on the Ashley. The name "Crowfield" was given to the property either by Arthur Middleton or his son, William. The name comes from Crowfield Hall in County Suffolk, England, owned by the aunt of Arthur Middleton. In August 1753 William Middleton advertised that he intended to go to England with his family and wished to dispose of his Goose Creek plantation. He defined his plantation as containing 1,800 acres of land on which rice, corn or indigo would flourish. He advertised his large brick house with many convenient outhouses and a near regular garden. Along with the house and land he sold to William Walter "furniture, china, plate and 300 books...."[125] Walter left the estate to his daughter in his will. Elizabeth Walter had married William Haggatt of London. The estate passed to his wife after his death, and she sold it to Samuel Carne of London. Carne conveyed Crowfield Plantation to Rawlins Lowndes of Charles Town for £2,000 sterling. Lowndes had a significant role in the history of Carolina prior to and during the Revolutionary War and as a state in the new republic. A temporary constitution had been adopted in March of 1776, and John Rutledge was elected president of South Carolina. Under the same constitution, Rawlins Lowndes was elected in 1778 to succeed Rutledge. It is not certain how long, if at all, Rawlins Lowndes lived at Crowfield.

It was near this time that William Dillwyn of New England visited Crowfield and wrote in his diary:

> S.F. and myself with a Negro boy for our guide went to the next plantation at which has been as much money expended in improvements as I believe has been the case anywhere in America. The Gardens, Fishponds and Walks occupy about 20 acres which has been well planned.[126]

William Middleton may have leased the property from Rawlins Lowndes. Middleton resided at Crowfield, but the record is not clear on which Crowfield estate he lived. Thomas Middleton, William's father, also owned an estate called Crowfield in Beaufort County. Thomas Middleton died in 1779 and Rawlins Lowndes sold Crowfield in 1784. Mr. Lowndes' advertisement in the Charleston *Gazette* gives a good description of Crowfield:

> To be sold that elegant most admired seat called Crowfield in the Parish of St. James Goose Creek four miles from the church of the said Parish and seven from that of Dorchester, it contains upwards of 1400 acres of land, has on it a very commodious dwelling house of excellent brick work, having twelve good rooms with fire places, in each, besides four in the cellar with fire places also and wants very little repair. The gardens are extensive, laid out in good taste and are in tolerable order. The Fish Ponds and canals are superior to anything of the kind in the State and abound with excellent fish. The pleasantness of the Situation, the good quality of the land the improvements and the vicinity to the Metropolis render Crowfield a most desirable abode where profit and pleasure may be as well combined as at any place in the State at the same distance from Charleston.[127]

THE PLANTATION COMMUNITY

Rawlins Lowndes sold Crowfield in 1784 to John Middleton, the youngest son of William Middleton, the former owner who had sold Crowfield when he moved to England in 1754. John Middleton had served in the Revolutionary War in Lee's Legion. John died shortly after his purchase of Crowfield in 1784, and the estate passed to his only child, John Middleton. This John Middleton retained the ownership of Crowfield until 1826. After his death the property was conveyed to Henry A. Middleton, Esquire, and remained in the hands of his descendants for many years.

The property was in the possession of Henry A. Middleton at the time of his death, and in March, 1876, the *Washington Chronicle* reported:

> Henry Middleton of Asheville, N.C., formerly of Charleston, S.C., died yesterday at the residence of his brother, Commodore Middleton, U.S. Navy, at the age of 79; he graduated at West Point 1816 but shortly after resigned his commission to engage in literary pursuits, married a niece of Sir Henry Pollock, resided a long time in England and France, and was the author of several works of political character; his father, the late Hon. Henry Middleton, was Governor of South Carolina and member of Congress in 1816 where he served until appointed to represent our government at St. Petersburg, his residence for 10 years. His grandfather was Arthur Middleton, one of the signers of the Declaration of Independence, and his Great grandfather Henry Middleton was one of the presidents of the first Congress in 1774. The father of the letter, Arthur Middleton, was one of the first Royal Governors of the colony.[128]

Crowfield is an outstanding example of how low country history can be hidden and forgotten. Today thick forests cover the gardens. The ponds and lake are covered with grasses and appear to be a swamp. Trees grow in the center of the house ruins. The Crowfield site is located between Interstate Highway 26 and Highway 176 adjacent to the City of Goose Creek. The area is so heavily covered by foliage that one would find it difficult to locate the estate even if he knew where to look.

The remains of the house and gardens are now part of a 3,100 acre tract owned by the West Virginia Development Company. The Crowfield tract is slated to become a housing development during the next 15 years, preserving the ancient ruins. A mound of earth standing approximately 15 feet is still to be found, though overgrown with trees. The brick foundations for the two privies are also prime archeological sites. There also remains a number of tall oaks which were part of the mile-long avenue. It is expected that the development of this area by the West Virginia Development Company will protect the remains and make it available for orderly public viewing.

THE OAKS

Most any visitor to old St. James' Church is aware of the beautiful and stately Avenue of The Oaks nearby. This was one of the homes of the Middletons. The plantation estate was granted in 1678 to Edward Middleton and Sarah, his wife.[129] For more than 116 years the plantation stayed in the family. It passed from Arthur Middleton to his wife, Sarah, to their son, Arthur Middleton (signer of the Declaration of Independence), to his son, Henry, and to his son, Thomas Middleton. In 1892 Edward Parsons of Kennebeck, Maine, purchased The Oaks. The original mansion house was built about 1700 and was the only one of the plantation homes owned by the Middleton family. The live oaks were planted, so it is said, in 1680. It survived the Revolutionary War, but was destroyed by fire in 1840. The Middletons were close to royalty as excerpts from the scrapbook of Mr. Frank Holmes indicate:

> Died at sea on the passage from London to Charleston, South Carolina, in October 1789, Lady Mary Middleton, the daughter of the unfortunate Earl of Cromartie and relict of the late Henry Middleton of S.C. The Earl had been banished from England for holding a correspondence with the "Old Pretender" who died at Rome in 1765 aged 78 years, his son Charles Edward at Florence in 1788 at an advanced age. His brother the Cardinal of York died at Rome aged 82 years.[130]

In addition, the Middletons served the state and nation in several capacities. One was a Governor, President of the Continental Congress, signer of the Declaration of Independence, Foreign Minister and President of the Provincial Congress.

The recipient of the original grant, Edward employed a French landscape gardener to lay out parterres, shrubberies and terraces. Edward's son, Henry Middleton of The Oaks and Middleton Place, owned 50,000 acres of land, 20 plantations and 800 slaves. He made his home at Middleton Place

THE PLANTATION COMMUNITY

on the Ashley and devoted much of his time to the cause of the American Revolution and to developing the grants at Middleton Place.

Henry Middleton gave the Oaks to his son Thomas.[131] Here Thomas' son Arthur was born. A tablet was erected to the memory of four generations of the Middleton family in St. James' Church. Arthur Middleton, the eldest son of the Honorable Henry Middleton, signer of the Declaration of Independence, is buried at Middleton Place and so is not mentioned on the tablet at St. James':

> To perpetuate the Memory of / Edward Middleton Esq. / Who arrived in the Province of South Carolina in the year 1678 / Settled at the Oaks near this Church / Was of the Grand Council of Carolina-Died in 1685 / And of his Son / The Honorable Arthur Middleton / For many years President of his Majesty's Council in, / and Commander in Chief of, the Province of South Carolina / Born in South Carolina in 1681 / Died 7th September, 1737 / And of the latter's Son / The Honorable Henry Middleton / A member of his Majesty's Council, & thereafter a President / of the first Continental Congress in 1774 / A member of the Council of Safety and President of the / Provincial Congress in South Carolina in 1775-1776 / Born in 1717-Died 13th June, 1784 / And of his Son / Thomas Middleton Esq. / A member of the Commons House of Assembly of the Province, and / thereafter of the Provincial Congress / Born 26th July, 1753-Died 19th August, 1797 / The last three of whom were residents of this Parish, and each / for many years of the Vestry of this Church; and rest as to / their earthly part without the Eastern wall of this / Church Adjacent to the Chancel / *Memoris nostra durabit si vita meruimus.*

The present Oaks plantation house is a 19th century white brick house built by Edwin Parsons and since remodeled in the Georgian style. Parsons built this house on the site of the Middleton's original home, and was one of the first to invest in the rehabilitation of one of the old Southern plantations. In 1930 Charles Sabin, former President of the Guarantee Trust Company of New York, purchased the Oaks and spent more than $100,000 in making it into one of the finest plantations in the South.

The house stands at the head of an avenue of oaks which runs for a quarter of a mile, shading the broad approach road. The house is one of the finest examples of Georgian architecture in America, and was designed by Ernest Flagg of New York. It was built in 1892 around the foundation of the original house, and has 18 rooms. The first floor consists of a living room, library, billiard room, three bedrooms and baths, kitchen, pantry, servant's dining room, main dining room, powder room and bath, drawing room and one other. The second floor consists of master bedroom, four bathrooms, two servants' bedrooms and a bath. In recent years a fine lounge called, the "Starlight Room" has been added. The house is used as the main attraction for a fine country club. The designer, Ernest Flagg, was also the designer of the Naval Academy at Annapolis, the Cochrane Art Gallery in Washington, D.C. and others. The classic front on the main house is considered one of the finest examples of Georgian architecture.

Just behind the house are sunken gardens with a well-designed rose garden on the side. Azaleas border the paths approaching the lake, resting amidst a grove of ancient live oaks. The plantation was the scene of William Gilmore Simms' novel entitled *Katherine Walton*.[132] It was also the setting of several scenes of the movie "Little Miss Rebellion," starring Dorothy Gish.[133] The house and the avenue of giant oaks were used to depict scenes of juvenile royalty, and revived all the colorful and stirring life of colonial Goose Creek.

WHITE HOUSE

Near the northern bank of Goose Creek, not far from Yeamans Hall, was the location of William Johnson's "White House" plantation. Prior to the American Revolution, William Johnson purchased the Vanderdussen plantation and built on the site of the Vanderdussen house.

Johnson was one of the "Liberty Tree Men" and was taken prisoner when Charleston fell to the British. He was sent to St. Augustine and his family was shipped off to Philadelphia. His son, Joseph Johnson, wrote of the journey from Philadelphia to Charleston after the war. Upon arrival at Charleston, the family visited with Mr. John Deas at "Thorough-good," while his father "went down on Goose Creek Neck" to inquire about his "farm on Red Bank." From the southwest part of his land, called "Vanderdussens,"

THE PLANTATION COMMUNITY

Dr. Johnson watched the British sack Charleston and destroy its fortification when the city was evacuated. The house was destroyed by fire. Later, temporary structures were erected on the site and were occupied by persons who farmed the area. Gravestones in the nearby woods mark the graves of Julia Giles, whose death occurred in 1885; William Barnett, in 1917; and Livinia Watson, who died in 1939. Other graves were unmarked.

In addition to the larger and better-known plantations, there were many others deserving mention. Live Oak Hill plantation, also known as Glen's, was situated west of Yeamans Hall. This tract was originally granted to William Murrell, one of the first settlers in the Province, who arrived about 1671. Part of Murrell's tract was conveyed to Thomas Ferguson.[134] This Thomas Ferguson was an active participant in the Goose Creek Council of Safety during the American Revolution.

Part of the original Murrell tract was eventually conveyed to John Glen. Glen was a successful merchant and Indian commissioner during the Colonial Period. He also acquired the plantation known as "Streators" on Charleston Neck. Just west of Oak Hill was the estate known as Cripp's or Langstaffe's. William Perryman was the first owner of this property, the recipient of a warrant in 1679.[135] By marriage the Cripp family gained ownership of part of the land. John Splatt Cripp was a Charleston merchant. On a map dated 1826 it was labeled as Langstaffe's. There was an old family graveyard on the estate. In the early years of this century some remains of a house foundation could still be seen.

Next to Brick House or Martindale and Fontainbleu was a tract accumulated from smaller parcels known as Thomas Mill's. A John Mill received a warrant for the property in 1677 and a grant for 70 acres on the north side of Goose Creek.[136] Mill became the owner of this property in 1720. He died in 1759 and conveyed the property to his children. Some old maps show a considerable number of buildings on the property.

Northwest of the Hayes plantation lay the large plantation known as Woodstock. On July 30, 1685 the Lords Proprietors directed Joseph West, Governor, to lay out to "Mr. Jean ffrancois De Genillat . . . three thousand Acres of land ffar with you are to pass Grants to the 2^d Jeane ffrancois d Genillat."[137] Jean Francois de Gignilliat was Swiss, and arrived in Goose Creek in 1685. The property passed to John Moore and in 1692 to Edward Rawlins. This property eventually passed to Thomas Bee, the first Judge of the United State Court for South Carolina. Bee died in 1812 and devised the Woodstock estate, with all the household furniture and stock, to his son Bernard E. Bee. Bernard was a graduate of West Point and an officer in the United States Army. Bernard E. Bee, Jr. served as a Brigadier General in the army of the Confederate States of America. He was killed at the first battle of Manassas in 1861. The elder Bernard E. Bee left his Woodstock estate in 1836 and took up a residence in Texas. The sale of his Texas property was used for educational purposes of Goose Creek children.[138] In 1886, a little of Woodstock could still be found. The old family mansion house was still situated near the South Carolina Railway line. The house was a large wooden structure in colonial style, with tall brick pillars in the front portico. A number of oaks were planted around it. In the 1880's there were remains of large gardens on the grounds where rice was produced and there was a drainage canal from the rice field down to Goose Creek. The 1886 earthquake destroyed most of the house, and by the 20th century it had virtually disappeared. The gardens were barely discernable at the turn of the century.

Next to Woodstock was Wolf's Castle or Keckely's, originally the home of John Bulline. At Keckely's was an old graveyard with a brick wall around it and with the stone markers of the Keckely family. Southwest of Keckely's was Charles Barker's and Spring Grove, and next to Barker's was Glaze's plantation.

CHAPTER VIII

THE POLITICAL HISTORY OF GOOSE CREEK,
1719 - 1783

The revolution which changed South Carolina from a Proprietary to a Royal colony signified more than a change in governmental design. The style of life in Goose Creek and South Carolina changed dramatically during the 50 years of Proprietary rule. Generally speaking, the Goose Creek frontiersmen had elevated their position to that of gentlemen planters by 1720. They were a special group of planter-merchants who, upon receiving large grants of waterfront property, had developed their early Indian trade into lucrative Charleston merchantile businesses. Dr. George C. Rogers made an interesting comparison in his book, *Charleston In The Age of The Pinckneys:*

> Since the eighteenth-century ideal was the landed gentleman, there was a tendency for retiring merchants to become gentlemen-planters. A principal settlement of such was at Goose Creek, eighteen miles up the Neck from the city, rather reminiscent of clusters of London merchants at Hampstead or at Newington Green.[1]

The gentlemen planters of Goose Creek did more than bring a new life style to the Carolina low country. They were planter-politicians who influenced the colonial government. They had successfully imposed the parish electoral system in Carolina through the passage of the Church Act in 1706 and even adopted the parish names from their home parishes in Barbados. They now worked within the structure of parish government to continue causing political change.

Yet seldom does change come about without resistance, and seldom does it occur in one community without affecting others. During the years from 1719 to 1783, the American colonies came of age. The colonial settlers rejected the mother country, established a home government and entered the international world as an independent nation.

These world-shaking events were exemplified in Goose Creek by general unrest which erupted into frequent hostilities. During these years a British war ship sailed up Goose Creek to kidnap a protest leader from his bed, the Goose Creek militia threatened open and armed rebellion, and

HISTORIC GOOSE CREEK

Goose Creek was invaded by a cadre of armed back-woodsmen demanding the right to vote. The finale to this period of unrest was an all out war between "red coats" and patriots, fathers, sons, brothers and neighbors. Goose Creek came of age through tests of war and rebellion and earned a place among the other communities which made up the new United States of America.

The parishes were political subdivisions as well as religious ones. The parish of St. James, Goose Creek, like the other newly established South Carolina parishes, had elections to send representatives to the House of Assembly. The church wardens acted as election managers and were appointed by the Governor and Council. Public notice of the election was given two Sundays before the election by posting it on the door of the parish church. Church wardens notified the persons elected by posting their names on the door within seven days after the election.[2]

A voter in South Carolina had to be a free white man of 21 years or older. He had to be a resident of the province for at least one year prior to voting and had to own land of 50 acres or pay 20 shillings a year tax. A representative had to be over 21 years of age, had to have resided at least a year in the parish and own 500 acres of land and ten slaves or personal property valued at £1,000.[3] The new Assembly was to consist of 36 members, four of whom were to be from St. James', Goose Creek.

The people of Goose Creek protested the need to travel all the way to Charleston for court service or to vote. This was remedied by the new Assembly when it passed an act in 1721 directing that a court be established at Wassamassaw for the parishes of St. James, Goose Creek; St. John, Berkeley and St. George, Dorchester. The courts would be in session for three days four times a year to hear criminal cases not extending to life or limb and civil cases not involving more than £100 sterling. No court houses were built in St. James' parish and the justices were untrained, causing many people to continue to go to Charleston for legal transactions.[4]

The election Act of 1721 apportioned the representation as follows:[5]

POLITICAL HISTORY, 1719-1783

Parishes	Acres	Average Acres per Taxpayer	Slaves	Tax-payers	Representation as allowed	Representation according to population.
Berkeley County						
1 St. Philip and Charles Town	64,265	220	1,390	283	4	6
2 Christ Church	57,580	538	637	107	2	3
3 St. Thomas and St. Dennis	74,580	661	942	113	3	3
4 St. John	181,375	1,885	1,439	97	3	2
5 St. James, Goose Creek	153,267½	1,432	2,027	107	3	3
6 St. Andrew	197,168	938	2,493	210	4	5
7 St. George	47,457	679	536	68	2	1
Colleton County						
8 St. Paul	187,976	935	1,634	201	4	5
9 St. Bartholomew	30,559	650	44	47	3	1
Granville County						
10 St. Helena	51,817	1,727	42	30	3	1
Craven County						
11 St. James, Santee	117,274	2,792	548	42	1	1
TOTAL	1,163,319	------	11,868	1,305	30	30

The problem with the courts was coupled with the continuing currency shortage, which almost caused a rebellion. For ten years after the Royal government was established, a continual debate over the issuance of currency took place. What the Goose Creek people wanted was either the issuance of more paper currency or a law which would make country produce legal tender. Governor Nicholson returned to England in 1725 and left the province in the hands of Arthur Middleton, then President of the Council. Middleton had been an advocate of the people during the last years of the Proprietary government, but now that he was acting governor he worked to uphold the Crown. Paper money and the problems resulting from the lack of it dominated President Middleton's internal administration. The tax returns for January, 1722 showed land and slaves owned as follows:[6]

HISTORIC GOOSE CREEK

Berkeley County	Acres	Slaves 7-60 Years
St. Philip's and Charles Town Neck	68,975	1,113
Christ Church	65,091	557
St. Thomas' and St. Dennis	91,420	775
St. John's and English Santee	182,659	1,271
St. James', Goose Creek	163,871	1,650
St. Andrew's	188,862	1,831
St. George's	52,710	469
TOTAL	813,588	7,666

With the ever-decreasing amount of paper money and the spread of counterfeiting, a popular movement for more paper money began to gain momentum. When the Council refused to budge from the King's orders, a group of protesters took matters into their own hands. Thomas Smith, a Goose Creek planter and a member of the Assembly, surfaced as a leader in opposition to the president and Council's currency policy.

Thomas Smith was a leader of the Commons House of Assembly and very popular with the people. He declared that "now there was necessity for a bold stroke, and that some men must be put in bodily fear."[7] A series of protest meetings were organized, and the protesters bound themselves to defend each other in refusing to pay their taxes and to continually work toward a liberal currency law. Thomas Smith drew up and presented a memorial to the President. In it the people complained of having to travel to Charleston and plead cases before unjust judges and having to pay legal fees where currency was scarce. The memorial called for a law making country produce legal tender or one producing a sufficient amount of paper money for provincial trade.[8]

The Goose Creek planters needed currency to pay debts and taxes. Often estates were sold at a fraction of their worth to pay taxes. President Middleton, angered by the petitioners, denounced their activities as being riotous and ordered the petitioners not to meet under threat of arrest. In retaliation, 200 armed men rode into town and delivered a petition to the President.[9] They were determined not to be arrested and were not.

As the protests grew in intensity, Thomas Smith became more and more adamant in his leadership. There began talk

POLITICAL HISTORY, 1719-1783

that the country, including Goose Creek, might rise in revolution. President Middleton was much concerned and took decisive action. He had warrants issued and sent constables up Goose Creek on a man-of-war to Thomas Smith's home at Yeamans Hall. There, at three in the morning, the constables burst into the home and pulled Smith from his bed. The arrest at Yeamans Hall had a traumatic effect on Smith's pregnant wife and was reported to have caused his daughter to fall ill for six weeks.[10] News of the event spread quickly. Smith was imprisoned and the countryside became furious. President Middleton attempted to dissolve the protest meetings. He had some success, but trouble continued as he lost more and more of his popularity. Several militia companies assembled at the call of the Assembly, but their sympathy was with the dissenters. The militia denounced the arrest of Landgrave Smith and became more of a threat than a help to the President.

The Goose Creek militia was commanded by Captain William Dry. Captain Dry was heavily in support of Landgrave Smith and was not quick to rally the militia to President Middleton. Middleton became alarmed and ordered the militia discharged from service. Immediately upon discharge, the Goose Creek militia reorganized itself into an independent company, much to the applause of the Goose Creek people.[11] Plans were made for retaliation. One plan was to seize Councilor Alexander Skene and to hold him in retaliation for the imprisonment of the Goose Creek planter Smith.[12] The situation became so serious that Charleston merchants persuaded President Middleton to reconvene the Assembly and thus induce the people to return to their homes. Once convened, the Assembly received a memorial from Smith requesting relief from his imprisonment. Soon afterwards, the Creek Indian uprising occurred, distracting the attention of the Assembly. Thomas Smith and his son returned to their plantation upon a security bond of £10,000 and their case never came to trial.[13]

The paper money controversy which was the cause of Goose Creek rebelliousness was partially resolved in 1730. All old bills were called in and £100,000 more of new bills were issued. The currency controversy was thus quieted for a while and threat of open rebellion from Goose Creek was silent for several decades. The Assembly of 1728 elected

Captain William Dry, who had taken a prominent role in the recent disturbances, as their speaker.[14]

St. James' parish, Goose Creek, was to remain closely associated with the political, social and economic developments of Charleston. Although many Goose Creek people were also merchants in Charleston and educated their children in the port city, Goose Creek was also stricken with many of the same problems confronted by the residents of the back country. Political representation, taxation and the maintenance of law and order were to be confronted as problems by the Goose Creek people as they were by the people of the Piedmont section of Carolina.

Representation was a controversial issue in Goose Creek. A writer in 1766 stated that there were 20 parishes and 50 members of the Assembly. He said that "the reason why no more parishes were laid out arises from political motives, as it would increase the number of assemblymen . . . ." The Assembly desired to manage affairs from the older sections where the established church was a fixture and the people had become homogeneous. The low country was a powerful faction.

The ever-increasing population in the back country resulted in the need for public service. Back country residents of the colony complained of a need for law and order and resented the lack of help from the Charleston-dominated government. The culmination of this dissatisfaction was the formation of a group called the Regulators to cope with crime due to the lack of courts and sheriffs.[15] Outlaws roamed the back country freely. There was a great deal of crime during June and July of 1767, which produced a crisis there. A Charleston newspaper reported the possibility of the back country being depopulated if law and order was not reinstated. The Regulators restored order themselves and did much to govern their own. According to author Richard M. Brown,

> The people were governed by their officers who decided all disputes over the Drum Head in the muster field. The country was purged of all villians. The whores were whipped and drove off. The magistrates and constables associated with the rogues, silenced and inhibited. Tranquility reigned. Industry was restored.[16]

During August and September, 1768, Charlestonians read reports of the so-called Regulator meetings. They were held to plan for back-country representation in the upcoming elections, and they generated rumors of marches on Charleston and other parts of the low country. The Regulators never marched on Charles Town but did, in at least one case, execute their plans to elect candidates to the Assembly in the Parish of St. James, Goose Creek.[17]

The Regulators marched on the Goose Creek polls. The church wardens were in charge of the voting and became so startled by the appearance of a large number of backcountry men that they didn't know what to do. The Regulators insisted that they had the right to vote as free holders within the parish. Recently drawn parish boundaries had excluded them from the newly established parish of St. Matthews, and the Regulators therefore came to Goose Creek to vote. The wardens "favored the liberty of the subject and the right of voting."[18] The Regulators voted, and the wardens left the validity of the election to the judgment of the Assembly. The Regulators dominated the Goose Creek poll and elected their choices: Moses Kirkland, Aaron Loocock and Tacitus Gaillard.[19]

Representation was becoming a serious problem. By the mid-1700's, more than half of the white population lived in the western parts of the colony, but Crown policy prevented increasing membership in the South Carolina Commons House of Assembly. It was not impossible to increase the number of parishes without increasing the number of assemblymen, however. In 1768 the representation of three parishes was reduced for the purpose of granting more to new back-country parishes. St. James' parish was permanently reduced from four to three members. Residents of Goose Creek complained bitterly about the loss of a parish seat. The complaints, however, were directed against the Crown's restriction on the size of the Assembly, and not against back-country representation.[20]

A freeholder in Goose Creek published an article on the question of representation. The position of the majority in the Assembly had been that the Assembly had the power of giving representation by legal enactment. That being the case, it also had the power to reduce the representation of a parish on the principle that the power that gives can also take away. The Goose Creek writer contended that representation rested on the English constitution. The right of community representation, he contended, could never be taken away.

The back-country repeatedly petitioned for representation during the 1760's. The establishment of the new parishes granted some relief for the back country but it was at the expense, in part, of Goose Creek. The Regulators, despite some temporary political success, were not to have relief from their problems until after the Revolutionary War. As long as they were part of colonial Carolina they were to suffer the lack of local government, adequate representation and the lack of a school system.[21]

A review of the active dissent of the Goose Creek planters reveals that problems with the British government, Proprietary or Royal, were present from the first settlement of the colony. In a broad sense, the American Revolution was not the same as the American War of Independence. The revolution lasted over 150 years, beginning when the first settler arrived in the new world. The problems that the Goose Creek men had with the Fundamental Constitutions, Proprietary instructions, currency, Regulators and despotic governments were not unlike problems faced by other Americans in other colonies. America had been settled by immigrants who generally were discontent in the Old World. They had come to America for a new lease on life. The Goose Creek people were like the frontiersmen in many other lonely frontiers in Virginia, Pennsylvania, or New York. They were a great distance from home rule and had to be independent to survive in the harsh frontier environment. Great distances diminish authority, and the people of Goose Creek suffered with problems similar to other Americans and aligned themselves with other revolutionaries to finally overthrow British rule. The revolution had started slowly, but progressed until independence was achieved.

The Goose Creek men had one revolution to their credit, having already ousted the Proprietors. They had gained control over the colonial legislature and later, aggravated during the 1760's by the presence of regular British troops within the colony, joined the armed rebellion for independence.

During the decade preceding the American Revolution, the Northern colonies suffered considerably from attempts by the British to enforce the mercantile system. The Naviga-

POLITICAL HISTORY, 1719-1783

tion Acts, the Stamp and Sugar Acts and the Townshend Acts were all measures taken by the British to maintain this economic system. These agitations were not directly felt in Goose Creek or in South Carolina, but there arose in Charleston a small group of patriotic dissenters who worked to keep the issues of protest in public view.

The complaints of the Regulators were but a few of those voiced by discontented colonists in the British new world. The people found reasons to resent the Crown appointed of salaried "strangers" (British civil servants) to political office here. Berkeley County planters began to refuse holding voluntary offices along side the salaried appointees. The appointment of Governor Boone in 1762 led to bitter controversy over the alteration of the 1721 election law and over the governor's obstinate and dictatorial behavior. It even became impossible to achieve a quorum in the 1763 Assembly, as many members absented themselves until the departure of Boone in 1764. Goose Creek representatives in the 1763 General Assembly were Peter Taylor, T. Wright, J. Mackenzie and J. Parker.[22]

Governor Boone was replaced by William Bull, who proved to be a popular and able local governor. He was not able, however, to make amends for the animosity left behind by Boone's mismanagement. Boone's placement of "unworthy" men from England in positions of honor (which the people felt should be filled by Carolinians) was not easily forgiven.

Christopher Gadsden and William Johnson were two low country men who led the opposition to the British Crown by keeping political issues in the limelight. They also had the support of many influential men in the country parishes. It was Gadsden and his followers who did much to publicize the grievances of the Northern colonies resulting from the Navigation and the Stamp Acts. An embargo on the port of Charleston during the Stamp Act was largely the result of the work of Gadsden and his Sons of Liberty group.[23] Political activists groups during that time were divided along merchant and mechanic lines. Rawlins Lowndes was a very popular member of the merchant class. He later owned beautiful Crowfield plantation in Goose Creek and served out the term of President John Rutledge after his resignation.[24]

HISTORIC GOOSE CREEK

The people of Goose Creek and the rest of Carolina were not nearly as affected by the Navigation Acts as were the Northern colonies. For some time they did well despite the regulations and were not particularly concerned about Parliamentary Acts which did not directly interfere with their own prosperity. The people of South Carolina later began to have more complaints against the Royal government and became supportive of the Charleston patriots. Much of the economy of Goose Creek was dependent on the production of rice, but a problem rose when rice production began to exceed the British demand. The success of Eliza Lucas in making indigo a profitable crop in the low country helped to lessen the severity of the problem, but the economy was threatened.

The controversy over the salaried appointments made by Governor Boone helped solidify resentment toward the Royal government. Gadsden and his followers used this to their advantage to help gather support for rebellion. The Stamp Act and the poor conduct of some English officials added fuel to the fire for the rebels. Gadsden and his followers began seeking support for an American Assembly composed only of Americans, and the people of Goose Creek were sympathetic.

One amusing legend about St. James' Church reflects the local spirit of the days just prior to the Revolution. The Reverend Edward Ellington was a staunch Loyalist. Once while he was conducting the church litany in an appropriate manner, he read, "That it may please thee to bless and preserve our sovereign lord, King George." The congregational response was supposed to be, "we beseech thee to hear us, Good Lord." There was silence instead, but moments later a loud response came from one pew: "Good Lord deliver us."[25]

Patriotism became strong in Goose Creek. Ralph Izard, a Goose Creek planter, wrote in 1774 from England to a friend who was managing his "Elms" plantation: "Nothing gives me so much concern as the thought that my people may want for clothes and blankets." He wrote of the possibility of using cotton, "which is produced in such quantities that some of it may be bought."[26] Izard was one of the most renowned patriots. He was a proud Goose Creek planter who brought prosperity, pride and dignity to his Goose Creek plantation, The Elms.

POLITICAL HISTORY, 1719-1783

After the repeal of the Stamp Act, the new Royal governor was well received in Charleston, but Christopher Gadsden continued his patriotic work. In 1774, meetings in Charleston and circular letters resulted in a July assembly of men who appointed a delegation of five to meet and discuss the situation between the colonists and the English Parliament at a general congress which was to take place in Philadelphia. In the meantime, a general committee of 15 mechanics and merchants from Charleston and 69 planters was appointed to take care of matters in Charleston. After a review of the situation, this committee decided there was a need for an election which would give each section or parish of the colony better representation. Charleston was to host 30 delegates, six from each parish. This body assembled in January, 1775.

In that month, delegates were sent to represent Charleston and the country parishes. Representing St. James, Goose Creek, were Thomas Smith, Sr., Col. Benjamin Singleton, John Parker, Benjamin Smith, John Izard and John Wright. These delegates resolved themselves into a Provincial Congress and pledged themselves to defend South Carolina.[27] Col. Charles C. Pinckney was elected president, and a general committee was appointed to conduct business until the next meeting.

Shortly afterwards news was received about the battle of Lexington, and the General Committee called for Congress to assemble. Henry Laurens was chosen to succeed Pinckney as President of the Congress. Plans were made to raise two regiments of infantry with which to oppose the British. Plans also were made for a Council of Safety to manage military affairs. The Council of Safety was to act as the executive branch of the government of the province. All had to profess obedience to the new provincial congress and were subjected to the justice of parochial and district committees.

The colony became divided, with some Carolinians remaining loyal to England (the "Loyalists") and many opposing the mother country and supporting the new provincial government. To put pressure on the Charlestonians, the patriots threatened confiscation of property and banishment of all who would not show some overt support for the new state. Some joined the patriots. Others who remained in Charleston and Goose Creek did not, and were to suffer at the hands of the patriot councils of safety.[28] Committees were formed to execute the directions of the Continental Association. The committee from St. James, Goose Creek, was composed of Benjamin Coachmen, Henry Smith, John Davies, James Streater, Alexander Mazyck, Benjamin Mazyck and Thomas Walter.[29]

The militia of South Carolina numbered about 14,000, consisting of 12 regiments of foot, one regiment in each district and county; one regiment of horse in the country, commanded by Col. William Moultrie of Goose Creek; and one artillery company. The provincial Congress also raised three additional regiments as an independent force.

There was much political divisiveness in the province, and in August an election was called to choose delegates to a new Provincial Congress. Most of the earlier congressmen were reelected. St. James, Goose Creek, elected Thomas Middleton, son of Henry Middleton, in place of Thomas Smith Sr.[30] Word was received that British troops were expected to arrive in September. In July, the Council of Safety appointed a committee to make the village of Dorchester an armed post. Powder and weapons were placed there for safekeeping. Early in November, Captain Francis Marion was ordered to take command of two companies of the Second Regiment. Captain Benjamin Smith commanded the Goose Creek company of the Berkeley Regiment of militia. He was directed to take the Dorchester post along with Francis Marion.[31]

The South Carolina Constitution was adopted by the Provincial Congress March 26, 1776, at which time that Congress resolved itself into the General Assembly of South Carolina. The Constitution provided for the election by the General Assembly of a President and Commander-in-Chief and a Vice President. John Rutledge was elected President and Henry Laurens Vice President. The legislative authority was vested in the President, General Assembly and a Legislative Council composed of 13 members to be elected by the General Assembly from its own membership. The new constitution gave St. James, Goose Creek, a total of six of the 202 seats of the Assembly.[32] Shortly thereafter, the British attempted an invasion of Charleston. Residents of Goose Creek were under Moultrie's command at the little palmetto fort on Sullivan's Island during the British threat of June, 1776. The Revolution was on its way.

The British failed to capture Charleston in 1776 and

POLITICAL HISTORY, 1719-1783

made no additional attempts for several years. In December, a new Assembly re-elected the President and Vice President and designed a new constitution. It was finally adopted in March of 1778, and provided for a Governor, a Lieutenant Governor and a Senate consisting of 28 members to be elected by the people in their respective parishes. The Legislative Council was dissolved.[33] A revenue act was passed by the General Assembly on September 9, 1779. Inquirers and collectors named for Goose Creek were Peter Smith, John Withers, and William Eckles.[34] The following were elected from Goose Creek: Senator John Parker, Representatives John Deas, Peter Bacot, Aaron Loocock, William Price, Benjamin Smith, and Peter Smith.[35]

By 1778 the British commanders, Lt. Colonel Banastre Tarleton and Major Ferguson, were successful in establishing a base of operations in Goose Creek, within easy striking distance of Moncks Corner and Charleston. In 1780, Sir Henry Clinton, with a naval convoy and an 8,500 man army, was successful in invading and capturing Charleston. By March 20 of the same year, the British had moved from John's Island to the Charleston Neck. At this time General Issac Huger with his 379 patriot cavalrymen were at Bacon's Bridge at the headwaters of Goose Creek. He moved with cavalry, Colonel Horry's dragoons and a small infantry unit to Moncks Corner. Clinton, attempting to sever Charleston from communication with the interior, sent Lieutenant Colonel Webster to join with Tarleton and with Major Ferguson's troops in Goose Creek. From there the British began a cautious march to Moncks Corner, where they engaged the American forces and defeated them.

Governor Rutledge ordered another election of the legislature in 1781. By this time both Goose Creek and Charleston were in the hands of the British. During the same year, General Nathaniel Greene agreed with General Sumter's plan to begin an expedition back into the low country to free it from British possession. Generals Sumter, Marion, and Lee's Legion were detached to move through St. James' parish down the Wassamasaw Road toward Goose Creek. His mission was to control Goose Creek and cut it off from British-controlled Charleston. Colonel Lee moved his regiment toward Dorchester. Upon receiving news that Hampton had suddenly appeared in Goose Creek, the British abandoned Dorchester, and Col. Lee captured a large amount of livestock, supplies and ammunition at the fort there.

Colonel Hampton arrived at the Goose Creek Parish church on Sunday morning, July 15, 1781, while the service was in progress. He captured some horses and also made prisoners of a number of those attending services. He then parolled the prisoners on their oath not to take up arms against the Americans. Colonel Hampton stayed but a short time in Goose Creek before he continued his march on the public road toward Charleston.

Berkeley County was the scene of many revolutionary encounters with the British. General Sumter's penetration into Berkeley and General Marion's guerrilla tactics in his home county kept the countryside active. Goose Creek remained occupied by the British during most of the Berkeley battles and was not the scene of major engagements.

The Legislature arranged to meet in Jacksonboro in 1782. General Greene moved his army to a position near Jacksonboro to protect them. The elected officials from St. James' parish were Senator William Logan and Representatives John Braddley, Alexander Broughton, Thomas Elliott of Wappoo, George Flagg and William Johnson. These men traveled to Jacksonboro and met in the Assembly on January 18, 1782.[36] Governor Rutledge's term had expired, but the countryside was in such turmoil that no election could be arranged. The Assembly thus chose their own executive officers: John Mathews to be Governor and Richard Hutson to be Lieutenant Governor.

The year the Jacksonboro Assembly met there were no major battles fought. General Cornwallis had surrendered to General Washington at York Town a year earlier and it only remained to make the proper peace arrangements. The people of Goose Creek, the rest of Berkeley County and all of South Carolina were soon to be able to celebrate victory.

Now that the long war was nearly over, the people of Goose Creek were faced with an even more devastating enemy: poverty. During the war, Goose Creek had been occupied by the enemy and had suffered at their hands. The "Red Coats" had done much damage, but had spared the old church because it displayed the Royal coat of arms. Slaves and stock had been stolen by the enemy, and crops had been destroyed. For many years the local men had left their plantations un-

POLITICAL HISTORY, 1719-1783

tended and at the mercy of natural disorder. There was hardly a plantation which had not been adversely affected by the war. In addition to the cost in material goods, the blood and energies of the Goose Creek people were lent to the cause for independence.

Because of the industrious efforts of Berkeley County historian Maxwell Clayton Orvin, the names of Goose Creek patriots are available in his book, *Historic Berkeley County*. Mr. Orvin compiled a list of Berkeley County patriots, many of whom were Goose Creekers. They all did their part to win independence for the American Colonies. The following were from St. James' Parish.

Colonel John Boddely was an adjutant in the Charleston militia in 1776, and served as a member of the General Assembly. Lieutenant Alexander Fraser from Goose Creek was a member of the House of Representatives in 1766 and 1778, and was a senator from St. James' parish in 1785. Major Alexander Garden from Otranto plantation was a cornet in General Lee's Legion in 1780. From March 1781 for the duration of the war, he served as aide-de-camp to General Greene. His father, the noted botonist, disinherited his patriotic son and left the country to return to England when the Revolution began.

Peter Gray was a Goose Creeker who was commissioned as a captain in 1778, and also served as a member of the State Convention of 1790. Captain James Graham was from Goose Creek. Lieutenant John Izard, whose father owned The Elms plantation in Goose Creek, was an aide-de-camp of General Isaac Huger. He was also a member of the 1775 Provincial Congress. Ralph Izard, owner of The Elms plantation, was a Representative at the Jacksonborough Assembly, served as a delegate to the Continental Congress and also served as a senator in the First Congress.

Lieutenant William Johnson was a Goose Creeker who joined hands with other patriots around an ancient oak tree on the outskirts of Charleston and pledged loyalty to the patriot cause. This ceremony was attended by patriot leader Christopher Gadsden's most loyal supporters. In Dr. Joseph Johnson's *Traditions* there is a graphic account of Lt. Johnson's reunion with his family during the war and his return to his house on Goose Creek:

HISTORIC GOOSE CREEK

> We reached the rice plantation of Mr. John Deas, called Thorough-good about twenty-two miles from Charleston on the Monck's Corner Road, and were there kindly entertained several days while my father went down on Goose Creek Neck, about twelve miles, to inquire after his farm and negroes on Red Bank. It was the lowest settlement in the neighborhood and was called White House, about thirteen miles by water from Charleston. Here he was happy to find that his negroes had faithfully kept together under their driver, had made a good crop of provisions, and had secured it from depredations by concealment in the woods. But as to the stock of horses, cattle, sheep, hogs, and poultry, it was all carried off except a colt which the plunders considered not worth taking.

William Johnson also served as a member of the General Assembly in 1781 and 1785.

Colonel William Mallard was active in the Revolution. In 1816 after the war, he served as treasurer of the road commissioners of the parish. He was a member of the General Assembly in 1826-27 and was an active opponent of the federal tariff laws in 1828. Lieutenant Stephen Mazyck was commissioned as first lieutenant of Captain Ravenel's company of the Berkeley Regiment and was also one of General Marion's men. Captain James Mitchell was a patriot soldier from the parish. Lieutenant John Parker from the Hayes plantation was a patriot who served as a senator from the parish in 1778. Captain Benjamin Singleton was a Goose Creeker. Lieutenant Richard Singleton lived at Wassamasaw and served in the First Regiment under Col. Gadsden.

Major Benjamin Smith was a captain in the Berkeley Regiment in 1777. He served as a Goose Creek member of the General Assembly in 1780 and as a delegate to the Constitutional Convention in 1788. Lieutenant James Smith was another Goose Creeker who served as a member of the Constitutional Convention. Captain James Stevenson lived at Wassamasaw, and Lieutenant Peter Taylor served with General Francis Marion.

Major Robert Thornley served as a Representative in the 1792-93 Legislature. Upon his death in 1805, the *City Gazette* stated that he was "an old, respected and useful citizen of this state: he served as an officer in the militia, from the beginning of the Revolutionary War to its termination, and was often engaged in the most trying and dangerous services, having been one of those who were most constantly and actively

POLITICAL HISTORY, 1719-1783

employed with General Marion, in opposing the British troops and tories, when this state was in its most reduced situation under their power . . . at the time of his death he was Senator for the parish of St. James, Goose Creek . . . ."

Captain Hugh Strain Winter, Major William Vance, Captain William Withers and Captain Richard Withers were patriots. Richard Withers' plantation in Goose Creek was seized by the British in 1780. Captain John Wright resided at Wassamassaw, and served as a member of the Provincial Congress in 1775. Major William Vance died in 1824.

Goose Creek men who served with General Francis Marion included John Brown, John Burbridge, George Cannon, John Deas, Andrew DeHay, John DeHay, Alexander Douglas, John Downing, Jones Douglas, Peter Bubose, William Logan, Robert Martin, John May, George Morris, Robert McCants and Thomas Owens. Other Goose Creekers who fought, though not with Francis Marion, were John Cooper, Charles Johnson, William Michaer and William Parker. Parker was also a member of the Legislature in 1786.

Marauding parties of British soldiers did much damage in Goose Creek during the period that Charleston was occupied. On one occasion two men went to Mr. John Parker's plantation in Goose Creek, called the Hayes. John Parker closed up his house and refused to let the men enter, and promised to kill them if they tried. The men went to Mr. Parker's storehouse and tried to break in, whereupon Mr. Parker shot and killed one. The other intruder ran off. Mr. Parker sent a letter to the commandant of Charleston to inform him of the fatality. The commander sent a return note saying he approved of the actions taken by Parker, and sent another soldier to the plantation to bury the marauder.[38]

There are stories which tell of more humane relations between the Goose Creek people and the British soldiers. Mr. John Deas of Thoroughgood Plantation had a direct confrontation with the British. Mr. Deas was called to his door by a British officer who entered his home and asked him to please accommodate his sick friend. The Deas family welcomed both of them and provided hospitality until the next morning. About a year later, when the British were withdrawing from the countryside to the city, two officers paid a visit to the Deas' home. They politely inquired as to the welfare of the family, and not being recognized as the sick and weary travelers of a year prior, stayed for friendly conversation for a number of hours. The officers then left, saying that the British army was passing nearby and they were aware of the mischief such a retreating army could cause. They had remained those hours to protect the Deas home. Then, having accomplished their mission, they thanked the family for their assistance a year before and rode off.[39]

Another party of marauders went by water to the old brick mansion of the Smiths near the mouth of Goose Creek. The house was tightly locked against the approach of the intruders. When they refused to leave, Mrs. Smith shot and killed one of them. The other carried the body to the boat and left. Such incidents were common during the war.

Goose Creek was in a serious state of economic collapse after the Revolutionary War, as was the rest of Carolina. What made matters worse was that the new American government was too weak to provide any kind of assistance. The planters were forced to rely on their own resources and energies for their recovery. The Goose Creek patriots began the task of rebuilding their wartorn plantations. The Goose Creek Loyalists were in many cases either banished from the colony or had their property confiscated. During the Jacksonboro Assembly in January and February, 1782, the Assembly established categories of loyalty which were to be dealt with by the Councils of Safety. They threatened banishment and confiscation for all who would not take an overt stand against the British. Some of the people in Goose Creek suffered at the hands of these patriot councils. This action, in some instances, threatened to bring about a complete overturn of property. In some cases commissioners took over control of confiscated estates and began to manage them, supplying slaves for public work and food for the patriot army.[40] Many relied on family ties and friendships to protect property from confiscation by both the patriot and Loyalist camps. Some even swapped loyalty at opportune times to protect their estates. Alexander Garden, Jr., whose famous father was a firm Loyalist, had been at school in England when the Revolution began. He took the oath to the King when he returned to South Carolina in 1780, but later switched to the patriot side. Garden was successful in getting the sale of his father's Goose Creek property postponed at

POLITICAL HISTORY, 1719-1783

the Jacksonborough Assembly. Edward Rutledge distrusted Garden and commented:

> Young Garden I suppose you know is with us, he is full of trouble, not on account of our taking of his Fathers Estate, but lest we should touch his Plantation at Goose Creek.[41]

In 1784 Garden was able to save his father's estate by getting it transferred from the confiscation list.[42] Gabriel Manigault, Jr. was able to save his property. Although he had signed the address congratulating the British victory at Camden, he reaffirmed his support for the patriots in time to save his property from confiscation.[43] Edward Rutledge was very outspoken in his condemnation of such fickle loyalty. To serve as representatives in 1783, Goose Creek sent Ralph Izard, Sr., George Flagg, John Braddeley, William Johnson, Alexander Moultrie, Captain James Stevenson, Thomas Middleton and Peter Smith. Benjamin Smith from Goose Creek served as a South Carolina Justice.[44] Some Goose Creekers made appeals to the House in 1783 for the return of confiscated properties.[45]

The legislators at the Jacksonborough Assembly valued the confiscated estates as a source of ready cash and "as a means of establishing a capital to build a present credit upon."[46] The preamble to the Confiscation Act stated that it was "just and reasonable" to use the property of Loyalists toward alleviating and lessening the burdens and expenses of the war, which must otherwise fall very heavy on the distressed inhabitants of the state."[47] In most cases it appears as if the Goose Creek properties were returned to the original owners.

Some Goose Creekers had had their properties seized ("sequestered") by the British because they were American patriots. Goose Creekers whose property had been sequestered included Ralph Izard, The Elms; William Moultrie, Windsor Hill; William Parker, The Hayes; and Richard Withers' estate.[48] These properties were easily returned to the rightful owners after the British left.

The rehabilitation of the Goose Creek property was much more difficult than the assignment to appropriate ownership. Many years of recovery lay ahead, and despite great efforts, the grand Goose Creek plantations were never again to realize the prosperity they had enjoyed during the colonial era. One year after the final peace, Ralph Izard wrote Thomas Jefferson from his Goose Creek estate. He commented that the "animosity and hatred" of the days of British conquest was the most baneful social effect of the Revolution in South Carolina:

> The British have deprived us of a great deal of our property. The inconveniences arising from their conflagrations and robberies will, however, in a short time be forgotten. The animosity and hatred planted by them in the breasts of our citizens against each other, is the most serious injury they have done us. Some joined the enemy from inclination. Others, in the most difficult times, from Compulsion, and believing the cause desperate and almost totally lost. Nine out of ten of those who received British protection I suppose to be of the latter description and had in the beginning shewn themselves both in council and in this field friendly to our cause. These can not, except in a few instances, forgive those who refused to bend to the power at that time existing in the State, and chose to commit their lives and property to the issues of the contest.[49]

It took many years for the bitterness to diminish among the Goose Creek people who were so directly involved in the war efforts. In addition to the destruction caused by the war, soil exhaustion had an irreversible effect on Goose Creek. A slow struggling recovery was to follow for 80 years in Goose Creek, which would then suffer a total collapse of its economy and culture after the Civil War.

CHAPTER IX

THE POLITICAL HISTORY OF GOOSE CREEK,
1783 - 1900

When George Washington took his oath of office, a new era in American history began. The Americans were victorious and a wave of optimism swept through the new nation. Along with the new freedom, however, was a grave responsibility for the new government. The economic foundation of the South was badly weakened. Depressed prices, unmarketable products, soil exhaustion and an unprofitable slave system portended an ominous economic future for South Carolinians. Thomas Jefferson was even talking of freeing his slaves and predicted with confidence the natural death of slavery.

Upon returning to their Goose Creek plantations, the planter-patriots were confronted with a new enemy even harder to fight than the British had been. The planters were to wage an on-going battle with poverty for many decades after the war. Few Goose Creek plantations had been untouched by it. During the British occupation, the plantations which had not been intentionally damaged had been neglected, were overgrown and badly in need of rehabilitation. The new American government could offer little assistance. In 1784, commissioners were sent to England to seek compensation for slaves and other property which had been carried off by the evacuating British army. William Logan from St. James' Parish, Goose Creek, was one of the South Carolina commissioners.[1] The long voyage to England and the troublesome negotiations netted no immediate compensation. Goose Creek, as the rest of the nation, was going to have to solve its postwar problems alone.

As a British colony, South Carolina had enjoyed many of the benefits of the British Empire. A bounty on indigo and naval stores had made that business very profitable in Goose Creek. The British government had also provided a bounty on rice production. This was of great advantage to the Goose Creek and Cooper River rice planters. The year of final peace between the United States and England, 1783, was also the year that the Goose Creek planter, Gideon Dupont, introduced the water-culture method of rice production.[2] This method of overflowing the fields with water at specific

141

intervals gave the Carolina rice planters a great advantage despite the absence of a government bounty. For nearly 100 years, Carolina rice was to be a highly profitable commodity on the world market. This was about the only progress made in Goose Creek agriculture in the years immediately following the war.

The profits from indigo were negligible and hardly equalled the expense of production. The Goose Creek slaves who were the basis for plantation society were no longer profitable without the availability of the British Empire's markets for agricultural goods.

Despite the wishes of Thomas Jefferson, the end to slavery was not in the foreseeable future. The introduction of Eli Whitney's cotton gin in 1793 made southern short-staple cotton extremely profitable. The agricultural revolution which brought great prosperity to the South came to be known as "King Cotton." Cotton had little economic effect on Goose Creek, however. The once-rich plantation lands which had provided rice, indigo, and foodstuffs for over 100 years were now exhausted. Planters did not have the advantage of scientific agricultural knowledge, and fertilizers and crop rotation were unknown. Cotton demands nutrient-rich soil, like the type found in the virgin bottom lands of the Gulf states. Even as early as 1750, Rev. Robert Stone wrote that Goose Creek lands were worn out and that the inhabitants were leaving.[3] By the 1790's they were not at all suitable for cotton production.

The production of naval stores, once a profitable commodity needed for the British Navy, was no longer a money-maker and any profit from livestock or corn production was barely enough for the maintenance of the plantation and family.

Unemployment received some relief in 1792 when the Santee Canal was begun. A requirement for the reestablishment of a sound agricultural system was economical transportation. The Cooper River system was a superb network of fresh-water streams and deep tidal creeks and rivers. It was almost a perfect means of travel from the plantations to the market. In 1770 a Commons House committee reported favorably on a plan for a canal from the Santee River to the headwaters of the Cooper River, and a company was chartered in 1786. The canal was to be 22 miles long, 35 feet wide and

POLITICAL HISTORY, 1783-1900

hold four feet of water. Locks were used to raise and lower the water levels. Some notable Goose Creek planters bought stock in the Santee Canal Company when it was incorporated in 1786. Aaron Loocock and Ralph Izard, both from Goose Creek, bought into the company. Aaron Loocock had a very profitable mercantile business in Charleston and Izard was a prosperous planter. With this and his connections with bonding interests through the New York Delancey family, Ralph Izard was able to maintain the prosperous dignity of his Goose Creek estate.[4]

The canal never proved to be very profitable, but its construction greatly relieved the dire economic problems of Goose Creek and Berkeley County for a while. The construction needed labor, and Goose Creek planters hired out their black slaves for cash paid annually to the owners. Both men and women were employed in this fashion.

Goose Creek also had earned the reputation of being unhealthy. Poor health was blamed on the swamp gases, but the recurring Goose Creek "fevers" were probably caused by malaria. Mosquitos multiplied easily in the swampy Goose Creek community. It was shortly after the Revolution that reduced attendance at the Goose Creek church caused regular Sunday services there to be cancelled. The church was used as a mission with only infrequent services for a number of years. As the population continued to decrease during the 19th century, the church was finally closed except for annual services.

On May 25, 1787 a quorum of 55 representatives from 12 states convened in Philadelphia to form a new constitution for the United States. Severe economic problems threatened to destroy the nation which, in the absence of strong federal leadership, was floundering in the world market and at home. The national tax system, the public debt and the nation's credit were presenting ever more serious problems. Symptoms of the economic crisis were exemplified in 1786 when impoverished back-country farmers in Massachusetts protested in what was known as Shay's Rebellion. The need for national leadership was paramount. A new constitution and President George Washington were to provide much of that leadership.

In 1787 representatives from each state went to Philadelphia and agreed to submit a new Federal Constitution to each state for ratification. A special convention of South Carolinians considered the document and ratified it on May 23, 1788. All of the Goose Creek conventioners voted for ratification: Ralph Izard, Peter Smith, Benjamin Smith, Gabriel Manigault, William Smith, John Parker, Jr., and John Deas, Jr.[5]

The nation was establishing a firmer federal foothold, and South Carolina followed suit. In May of 1790 a state convention met in Columbia to adopt a constitution for the State of South Carolina. Delegates from St. James' Parish, Goose Creek, were Aaron Loocock, John Deas, Peter Gray, Nathaniel McCants, William Allen Deas, James Smith and Thomas Parker.[6]

As the new state entered the 19th century, symptoms of discontent with some Federal policies started to be revealed in protest meetings held in St. James' parish. The extent of the sovereignty South Carolina was to have in the republic was an early issue which was to be contested until the Civil War. Federal policies regarding internal national improvements, tariffs and slavery were to be in the political forefront in the parish. The Goose Creek people were to be as active in their rejection of federal authority as they were rejecting the Proprietors and Royal government.

Tariffs were import taxes imposed to protect young and inexperienced Northern industries. Although the tariffs had a positive effect by making American manufactured items competitive with those from England, the Southern merchants, many with new cotton interests, were much in opposition. They resented paying higher prices for imported manufactured items. Southerners were large consumers of manufactured goods. They were greatly alarmed in 1828 when the federal Congress imposed a very high tariff on the nation. Southerners referred to the 1828 tariff as the "Tariff of Abominations."[7] Several Southern states protested formally, and in South Carolina the flags were lowered to half-mast. "Let the New England beware how she imitates the old," one South Carolinian said in an eloquent protest.[8]

The people of Goose Creek were infuriated. Goose Creek was a part of the old South, and one of the least flourishing sections of the young nation. The Northeast was reaping profits from tariff-protected industries; the West was experiencing rapid population growth with accompanying prosperity and the new Southwest was producing shiploads of cotton. The old South, in addition to its own problems, was faced with what it perceived to be unfair federal laws. The people of Goose Creek protested heatedly.

A protest meeting against tariffs was held at the Wassamasaw Chapel by Goose Creek citizens. Captain Nathaniel Lawrence presided, with Coswell Mims acting as secretary. John N. Davis, Thomas Blackman, Dr. John Williams, West Williams, Thomas Fauling, George Crawford, Jacob Barker, John Shuler, Isaac Bradwell, S. Shingler, Captain A. Gillon and Colonel William Mellard were chosen to serve as a resolution committee. They produced the following:

PREAMBLE

We the people of this Parish, have, for a long time, been silent spectators of the great political movements, which have agitated the union, and distracted her councils; but being a part of the great human family, and having a common interest with all, we feel it a duty to ourselves, our country and posterity, now to give expression to our opinions and feelings. We have, with deep concern, witnessed the bold and rapid encroachments of the general government upon the authority and sovereignty of the states, in passing of the tariff imposing duties, not for the purpose of revenue, but for the protection of manufacturers, to the injury of our revenue, and to the ruin of our commercial and agricultural interests. We have looked into the federal constitution, and have no where, seen the power delegated to Congress to favour and protect any particular branch of industry, particular class of citizens, or particular sections of the union, at the expence of other branches of industry.

RESOLUTIONS

1. Resolved, that the act, establishing the constitution of the United States, was the act of the people of the several states, as states, and not of the people of the United States in their aggregate capacity.

2. Resolved, that the doctrine of the federal constitution emanating from the people at large, and not from the states, is anti-republican, false and dangerous; and would break down the barriers which separate the powers of the general government from those of state governments.

3. Resolved, that the power claimed and exercised by Congress, of constructing Roads and opening canals, under the doctrine of the general welfare, presupposes a sovereign state to have no controul over its own soil, and is a downright heresy.

4. Resolved, that the State Legislature of 1826, has rendered itself memorable and illustrious, by reclaiming public opinion from the dangerous creed of the latitudinarian disciples of the present day.

5. Resolved, that Congress has exercised powers in passing the Tariff, not delegated by the Federal Constitution.

6. Resolved, that we will, as far as practicable, live upon our own resources, by raising our own stock and manufacturing our own clothing; and we recommend the general use and wear of homespun to our fellow citizens.

7. Resolved, that we place the most implicit confidence in the legislature of this state, and we will cheerfully adhere to any constitutional mode of relief which may, by it, be recommended.

8. Resolved, that the Members of Congress from this State, have faithfully and ably discharged their duty, in representing the sentiments of their constituents on the subject of the Tariff.

On motion, it was Resolved, That the proceedings of the Meeting be published in the Charleston Mercury.

The Meeting adjourned, and the assembly partook of the vicinity in which the meeting was held, and immediately retired.

NATHANIEL LAWRENCE, Chairman.
Coswell Mims, Secretary.[9]

As a result of a number of such meetings throughout the state, two political parties evolved in South Carolina, both in opposition to the tariff. The parties differed on the methods of opposition. The States Rights and Free Trade Party (hereafter referred to as the States Rights Party) desired complete nullification of the tariff laws. The other party was known as The Union and States Rights Party (hereafter referred to as Union Party). They were not in favor of complete nullification. The States Rights party was supportive of nullification even at the risk of revolution and war. In the 1832 general election two Goose Creek Union Party candidates were elected to the Legislature. They were John N. Davis (senator), and J.L. Strohecker (representative).[10]

Despite the meetings of the Nullifiers in St. James' parish, the Unionists won by a moderate margin. St. James', Goose Creek was one of only 11 districts where the Unionists elected all of their candidates.[11]

After the election, the Governor called for an extra session of the legislature to meet with the newly elected

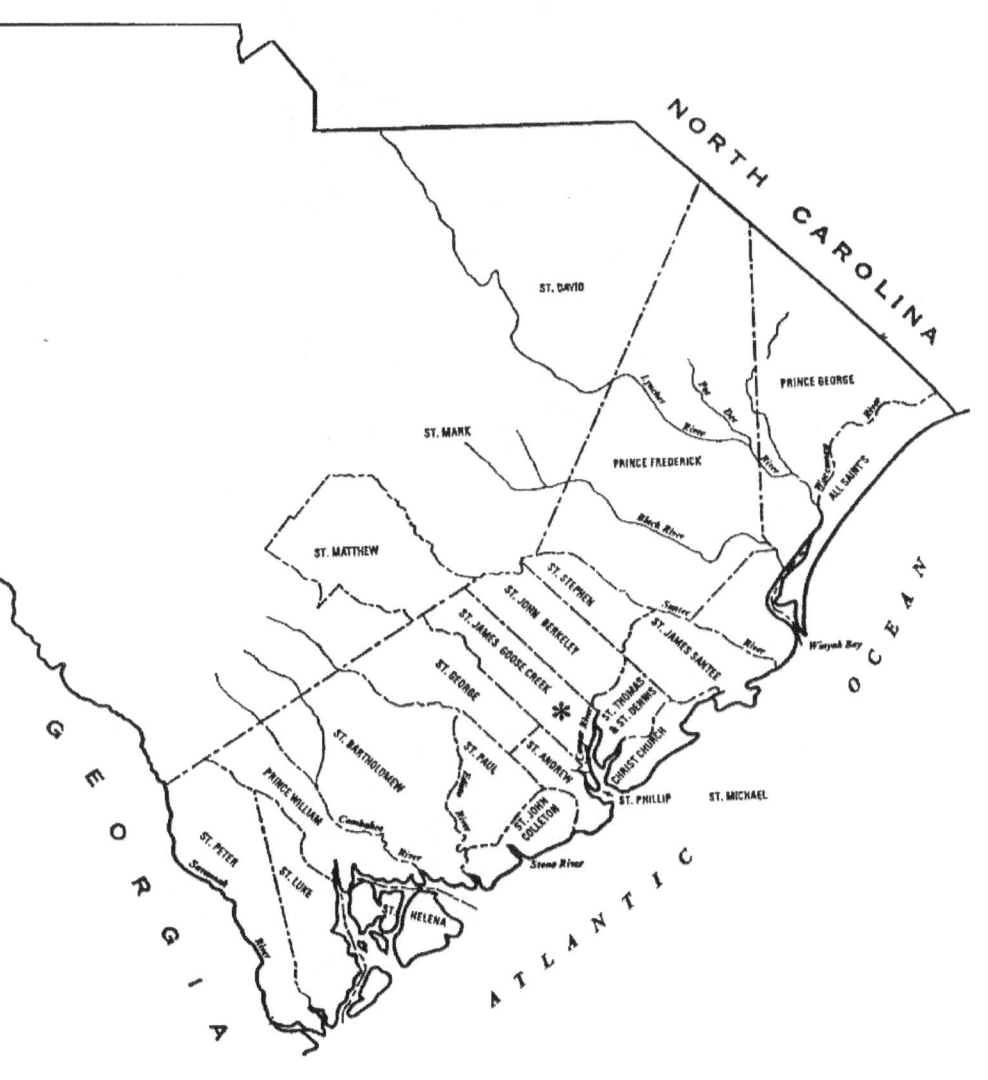

The Parishes of South Carolina in 1790.
— *Courtesy of the University of South Carolina Press.*

Landgrave Thomas Smith, Esq., one of the "Goose Creek Men" and a Proprietary Governor of the Province of Carolina.
— *Courtesy of Harper & Row, Publishers, Inc.*

Medway Plantation house, acquired by Landgrave Smith through his marriage to Sabina, widow of John D'Arsens, Signeur Van Wernhaut in 1687.
— *Courtesy of Harper & Row, Publishers, Inc.*

The Hon. Arthur Middleton, Esq., 1742-1787, a signer of the Declaration of Independence.
—*Courtesy of the South Carolina Historical Society.*

St. James' Church, Goose Creek, as painted by Charleston artist Charles Fraser between c. 1790-1806.

—*Courtesy of the Carolina Art Association.*

The interior of St. James' Church, showing the Royal Arms above the pulpit.

—*Courtesy of the South Carolina Historical Society.*

The Rev. Francis LeJau, D.D., 1665-1717, Anglican minister to Goose Creek from the Society for the Propagation of the Gospel in Foreign Parts, London.

—*Courtesy of Duke University Press.*

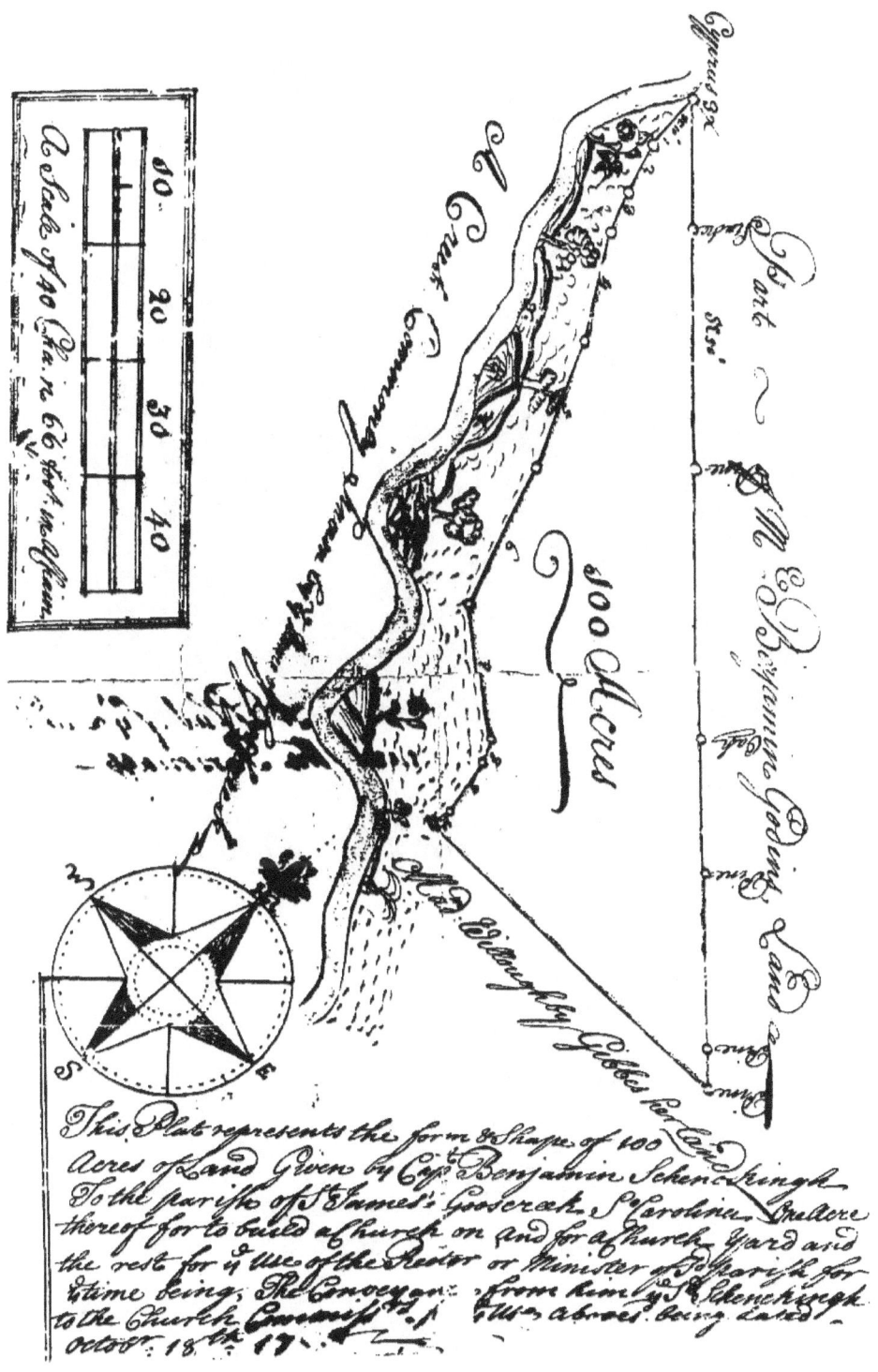

The plat of Capt. Benjamin Schenckingh's 1706 gift of 100 acres of land to the Parish of St. James for use as the church site and glebe lands.

—*Courtesy of the South Carolina Historical Society.*

The Hayes or Ingleside's Plantation house, former home of the Parker family. The land was originally granted to John Parker in 1702.
—*Courtesy of Harper & Row, Publishers, Inc.*

Yeamans Hall Plantation house, built about 1693. The original land was granted to Lady Margaret Yeamans in 1674.
—*Courtesy of Harper & Row, Publishers, Inc.*

members. Three days later a bill was passed calling for a convention of delegates to meet November 19. To this convention Goose Creek sent Isaac Bradwell, Jr. and G.H. Smith.[12] Five days later the convention passed an Ordinance of Nullification with all Goose Creek delegates voting in favor. Great fear of Federal retaliation caused special provisions to be taken for defense and all officers (except legislators) were required to take an oath of allegiance to the new ordinance.

The Union Party protested against the Nullification Ordinance and the Oath of Allegiance.[13] The Unionists began to organize military companies loyal to the President of the United States, while the Nullifiers established arsenals and military depots. The entire affair became quite ominous until it was finally quieted by a compromise tariff. The Federal compromise was to be short lived, however. The tariff issue was to be raised again as a primary grievance leading to the Civil War.

It was about this time that Northern abolitionists began to strengthen their ranks and call for an end to slavery. The inhumanity of slavery, which many Southerners perceived as a necessary evil, caused antislavery societies to arise throughout the nation. Northern abolitionists intensified their social reform movements in the 1830 and 1840's. Additional momentum was gained when the slaves were freed in the British Empire during the 1830's. Some extremists such as William Lloyd Garrison greatly alarmed the slave-dependent South. In his militant newspaper *The Liberator*, he made a frontal assault on the Southern slave owner.[14] This was the beginning of a 30 year verbal battle over slavery that would finally culminate in the Civil War. As the abolitionist movement gained momentum, the Southerners, bound to the institution by tradition and economics, were forced to take their stand.

The Southern states retaliated by organizing in opposition to the abolitionists and by organizing their defenses against possible Northern aggression. The slavery issue was of the gravest concern in the Carolina low country. Less than 25% of the population was white, and the economy was dependent on slave labor. The Goose Creek people were adamantly supportive of slavery. The small farmers and those on the beautiful old Goose Creek plantations had been struggling against adverse economic conditions for decades and were in no position to abandon their source of cheap agricultural labor. The objections of the Northern abolitionists meant economic collapse of the Goose Creek plantations. In retaliation to the abolitionists, a meeting was called in Summerville in August of 1835. It was resolved during this meeting to denounce the actions of the Northern abolitionists. Summerville was in St. James' parish, and the meeting was attended by the concerned people of Goose Creek.[15] Goose Creek and Dorchester citizens met at the Cypress Camp Ground on September 9, 1835 to hear the report from the August meeting in Summerville. At Cypress the citizens again resolved to resist the activities of the "Northern fanatics."

The following citizens were appointed to serve as a committee of vigilance: Isaac Bradwell, Esq., Chairman; Capt. Thos. Mims, J.J. McCants, J. Smith, Dr. J. Wilson, John Inabnit, J. Varner, G. Smith, John Brownlee, Isaac Murray, Joseph Inabnit, C. Mims, Dr. R.H. Jones, John Cockfield, Wm. Riggs, Richard Minus, Dr. Bradwell, John Plat, B. Earnist, R. Chinnus, R. Stephenson, Secretary.[16] Communication was so slow and unreliable and abolition was so important that there was a need for such a committee to keep the community informed about the developments.

In December of 1850 the State Legislature authorized an election to be held October 13, 1851 to choose delegates to a convention to assemble in Columbia to consider the abolition issues. Delegates to the convention from St. James', Goose Creek were W. Williams and Isaac Bradwell, Jr.[17] Protest meetings became common and now began to hint at the possibility of secession. A meeting was held in St. James' parish, Goose Creek, on July 13, 1851, at which another resolution to defend slavery was drawn.[18]

An incident in 1855 took the issue of slavery off the minds of the people for a while. The first railroad strike in the state occurred in Berkeley County near Goose Creek between the Northeastern Railroad and its workers. The workers marched to Charleston, armed with clubs and pistols. They were met with resistance at the city limits by the sheriff and some concerned citizens, and returned to the railroad construction site. A military detail was dispatched from Charleston to serve warrants against the striking workers.

24 of them were arrested and held for trial on riot charges. This action ended the strike.[19]

Slavery and tariffs, two issues so deeply rooted in southern economics, were the two main causes of the Civil War. That great war, known in the South as "The War For Southern Independence," threatened to divide and weaken a nation which had endured the struggle and resulting problems of its own independence 90 years earlier.

The Southern states seceded from the union for a multitude of reasons. Political influence in Congress had moved away from the South. The settling of the West had brought anti-slavery congressmen from the new states to Washington, and Harriet Beecher Stowe's masterpiece, *Uncle Tom's Cabin*, had placed popular support firmly behind the anti-slavery movement in most parts of the nation. The South was in a desperate situation, and the people of Goose Creek seemed to react as adamantly as any other Southern community.

On September 16, 1851 a large meeting of the citizens of the parish of St. James, Goose Creek, met at the Wassamasaw Chapel. Col. T.B. Earnest called the meeting to order. The assembly elected the Hon. John Wilson as chairman and J.J. Browning and George C. Smith as secretaries. At this meeting they resolved to cooperate with all of the Southern or slave-holding states in resisting the encroachment of tyranny, and "maintaining our just rights." They pledged trust and confidence in others who, with themselves, were threatened by a common danger. During the same meeting it was resolved that it would not be proper or in good faith for South Carolina to secede alone.[20] Reminiscent of the rebellious days of the American Revolution, a Committee of Safety and Correspondence for the parish was appointed: Rev. Stephen Williams, Rev. West Williams, Benjamin Godfrey, George Crawford, Thomas Mims, William McWilliams, Col. Thomas J. Mellard, Captain S.C. Warnock, W.B. Thomas, Albert Clark, Hamilton Hart, Wm. Martin, Senr., Wm. Whaley, J.J. McCants, Col. J.B. Earnest, J.J. Browning, G.C. Smith, H.T. Browning, Rev. A.G. Sims, J.T. Crawford, Hon. John Wilson, and John Lawrence.[21]

A state convention was called for December 17, 1860 in Columbia for delegates from throughout the state. The purpose was to consider the ever-threatening encroachment of the Northern abolitionists and secession from the Union. From Goose Creek, John N. Shingler and C.P. Brown were sent.[22] The convention moved from the State capitol at Columbia to Charleston because of a threat of smallpox. On December 20, 1860, the conventioners met at the St. Andrew's Society Hall, with 169 delegates attending. The Ordinance of Secession had been drafted. The coventioners heard it read while remaining politely silent. By unanimous vote the ordinance was approved. "The Union now subsisting between South Carolina and other States, under the name of the 'United States of America' is hereby dissolved."[23]

These 20 words were to affect the lives of every Carolinian. Shortly thereafter, other Southern states joined with South Carolina to form the Confederate States of America. The work of the conventioners turned Charleston into a joyous celebration. From the windows of the *Charleston Mercury* newspaper office, hastily printed sheets were tossed which read, "The Union Is Dissolved."[24] Flags waved, cannons roared, bonfires were lighted and people screamed the news throughout the streets. Military companies organized immediately, arms were gathered and the most popular toast was "Damnation to the Yankees."[25]

One company of Goose Creekers was the Wassamassaw Cavalry. The Confederate service of this company was summarized in the Charleston *News and Courier* (August 17, 1877) as follows:

> The Wassamassaw Cavalry was organized . . . in 1857. T.H. Winter was the first commander, and subsequently served as one of its lieutenants during the War Between the States.
>
> The company, with Dr. J.C. McKewn as captain, entered the Confederate service in January, '62, on the coast of South Carolina, in a battalion formed by companies commanded by Capts., Frank Hampton, Earle, Dean, Williams, and Westfield, In July, '62 the battalion was ordered to Virginia, and with other companies from the State formed the Second South Carolina Regiment, commanded by Gen. M.C. Butler, as Colonel. The company, with the regiment, remained at the front in Virginia until the spring of '64 when it was ordered to South Carolina to recruit horses and men. The following November the company was the defense of that city until the spring of '65, when the Confederates were forced into the interior of the Old North State, and its members, like all other Confeds, were invited to return to their homes and be loyal citizens of Uncle Sam.[26]

POLITICAL HISTORY, 1783-1900

The cavalry flag was left at a house near Richmond, Virginia. It was made of blue and white silk with a palmetto tree and the motto, "The brave may fail, but never yield." The words "Wassamassaw Cavalry" were written on the silk. Along with the summary of the cavalry's history, the newspaper requested information regarding the whereabouts of the flag.

No Civil War battles were fought in Goose Creek or elsewhere in Berkeley County, but the Goose Creek people felt the effects of the war. On April 19, 1861, President Lincoln issued a proclamation stating that a blockade of the Southern ports was in effect. At first this was only a paper blockade, but eventually Charleston harbor was closed. The "Stone Fleet," so named because the ships were loaded with granite, was sunk in Charleston harbor by the Union Navy to prevent the flow of harbor traffic. This and the U.S. Navy completed the blockade. A shortage of almost everything touched the lives of almost all low country residents. By early 1862 there was a shortage of shoes. Prices rose with the depreciation of Confederate money. In 1863 corn was selling for $2.25 a bushel and bacon $1.00 a pound. By 1864 bacon rose to $5.00 a pound, butter $6.00 a pound and sugar $8.00 a pound. Most things were just not available. A pair of boots reached the price of $250.00 a pair.[27]

Human energies not engaged in armed service were called upon to defend the city. Most of the Goose Creek women and those of the countryside near Charleston took refuge in the city. The women of Charleston worked gallantly in its defense. Captain Wagner of Fort Moultrie called upon the women of Charleston to produce several thousand cartridge bags in 24 hours on one occasion. The women worked late into the evening to meet the challenge, and the bags were delivered. They supplied bags made out of their petticoats and pillow cases.[28] Slaveowners of Berkeley County were called upon to furnish slaves to erect breastworks on Charleston Neck to prevent an invasion of the city by land. The *Charleston Daily Courier* reported the daily movement of Union troops and the impending invasion of the Charleston low country in 1863. Three Goose Creek men, Keith Brown, B. Rhame, and C.W. Glaves were appointed to procure slaves and send them to work on the Charleston Neck breastwork.[29] No battles were fought in the parish, but many

HISTORIC GOOSE CREEK

Goose Creekers lent their service to the Confederacy.

Captain Carston William Vose was captain of the Goose Creek company attached to the 18th Regiment. Some of the Captain Vose's family still live in Goose Creek.[30] Vose immigrated to St. James' parish, Goose Creek from Woldsdorf, Hanover, Germany, where he was born in 1806. He had stayed a short while in New York, New Orleans and Charleston before he married Mrs. Brickman and came into possession of a plantation on the State Road at the 18 Mile House. This house, located on the main road from Columbia to Charleston and only one day's travel to the city, was a favorite stopping place for travelers. Cattle and hog drovers would stop at the 18 Mile House for boarding and sometimes dispose of their livestock for subsequent resale. A family account of Captain Vose recorded:

> Captain Vose had a large share of "the milk of human kindness." The footsore traveler on the state road could always find rest under his hospitable roof and the poor man a friend. It may be truly said that he has been "gathered to his fathers, having the testimony of a good conscience, at peace with his Maker and in perfect charity with the world."

Captain Vose had seven children by three marriages. Although he was never called to lead the Goose Creek company into battle, his son John George Vose participated in numerous southern engagements during the Civil War. A review of the son's experiences reflects on the period, the war and life in general in the Goose Creek area during the war years. Captain Vose moved his family to Summerville in 1852 and built a store there two years later. Summerville was then within the boundary of St. James' parish. It is from Summerville that John George Vose joined the Confederate forces.[31] He recorded his personal account of the war from memory:

> By the next summer my father bought a house in Summerville, S.C. After that, our summers were spent there. Summerville was then a summer resort for the planters in that neighborhood, as it was considered unhealthy on the plantations in the summer. Our overseer, Mr. Moses Gibson, stayed on the plantation all the year. I was a great favorite of his and always slept with him. I do not recall how I spent the winters up to this time. During the summer I attended the town school. When I was about 12 years old,

POLITICAL HISTORY, 1783-1900

> I attended school in Charleston kept by Rev. Muller, who was also pastor of the German Lutheran Church. I also attended that Sunday School and Church. Where I never was much on German. I could read and understand a little, but have now forgotten all. I then went to the Charleston High School. The latter part of 1869 I went to Newberry College primary department and in a short while was in the preparatory department. This was 1860.
>
> My teacher, Professor Gus P. Pifer, A Virginian, took quite a fancy to me and invited me to spend the Christmas holidays with him in Virginia. I wrote home and Pa sent me the money for the trip, but just then the secession excitement was running high and Professor Pifer decided not to go. That put an end to the trip, but as I had the money for the trip, a tick struck me to invest some of it in a trip home — which I did. I got up about 9 o'clock at night and found the whole family making a flag on a Palmetto tree and the words "Southern Republic" sewed on under the tree. You see, the state had just seceeded! That flag was hung across the road in front of Pa's store the next morning and I expect it was one of the first flags of the Confederate States . . . .[32]

John George's personal accounts are remembrances of long marches, days on freight trains, hunger and comrades in war. His arrival home is of interest:

> We got to Summerville in early afternoon. I made straight for home and found some of the home guard at our store, but Pa was at home in bed — had been kicked by a mule. I tell you there was some rejoicing!
>
> Alex and I were both in a dilapidated condition, especially our clothing, but we soon washed up and, in a few days, I was rigged out in a pair of Pa's pants. He was an old-timer and his pants were homemade (he never wore store clothes). He weighed around 200 pounds, so you can imagine the figure I cut in his pants. A little later he gave me two suits and a pair of shoes. It took me some time to become accustomed to store clothes as I had been in uniform quite a while.[33]

The race issue after the war was a difficult adjustment for the white land owners. The accounting of John George Vose sheds some light on the problem and the attitude of the day:

> I must say something about Alex right here. His skin was black but a truer heart never beat. We were children together, we played together, we grew up together, we thoroughly knew each other and loved each other. There was nothing too good for Mass' George or Sonny, as he some-

times called me. He was true to the last. He had every chance to go to the Yanks; but, no, he returned home with me and remained for quite a while just as if he did not know he was free.[34]

Captain John George Vose died in Summerville on August 11, 1884, at the age of 78. At the time of his death, he was the oldest resident of Summerville.

War-torn Charleston and its southern neighbors were witness to destruction and poverty. The handsome cities of the Old South, Atlanta, Richmond and Charleston, were never again to enjoy the great civilization of antebellum days. Charleston and its surroundings were scenes of destruction. Banks and businesses were closed, runaway inflation was persistent, the educational system was disrupted, and agriculture was crippled. The people of Goose Creek suffered no less than most old Southern communities. They had not felt the direct onslaught of Union soldiers but they had felt the impact of economic collapse and the passing of the southern civilization. Recovery was dreadfully slow.

There was little sympathy for Charleston in the Northern states. Even before Charleston was captured, the *New York Tribune* published:

> "Doom" hangs over wicked Charleston. That viper's nest and breeding place of rebellion is, ere this time, invested by Union Arms — perhaps already in our hands. If there is any city deserving of holocaustic infamy, it is Charleston. Should its inhabitants choose to make its site a desert, blasted by fire, we do not think, many tears would be shed. Travellers of to-day are quite undecided as to the location of ancient Carthage; travellers of 2862 may be in the same doubt about Charleston.[35]

A letter from General Holleck in Washington to General Sherman read: "Should you capture Charleston, I hope that by some accident the place may be destroyed and if a little salt should be sown upon its site, it may prevent the growth of future crops of nullification and secession."[36]

On February 14, 1865, the war was near its end. General Beauregard sent instructions for the evacuation of Charleston. As Charleston fell to the Union army, the evacuating Confederates passed near Goose Creek. The troops in Christ Church parish went by steamer to Strawberry Ferry, about six miles above the Goose Creek church. From there they went by way of Cordesville to St. Stephens.[37] The surrender at Appomatox

POLITICAL HISTORY, 1783-1900

was only a few months away. The low country was in shambles.

The problems of post-war Goose Creek were formidable. The need to revive business, transportation, and investment capital was of immediate concern. No federal aid was to be expected, and for a long time none came. Goose Creek's precarious economic position was further aggravated by the development of the share-cropping system and the crop lien system of finance. After the war, hard-pressed creditors began demanding interest and principal payments on mortgages. Many were forced to sell parts of their land in order to finance cultivation of the rest. Under the share-cropping system, the land was divided into many small holdings resembling small farms but actually parts of single plantations. Attaining a small plot of land was a big achievement for Goose Creek black men who so recently were on labor gangs during slavery days. To make matters worse for the local economy, it was impossible even to get the crops planted unless a merchant advanced the seed, capital for equipment and even money for necessities such as food and clothing. The entire South suffered due to the lack of capital and cheap labor. Most large estates were sold in pieces to pay taxes, purchase equipment and pay for everyday necessities. Eventually most of the Goose Creek land was divided into small holdings. The 1870 post-war census reveals that almost all of the land in Goose Creek was held by illiterate black farmers.[38]

Political problems complicated the economic ills. Radical political parties kept many whites from the Southern polls. Encouraged by the Northern radicals, blacks dominated politics. South Carolina was readmitted to the Union June 25, 1868, but it wasn't until eight years later that "conservative" government returned to the state. General Wade Hampton was elected governor of the State in 1876. A state census taken in 1875 showed the population of St. James, Goose Creek, to be 23,142, with 4,026 whites and 19,116 blacks and 3,320 total registered voters.[39] The census for Goose Creek was extremely exaggerated because the count included people on Charleston Neck from the city limits to Six Mile and as much of the parish of St. Andrew as lay on the east side of the Ashley River. The figures, although exaggerated, reveal a nearly four to one black-to-white ratio.[40]

HISTORIC GOOSE CREEK

Political rallies were tumultuous during the years of Reconstruction. Bitter feuds were common between the Republicans (mostly black) and the Democrats (mostly white). The Charleston *News and Courier* quite obviously favored the Democrats. On September 1, 1876, it reported on a political rally at Strawberry Landing near Goose Creek. Strawberry was a black Republican stronghold with between 600 and 700 black voters to approximately 25 white. The Republicans accepted a Democrat challenge at the podium, and large numbers of Republicans and Democrats met for the rally. The so-called Radical Republican stronghold was invaded by cheering Democrats, many of whom came from Charleston on the steamer *M.S. Allison* via the Cooper River. Arriving on horseback to lend support to the outnumbered Democrats was the Hampton Social Mounted Club of Goose Creek and the Mt. Pleasant Mounted Club. The Goose Creek club consisted of 30 men under the command of Captain George M. Thorin. Major Huguenin commanded the 25 mounted men from the Mt. Pleasant club. At the rally they were confronted with hundreds of bystanders. Some people were armed with muskets, rifles, shotguns, swords and bayonets.[41] Major Barker from Goose Creek was in command of the mounted men. He instructed the men to keep peace and to prevent any "colored" person from being intimidated.

It appears as if many black citizens desired to join the Democrats but were threatened by the black Republicans. Major Barker's mission was to show willingness to protect any black man who wanted to join the Democratic Party. In spite of the foreboding appearance, no violence resulted during the meeting at Strawberry. There were some very heated exchanges of words by the various speakers, but they all culminated in a loud crash when the speaking platform collapsed.[42]

Prior to the Strawberry debate, Major Barker had purchased 25 navy revolvers for his men. During this period the most formidable armed force in Goose Creek was the social mounted clubs. They were organized under the guise of hunting clubs, but to many outnumbered whites, the clubs offered a great deal of security. The Wassamassaw Mounted Club was organized with T.S. Browning as the captain. This club was also referred to as the Centennial Democratic Club of St. James, Goose Creek.[43] The first meeting was September 8,

POLITICAL HISTORY, 1783-1900

1876, with Mr. C.W. Sanders as secretary. The mounted clubs kept the communities armed and independent of the Republican and black state government. This was a period of frequent political rallies in Goose Creek and its environs. One incident which included many Goose Creek people erupted in violence. A rally near Goose Creek was a typical debate which erupted into a shouting match. A group of blacks appeared with clubs and a few guns they had hidden in an old abandoned house. A riot ensued during which many people were injured and a few killed. There is no record of any of the Goose Creek people being injured.

Republican Governor Chamberlain tried to disband the rifle and mounted clubs but they continued to have a great deal of popular support. In the state-wide election in 1876, Wade Hampton was elected to the governorship. This was victory for the Democrats and it marked the end of the Radical Reconstruction period. White people's faith in state government returned when the new governor replaced the Radical trial judges with Democrats. In St. James, Goose Creek, he appointed H.H. Murray as Trial Justice.[44]

General Wade Hampton was the Democratic candidate for governor again in 1878. Many people from Goose Creek attended a Democratic rally in Bonneau on October 2, 1878. The Goose Creek Democrats boarded the train at Mt. Holly and Strawberry for a cheering ride to Bonneau. The Strawberry Democratic club with their president, Dr. O.C. Rhame, was accompanied by many black supporters. The Democrats wore red ribbons, red shirts or red pieces of cloth to signify unity. Although the Berkeley precincts were carried by the Republicans, the state as a whole was carried by the Democrats. Wade Hampton and his Red Shirts were reelected.[45]

January 3, 1882, a mass meeting of citizens from Goose Creek and Colleton County was held in Summerville.[46] It was called by State Senator Fishbourne of Colleton, who denounced the so-called stock law and wanted to petition the governor against enforcement of it. In Goose Creek, as in the rest of the low country, it was the practice to allow livestock to roam at large. This made it necessary to fence in the crops to keep the livestock out. As more and more of the land was cultivated and as the large plantations were developed as small farms, many requested a law to compel livestock owners to fence in the animals.

HISTORIC GOOSE CREEK

A great deal of debate arose in regard to the stock law issue. Many contested that the poor man would surely go broke if he had to purchase enough fence for his acreage. Despite much debate, a stock law was passed by the General Assembly in 1881. All cattle were to be fenced from that time.

In 1882, Charleston County was divided, and the name Berkeley was restored to part of it. Mt. Pleasant was named the new county seat of Berkeley. In July of that year the Democratic party of Berkeley County had its first convention at Alhambra Hall in Mt. Pleasant. Goose Creek delegates to the Mt. Pleasant convention were G.W. Shringler, T.T. Connor, Dr. J.B. Wiggins, Dr. O.C. Rhame, L.S. Browing, George Conner, Charles Boyle, R.S. Pringle and T.H. Smith.[47] Mr. Charles Boyle was elected chairman of the temporary convention. A committee composed of one member from each parish assigned representatives to the state convention. Of the twelve state delegates, Goose Creek was to have three: T. Henry Smith, George W. Shringler and Charles Boyle.[48]

In the county election of November 7, 1882, T.H. Smith was elected County Chairman and Dr. T. Wiggins elected coroner, both from Goose Creek.[49] The political division in Goose Creek was strongly aligned racially. Almost all the whites were Democratic, but split over the stock law issue. In 1882, the predominantly black Republicans also split into two factions. T.S. Browning, R.S. Pringle and Charles Boyle of Goose Creek were elected in 1886 as Representatives from the county.[50] County officials from Goose Creek in 1888 were Representatives Robert S. Pringle and T.W. Wiggins.[51]

This was a time of political unrest in South Carolina. In 1890 the Republican and the Democratic parties disagreed among themselves on many issues and each one split into two parties. This gave the area four parties besides the independents. The majority of the residents of Goose Creek supported one of the two factions of the Democratic party.

1895 was a good year for the people of Goose Creek: the cotton crop was the best since the Civil War. The political situation had settled down and the people were without any major turmoil. One of the favorite occasions of the farmers was the annual cane grinding day held each Autumn. Stalks of sugar cane were fed through large steel rollers powered by mules. The cane juice was squeezed out by the rollers and boiled to make sugar, candy and other sweets. There was

POLITICAL HISTORY, 1783-1900

dancing to fiddle music, games for the younger people, and gossiping for the older generations.

The area of Goose Creek was further reduced around 1896 when a large portion of the parish was assigned to newly established Dorchester County, including the town of Summerville. At this time there wasn't much to the town of Goose Creek. The planters had left and the plantations were either non-existent or run down. The only real town in the parish, Summerville, was assigned to Dorchester County. St. James' Parish, Goose Creek, received three magistrates by an act of the Assembly approved March 3, 1899. One was to reside in the upper portion, one in the central portion and one in the lower portion.[52]

During the decades following the Civil·War, less and less historical significance is attributed to Goose Creek until the second half of the 20th century. In fact the Goose Creek community lost much of its identity. The old parish boundaries were no longer used for civil or legal administration and were hardly discernable except by local historians. During the last years of the 19th century, almost all of the old plantation buildings and grounds were reclaimed by the natural pineland and marsh. A few remnants of stone walls and gardens remained, along with stone grave markers to remind residents of the proud and prosperous community which once flourished. Save for the name of the creek itself, the community identity almost vanished, leaving old St. James' Church as a monument to the former community center.

New settlements with new identities began appearing in the Goose Creek area. Rail lines were of new economic importance during the second half of the 19th century. Mt. Holly was such a rail stop with a station, a post office and a general store. Nearby black communities of small farms found new identities centered around country churches like Casey Church near Mt. Holly, Grove Hall, and St. Paul's, where Boulder Bluff now stands. Most newspapers during this period refer not to Goose Creek but to Mt. Holly. It appears to have supplanted the old Goose Creek community at the turn of the 20th century.

CHAPTER X

EDUCATION AND SCHOOLS IN GOOSE CREEK BEFORE THE 20TH CENTURY

Many of the early Goose Creek settlers were educated people. As soon as they satisfied their basic survival needs, they promoted moral and literacy improvement for themselves and their children. Although the early settlers recognized the need to provide for education, few schools appeared in Goose Creek until well into the 20th century. The small number of schools during the 17th, 18th and 19th centuries does not mean that there was an absence of education. On the contrary, there is much evidence that intelligence and literacy were common among many professionals, government leaders and others living in Goose Creek during the Colonial Period. It wasn't until Reconstruction that Goose Creek witnessed an almost complete absence of formal education. Goose Creek remained in that condition until well into the 20th century.

The earliest educational efforts in Goose Creek were provided by the family. Later the church, private tutors, Charleston private schools and eventually the colonial and State legislatures provided whatever formal education was to be available for the residents. At first, education in Goose Creek had little to do with schools, teachers or books. The earliest education was simple culture borrowing. Valuable lessons in hunting, farming, fishing and travel were learned from the Indians.

The family was the primary educational institution in the Goose Creek frontier. The Goose Creek family (like those in Europe) was headed by the father, but unlike the European families, it was not a large family of extended kinship. The large extended families of Europe had been broken and divided by the voyage to the new world frontier.[1] For the families who first went to Barbados and then came to Goose Creek, or the Huguenots who left France for religious freedom, the old European extended family was forever broken into smaller nuclear family groups.

A review of early land grants shows that some large families came to Goose Creek. As these families had ready access to land, they could be self-sufficient and need not rely on the colonial settlement except for a few of their survival needs. The Goose Creek families were absorbed into the frontier,

EDUCATION AND SCHOOLS

and became relatively isolated and independent. The head of the household was solely responsible for the protection and education of his family members. The most important figure in the transfer of knowledge and culture was therefore the father, and the family was the primary educational institution.[2] It taught the child survival and social skills, spiritual values and gave vocational training.

In addition to the family, the nature of Goose Creek society greatly influenced the style of education. Goose Creek had a plantation society which existed without a community center. One of the notable results of this system was the lack of any town-centered life. There were few centrally located children to make the establishment of community schools practical. The absence of a town or community center, the isolation of the independent family units and the idea of gentility which evolved from the planter society did not encourage the promotion of public schools.

The plantations were large, self-sufficient, independent and connected to each other with poor roads or none at all. The community was loosely tied together by the river and the creek which provided the most efficient means of transportation and communication. The whole parish of St. James, Goose Creek, was large, and many settlers did not have access even to travel by water. Public schools were not practical, and formal education was simply not available to the average settler. A Goose Creek gentility governed the education of the upper classes. Although the plantations were somewhat isolated from each other, they were not far from Charleston. The same water system which provided the loose unity in Goose Creek also made Charleston accessible to the wealthy planters. They used the private schools and tutors in Charleston. Because many of them were also merchants, their business often brought them to Charleston, making it even more convenient to educate their children there.[3] From about 1730, Charleston had a number of private schools for boys and girls of all ages. Charleston also provided experienced teachers of language, music dancing and other "polite arts." The following is a partial list of school masters and mistresses who advertised in the *South Carolina Gazette* from 1732 to 1775.[4] The year following the name and subjects taught is the year the advertisement first appeared.

HISTORIC GOOSE CREEK

Mrs. Salter (Music).........................1734
The Widow Varnod (French, embroidery)........1734
Mary Hext (Needlework, writing, dancing,
    music, arithmetic........................1741
Ruth Lowndes (Plain work, reading)............1743
Elizabeth Anderson (Writing, music, dancing,
    drawing................................1749
Jane Williams (Navigation, trigonometry)..........1747
Charles Walker Fortescue (Latin, Greek,
    rhetoric, logic, natural philosophy,
    trigonometry, geometry, astronomy,
    geography, chronology, mensuration,
    surveying, navigation, dialling)..............1747
William Mason (reading, writing, arithmetic).......1757
Jonathan Copp (geography, history, Latin).........1760
Andrew Siri (French, Italian, bookkeeping).......1767
Joseph Feltham (Writing, arithmetic)............1770
Ann Sage (Writing, arithmetic, drawing,
    music, embroidery, needlework)..............1774

According to a study of the *Gazette*, which was published in Charleston, more than 400 advertisements relating to schools and schoolmasters appeared from 1733 to 1774.[5]

The church was more explicit in its educational function than the family or community. In the 18th century, religion and education were inseparable. The prosperity and ralatively dense population of the colonial parish of St. James, Goose Creek resulted in the continual attention and support of the Society for the Propagation of the Gospel in Foreign Parts.[6] This missionary society (the S.P.G.) was established in 1701 as an auxiliary of the Anglican Church. It was active in promoting education in all the Southern colonies except Virginia.[7]

This support resulted in the early construction of a church, the appointment of a number of Anglican ministers, the hiring of a school master and the later construction of a church-supported school house. The colonial parish vestry invested a number of endowments and subscriptions to provide education for the children of the parish. The vestry support of education decreased at the close of the Colonial Period, the result of the Revolutionary War, discontinuation of S.P.G. support and the infrequent use of the church. Despite these setbacks, the vestry continued to use its school funds to provide for the maintenance of schools until the outbreak of the Civil War. The efforts were resumed after the

EDUCATION AND SCHOOLS

war, through financial assistance to worthy parish youth who wished to attend private academies and colleges, and continued into the first two decades of the 20th century.

The society sent missionaries to Goose Creek, the first being the Rev. Samuel Thomas. The S.P.G. based its missionary programs on the assumption that the development of the Negro slave was identified with the success of the white man. The S.P.G. missionaries instructed both races, as they believed education was inseparable from Christianization. This philosophy was the first step in making it possible for blacks to become Christians, literate and to eventually establish their own churches and institutions.[8]

The Reverend Samuel Thomas began his missionary work in St. James' parish teaching the slaves in 1695. He was so successful that in ten years he was to identify 20 black communicants able to read and write.[9] His success was not met favorably by all. Thomas Nairne, an Indian agent, wrote in a letter August 20, 1705:

> By a private paper I received in Charlestown containing an account of the Society's transactions. I perceive their good ... intentions ... are quite perverted under the notion of converting the Goose Creek negroes as a work good and necessary ... All Carolina laughs at that untruth ... which ... is an action highly base and dishonorable for people who have the best estates in this country and such numerous families of negroes to employ that men and money designed for the poor Indians, (is used) to instruct their slaves.

In addition to Captain Nairne, the Rev. Robert Stevens of Goose Creek said he had heard:

> ... that Mr. Thomas is instructing the negroes of Goose Creek. I live at Goose Creek, but know no negroes that he ... instructed any other way than by his now and then preaching ... where there might be 5 or 6 Christian negroes ... for I know of no more in Goose Creek ... Three or four of those negroes may read, yet it is but sorrily, and I am informed they have books.[10]

Reverend Stevens also commented that the missionary had presented Bibles and prayer books to the slaves. He said that if the master wanted this done they would have surely spent their own money and not that of the missionary society. Mr. Thomas' success in teaching the slaves made the S.P.G. aware that Negroes had the ability to learn quickly.

Rev. Thomas' successor was the Reverend Francis LeJau. He greatly expanded the missionary efforts, and expressed the need for schools to the missionary society from an early date. He and his wife opened a school at their Goose Creek home.

LeJau's educational program for the slaves was very successful. It was apparent that many Negroes wanted education and were capable of learning quickly. Rev. LeJau was an able teacher. He explained some of the obstacles he faced in his letters to the S.P.G. Some masters feared that an educated slave would be rebellious. Some worked the slaves on Sunday, and Indian traders saw folly in doing much more than enslaving the Indians. Dr. LeJau instructed the slaves once a week, but questioned the wisdom of his labors under the existing conditions. He wrote the Society:

> . . . the children of this parish are well acquainted with their catechism; but as I feared the negros and Indian slaves should not be sent to be instructed. I must give the melancholy account that it has so happened; yet I will take all opportunities, and will use all means as God pleases to enable me to secure those poor souls. Their working upon Sunday for their maintenance, and having wives or husbands at a great distance from their plantations, in my humble judgment does much harm and hinders much good. . . .Several sensible and sober slaves have asked me also to be baptised and married according to the form of our Holy Church. I could not comply with their desire without the consent of their Masters, but I have exhorted them to perseverance and patience. I also humbly desire to be directed therein: the masters are willing, most of them.

Reverend LeJau suggested that the slaves masters help him choose men of intelligence and of stability to become literate leaders. The idea of student selection is most interesting because it is the forerunner of the academic "track" system of the 20th century. He proposed that some slaves might devote themselves to book learning, while others might best be left to crafts and manual skills.[12] According to LeJau, it was much easier to see the adoption of the white culture by the Negro than by the Indian. The Indian remained aloof and did not openly respond to instructional efforts. The black slave made a more ready response.[13] He had a master, whose directives he was compelled to follow. The rich African languages and expression lent itself to Americanization and adaptation.[14]

EDUCATION AND SCHOOLS

Convinced that his educational program should be expanded, LeJau advised that additional workers be sent to the colony. He recommended that the S.P.G. send a school master to Goose Creek for the white children.[15] In 1710, Mr. Benjamin Dennis was appointed, and arrived in 1711.[16] Shortly after his arrival, Mr. Dennis broke his thigh-bone and became ill. By February of 1712 little progress had been realized toward starting a school. He wrote that nothing had been done . . .

> . . . as to fixing a school as yet . . . it will be a tedious work . . . as health will permit me, [I] have taught such as have been sent . . . I have at present 18 scholars, four of which are blacks. Two of them being children of one man who was born in Portugal and there baptized, but now goes to Church and is desirous of learning arithmetic etc. . . .[17]

Mr. Dennis' school was used to serve Negroes, Indians and white children. In 1712 he had 29 scholars, including two Negroes. The next year 30 attended, with one Negro, and in 1714 he had 23 students, including one Negro.[18] This success was interupted in 1715 by the Yemassee Indian War. The school was closed and Benjamin Dennis joined the force hastily assembled to defend the province. He was discharged from this service by Lieutenant General Moore on August 25, 1715 in order to start the school again.[19] The school reopened August 29 with four pupils. He wrote the S.P.G. on September 2 that six more scholars had come, but that the misfortunes of the war had caused many to move to Charleston. He asked permission to move to Charleston where he could have more pupils and be a greater service.[20]

The Goose Creek schoolmaster received an annual salary of £20 from the S.P.G., which also provided him with "one Doz. of Testoments, one doz. of Common Prayer Books; one doz. of Lillys Grammars, three doz. of Primmers and two copys of Dr. Talbots' Christian School Master."[21] The S.P.G. apparently intended for the schoolmaster to instruct the scholars primarily in Christian piety. Dennis taught his pupils grammar, reading, and simple arithmetic. The bulk of his instructional time was used for teaching the principles of Christianity.

Reverend LeJau was very worried over the lack of education in Goose Creek. His concern was especially aimed at religious Dissenters. He requested that the S.P.G. send "some

Writings tending to Confound Atheists and Freethinkers." He was sent several orthodox works: Bishop Wilkins' on natural religion, Woolsey against atheism, Leslie on the Deists, and a translation of Grotius De Veritate. The Baptists in Goose Creek were a concern to LeJau. He described them as "cunning and artful . . . dangerous only to the ignorant." Education was considered the best vehicle for "true" religious guidance.

The good intentions of the church and the S.P.G. alone failed to fully support Benjamin Dennis as schoolmaster. The people of Goose Creek did not contribute enough money to support a teacher, and money from the public treasury was necessary to help support Mr. Dennis while he taught there.[22]

The South Carolina colonial government took measures to establish and support schools in Goose Creek. A law passed in 1695 provided that poor children be bound out as apprentices to learn a trade and become productive citizens.[23] In 1710 an act was passed which provided that various bequests which had been made for the establishment of a free school be placed under the control of a board of trustees. Doctor LeJau represented Goose Creek among the trustees.[24] They were empowered to build a school and employ a master capable of teaching Latin, Greek and the "useful parts" of mathematics.[25] Since little was accomplished under this act, the Legislature provided two years later that £100 be appropriated annually from public funds to pay the schoolmaster's salary. Benjamin Dennis was specifically cited as being in need of financial aid.[26] 12 pupils were to be admitted free of tuition and the others were to pay tuition at the rate of £4 a year.[27]

The schools provided by this legislation were a progressive change from the old Latin grammar school program. The course of study was much like that of later academies. The schoolmaster was to teach Latin and Greek, but provision was made for an usher to teach writing, arithmetic, and business accounting. The usher's salary of £50 was also to be paid out of public funds and he was required to teach such persons as were appointed to receive free education without charge.[28]

The Act of 1712 also authorized the vestry in each parish to draw upon public funds up to £12 to build a school

EDUCATION AND SCHOOLS

house and £10 per year to pay the master's salary.[29] It granted the vestry of St. James' Church the authority to nominate two or more persons to be overseers of the poor of the parish. Their responsibility was to provide some maintenance for the poor and to apprentice poor youngsters until they became of age. Education through apprenticeship was encouraged by law.

During the Colonial Period, school legislation in South Carolina provided only marginal support for apprenticeship and schools. Class lines in Goose Creek were distinctly drawn, with the gentility sending their children elsewhere for schooling. Public schools in Goose Creek were considered charity, as they were in most of South Carolina. This colony had no laws like those in New England, which required the establishment of schools or provided for their support through taxation.

Although the Act of 1712 was an attempt to provide educational opportunities, it had little impact. A later act (1722) gave the justices of the parish authority to purchase land, erect free schools and to assess the property and slaves in each parish for the support of its school.[30] Without direct taxation to support education, little progress could be made. This act had little impact on the educational situation in Goose Creek.

The lack of resolve for supporting public schools by taxation placed much of the educational burden on the S.P.G., private contributions and tuition. Early in the 18th century, there were approximately 1,000 people residing in St. James' parish.[31] St. James' Church and the missionary society took the lead in education. As noted earlier, Dr. LeJau had continually requested that the S.P.G. support a secular school in the parish, and Benjamin Dennis was sent in 1710.[32] In 1728 the Reverend Richard Ludlam died, leaving his entire estate to the support of a school in Goose Creek.[33] Rev. Ludlam served at Goose Creek from 1723 to 1728, and instructed large numbers of slaves. He, like his predecessors, was confronted with the problem of slave masters who disapproved of his work. In 1725 Ludlam wrote about treacheries of some slaves ("secret poisonings and bloody insurrection") who had been instructed in Christianity. In 1726 he baptized 11 Negroes and the following year he reported the total number of slaves to be 1,500. He baptized five more that year. Upon his death in 1728 he embodied in his will a dream he had for the parish.

In testimony to his regard for the missionary society and his sincere affection for the Goose Creek parishioners, he bequeathed all of his estate to the S.P.G. in trust, "for erecting and maintaining a school for the instruction of the poor children of this parish."[34] The money was not immediately used for this purpose. On August 23, 1742, the Society informed St. James' vestry that £592 7 shillings 6 pence sterling was collecting interest at 10% annually, and that there were still some unsold lands which would add to this total.[35] The Society requested that the vestry inform them of the estimated cost of erecting a school house according to the will of Mr. Ludlam.

The vestry considered Mr. Ludlam's bequest insufficient to build and maintain a school. The money was held with interest, and the vestry proposed to raise a sufficient sum by contributions from the parishioners. In 1744, the following paper was circulated in the parish.[36]

> Whereas nothing is more likely to promote the practice of Christianity and Virtue than the early and pious Education of Youth. We, whose names are here underwritten, do hereby agree and oblige ourselves, our Executors and Administrators, to pay yearly for three years successively, viz: On or before June 18th, 1745, 1746, 1747, to the Rev. Mr. Millechampe, or to the Churchwardens for the time being, the several and respective sums of money over against our names, respectively inscribed, for the setting up of a School House in the Parish of St. James, Goose Creek, on the land for that purpose purchased for instruction children in the knowledge and practice of the Christian Religion, and for teaching them such other things as are suitable to their capacity.

	£		£
S. Middleton	100	W. Blake	100
Wm. Middleton	100	Cornelius Dupre	5
John Morton	60	Alexander Dingle	5
Zach. Villepontoux	50	Stephen Bull	5
Peter Taylor	25	G. Dupont	7
Thomas Middleton	50	Henry Izard	60
Richard Singleton	20	James Kinloch	40
William Allen	25	Gideon Fourcherad	10
Martha Izard	20	Mag. Eliz. Izard	30
Mary Izard	20	Maurice Keating	10
Susanna Lansac	10	James Bayley	10
Jane Morris	20	Joseph Hasfort	15
Joseph Norman	20	James Marion	5
Richard Tookerman	5	Peter Porcher	15
Benjamin Mazyck	15	James Singleton	10
Paul Mazyck	50	Isaac Porcher	5

EDUCATION AND SCHOOLS

Robert Brown	15	Benj. Singleton	10
William Wood	8	Rachel Porcher	5
Robert Adams	5	Thomas Singleton	10
Peter Taylor	100	Benj. Coachman	100
John Channing	100	Thomas Smith	50
C. Faurcheraud	100	Henry Smith	50
Robert Hume	100	Sedgewick Lewis	25
John Parker	70	James Lynch	30
W. Withers	50	James Coachman	40
Benj. Smith	50	John Deas	100
John Fibbin	30	Rebecca Singleton	25
John Mackenzie	100	Peter Tamplet	50
John Moultrie Jr.	100	Joseph Dobbins	25

Apparently a school house was not erected at this time despite the generous contributions. On January 13, 1756, the Reverend James Harrison, the parish priest for four years, wrote the Society that the subscription for the school house had been raised, land bought and bricks made. This letter was nine years after the above subscription request notice was circulated.[37] Rev. Harrison urged the Society to continue its work toward erecting a school. Again nine years later, in 1765, Mr. Harrison wrote the Society to transmit the accounts of the Rev. Mr. Ludlam's legacy.[38] Mr. Harrison informed the Society that the parish had raised £200 sterling which they agreed to contribute if the Society consented to the following proposals, which it did.

    I. That the Parish shall choose annually three Parishioners of which the Rector shall always be one, to be the Visitors of the School, to inspect the conduct of the Master, and to examine what progress the Scholars have made in their learning.

    II. That if any Schoolmaster sent by the Society shall neglect the Instruction of the Children, or by any immoral behavior or otherwise, shall become unfit for or incapable of performing his proper duty, then the said Visitors, or two of them, (provided the Minister of the Parish be one) shall inform the Church-wardens and Vestry for the time being of such neglect, incapacity, or unfitness. And if upon just inquiry, the majority of the Churchwardens, and Vestry, shall find the Master to be negligent, unfit, or incapable, it shall be in the power of the said majority to suspend, displace, or remove the said Master, as shall seem to them most proper, acquainting the Society there-with by the first opportunity and giving their reasons for so doing.

    III. That as by the death or removal of the Master, considerable time will elapse, before the Society can be made acquainted therewith, and supply the vacancy, the Vestry shall have power to nominate a substitute to perform the Office of School Master during the suspension, allowing him any sum not exceeding the half of the Salary till the

HISTORIC GOOSE CREEK

Society's pleasure be known, and in case the vacancy shall happen by death, to allow the Person who afficiates any sum not exceeding two-thirds of the Salary.[39]

Adding to the support of the Goose Creek school was a bequest from Mr. Peter Taylor in 1765. He gave the vestry £100 sterling to be paid for the erection and maintenance of a school after his death.[40] His bequest was to be held at interest for the school, with remaining money for the education of poor children in the parish.

The vestry of St. James', Goose Creek, was incorporated on March 28, 1778 in order to enable them "effectually to put in execution the trust reposed in the Society for the Propogation of the Gospel in Foreign Parts, by the last will and testament of the Rev. Mr. Richard Ludlam, deceased, according to the pious intention of the Testator, and to settle the accounts of the Rev. James Harrison."[41] Harrison, the church minister, was leaving the parish and submitted to the vestry all the accounts belonging to the Ludlam Fund, totalling £15,272 2 shillings.[42]

The Ludlam Fund depreciated considerably during the Revolutionary War. Much property damage was done by the British, and valuable slaves were carried off. A brick school house was finally built in 1802 and used for many years. The Revolutionary War took its toll on the Goose Creek community and, coupled with other factors, the church membership declined after the war.[43] Due to financial difficulties, the vestry petitioned the Legislature for permission to sell the tract of land. This was granted, and the school was sold in 1828.[44] The structure was used for a dwelling and was still standing in 1859,[45] but later fell into ruin and was overgrown by bushes and trees. The foundation could still be traced during the first decade of the 20th century.

In 1828, the vestry decided to establish two schools, one in Groomsville in the lower part of the parish and the other at Wassamasaw Chapel.[46] There is a record of a gift of 40 acres on Wassamasaw Swamp from Landgrave Thomas Smith in 1728 for the use of a free school.[47] One of the parish schools was established at that site. Two school masters were employed for the two schools at a salary of $300 annually. Mrs. E.A. Poyas visited the Groomsville school and wrote, "Returning from thence to Whitesville, St. John's we drove close to the old brick schoolhouse where a young man

EDUCATION AND SCHOOLS

had collected a few scholars of the lower class, from Groomsville and the neighborhood." The school was located in the same vicinity as the Goose Creek Chapel of Ease. In 1847 the vestry elected trustees to provide supervision to the school. The Rev. C. Wallace was requested to investigate the schools, due to the failure of the trustees to do so. He did so, and recommended instructional changes and that new books be purchased, to be owned by and kept at the school. William Waterland, teacher at the Wassamasaw school, was very progressive in at least one instructional area. He made a particular point to teach English gramatically. It appears as if he was the first to do so in America, according to available records.[48] The Groomsville and the Wassamasaw schools provided instruction for more than 30 children a year, and as many as 42 attended in 1858.[49]

In 1859 the vestry used the Ludlam Fund to pay the St. James academy $200.00 for the education of 12 poor parish scholars.[50] The two church schools were maintained until the Civil War. The vestry made yearly reports to the legislature after 1843 on the use of the Ludlam Fund for educational purposes. Near the onset of the Civil War, vestry treasurer Dr. Henry R. Frost made the following report showing the financial resources of the parish for support of education:[51]

STATEMENT OF SCHOOL FUND

424 State Bank Shares	$10,600.00
7 South Carolina R.R. Shares	315.00
City 6 per Cent Stock	2,100.00
State 6 per Cent Stock	1,400.00
Premium	116.00
	$14,531.00

General Bernard Bee gave to the vestry 4,605 acres of land in the Milam Land District in Texas for payment of a bond debt of $3,379.00 borrowed by him from the Ludlam Fund.[52] The confusion and disorder of the Civil War had caused much of the Texas land to be taken for possession by settlers. Some of the land had also been confiscated for taxes. In 1873 the vestry attempted to recover the land but was not entirely successful. In 1882 it began corresponding with a legal firm in Galveston, Texas, who agreed to attempt to recover the lands upon condition of receiving one half of the amount realized from the sale of the whole. A large portion of land was recovered in 1882, and after paying the legal fees the church received $5,000.[53] This amount was invested in the Ludlam Fund with the interest to be used for education. Even well into the 20th century, the Ludlam money was used for the education of worthy white parish scholars.

This tradition of educational support continued during the period from 1872 to 1925.[54] The vestry was inactive during the Civil War, but resumed its activities in 1872 with efforts to evaluate the Ludlam Fund and reclaim the Texas land. Although the vestry discontinued its support of the two church schools, it did continue to use the Ludlam money as it was intended. More than ten children received financial assistance to attend school during the period 1872 to 1905.[55] These scholars received Ludlam money to attend Porter Academy in Charleston;[56] Pinopolis Academy, near Moncks Corner;[57] The Confederate Honor College and Union College.[58] Union College was in Schenectady, New York but the other schools were local.

The St. James' vestry role in providing for education was coupled with increased efforts on the part of the State to provide for free education after 1811. In 1811, a South Carolina act to establish free schools throughout the state resulted in educational opportunities in the parish on an intermittent and limited basis. Despite limitations of the vestry and the State, these two institutions provided the majority of education for white parish youth until the 20th century.

In accordance with the 1811 "Act to Establish Free Schools Throughout the State," the people of St. James' Parish, Goose Creek, were entitled to three school commissioners. The number of schools were to be equal to the number of members sent to the House of Representatives from each election district.[59] The primary elements of learning: reading, writing, and arithmetic, were taught in these schools. Any child was entitled to attend free of tuition, but in case of an overload, preference was always to be given to orphans or children of poor parents. The State treasury was to pay $300 each year for the support and maintenance of each school.[60] School commissioners were appointed by the legislature to serve three-year terms and to oversee the schools in each district. The commissioners had the authority

EDUCATION AND SCHOOLS

to appoint school masters and to schedule the time and place of instruction.[61]

In accordance with this act, the Goose Creek school commissioners were confronted with the task of providing free education for the children of the parish with an annual state allotment of $600. The commissioners used this money to hire teachers at the salary of $25 dollars a month[62] and provided instruction in various parts of the parish.

Both men and women were employed at the free schools. Most of the teachers were South Carolina natives, but one was born in Ireland and one in Florida.[63] Despite the limited income, one teacher (Mr. James P. Hughes) accumulated an estate worth $2,000 after more than 20 years of teaching.[64] These teachers taught in schools which changed locations during the year and from year to year to provide some educational opportunities in most parts of the parish.[65] Most school terms lasted from three to six months at any one location, with class sizes ranging from one to 39.[66] It was not unusual, however, to find some schools staying in session from nine to 12 months. Class size and length of school term varied widely, as did the locations of the schools.

The commissioners' efforts to provide for education in a parish that ranged from what is now Orangeburg County to the back-waters of the Cooper River used as many as 39 different school sites.[67] They ranged from Wassamasaw and Holly Hill in the western part of the parish to Goose Creek in the eastern.

Some schools were reported to the legislature by number instead of name, making it possible that there were even more than 39 different sites. Some had very similar names such as Targate, Target, Tarhill, Tarkiln. These four names may be referring to the same school. It is evident that these sites were many, changed often and were seldom at the same location two years in a row.

It is doubtful that any school houses were constructed for the use of the free schools. The type of buildings used for them varied. The Gasquette Meeting House was used in 1836.[68] A chapel, a church, and even a building which was formerly a tavern was used in 1856.[69] Beginning in 1854, schools were listed as either free or assisted.[70] Of the ten schools reported in 1854, six were reported as being assisted. $4 a quarter was charged each student in 1858. Besides tuition, the St. James' Church vestry paid $200 to the St. James Academy, (a public academy) in 1859 for the purpose of sending twelve scholars tuition-free.[71]

The 1811 act required teaching reading, writing and mathematics. St. James Academy was the only academy in the parish during this time, and was probably intended to provide some secondary instruction. No private academies were incorporated in the parish. The scholars received education in the "three R's" and had limited opportunity to attend secondary school. The St. James' parish scholars enjoyed a relatively short school term and rarely had a school in the vicinity of their homes two years in succession.

The state-supported schools and the two schools supported by the vestry provided almost all of the formal education received by the children in the parish. Other private or tutored instruction was probably available to some extent. Out of the 244 children who attended school in 1859, 192 attended the state-supported schools.[72] Approximately 40 attended the vestry-supported schools. The remaining students most likely attended some other private school. The large majority of students in the parish attended either a state-supported or St. James' vestry-supported school.

These schools were generally used for the poorer children of the community. The English practice of employing a tutor was generally used among the large planters of Goose Creek. A tutor was a common resident of the old Goose Creek plantation (now known as Yeamans Hall) and of Medway. John Parker, the rich Goose Creek planter residing at the Hayes plantation, advertised in the *Royal Gazette* in 1781 for a schoolmaster "who can teach the English Language grammatically.'[73] The tutors were usually competent persons who would perform other duties such as keeping the estate accounts besides teaching the children. The tutors would often teach not only the family children but also those of the planters' neighbors. In some instances school houses were erected on some Goose Creek plantations. An excellent example of one is found at Goose Creek's Medway plantation. It is a charming little building set aside from the main house, and served as a schoolhouse during the flourishing plantation days. It is impossible to determine how many children received their education at such schools, but it is likely that such education was common. Plantations were

EDUCATION AND SCHOOLS

typically large, isolated and relatively self-contained. A plantation school site was a reasonable method of providing education in the rural environment. Separate school houses on the plantations were probably rare, however. A part of the house or the shade of an oak tree probably was sufficient as educational facilities. The research of Judge Henry A.M. Smith made no mention of other schoolhouses in his report on the Goose Creek plantations.

Although there is much evidence that the Goose Creek planters were relatively well educated, the S.P.G. missionaries were appalled by the ignorance of the Goose Creek people. Despite this contradiction, it is plausible that the Barbadian and French planters maintained a relatively high cultural level during the Colonial Period. The ravages and chaos of the Revolutionary War resulted in a decline of culture and prosperity in Goose Creek. There was another slow decline during the first half of the 19th century, and finally a collapse of the economy during the Civil War. The once-prosperous Goose Creek community suffered severe cultural and economic destruction as a result of Reconstruction policies following the Civil War. Drastic changes in the social and economic characteristics of the people of Goose Creek resulted in subsequent changes in education.

The Civil War meant the end to the planter society and the landed gentry. The war also changed the nature of the people who owned the land, provided professional services, leadership and education in the community. In 1850, ten years before the war, there were 1,857 free inhabitants in the parish. Most of the adult white male inhabitants reported their occupations as planters. There were also midwives, blacksmiths, mechanics, surveyors, wheel rights, wood cutters, capitalists, toll-gate keepers, pump menders and many laborers. Thomas Mims, George Smith and Henry Nichole were school teachers. Thomas L. Gilson and Tamil Hamilton were physicians. There were 370 families living in 295 households. Ten years later, just before the war, the same general trend was followed. Mr. J.P. Hughes, John Gadsden, M.E. Woode and Nelson Joiner were school teachers. There were four physicians in the parish, along with skilled workers such as watchmakers and coach makers. The professional and skilled workers in Goose Creek virtually disappeared as a result of the war. The 1870 census reported the total absence of the planters, the gentility and the professionals. After the war almost all residents were reported as being unable to read and write. Goose Creek was populated by small farmers, farm laborers, phosphate laborers and railroad workers. There were no teachers, doctors or other professionals reported there in 1870 or 1880. In 1880 there was a much smaller population in Goose Creek. Almost all residents were black. Many reported their occupations as being railroad workers, phosphate workers, small farmers and laborers. Few schools, poorly trained teachers and little educational funding resulted in a deplorable state of public education. Goose Creek was no different from the other communities in Berkeley County. In 1885 a number of citizens interested in education were concerned about inadequacy of the public school system in the county. Because the population was mostly Negro, Berkeley was often referred to as the "Black County." A letter from a resident in St. Stephen's parish in 1886 expressed dissatisfaction:

> The meager renumeration of our teachers leades men of ability and competence seek a new field of labor and leaves us but a scanty number of half-educated teachers who perform their task simply as a matter of duty . . . .

The public system of education in Goose Creek remained relatively unchanged during the years from 1865 to 1960. The one or two-room rural school house was the common source of education in Goose Creek until the influx of people, business and prosperity in the 1960's.

CHAPTER XI

ST. JAMES' CHURCH, GOOSE CREEK

> I love your Parish, and most of all its romantically situated Ancient Church, St. James'. Its antiquated appearance, the death-like silence that prevades its immediate vicinage, and the time-worn, moss-covered tablets of those who there sleep the quiet sleep of death; of those who shall never be awakened from their leaden slumbers, until that awful day arrives, on which the great Jehovah will command the wide earth and the deep sea to yield up its inmates.[1]

Old and beautiful St. James' Episcopal Church is an inseparable part of the long history of Goose Creek. A beautiful monument to antiquity, the church survived the ravages of time and remains stately amidst the non-attending residents of contemporary Goose Creek. It stands as it did when it was first built in 1714 on the banks of Goose Creek, across the water from once-spacious Otranto plantation. An informal investigation revealed that relatively few people in the local community have visited the old church and have consequently missed a chance to take a mental journey into the past. Hundreds of motorists pass the historical site daily as they drive to and from work.

Turning from Highway 52 onto the Old State Road, one crosses the creek where a ferry once carried pedestrians and horsemen over the open water. A busy tavern once stood immediately past the bridge on the left, from which the church ministers could hear the ribaldry (much to their disdain). Turning right just past the bridge, a few hundred yards through undisturbed pine woods is the place which was the center of the planter community.

> There are other sacred edifices in America larger and statelier than the little chapel near Otranto; but is greatly to be doubted whether there is anywhere on this continent another church, chapel, or meeting house more interesting to those to whom the past is a book to be read and pondered than St. James Church, Goose Creek.

Much of the church's history is contained in the work of a church vestryman, Dr. Joseph Ioor Waring. Dr. Waring prepared a brief history of the church in 1909, at the request of the vestry. Some of the information in this chapter was gathered from the book. For more than 250 years the church vestrymen have strived to maintain the church, its grounds and its long history.

The church building is evidence of the prosperity of the colonial community. It is of brick, 50 feet long and 40 feet wide. It now has a slate roof and rough-cast walls. There are 13 arched windows and two side doors, with one main entrance. The keystone over each window is decorated with a cherub's head and wings of stucco. The main entrance has five bas-relief hearts. Over the front door is a model of a pelican feeding her young. This is the symbol of The Society for the Propagation of the Gospel in Foreign Parts, the society which sent missionaries to the Goose Creek wilderness. The pelican is feeding her young by tearing meat from her own breast, symbolizing the sacrificial acts of charity of the missionary society. The exterior S.P.G. symbol was placed over the door in 1907 to replace the original one, which can be found stored inside the church. The 1907 model was designed by Mrs. Lee Honour of Charleston as a work showing her love for the old parish.[2]

A small robing room is under the stairs leading to the gallery. Inside the church are 24 pews of the old square box pattern. The aisles are paved with flagstone, leading to a tall elaborate pulpit, which is ascended by winding stairs. A huge sounding board is located above it. A replica of the handsome pulpit is a main attraction today for tourists at Charles Towne Landing, in Charleston. Across the entire expanse from the pulpit is the gallery, located over the main entrance. Within the chancel rail is a small reading desk and a communion table. Behind the chancel is the Royal Arms of Great Britain, supported by four Corinthian pillars. The arms are painted brilliantly in red, blue and yellow. It is reported that British soldiers who camped on the church grounds during the Revolutionary War spared the church because it displayed these arms.[3] They are those of the three King Georges, and show the white horse of the Royal House of Hanover.

Two marble tablets are found on each side of the chancel, bearing the Decalogue, Apostles Creed and the Lord's Prayer. These were presented to the church by William Middleton in 1758.[4] Several memorials are also found on the walls. One is the arms of and testimonial to Col. John Gibbes and Jane Gibbes. The others are memorials to Ralph Izard and Peter Taylor (see Appendix B).

THE PARISH CHURCH

In front of the gallery is the hatchment (arms) of the Izard family. In accordance with the English tradition, the hatchment was presented in front of the coffin when the head of the family was buried and later hung upon the wall of the church. The one in Goose Creek Church is one of only two such hatchments in American churches.[5]

The church building was the product of a prosperous community. The rich lands and forests in the area of Goose Creek were eagerly sought by the English and French settlers. The creek and river afforded easy transportation, and Goose Creek's distance from the sea provided safety from pirates. Soon after Charles Town's first settlement, the Goose Creek area became the most prosperous and populated community outside the city.[6] These people were mostly English Barbadians and French Huguenots. Both groups were inclined toward the Church of England and combined their efforts to erect and support the church.[7]

The first missionary to the Goose Creek people was Reverend William Corben, A.M.[8] The people were without a minister and religious services until his arrival in 1700. He had formerly served at the Chapel of Bromley, St. Leonard in Middlesex, England. The Rev. Mr. Corben worked in Goose Creek until he returned to England in 1703. The Church of England had organized a very dynamic and influential organization known as the Society for the Propagation of the Gospel in Foreign Parts. The S.P.G. found in 1701 that more than half of the 7,000 colonists, not including the Negroes and Indians, were without religion, the only church being in Charles Town. There were no schools and only a few Dissenting teachers.[9] The S.P.G. sent the Reverend Samuel Thomas as their first missionary to Goose Creek in 1702.

Reverend Thomas had a most miserable voyage to America. In his own accounts he recorded that in the passage down the English Channel he was "forc'd to lye upon a chest," and "after many unfortunate and humble perswasions" he at last obtained leave to read prayers daily, but he was "curs'd and treated very ill on board."[10] At Plymouth he almost died from an illness, but recovered well enough to sail to Charles Town. After "12 weeks and 2 days at sea" he arrived in Charles Town on Christmas Day, 1702.[11] His purpose was to bring the gospel to the Yemassees, and the S.P.G. voted for him "to be laid out in stuffs for the use of the wild Indians."[12]

HISTORIC GOOSE CREEK

The Indians were, at that time, quite hostile. The colonial Governor refused to send him among the Indians and retained him as his chaplain. He was then assigned to "the care of the people settled upon the three branches of Cooper River."[13] Goose Creek was the largest and most populated community outside Charleston and it was there that the Rev. Mr. Thomas began his work. He lived with Governor Nathaniel Johnson at Silk Hope Plantation on the Cooper River. The Governor and Council wrote to the S.P.G. expressing their gratitude for the S.P.G.'s work with "our pour infant church in this Province," and their pleasure at the arrival of Mr. Thomas.

Rev. Thomas found only five communicants when he arrived, but through his efforts the number increased to 32. In a letter dated May 3, 1704, he wrote:

> The town minister has a very noble maintenance out of the public treasure, but we country ministers having nothing to trust to, but only a small and uncertain subscription. The country stands in need of more ministers, especially of one for a place called Goose Creek, a creek the best settled with Church of England families of any in Carolina. . . . The congregation was so numerous that the Church could not contain them, many stood without the door.

Shortly after his arrival he had written the S.P.G.:

> the neighborhood here to who I preach every lord's day . . . are an ignorant but well inclined people, who seem to want nothing to make them pious, but the common assistance of God's Holy Spirit, Ministers and Ordinances.[14]
>
> The next parish to Charles Town is Goose Creek, one of the most populous of our country parishes, containing, (as near as I can guess) about one hundred and twenty families. Most of the inhabitants are of the profession of the Church of England, excepting about five families of French Protestants, who are Calvinistic, and three families of Presbyterians, and two Anabaptists . . . The number of communicants was about thirty, of whom one was a Christian negro man. The Church at Goose Creek was well frequented as any of our ministers officiated there. The number of heathen slaves in this parish I suppose to be about two hundred, twenty of whom I observed to come constantly to Church, and these and several others of them well understanding the English tongue, and can read.[15]

Although the people of Goose Creek had been accused of refusing to Christianize and educate the slaves, it appears that Rev. Thomas' letter refutes the charges.

THE PARISH CHURCH

Reverend Thomas brought his family from England to Goose Creek in 1705. He died shortly after returning with his family, but not before he laid a sound religious foundation for his successors.[16] A year later the parish of St. James, Goose Creek, was organized. On November 30, 1706, an Act of Assembly established the parish and defined its boundaries.[17] Following the death of Rev. Samuel Thomas, the S.P.G. sent a native Frenchman for his replacement. Reverend Francis LeJau, D.D., arrived in October of 1706.[18] He was a native of Angers, France, and was a canon in St. Paul's Cathedral in London. Francis LeJau was born and raised as a French Huguenot. He was ordained by the Anglican Bishop of London and came to Goose Creek to officiate in the Anglican Church, and found a large congregation of Frenchmen there. It was during his ministry that the Goose Creek Huguenots joined St. James' church.

The French were second only to the English Barbadians in shaping the development of Goose Creek. At a very early date there was a French church among the many French plantations and settlements. From 1685 onward, the French population of Carolina became increasingly significant. The Huguenot settlers in South Carolina divided into four groups. Some settled at Charlestowne, some at Orange Quarter in the Parish of St. Thomas and St. Denis, the largest group settled on the Santee River and the smallest group of the four settled at the head of Goose Creek. In 1699, Peter Girard gave the number in Goose Creek as 31.

As early as 1695, the relatively large Goose Creek French settlers undertook establishing a place of worship. The earliest mention of a French congregation in Goose Creek is in the will of Anthony Prudhomme dated 1695, in which he bequeathed a cow and two heifers to the people who worshipped there.[19] One mention of the church itself is on a map made by Joseph Purcell, surveyor of the Parker or Fleury plantation in 1785.[20] He designated the site as the "Remains of a French Church." The church apparently owned no land, not even the site upon which it stood, and little is known of its history. The building was located about four miles northwest of St. James' Church and one and one-half miles from Ladson's Station. A granite cross erected by the Huguenot Society of South Carolina now marks the spot. It was located on a tract of land granted to Abraham Fleury de la Plane in 1696.[21]

Judge Henry A.M. Smith, a low country historian, wrote that James Gignilliat, who lived in the immediate area of the church, was one of the early ministers or perhaps the only minister of the church.[22] Judge Smith visited the site near the close of the 19th century and found some bricks which may have been from the pillars, and the remains of a few unmarked graves. It is evident that the French were absorbed by the established Anglican church and became active members of St. James'.[23]

Upon his arrival the Rev. Francis LeJau found that the parishioners were collecting materials for the construction of a church and parsonage. In 1708 Benjamin Schenckingh gave a gift of 100 acres of land to the church. The original land plat is still in the possession of the vestry:

> This plat represents the form and shape of 100 acres of land given by Capt. Benjamin Schenckingh to the Parish of St. James, Goose Creek, South Carolina. One acre thereof for to build a Church on, and the rest for ye use of the Rector or Minister of said Parish for ye time being. The conveyance from him ye said Schenckingh to the Church Commissioners for ye use above, being dated October 18th, 1706.[24]

The first wooden church was built on another tract of 16 acres given by Benjamin Godin.[25] Soon afterwards, the church wardens and vestry were sworn into service. Curious oaths were taken by the first church officers, proclaiming the absence of transubstantiation of bread and wine to the body and blood of Christ and the rejection of Papal authority.[26] The church parishioners met on Easter Monday, April 14, 1707, to elect Reverend Francis LeJau as Rector. The election was confirmed December 14, 1707, according to the Church Act. The first wardens were Robert Stevens and John Sanders, and first vestrymen were Ralph Izard, George Cantey, Captain James Moore, Arthur Middleton, Captain John Cantey, William Williams and Captain David Deas.[27]

In 1707, the parish of St. James, Goose Creek, contained approximately 1,000 persons. During the first year of his work, Reverend LeJau baptized 21 children, and 19 more during his second year. There were 35 communicants.[28] Reverend LeJau was held in high regard by the people of Goose Creek and worked diligently to educate and baptize the black slaves and Indians. He won the esteem and love of the people by abolishing the customary baptismal fee which most were

THE PARISH CHURCH

unwilling or unable to pay. To show their respect for him, the parishioners subscribed £60 yearly in addition to his regular S.P.G. salary.[29] Dr. LeJau informed the S.P.G. that the moral character of his parishioners had improved and reported that his church was well attended. He had to report, however, that there were still among the community "some few atheistical persons, and scoffers at all revelation." Despite many hardships, Reverend LeJau wrote a very optimistic letter to the S.P.G. on February 9, 1711:

> Upon the 1st Sunday in Advent I baptized 4 adult negroes two men and two women with the caution of which I had the honor to give an account to the Society. The ceremony was done after our devine service to the satisfaction of some pious masters. Some others did not like it so well at first. Their chief argument was from the inpossibility of bringing the slaves into a right order. I have exhorted them to begin and try and I thank God we see some good success, and an appearance of better in God's own time. They come sometimes 40 or more to Church, I intend to catechise them again when I have done instructing our white children. I believe 'tis best to wait a little, except in case of danger. I endeavor always to act by the consent of the masters. The spiritual state of my parish 30th June 1710 to February 1st instant is 17 children baptized, an adult white and sensible man and 4 adult negroes, 3 marriages and 8 burials. Concerning the communicants I have admitted five that had not received the Holy Communion before. Our constant number is 30 among whom five negroes. In all I believe I have 50 and more communicants....
> Give me leave before I end my letter to beg of you whether I might presume to ask of the Society a little present of 2 or 3 yards of ordinary linen for the negroes who are baptized by me and continue to live in an edifying manner. I humbly think such an encouragement would do good among them and others....[30]

LeJau received any slave child into the Church who was presented by the master. Adult christian Negroes could also have their children baptized if both parents had been baptized. Upon the advice of the S.P.G., he began to baptize any slave child if presented by parents, even if only one parent had been baptized and received into the church.[31] On Easter, 1712, there were 37 communicants at the church, five of whom were Negroes. By August of 1713, LeJau had increased the members to 60 with five Negro men and two women. His reports indicated that their numbers continued to increase yearly.

HISTORIC GOOSE CREEK

Before the outbreak of the Yemassee Indian War in 1715, the Rev. Mr. LeJau convinced the S.P.G. to send the first school master to Goose Creek.[32] This was a continuation of the educational concerns of his predecessors and the beginning of a long church tradition of formal education for the parishioners.

During the last years of Reverend LeJau's service to Goose Creek, the present brick church was constructed. By 1714 the number of church communicants had increased to 70 whites and eight blacks.[33] The congregation was too large for the old wooden church, and in 1714 the brick structure and parsonage was erected. In 1717, Reverend LeJau became ill, and after a long and painful illness, he died on September 15. He was buried at the front of the chancel. The following is inscribed on a marble tablet over his grave:

> Here lyeth the Body of / the Rev. Francis LeJau, / Doctor in Divinity, of / Trinity College, Dublin, / who came to this Province / October 1706, and was one / of the first Missionaries / sent by the Honourable / Society to this Province, / and was the first Rector / of St. James' Goose Creek. / Obijt 15th September 1717, / Aetat 52. To whose memory / this Stone is fixed by his / only son Francis LeJau.

Upon the decease of Dr. LeJau, the vestry applied to the S.P.G. and the Bishop of London for another missionary. They stated the great loss which the parish had sustained in the death of their rector and declared him to have been a "good, pious and learned minister, by whose doctrine and conversation many have reaped much profit."[34]

A large and beautiful Book of Common Prayer was presented to the parish in 1717 by Abel Kittleby, Esq. of the Middle Temple, London, Landgrave of Carolina. During the pastoral vacancy in the church, it was served by the Reverends Guy, Hasell and Tustian. There was no bishop in the province, and consequently the church had never been consecrated. The vestry did not want the church to be used for secular purposes, so it resolved on July 14, 1719, that the church was to be used for worship only.

On July 14, 1719, a resolution was passed by the vestry providing that the first two lower pews of the middle two rows be used by the wardens and vestry only. A visitor to the church today can recognize these pews by the brass identification plates. The resolution also reserved one pew to Arthur

THE PARISH CHURCH

Middleton and his heirs, due to his help with the church construction and his donation of land for the parsonage.[35] The same reservation of a pew was made to Benjamin Schenckingh and Benjamin Godin for their land contributions. Pews were also allocated to Col. James Moore, Roger Moore, Mrs. Anne Davis, Benjamin Gibbes and John Gibbes.[36] The remaining pews were sold, according to custom.

The S.P.G. sent the very unpopular Rev. Francis Merry to Goose Creek in 1720. The vestry wrote S.P.G. that they disapproved of him. "Mr. Merry's behavior is so indiscreet that the parish can not elect him," that "his Excellency Governor Nicholson and all the clergy were very sensible of how he had behaved himself, etc."[37] The S.P.G. recalled Mr. Merry and invited Rev. Thomas Marritt to hold services until the S.P.G. sent a replacement.

The S.P.G. sent the Rev. Richard Ludlam, A.M., to Goose Creek in 1723, and he was immediately elected Rector August 31, 1723. The public treasury paid his yearly salary of £100 in Carolina currency. Rev. Ludlam enjoyed a handsome parsonage house of brick and a piece of land of about 100 acres. Rev. Ludlam became much loved and was well respected by the parishioners.[38] He spent much of his time and energy converting and teaching the slaves, who were at that time mostly African-born. He reported to the S.P.G. that his parishioners were "sober, well disposed, and attentive to public worship," and that the people continued to bring their children to be baptized, and that many "devoutly received the Lord's Supper." Upon his death in 1728, he bequeathed his estate of approximately £2,000 currency to the establishment of a school for the poor.[39]

The following entries were recorded by the Rev. William Guy in the register of St. Andrew's parish: "Buried Sept. 29th, 1728, Mrs. Ludlam. Buried Oct. 12th, 1728, Mr. Ludlam, Rector of St. James, Goose Creek."[40] The Rev. Ludlam followed his wife to the grave within twelve days. Although it is probable that they were buried at St. James' Church, no marker can be found today.

The Society appointed the Rev. Mr. Thomas as Rev. Ludlam's successor in 1729. He was unfortunately drowned while embarking near Sheerness, England.[41] In 1730, the S.P.G. sent Rev. Lewis Jones of St. Helena's parish to St. James but he was soon ordered to remain at St. Helena's. The

Rev. Timothy Millechampe, A.M., was sent by the S.P.G. in 1732 and immediately elected Rector. Rev. Millechampe returned to England in 1738 and remained there until the following year. In 1744 he returned again to England, and was presented with a testimonial from the vestry upon his departure. (See Appendix C.)[42]

Mr. Millechampe was in bad health and remained away for years. The absence was much regretted by the church parishioners, as the church had only occasional services of any minister. The vestry wrote to the Bishop of London and the S.P.G. on July 12, 1748, complaining of the absence of Mr. Millechampe and requested that another missionary be sent in his place. In the meantime, Mr. Millechampe had recovered his health and had become rector of the Parish of Colesbourne in the Diocese of Gloucester. The S.P.G. relieved Mr. Millechampe of his mission in Goose Creek.[43] Services were held temporarily every month by alternating ministers including the Reverends Guy, Durand and Cates.

During the years that Reverend Millechampe officiated, the instruction of the parish. Negroes suffered much as a result of his illness and absence. Millechampe complained in 1734 that he was able to baptize only one Negro man, and in addition several books had disappeared from his library, probably stolen.[44] On October 15, 1741, he reported to the S.P.G. that there were 2,160 unbaptized Negroes and 20 Indians in the parish. There were 91 white families, ten of whom were Dissenters. He reported in 1742 that there were 98 families and 2,752 slaves. On Christmas day in 1742, 20 white and two Negro communicants attended service.[45]

Reverend Robert Stone succeeded Millechampe at Goose Creek in 1748. He was at first very alarmed by the unhealthy conditions and commented that he had buried eight people in the first nine weeks he was in the parish. Two years later his impression of Goose Creek had improved. He wrote with new confidence and optimism:

> ... The beginning of Lent last year I set apart the afternoons on Sunday for the instruction of negroes, and continued to do so until was [taken ill]. Such numbers crowded the church before, that they were very off[ensive] to the whites. To show how acceptable it was to them, they sent six of the old men with a present of poultry to thank me. I returned their present and told them I should be well satisfied for my pains, if they would make good use of it. I have

THE PARISH CHURCH

> received thanks from several of their masters and mistresses who thought that they behaved much better since they frequented the church. As soon as I was recovered they came and desired me to do like again. Which I shall always comply with whilst health will permit. I have baptized since my last only two grown blacks and seven white children....[46]

Reverend Stone died in 1751, and was buried in St. Philip's churchyard in Charleston. Rev. Jonathon Copp arrived in Goose Creek from Georgia in February 1752, but the S.P.G. had already appointed Rev. James Harrison, A.M. Reverend Harrison arrived in December and was elected by the vestry, which came to appreciate his service and allocated more than £340 currency for him to "purchase a negro for the use of the Parsonage."[47]

Rev. Harrison wrote to the S.P.G. that enough money had been raised by subscription and the Ludlam Fund over the years to build a school house. He also informed them that in 1757 many persons had brought their children from up to 280 miles away to be baptized by him.[48] He had 30 white and 17 Negro communicants. The following year William Middleton presented the church two marble tablets inscribed with the Decalogue, Apostles' Creed and Lord's Prayer, which were placed on each side of the last window. The S.P.G. reported on the condition of the parish in 1758:

> ... it is impossible to ascertain the exact Number of white Inhabitants of that Parish, as it is unbounden to the North West; and those unfortunate People, whom the Terrors and Calamities of War drive from the more Northern Provinces, are continually changing their Places of Residence. Mr. Harrison is informed by some, who have brought their Children from 80 to 200 Miles Distance to be baptized, that there are about 30 Families scattered about here and there among them. The Number of Communicants within the more settled Part of the Parish, is 30 Whites, (10 of them added within the last Year) and 17 Negroes; and he had baptized 13 White and 3 Negroe Children and 7 adult Negroes in that Year, Mr. Harrison adds, that Mr. Peter Taylor a good and worthy Parishioner hath made a Present of a Negroe Girl for the use of the Minister of that Parish, as a small Encouragement to him for his endeavouring to propagage the Gospel among the slaves of the Parish; (to use the Words of the Entry of this Donation in the Vestry-Book) and Mr. Harrison promises, that his sincere Endeavours in this good Work, as far as is consistent with other Duties incumbent on him, shall speak his Gratitude for this Benefaction.[49]

HISTORIC GOOSE CREEK

In 1758 Rev. Harrison wrote to the Society that his congregation had increased, that he had 26 white and 20 black communicants, and that he had recently baptized 18 white children and five adult Negroes.[50] In 1761 he recorded that the war with the Cherokee Indians had caused many of his parishioners to move to the "Northern Provinces." The S.P.G., in a summary of the Rev. Mr. Harrison's letters of that year, included that:

> ... by the Calamities of the War with the Cherokee Indians, the Number of Inhabitants in his Parish is considerably lessened, many of the unfortunate People, who were driven from their Settlements, having retired to the Northern Provinces, to procure that Protection and Maintenance, which they saw but little Liklihood of in South Carolina. He has 31 white, and 26 Black Communicants; has baptized since his last 15 Children, and 2 Adult Negroes.[51]

Power of attorney was sent from the S.P.G. to the vestry to use the money left by Reverend Ludlam, in combination with their own, for a school. The Reverend James Harrison, Robert Horne, Benjamin Coachman, and John Parker were appointed attorneys.[52] Mr. Peter Taylor left additional money for the church school in 1765.[53] On November 7, 1744, Rev. Harrison notified the vestry that he intended to resign. He commented on the great flow of people in that section of the province. The church and parsonage were located near a well-traveled road. Travellers would cross the creek, visit the tavern near the creek crossing and would pester the minister for lodging and entertainment. Rev. Harrison finally moved to St. Bartholomew's parish.

Upon the departure of Rev. Harrison, the Rev. Edward Ellington of St. Helena's parish was elected Rector. In 1778 the vestry was incorporated to enable them, in their words, "effectually to put into execution the trust reposed in the Society for the Propagation of the Gospel in Foreign Parts, by the last will and testament of Rev. Richard Ludlam, deceased, according to the pious intention of the testator, and to settle the accounts of the Rev. James Harrison."[54] Rev. Harrison submitted to the vestry all of the Ludlam Fund papers and accounts to the amount of more than £15,272.[55] The Ludlam Fund depreciated greatly during the Revolutionary War, but there was enough remaining to erect a school. A deed dated March 28, 1778, refers to the conveyance of twelve acres of land from Henry Middleton to the church ves-

THE PARISH CHURCH

try.[56] The land was transferred to the church with Benjamin Coachman and Benjamin Mazyck representing the vestrymen and wardens. It was conveyed by the giving and receiving of "a twig and a turf."[57]

The Reverend Edward Ellington was rector of the church during the chaotic years of the American Revolution. Charleston was occupied by the British and the parish was within the British lines. Reverend Ellington proceeded to use the prayer in the litany for the King of England. During the period of British occupation, one parishoner told the priest that if he used the prayer for the King, the member would throw his prayer-book at his head. The threat did not prevent him from using the prayer the following Sunday, but the promise was kept, and Reverend Ellington was the target of a hurled prayer-book. The gentleman had executed his threat, and as a result, Ellington refused to hold services following the incident.[58] The church was not used for services after this incident until after the war. It was visited by British troops, but was the only country church which was not profaned by the British army. Some churches were converted into garrisons, hospitals or barracks and some were burned. The kind of treatment by the British is attributed to the presence of the Royal Arms which remained over the altar. Of those arms, it was said that "not the sternest Republican would now wish to see these symbols of regality removed, when it is known that they saved the temple of God from the violence of a mercenary and ruthless soldiery."[59] Of the Good Reverend Ellington, Doctor Joseph Johnson wrote:

> Mr. Ellington was pious, talented eloquent, and zealous in his parochial duties. His easy, polite and sociable deportment rendered him a welcome guest in every family circle — he was one of the most engaging in every social assemblage of that then genteel, hospitable and populous neighborhood. He was particularly suited to the manners and customs of the Carolinians, commanding their respect, esteem and confidence, as a man and as a minister. His pleasantries appeared to be the overflowings of a well-stored mind, with universal benevolence and a conscience void of offence towards God and man. He would occasionally say that he believed he did more good, professionally, during his domestic visits than by his preaching. His preaching, too, was of the very highest order; he was one of the best pulpit orators that I have ever heard. In the strife and warfare of the revolution, he could not but feel a lively interest, but he took no part in it; he

bowed with humility to "the powers that be," and endeavored to promote peace on earth and good will towards men.[60]

Reverend Ellington was more than just a good minister. During his residence near the Goose Creek bridge, the bridge was torn down to begin construction of a new one. He realized the great inconvenience the lack of a bridge caused so many travelers. Many were not aware that the bridge had been demolished, and upon traveling that far, were forced to retrace their paths and take a rather bad road around the head of Goose Creek swamp. This was a matter of considerable distance. The Reverend procured a flat boat and employed men to provide a ferry service, charging a fair crossing fee.

One wagoner complained greatly one day upon having to pay a fee for such a short crossing. The priest admitted that he had no authority to charge a fee as there was no act of the Legislature providing for it, but he reasoned also that he was under no obligation to provide the service. The customer paid, begrudgingly, still murmuring about the short crossing. A few days later the same man returned and called for a crossing for his wagon and team. Mr. Ellington instructed his ferryman, who loaded the wagon and team. Instead of crossing directly, the ferryman took the ferry up and down the creek until the wagoner became quite tired. The rector then asked him if he had gotten a long enough ride for his money. The customer was quick to agree. Mr. Ellington assured him that the whole business was to give satisfaction, and the crossing was voluntary if they crossed at all.[61]

The Reverend Ellington resigned in 1793 and moved to Savannah, and the church was without a minister until 1796, when the Rev. Milward Pogson was elected. He served until he resigned on February 26, 1806. Rev. Pogson was the first minister to be ordained in the Diocese of South Carolina.[62] Bishop Smith ordained him a deacon on December 20, 1795, and priest on December 19, 1796. He married Miss Henrietta Wragg, and is buried at St. Philip's Church where a slab marks his resting place. A humorous story about Reverend Pogson tells that the good Father Pogson could not refrain from his favorite sport of fishing, even on Sundays. One Sunday morning while walking to church carrying his sermon under one arm and his fishing pole on his shoulder, he stopped on the bridge to test his luck. Upon hooking a large trout, he forgot

THE PARISH CHURCH

his sermon and allowed it to slip into the water. The current was strong and it floated away. The minister had his trout but his congregation had no sermon that day.[63]

A sketch of the church, viewed from the parsonage, was drawn about 1800 during the time that Reverend Pogson officiated. The sketch, by artist Charles Fraser, shows that the parsonage stood on a slight hill which was northeast of the present road where it curved toward the church. There was still evidence of an older road which, according to a low country custom, led directly to the church door. The sketch also shows a small vestry building where parish business was conducted and where coachmen could take shelter.[64]

Rev. Pogson's resignation was followed by the election of the Rev. John Thomson. He served only two years before going to England in 1808, and was the last regular minister at St. James' Church.[65] It was believed that the swampy Goose Creek area was unhealthy, causing the planters to leave the parish in the Summer, leaving need for church services only in the Winter and Spring. The church became less and less active during the 19th century, with the congregation becoming smaller as many planters left the parish.

The vestry remained active during the 19th century, building a brick school near the church in 1802 and maintaining two parish schools beginning in 1828.[66] The vestry continued to provide for occasional services at the church. In 1825, the Reverend C.P. Elliott, deacon, was a missionary and Rector the next year. He reported that only four or five communicants lived in the area among seven or eight families. Although the population was small, the Reverend Elliott conducted services every second Sunday, and in 1826 every Sunday until he resigned in March of 1826, leaving for Cheraw. Major Edward H. Edwards was church deputy in 1832.

The church vestry collected $800.00 for rental on three acres of land leased to Mr. C. Miller for a number of years. The lease had been transferred from Mr. Miller to Gen. E.H. Edwards, and upon his death, it reverted back to the vestry. This money was used to repair the old church, which had fallen into a state of ruin over the years.[67] John Lucas was contracted with to repair the church to its former condition for a fee of $500.00. St. Michael's church in Charleston graciously offered to defray the expense. The walls had cracked with the years, and had to be bound together with iron bands.

HISTORIC GOOSE CREEK

Iron rods were also placed through the church to pull the walls together, and strengthen the roof, which had split. The church was replastered inside and the rough-casting on the outside was repaired. The building was also re-roofed, as the shingles needed repair.

The old church has often been the object of vandalism. The 1844 contract also called for repair of the Coat of Arms which had been defaced: the lion's tail had been carried off. The pulpit stair-rail was replaced, the flooring was relaid and the pews cut down to remove the rotting lower sections. The nearby forest had grown so close to the building that it produced 30 cords of wood when it was cut away. The beautiful S.P.G. pelican and her young was also broken, and was replaced after much effort to duplicate it. All of this work was completed in April 1845,[68] and the vestry requested Bishop Gadsden to consecrate the building. It had never been consecrated because there was no bishop in South Carolina during the Colonial Period. Bishop Gadsden performed the service on April 17, 1845, and was assisted by the Rev. A. Fowler.

In December of 1845, regular services by a missionary were started again. Reverend Philip Gadsden, Rector of St. Paul's, Stono and St. Paul's, Summerville, and later the Reverend J.W. Taylor served as ministers to the church. These services continued for many years until after the Civil War. An unusual episode in the church's history occurred during the last years of that war. The Reverend L. Phillips was the minister of St. Stephen's church on Anson Street in Charleston. The church was shelled and received considerable damage from the battling armies. At the suggestion of a member of St. James' Church and with the Bishop's approval, the Reverend Mr. Phillips conducted seven services at the Goose Creek church. He also conducted seven services on the plantations for the slaves and baptized 23 Negroes. He believed the Goose Creek area to be an excellent community for missionary work, but after the war he did not continue service for long. During the Civil War the records and the communion silver were lost. During the turbulent years of post-war Reconstruction, the church fell into the hands of the local blacks, and it was not reopened until 1876. The church suffered considerably during the war. Wear and tear from the natural elements, vandalism, malicious mischief and the earthquake of 1886 kept the vestry busy raising funds to contract for repairs after

THE PARISH CHURCH

the Civil War to the present.

After Reconstruction, the church was used intermittently, usually for special Easter services. For these occasions, the Atlantic Coast Line Railroad would operate a train to carry Charlestonians to the old church. A service was conducted on April 22, 1900, and a large congregation was present, with the Rev. Henry J. Mikell officiating. The vestry present included Doctor Parker, Mr. Dwight Stoney, Dr. Joseph I. Waring and Samuel Stoney.[69] In 1909 the vestry was composed of Francis LeJau Parker, M.D., and S. Porcher Stoney, wardens; with Samuel Gaillard Stoney, Joseph Ioor Waring, Edwin Parsons and Francis William Holmes as vestrymen.

Rev. Robert Wilson, D.D., rector of St. Luke's Church, Charleston, conducted an interesting service Sunday, April 12, 1896. The church was well filled with many old parish families to witness the dedication of a white marble tablet, which reads as follows:

> St. James Parish, Goose Creek
> Established by Act of Assembly
> November 30th 1706.
> Organized April 14th 1707.
> First Church built about 1707.
> Present Church built about 1713.
> Church consecrated April 17th 1845.
>
> Rev. Francis LeJau, D.D., 1707-1717.
> Rev. Richard Ludlam, A.M., 1723-1728.
> Rev. Timothy Millechampe, A.M., 1732-1748.
> Rev. Robert Stone, A.M., 1749-1751.
> Rev. James Harrison, A.M., 1752-1771.
> Rev. Edward Ellington, A.M., 1775-1793.
> Rev. Milward Pogson, 1796-1806.
> Rev. John Thomson, 1806-1808.

Another service was conducted Sunday, April 17, 1904, to commemorate the arrival of the first S.P.G. missionary, the Rev. Samuel Thomas. The address was delivered by Col. John P. Thomas, a descendant of the first missionary. On Sunday, April 22, 1906, a service was conducted by the Bishop of the Diocese of South Carolina, the Right Reverend Ellison Capers, D.D., commemorating the 200th anniversary of the establishment of the parish of St. James, Goose Creek, by an Act of the Assembly. At this time a marble tablet was dedicated by the Bishop in memory of the Rev. Richard Ludlam. It was unveiled by two children who were being educated by the fund left by Rev. Ludlam in 1733. The Ludlam tablet reads as follows:

> "The memory of the Just is Blessed."
> Reverend Richard Ludlam, A.M.
> Elected Rector of this Parish
> August 31st, 1723
> Died in 1728
> Zealous and faithful in the discharge of his duties, he merited and won the esteem of his people. As a mark of affection for his Parishioners, he bequeathed his entire estate, amounting to £200 in trust. "For erecting and maintaining a School for the poor children of this Parish."
> This gift known as the Ludlam Fund has for one hundred and seventy-eight years been used for educating deserving children.
> It stands a living monument to this good and generous man.
> "To do good and to distribute, forget not."
> This Tablet
> Is erected by the Vestry
> On the two hundredth anniversary of the establishment of this Parish.
> April 28th 1906.

Below the inscription appears the names of the wardens, Francis LeJau Parker and Samuel Parker Stoney; and of the vestry, Isaac Dwight Stoney, Joseph Ioor Waring, Samuel Gaillard Waring and Edwin Parsons. After the service, an address was delivered by the Honorable Henry A.M. Smith about the parish of St. James in its early days.[70]

The railroad was the most commonly-used method of transportation to the church during the first decade of this century. On April 23, 1906, the *News and Courier* reported that seven train coaches were used for the ride to Goose Creek.[71] As many as 700 people attended another year. It was a pleasant ride by coach, and a pleasant walk from the rail stop, over the creek bridge, to the church. By 1925 the motor car had replaced the train, but the popularity of the annual service remained.

Professor Francis L. Holmes owned Ingleside plantation, located near the church. He took great interest in the affairs of the parish and was largely responsible for the maintenance of the church during the mid-19th century.[72] He enjoyed bringing his houseguests to visit the church and to relate its

THE PARISH CHURCH

history to them. He served as a member of the vestry and did much to restore the building. On August 31, 1886, the church was badly damaged by the earthquake which devastated the low country. The front section of the church suffered much damage when the gable fell out entirely. Part of the east gable crumbled, and the walls were badly cracked.[73] The old memorial tablet and the Royal Arms over the chancel were also broken. Restoration work was begun immediately, but the broken Royal Arms seemed impossible to restore. Years before, however, the daughter of Professor John McCrady had painted a copy in oils for the use of the New England Historical Society. The painting was obtained and from it the restoration was made.[74]

By the turn of the century the church was again in good repair, with great pains having been taken to restore it to its original condition and appearance. Forest fires were a threat, so the shutters and doors were covered with iron and the roof with slate, making it almost fireproof. The slate roof may have been a gift from two Englishmen residing in Charleston. One of the men responsible for replacing the shingle roof was Cowlan Gravely. Vandals have also done damage to the church over the years, and a *News and Courier* report of April 20, 1925, referred to the "marks of vandals."[75] Today, access to the old structure is granted only under supervision, and the church yard is protected by a brick wall and an iron gate. The exterior was painted about 1931 in accordance with a sketch made in 1803 by Charles Fraser, the celebrated Charleston painter of miniatures.

Inside the protective brick wall is one of the oldest, most interesting and informative graveyards in South Carolina. It is much like an outdoor museum in which a visitor can derive hours of historical adventure. A great store of local history, literature and art is preserved in the natural outdoor setting of the cemetery. This is one of several "graveyard museums" in Goose Creek.

The Church of St. James, Goose Creek, and its cemetery is recorded on the National Register of Historic Places. Because it is protected, many grave markers from other Goose Creek sites have been moved to the church yard. Within the protecting wall of St. James' cemetery are 27 graves, 26 of which are marked with tombstones. The grave markers contain large amounts of historical data. Thirty-seven names of deceased persons are recorded on these stones as being interred in the cemetery. To this number can be added other parishioners buried there, as recorded on memorial plaques on the interior walls of the church, and also the Reverend LeJau, who is interred at the foot of the altar.

Of the 37 persons known to be buried in the cemetery, 21 are male and 16 are female. Three infants and three children are among the 37. The earliest death recorded by the inscriptions is that of Doctor Robert Brown, Esq., who died in 1757. The oldest person buried there is Mrs. Mary Mazyck, who died at the age of 82 years. Using the tombstone data, one can determine the average male lifespan as being 38 years, and the average female as 40 years. Mary Mazyck was a most unusual person to have lived to the ripe old age of 82.

A visitor entering St. James' Church cemetery through the iron gate will find the testimonial stone to Thomas Bromley immediately to his right. Bromley appears to have been buried upon his request in a part of Peter Manigault's Goose Creek estate known as "Steepbrook." Peter Manigault's grandson, Charles, seems to have moved the stone to the house he purchased from William Drayton at 6 Gibbes Street, Charleston, probably in 1836. The stone remained there until the owner of 6 Gibbes Street, Mrs. F.G. Boggs, moved it to St. James' churchyard. The stone has been worn and weathered so badly through the years that the inscription is almost totally illegible. (See Appendix D.)

Thomas Bromley was an attorney of Charleston, but was an Englishman by birth. He appears to have been an intimate friend of Goose Creek planter Peter Manigault. He died at Manigault's country home in Goose Creek from an attack of fever. Mrs. Manigault's diary stated simply that, "Mr. Bromley died." The *South Carolina Gazette* for August 26, 1765, stated, "Last Thursday morning after a short illness [died], Thomas Bromley, Esq., clerk assistant to the hon. Commons House of Assembly of this Province; and next day his remains were interred, without any funeral pomp, agreeable to his own request, on the plantation of Peter Manigault, Esq., Goose Creek, attended by a number of his particular friends." It appears that Bromley was a bachelor and died without heirs. His personal property indicated that he was a man of some wealth and good taste. He had one slave named Frank. It appears from his epitaph that he enjoyed his friends

THE PARISH CHURCH

and merriment.

Standing near the stone of Thomas Bromley is the marker of Dr. Robert Brown. Dr. Brown was buried at St. James' Chapel of Ease, which fell into ruin during the Revolutionary War. Dr. Brown's stone was removed to the Goose Creek church. The inscription reads: "In Memory of / Dr. Robert Brown / who departed this Life 25th Nov. 1757 / Aged 43 years." The third grave site, located next to Dr. Brown, is that of the infant child, William Senkler: "Sacred to the Memory of / William Senkler Son of / William and Elizabeth / Sinkler He died on the / 15th July 1814 aged 3 weeks." Moving counterclockwise around the church, one finds the grave of Elizabeth Ann Smith. The tombstone reads: "Here. lies the body of / Elizabeth Ann Smith / The Amiable and / Deservedly Beloved / Wife of Captain / Benjamin Smith who / died the 26 March 1769 / Aged 27 Years Also / Their Daughter Mary / Smith Who Died September / 9th 1768 Aged 3 Years / 5 Ms & 8 Days." Mrs. E.A. Poyas wrote, "The father [of the daughter, Mary Smith and husband of Elizabeth Ann Smith] was then thirty four when he became a widower; his title was Major at the time of his union with Catherine Ball in 1773.[76] (See Appendix E for other tombstone inscriptions.)

Four grave markers were brought to the Goose Creek church from Windsor Hill, the home of the famous Moultrie family. Windsor Hill is located near what is today known as Pepper Hill, and was once considered part of the Goose Creek community. William Moultrie was the second son of Dr. John Moultrie who immigrated to South Carolina. Moultrie was born in Charles Town on November 23, 1730. His first wife was Elizabeth de St. Julien. After the death of Elizabeth he married Mrs. Hannah Lynch. William Moultrie served as Public Treasurer of South Carolina, and was elected a member of the Commons House of Assembly on October 29, 1754, and on three other occasions. He was appointed by Lieutenant Governor Bull as a captain in the South Carolina Provincial Regiment in the Cherokee War in 1760. He later served as a major in the militia regiment of horse in 1773, and in 1774 and 1775 as colonel. William Moultrie was also deputy to the First Provincial Congress of South Carolina and the Second Provincial Congress in 1775 and 1776. He became a member of the first General Assembly of the State of South Carolina in 1776. He was also elected member of the Legislative Council, and by the time of the First Provincial Congress as colonel of the Second Regiment of South Carolina. He was commissioned by the Council of Safety June 17, 1775, and commanded the forces on Sullivan's Island on June 28, 1776, when victories were won against a British fleet and army. Moultrie commanded troops at the unfinished fort, and after his victory he and his regiment were made part of the Continental Establishment.

The fort on Sullivan's Island was later named in his honor. He was promoted by Congress to Brigadier-General, and on September 16, 1776, was elected the first State senator from St. John's, Berkeley, in 1778. He commanded forces which engaged in numerous encounters with the British. He helped defend Charles Town in 1780, and after the surrender of the city, he was captured by the British. On October 15, 1782, he was promoted to Major-General, and served until the end of the war. He was elected Governor of South Carolina in 1785, and served two years.

The General was elected again in 1794 to serve two more years, and died September 27, 1805. His *Memoirs of the American Revolution* is a valuable contribution to the history of the war and the period. His grave marker may be found at St. James' church, and reads as follows:

> William Moultrie / South Carolina / Major General Continental Army / December 4, 1730 / September 27, 1805 / Thanks of Congress.

General Moultrie was buried in an unmarked spot in the family graveyard at Windsor Hill Plantation. Moultrie's grave was identified through the laborious efforts of the Huguenot Society of South Carolina and its president, the Rev. Canon Edward B. Guerry. William Moultrie was then reinterred at Fort Moultrie on Sullivan's Island. Most of the grave remains, including parts of the coffin, are buried at St. James' church, but bone slivers of the General were buried at Fort Moultrie.

William Moultrie's son, William Jr., was born August 7, 1752. He was appointed a second lieutenant in the Second Regiment in 1775, and to first lieutenant and later captain. William married Hannah Ainslie in 1776, and was elected a member of the House of Representatives of South Carolina in 1781. He died December 11, 1796, at his home at Windsor

THE PARISH CHURCH

Hill in St. James' parish. (See Appendix F for inscriptions of the Moultrie family from Windsor Hill.)

There was a Chapel of Ease belonging to the parish, located about seven miles below Strawberry Ferry and about seven miles from the Goose Creek church. It was a brick building built in the shape of a cross on one acre of land donated for that purpose by Mr. Dutarque.[77] There is no record of when the chapel was built. The parish was so large, the people scattered so widely and transportation so slow and difficult that it necessitated the construction of such chapels to accommodate parishioners living a distance from the parish church. Mrs. E.A. Poyas wrote about the "Yeamans Hall" Smith family journey to Sunday worship at the Goose Creek church as follows:

> By crossing the carriage and horses in a flat, and having the family rowed over the creek in a fine canoe, Mrs. Henry Smith and daughters had only a few miles to ride. But your mother loves to believe, as the old negroes have told, that "Massa stayed at home and kept sarvace with old Misses, his mama."[78]

The Chapel of Ease provided conveniences for some worshippers. Although there is no record of the exact date of its construction, there was a figure resembling 1721 appearing on one of the bricks.[79] Frederick Dalcho wrote in 1820 that, "There are several tombstones around it; the oldest inscription upon them, that is legible, is 1757."

It appears from a road law that the chapel was standing in 1725.[80] Judge Henry A.M. Smith reported that the chapel was probably destroyed during the Revolutionary War.[81] Nothing remains today except an historical marker on old Highway 52, not even an old brick. There is, however, an overgrown earthen mound where bushes and vines may be hiding bits and pieces of ruins. Even the grave markers are gone now, but some of the inscriptions were recorded and published. (See Appendix G.)[82]

> The Chapel of Ease, belonging to your Parish, stood about seven miles below Strawberry Ferry; a brick edifice in the form of the Roman Cross. After a few years use, it was accidentally burned down. I visited the ruin some four years age, and read the inscriptions on ancient tombstones; amongst the names there recorded, you will find those of Broughton, Broun, and Deas. The Baptists have a neat

wooden church adjoining the ruin, from which they have used a few bricks for their steps. That glebe of one acre of land, had been presented by Mr. Dutarque of unfortunate memory, he and his family having afterwards fallen into fatal delusion. There is no record of the time when the chapel was built, something like the figure of 1721 appears on a brick; and, from a road law, we find that it was standing in 1725. The oldest inscription on a tomb there, that is now legible, is 1757 — it is that of Mr. Nathaniel Broughton, of Mulberry Castle, in St. John's Parish; son of Colonel Thomas Broughton, who built the castle, commencing in 1714, and the grandson of Governor N. Johnson, who died in 1713.[83]

Today the annual service at St. James' church is an experience in timelessness. It seems that some things change very little. The old church is a true monument to the labors and love of the Carolinians for their land, families and friends. Economic forces and the ravages of war caused the once prosperous community to wane to the point where the church lost much of its usefulness. There remains, however, a very strong sense of pride for the old church and for what it represented. Frederick Dalcho's history of the Anglican Church in South Carolina reveals the special spirit that the ministers brought to Goose Creek. They left their homes and cast their lots with the frontiersmen in the wilderness. The ministers were not the dregs of the Anglican Church. In many cases they were men of learning and ability. Of the eight rectors of the church, one was a canon of St. Paul's Cathedral and had the Doctor of Divinity degree, while five others had earned their A.M. degree.[84]

The country church was the social center of the neighborhood. Owing to the scattered nature of the plantation society, the poor condition of roads and the difficulties of travel, people found it difficult to visit each other. Sunday was eagerly awaited: a day to see neighbors and friends. On Sunday mornings before the service, men would gather around the front door to discuss crops, politics or the latest horse race. During the recess between morning and evening prayers, a mid-day meal was enjoyed in picnic fashion beneath the live oak trees near the church. The church meant much to the people of Goose Creek. It was in many ways the home of patriotism during the Colonial Period. It was the established church of the state and promoted a strong spirit of loyalty to constituted authority. Even when the trials of the Revolution

THE PARISH CHURCH

approached, the patriotic spirit of the American cause was felt among the church patrons. You could find more communicants at the old church than could be found at Charleston's St. Philip's on Easter Sunday, but now it is a monument to colonial Goose Creek, and only occasionally now a place of prayer.

CHAPTER XII

GOOSE CREEK GHOSTS AND LEGENDS

Ghosts, goblins and various forms of apparitions have always had their place in American history. Most of the spirits which have delighted and frightened the American people for hundreds of years have been poorly documented but have reappeared during every period of history. Almost all of the stories, from those of the headless horseman of Sleepy Hollow to the more real ones of witches and demons in Puritan New England, have come down to us with at lease some basis in fact.

Goose Creek, from its earliest period, had its share of unexplainable phenomena. Its 300 year history has produced some of the most interesting tales one could find anywhere. Goose Creek has several ghosts, a most unusual wedding, and even a premature burial story; tales which rival those conjured up by Edgar Allen Poe. The Goose Creek legends are based on fact. The stories are about real people, real places and with an accurate fix on the time of their occurrence. If fact gives way to fiction somewhere in the tale, it is for the reader to decide. Those who might doubt the authenticity of the reports should make a visit to old St. James' church or old Medway house. Even the most unimaginative visitor to either place will most likely be noticeably moved by their eerie timelessness. Both places have their ghosts. A moment of silence at these places may be broken by the rustling memories of colonial planters. Listen for the sounds of the frequent horseman on the muddy road near the church, the call of the ferryman crossing the creek, and the activity that was commonplace around the tavern near the church. Occasionally visitors to the old Medway House look from the front lawn and catch glimpses of a ghostly figure through the small panes of the upper front window. It's easy for visitors to the old church to hear the past and feel the realities and the unrealities forgotten by most during the last 300 years.

MARY HYRNE OF GOOSE CREEK PLANTATION

Yeamans Hall Plantation, once known as Old Goose Creek, is one of the most interesting Goose Creek houses. The mansion on the creek was originally built as a defense against the Indians. It was surrounded by breast-work and

GHOSTS AND LEGENDS

was equipped with gun portholes in the foundation. For the purpose of withstanding long sieges, a well was dug underneath the house, and a tunnel running from the house to the river supposedly provided hidden escape or entry. The old house is a perfect home for ghosts and spirits. It had trap doors, secret chambers and all of the necessities for a good ghost story.

On the back porch there was a small room with an entire double floor and trap-door. Here the family could conceal valuables if threatened by Indians. As the years passed, this secret place was forgotten by most, except for a boy called Paul. This slave boy began hiding here during the day, and made mischief at night. For three weeks the house mistress feared the young boy drowned or kidnapped. From that time on it was called Paul's hole.

This quaint old plantation possesses a haunting spirit which has been reported time and again for almost 200 years. The last sighting of the spirit was only a few years ago. The first sighting is told as the story of Mary Hyrne. It was a custom in colonial days for families of means to hire private teachers for the education of their children. Public schools were extremely rare and the occasional church-sponsored school was often inaccessible to many of the remoter plantations. Such was the case when Mrs. Latham left her native Ireland to seek employment as a governess in Charleston. Widowed and without means of support, she underwent the ordeals of the voyage with hopes of teaching in the distant land of opportunity.

Upon arrival she immediately learned of the Old Goose Creek plantation, where she could teach four little girls. The journey was by coach over miles of rough dirt and clay roads. Although it was a pleasant change to travel this way after such a long ocean voyage, it was a tiring experience for the new governess.

Old Goose Creek plantation rested at the goose-neck bend of the creek for which many believe it was named. The glassy creek and the wide expanse of open marsh on which the plantation rests retains some of its timeless beauty even today. For Mrs. Latham, all of this and the moss-laden oaks were very strange and beautiful. She had never seen such in her native Ireland.

Upon arrival, Mrs. Henry Smith and her small daughters helped settle the new governess into her accommodations. Mrs. Smith's husband had died some years before, and the family had settled on the first floor of the old estate. Mrs. Latham was to occupy the second floor and Mrs. Smith offered to have one of her servants sleep there so the governess would not be alone.

"Oh, really, Madam, I will not be afraid to stay up there. What could possibly happen to me? I beg you, don't give it a thought."[1] Mrs. Latham moved onto the second floor with her possessions to be alone in her room overlooking the marsh and the creek.

The next morning was Sunday. The family gathered downstairs with the servants to read the Sunday service. Mrs. Latham remained upstairs to read *The Turkish Spy,* a novel she had brought with her to gratify her interest in romance.[2] The morning service was suddenly disrupted by the trembling and wide-eyed appearance of Mrs. Latham on the stairway. She cried out hysterically, "Who was that who just went out?"[3]

The family and servants were startled and amazed by the interruption. No one could pass by without going through the hall, and none had. Mrs. Latham was shaken and unconvinced by the family logic, so the party searched for the mysterious visitor.

After some calming, the governess began to relate her experience, which she would retell for years to come. She had been sitting in her room, reading of romance, when she heard a disturbance in the outside hall. She listened intently as footsteps approached her door. The door opened slowly to reveal an old lady dressed in a black gown with a muslin neckerchief crossed on her breast. Her head was covered with a white cap.

Mrs. Latham was puzzled because she knew nothing of this elderly occupant of the house, but she remained polite and invited the lady in. Receiving no response she repeated, "Come in, won't you?" There was still no response, only a disapproving glare. Mrs. Latham moved toward her as the mysterious lady moved slowly off. A cold draught seemed to fill the room, recounted the governess. She was repelled but at the same time incredibly attracted to the lady. She was drawn by a strange force to follow her as she glided several paces ahead to the next room then the one beyond. There the old lady seemed to vanish. A panic filled the governess as she ran back through all the rooms, thinking she had someway missed her. But she was to be found nowhere.[4]

After telling her experience she was not to be pacified by the assurances of the family. She was surely not mistaken about the strange visitor and she gratefully accepted the offer to have someone sleep upstairs so she would not be alone.

Sunday was a gathering time for the family and so the following Sabbath Mr. Benjamin Smith came to visit his brother's widow. The new governess was immediately upset by the appearance of Mr. Smith. She became hysterical, crying out, "You are like her. Heaven help me, you are the living image of the lady who glared at me!" Mr. Smith seemed to immediately understand the lady's alarm and talked gently for some time to calm her tears.

"My mother, Mary Hyrne, spent the last years of her life in these rooms upstairs," he told her. "She seldom came down, and it was customary for the family to take their work or books up there to sit with her. She was a dear old lady and kind. In the closet of one room she had many little partitions built, in which she kept sugar dainties for her small grandchildren."[5]

Mr. Smith explained that his deceased mother was no doubt concerned about the influence Mrs. Latham might have on the minds of her granddaughters. The governess was reading a romantic novel on the Sabbath instead of attending the family worship service. His very pious mother had returned to protest and express her concerns for the children's welfare.

Mary Hyme never again appeared to protest the presence of the Irish woman who became a faithful and pious governess and lived to teach four generations of Smiths and children of other Charleston families. She also found romance and married again. She retold the story of Mary Hyrne's protest many times and delighted in having such an exciting story to tell.

This delightful story of the ghost lady of Old Goose Creek is based on a considerable amount of historical fact. Mary Hyrne was the only daughter of Colonel Edward Hyrne and his wife, Elizabeth. Their daughter, Mary Hyme, married Thomas Smith, the second Landgrave, and lived her life at the country mansion overlooking the waters of Goose Creek.[6] In her later years she was sickly, and spent most of her time confined by bad health on the second floor of the country mansion. There she would entertain her grandchildren with baby houses, doll's parties and sugar dainties. It is reported that her son, Benjamin, strongly resembled his mother and that was the reason he so alarmed Mrs. Latham when he came to visit.

Mary Hyrne Smith died in 1777 at the age of 80 years. Although many years have past since the Ghost Lady of Old Goose Creek appeared before the young governess, there are many who still sense her presence on the plantation grounds. In this century a very fine country club has been developed on the spacious grounds. One day some Charleston ladies were decorating the central club house for the enjoyment of the homeowners. One of the party was temporarily separated from the others. She was puzzled to see an old lady approach her with a glare and then turn away.

"Who else is here with us?" she questioned. "It was an old lady in an old-fashioned black dress with a muslin neckerchief and a little white cap." "Who could she be?"

She was answered in a voice full of respect, "It was Mary Hyrne — protesting again."

"Not a word she begn'd to say,
But like a spectre stalked away."[7]

THE MORBID TALE OF MISS COLEMAN

There is a rather rare old book printed in New York City that contains one of the most curious stories about St. James' church. Only 100 copies were printed. *The Goose Creek Church, A Morbid Tale* was published in 1901. No author's name appears on the work.

According to this quaint old book, Charles Carrington had a strange experience at the church. It seems that he had become weary at a house party, and wandered away for a walk. He walked to the old church, which at that time was surrounded by a ruined wall and an old iron gate. A drizzling rain forced the weary wanderer through the grave yard and into the protection of the gloomy church structure. A queer sense of presence made him grow uneasy as he heard footsteps approaching. He was met by a solitary young woman who knelt in prayer for a few moments and then introduced herself as Miss Edith Coleman. She was one of the members of an old Goose Creek family. Her ancestors were buried in the family vault outside of the old musty church.

A rather strange conversation ensued when Carrington confessed that a strange fear had crept into him. Miss Coleman spoke of death and fear. She explained the folly of fearing death and of fearing the dead. Surely, she said, the dead can do no harm, and life is as great a mystery as death. Mr. Carrington was not consoled by her reasoning. He feared the graves, the vaults, the markers of death and heavy sense of ghostly presence in the old church. Miss Coleman showed her family vault to Carrington and spoke of her father's insistence that all family members be buried in it.[8] Charles Carrington returned to the dinner party to tell the story of his church visit. He asked his host about the old church and the lady he met.

> "Why, surely that must have been the Goose Creek Church," broke in his hostess. "It is quite an historical bit, dating back somewhere about 1670. Did you notice the arms of England over the altar? That is something hard to find in America to-day...."[9]

Charles Carrington made daily visits to the old church to meet with Edith Coleman during the following week. Their conversations, as might be expected, led to romance, although Edith remained aloof from Charles' earnest pleas of love. She spoke of such serious aspects of love that it puzzled and frightened him.

"Would our love outlive the fires of youth when the finger of time had placed its seal of age and decay? No, no, a thousand times no! Man's love droops, then fades and dies."

The intensity of her words startled him, but he could not draw back.

"Put me to any test, Edith," he cried, taking her unresisting hand and looking longingly into her face, she laughed her low, sweet laugh.

"You swear it?"

"I swear it!"

"Then follow me."[10]

He followed her to her family vault, where she mysteriously disappeared. He had only looked away for a second. Where had she gone? She couldn't have entered that dreadful vault? With nervous strength and energy, he grabbed the iron vault handle and in a burst of force broke the rusting lock.

The door fell outward and something which had evidently been leaning against it fell in a confused mass at his feet. He could not comprehend what was lying before him. Breathless from his burst of strength and his fearful state, he could only stand and stare at what lay at his feet. It was a human body. He put his hands up to his eyes and for a moment stood there swaying. Then with a moan he fell forward upon his face beside that awful heap.[11]

For months following this dreadful experience, Charles Carrington lay near death with a raging fever. He remembered nothing at first, but the ghastly details of his experience slowly returned to his memory. When he regained his strength, he returned to his host to investigate the event that had so tormented him. His rescuers told of finding him at the church.

> "Well, there they found you lying on your face in front of the Coleman vault, but that was not the terrible part. The door had been forced open and alongside of you lay the body of Edith Coleman."
> "The body was in a horrible state of decomposition, so the men said."[12]
> "She was the eldest daughter of Mr. James Coleman, who is our nearest neighbor. Some months ago she died and was buried in the family vault . . . ."
> "I was at the funeral, and the life-like look of Edith was even then commented upon. The upper part of the coffin lid was off, so that those present might have a last look at the girl. I remember now wondering at the time if she were really dead and how awful being buried alive would be. Of course not for one instant did I imagine that such a thing could happen, but you know how queer thoughts will sometimes intrude themselves."
> "Now, bearing this in mind in the light of subsequent events, it seems as if there could be no other explanation than that she was still alive when the coffin was placed in the vault."
> "By some oversight the lid could not have been securely put on, for this was found off. The torn lining and the plain marks of fingernails showed conclusively that there had been an awful struggle for breath and life. It would appear that the girl had had strength to force the lid, to drag herself as far as the door of the vault and there on her knees before it her strength had given out and she had died. It is almost too horrible for words. To think of the agony that poor creature must have suffered when she found that her almost superhuman efforts were in vain, that she was barred in and had to die."[13]

GHOSTS AND LEGENDS

Charles Carrington never told of his meetings with Edith nor offered explanation for his mysterious accident. He left the plantation of his host, returned to his home and never visited the old church again.

This story, like so many Goose Creek stories, has some basis in historical fact. There is a story of such a premature burial. It seems that a young woman was buried in a vault near the front door of the old church. A young slave boy had the task of bringing water to the church daily. He heard cries and screams from the newly sealed vault that so frightened him that he was at first afraid to tell of his experience. When he finally told his master, the vault was reopened and the startled observers found that the young woman had torn her way out of the wooden coffin, only to die imprisoned by the walls of the brick vault.

The vault across from the front church door is marked by a marble slab which reads:

> Here Lies the Body of
> Elizabeth Ann Smith
> The Amiable and Deservedly
> Beloved Wife of Captain
> *Benjamin Smith*
> Who died the 26 March 1769
> aged 27 years
> also Their Daughter
> Mary Smith Who Died
> September 9th 1768 Aged 3 Years
> 5 Ms and 8 Days.

The name of the young woman on the Goose Creek vault is not the same as that of the woman met by Charles Carrington. There is no documentation of the authenticity of the reports of the premature burial, nor good reasons for the difference in names.

THE GHOST OF "OLD BANDISON"

During the colonial era the American colonists were called upon time and time again to assist in many of the wars the British engaged in against the Spanish and the French. In 1739, General Oglethorpe attacked the Spanish at St. Augustine. The Carolina Regiment was an auxiliary force supporting Oglethorpe whose officers were Colonel Alexander Vanderdussen of Goose Creek and Lieutenant Colonel Francis LeJau,

HISTORIC GOOSE CREEK

son of the Goose Creek minister.[14] Little is known of Colonel Vanderdussen before this time, but he had been in Carolina as early as 1731. He owned lands in Goose Creek and was a member of the Commons House for St. James, Goose Creek. Like Oglethorpe, he had seen service in foreign wars and was esteemed as an experienced soldier.[15]

Colonel Vanderdussen continued as a member of the Commons House for many years and was later one of the King's Council. He died in England in 1759, leaving no family. After his death the house was supposedly haunted. The probability is that it became the resort of runaway slaves who were interested in spreading the report. Local blacks would say, "If you go there Old Bandison will catch you." They meant Col. Vanderdussen, the former owner, who lived in great style in the house he built on Goose Creek. He built a dairy and had a row of fine mulberry trees which he likely cultivated for the production of silk. He is reported to have been a severe master and his reputation was spread by the neighboring blacks who contend that old Vanderdussen did really "revisit the glimpses of the moon, making night hideous."[16] The house was afterward rebuilt and occupied by William Johnson who reared a large family there, undisturbed by ghosts. Among the family was the Honorable William Johnson, Associate Justice of the Supreme Court of the United States.[17]

"MAD ARCHIE" CAMPBELL

Captain Archibald Campbell was an officer in the King's army during the Revolutionary War. During the period of British occupation of Charleston, Goose Creek was within the British lines. St. James' Church was familiar to the British soldiers and was used as a place of worship during the war. In 1780 the old church was the scene of the most unusual wedding of Mad Archie Campbell and Paulina Philps.

Captain Campbell was a young officer who had the reputation of being a proud and swanky soldier. He was a man of his word, but also a man who would act presumptuously. In 1780 he attended a Tory ball in Charleston. The British had invited Whig ladies to attend, but because of the occupation and the strong feelings of loyalty, none did so. It was at this ball that Captain Campbell met the daughter of a prominent South Carolina family, Miss Paulina Philps. He was roman-

GHOSTS AND LEGENDS

tically taken by the young and beautiful Paulina. Miss Philps was not interested in the young captain and ignored him for another man at the ball. The young captain, chided by his army friends, challenged his comrades to a wager.

"I intend to marry the lady," he stated in a voice just short of a shout. He was rebutted by a burst of laughter. "I'll wager," said one of Archie's friends, but Archie took the initiative to make the bet. "Nay, gentlemen. It is I who will wager, my Arab filly to your £50, that within three days I will be married to the lady and with her consent." His wager was quickly accepted.[18]

The following day, Captain Campbell went to 43 East Battery to offer a sunny ride to the lovely Miss Philps. She appeared anxious to ride about in the fine gig, which was a sure show of respectability. They rode off from town rapidly until they were riding through the countryside. The young Captain drove his steed faster and faster, over the fearful pleas of Miss Philps. They finally arrived at an old bridge, and after crossing over, young Paulina first saw the ancient Goose Creek church.

During that time the Reverend Edward Ellington was minister of the church. He was called to the door of the rectory, whereupon the wild-eyed captain announced his intentions to be married to the lovely lady. The good Reverend, noticing that she was nearly faint, protested, "Not without the consent of the lady." Mad Archie immediately lived up to his reputation, drew his pistol and shouted, "Unless you comply, you shall be instantly shot, and the lady's virtue could only suffer in consequence. I say, sir, make haste!" When he pointed the pistol at Paulina Philps, she hurriedly consented.[19]

After the nervous wedding, the proud husband drove his new bride back to Charleston at a modest pace. The young girl lost most of her fear and apprehension and told her family: "Until we arrived at Goose Creek, I had never thought seriously about marrying Captain Campbell. Indeed, I supposed his wild talk to be only a soldier's way of making love."[20] She told her friends that when Campbell was particular in his attentions, and flattered her, she had considered it nothing more than what all the British officers were in the habit of doing. That day at the church surely had changed her mind. Mad Archie won his wager of £50 and his beautiful bride. Paulina and Archie spent a year of marriage at Exeter Plantation. They had one daughter and lived happily for a short time.

At the battle of Videau's Bridge, the advanced companies of the British and American armies met near the club house at the bridge. During the battle, Captain Campbell was unhorsed, either by falling or by the death of his horse, and was forced to surrender. He was seated on a root of a tree, guarded by a sentinel. A few moments later he tried to escape, and despite his guard's warning he continued to run. He was shot in the back and killed.[21]

The lovely Paulina reportedly died soon afterwards. The spirits of Mad Archie and Paulina have never left the low country. There are reports of his return to the old church and Exeter plantation. When the night falls soundly on the river, some say they can hear the stealthy rustling of spirits.

THE GHOST OF MEDWAY

Ghosts abound at the old Medway house on Back River. Of all the eerie spots of Goose Creek, Medway is without rival. "It was just the place for ghosts to walk, for strange voices to be heard, for unusual things to happen," said John Bennett, author of *The Treasure of Pierre Gailliard.* In this book of treasure and intrigue, Bennett immortalized the atmosphere of Medway Plantation. He revived the eerie sense of desolation and haunting allurement found within the walls of the well-built old house. Of the countryside, he wrote:

> ... we rode through a desolated country, from which the old plantations had almost vanished; even the brick foundations of the ancient houses had been carted away by the negroes to build crooked chimneys to their cabins, after the great plantations had been destroyed during the war. The old corduroy road was half sunken into the bottomless swamp ....
> Of the sturdy, daring Frenchman, who faced savages and war, carved out a fortune by industry, only to die in agony on a tree, as spies and traitors die, there was left, only a few years ago, but a fallen tomb, a tombstone split from end by vandals, and used as a stand for bee-hives by negroes. Beneath the dust of fallen leaves, the vines and moss which gather, one can just make out "Here Lyeth Ye Bodye" ... the name has vanished away.
> ... It was certainly true that there was something ghostly and sad and strange about the whole demesne.[22]

GHOSTS AND LEGENDS

Many ghosts are said to walk in the low-ceilinged rooms of old Medway. They are protected by thick walls with large fire places and narrow windows. The Medway house is situated on expansive plantation grounds approached by miles of entrance road, bordered by tall pines and moss-ladened live oaks. The old home sits on an expanse of well-kept lawn spreading down to Back River. The house is the oldest one of record in the state, and was constructed in 1686 just 16 years after the colony at Charles Town was founded. It was built by Jan Van Arrsens for his wife, Sabina de Vignou. The high dutch gables of the home were fashioned to induce evil spirits to walk down and leave the house in peace. Van Arrsens did not live long to enjoy his home on Back River. Upon his death his widow married Landgrave Thomas Smith who was governor of Carolina. They had no children. The Landgrave died at the age of 46 and was buried on the plantation grounds. There is no trace of Van Arrsens' grave. Langrave Smith's is marked by a marble slab.

The old Dutchman returns to the ancient house to assert his possession. One who has enough nerve to sleep in the upstairs bedroom on the south side, a part of the original structure, is likely to wake in the night to see old Van Arrsens seated before the fireplace smoking his pipe. He sits contently there enjoying both his pipe and his home.[23]

Downstairs there is another ghostly visitor — that of a beautiful girl whose heart was broken by the death of her husband while he was hunting. The Medway Plantation grounds abound in deer, wild turkey and other animals, and hunts have been held there for hundreds of years. At one such hunt, a gathering of deer hunters and their wives, including a young couple, met at the ancient home. The young girl had a fear of the hunt and begged her husband not to go. She had a foreboding fear of disaster as she watched him leave with his comrades. Near dusk the hunters returned, carrying an improvised stretcher. The girl's eyes fell upon it and saw the lifeless form of her husband. They took her home, where she died shortly thereafter. For many years she has haunted the spot where her heart had died at the sight of her husband's stretcher. Night after night she comes back to the place of her anguish to wait for her young husband. Some have reported that the hunter's bride comes and stands by the north window to peer through the small panes of glass. Others say they have heard only the rustling of her gown as she waits.[24]

Another story is of a romantic young lady who is sometimes still to be seen waiting to see the spirit of her lover, who promised to appear to her after his death, but never did. It seems that old Mr. Samuel Marion and young Miss Polly Seed believed the possibility of a dead friend reappearing to a loved one. They promised each other that whoever was to die first was to return to meet the other in the upper north room. After the old gentleman died, Miss Polly waited patiently one day in the north room, but the meeting was not kept.[25]

Many other ghosts and apparitions abound in the old plantation and grave sites in Goose Creek. There is old "Pontoux," the ghost of Parnassus plantation on Back River.[26] He haunts the cool spring and is reportedly the spirit of Zachariah Villepontoux, the Goose Creek church vestryman.

The old Goose Creek plantations, churches and graveyards abound in mystery. The swampy Goose Creek water and dense pine and oak forests stir the imagination and provide ideal settings for ghosts. Visitors who possess enough nerve and desire can still visit the old sites at dusk and may be able to feel the spirits of old Goose Creek.

CHAPTER XIII

GOOSE CREEK IN THE 20TH CENTURY

People living in Goose Creek during the first half of this century probably could not foresee the dynamic potential of the rural countryside. From 1900 to 1950 the community was little more than a handful of residents clustered near country churches. The small black settlements had community names such as Grove Hall, Casey, Bowens Corner, Mount Holly, Back River, Howe Hall and Liberty Hall.

Besides the ten to 20 acre farms, there was an occasional lumber or grist mill, a few general stores and a number of small white-washed churches.[1] Charleston and Berkeley newspapers prior to 1950 rarely referred to the area as "Goose Creek." This name was generally applied to the creek itself and the reservoir that provided drinking water to Charleston County.

Goose Creek's potential lay dormant until the economic pump was primed by federal money. After World War II, federal military interests brought the immigration of thousands of military and civil servants. Secondary commercial interests and the subsequent flow of investment capital followed.

This influx of people came to a community that was dominated by black social, economic and religious institutions but the sheer number of newcomers quickly supplanted the black community. Little has been done to preserve the history of black Carolina, unfortunately, and even less to preserve the rich history of black Goose Creek. Widespread illiteracy among Goose Creek blacks and failure on the part of the Goose Creek whites to record day-to-day events have resulted in a shortage of information for this period. Little physical evidence of the rural history remains and the older residents are passing from this world, taking with them countless stories of old Goose Creek and bygone days.

The Goose Creek blacks lived harmoniously with their few white neighbors. Generally speaking, the remaining black residents speak favorably of the byegone days. They recall the days as being happier than life in the 1970's. There was a strong sense of black independence although white supremacy prevailed, as the mills and the stores were all white-owned.

The rural blacks depended on the white-owned businesses for products and services not available from the land.

215

The Goose Creek black usually owned his small farm which provided a large measure of independence, but relied upon part-time employment to supplement his agricultural income. Many found full or part-time work in the fertilizer, brick or lumber businesses in or near Goose Creek. Although the Goose Creek black was traditionally subservient and often economically dependent upon the white minority, he owned the vast majority of the lands and was the master of his own immediate settlement.

Clearly the most important institution in Goose Creek was the black church. It performed many important functions besides providing religious guidance, and was an agency through which the community organized itself. The church leaders were decision makers, social workers and community administrators. Every black Goose Creek subsection had a church. There were no other institutions to provide political or civil leadership. Some communities were very small, with hardly a dozen families in the congregation. Bowens Corner was such a settlement. Others like Casey, Grove Hall or Howe Hall contained several dozen families who made up large church congregations. The church ministered only to the local neighborhood, resulting in the absence of any community cohesiveness in the greater Goose Creek area.

The black clergyman was the most important community leader. According to the 1906 census of religious bodies, almost all black Carolinians were affiliated with a church.[2] Most of Goose Creek's churches were of the African Methodist Episcopal, Episcopal or Methodist Episcopal denominations. There were no white churches in the immediate area and no significant white institutions. The churches offered the black Carolinians their most meaningful opportunities for exercising independence. Aside from serving as a training center for community leaders, the church also influenced education by exercising considerable control over the schools, the teachers and the students.

Casey was a typical black Goose Creek settlement. It was located between State Highways 176 and 52, adjacent to the Mount Holly plantation. Casey appears to have been first settled sometime during the Reconstruction period. Some Casey natives tell of a freed slave of that name who set up a tent from which he preached to the locals in the area.[3] This small assembly contained enough consistent worshippers to

THE 20TH CENTURY

give some permanence to the settlement, and Casey built a log and mud cabin which served as the first permanent community church. A strong community spirit developed which was centered upon the church. It was isolated to a large extent, and became almost entirely self-sufficient. By 1970 the Casey settlement was being replaced by hundreds of homes and apartments that make up Foxborough subdivision.

Casey was bounded on three sides by roads. South Carolina State Highway 176 was, in the late 1930's, a dirt road. On that road, near where Highway 52 and Highway 176 intersected, was a grist mill that serviced the community for many years. Highway 52 was a single lane base-rock road until the late 1930's. The Old Moncks Corner Road was Casey's main thoroughfare. Casey was landmarked by a number of structures that in many ways symbolized the values of the black settlement. The old Casey church was a beautiful white wooden building which replaced the earlier log structure. It was not unusual to find more than a hundred worshippers in the congregation on Sunday morning. The church's foundation can still be found near the Old Moncks Corner Road next to the Casey cemetery. The church was destroyed by arson in 1977. The Casey cemetery contains dozens of grave sites; the silent stone reminders of the Casey people of bygone days. There is an impressive stone and monument to the church which reads:

> In Loving Remembrance / Our Dearly Beloved Pastor / Reverend Wm. Evans / The Founder of Caice [Casey] Church / Born in 1822./ Died in 1887 / Aged 65 years. / Servant of God well Done / Thy Glorious Warfare is Past / The Battle Fought, The Race is Won / And Thou Art Crowned at Last.

Next to the church stood the Casey school house. This wooden structure was the sole source of local education for the black scholars during the many decades of segregation. A chimney remains where the three-room school once stood.

Across the Old Moncks Corner Road from the church stood the Casey fellowship hall where many of the community decisions were made after lively debates. "Sanctified people" would have revivals there upon payment of an appropriate fee.[4] Not far from there stood a second smaller assembly hall. Here large groups would crowd inside to make community decisions and plan projects. Scattered within a short walking distance of the church were the several dozen homes where the people of Casey raised their families.

Mrs. Loretta Parsons came to Casey in 1930 at the age of nine, and spent her life in the rural environs of Casey and Mt. Holly. Her favorite memories are of the Old Moncks Corner Road, the bubbling spring, and the places where she played as a child. From these memories it seems that Old Moncks Corner Road has since lost most of its splendor. It was once a country avenue with a natural green median between the carriage ruts. A green tunnel of foliage unfolded overhead and kept the road cool and breezy in the summer. Just a few yards from the eastern side of the road was a natural spring which fed a land-locked pond. It was a favorite fishing spot and offered cool, bubbling refreshment. The spring water was brought to the church and homes daily.

Some of Mrs. Parsons' favorite memories are of the church services. Sunday service was a day-long event. Morning and evening services were attended by dozens of worshippers who, prior to the late 1940's, arrived by horse and buggy or on foot. The residents put on their best clothes and behavior for their favorite day of the week. The second Sunday in June was Children's Day in Casey. On this day children came from as far as Summerville and Moncks Corner, many on wagons lined with boards for bench seats. The typical Sunday picnic was made special that day with plenty of lemonade, cookies, cakes and covered dishes. Meals were cooked over a wood-burning stove in the Friendship Hall near the church.

An early, full-time minister to the African Methodist Episcopal Church at Casey was Reverend Hayward from Sumter.[5] Arriving by train at Mt. Holly, he served the church for approximately twelve years during the 1930's and 1940's. Reverend C.J. Mack succeeded Reverend Hayward, and was succeeded by Reverend Pyatt. Reverend Pyatt's ministry was tainted by a fund-raising problem. It may have been little more than a bookkeeping error, but some contended that all of the money raised for the rehabilitation of the church was not spent in the proper manner.[6] The church was rebuilt to some extent at that time. It was a large structure with stained glass windows, a chorus loft and a beautiful ministry platform.

Some of the most frequent worshippers at Casey were Elizabeth Salley, C.J. Bryant, Pauline Gourdine, Wooford Johnson, Frank and Willie Mae Cohens, Frank Sass, Sr., Janie Mae Bryant Jefferson and their families.

THE 20TH CENTURY

The Casey school was the only local institution of formal education. It was open two months before and two months after Christmas, with some classes also conducted in the meeting hall. Mrs. Sadie Franklin, Mrs. Nathalie Chisolm and Mrs. Earlene Jefferson taught at Casey. These educators were still well-respected teachers in the Goose Creek public schools in the late 1970's. Children from the black communities at what is today Boulder Bluff, Mt. Holly and Liberty Hall, walked to Casey school.[7] A small school on Howe Hall Road served the children of that section, and at one time there was a one-room school at Bowens Corner. There was also a school for black children at Grove Hall about three miles from Casey and a place for "mixed blood" children at Varner School on Highway 17A.[8]

The schools in these communities were the product of cooperative efforts. The teachers provided all social services from the school house. Men like the Reverend James Harris, supervisory principal at Casey, directed the entire social service program for the isolated community. Educators worked to improve health and road conditions, and worked with church men to revitalize or organize the local church.[9] The teachers were second in community importance only to the church minister.

Students wishing to attend secondary schools had to board with friends or relatives in Moncks Corner or Charleston. A 15-mile bus ride to either locale cost 20¢, making such arrangements much too expensive for students. The Berkeley Training High School in Moncks Corner was started in 1921, and the building housing it was enlarged from time to time as admission applications increased. Under the supervision of Principal R.E. Ready the school became an important Berkeley County educational institution.[10] Rural educational services were greatly improved in 1954. At that time the schools at Casey, Grove Hall, Howe Hall and Bowens Corner were combined and the students served by a new school built on Howe Hall Road. Mr. L.C. Mahoney served as the first principal of the new Howe Hall school.[11] Many Casey graduates attended Berkeley Training School and are making contributions to contemporary Goose Creek. Casey school burned in 1966, this being the seemingly usual fate of most old Goose Creek structures.

The Goose Creek subsection was nearly self-supporting.

HISTORIC GOOSE CREEK

Almost all necessities of life were produced locally. Wheat, cotton, peanuts, hay, rice, sugar cane, tobacco, corn and almost every variety of garden vegetable were grown. Work was available producing pulpwood, firewood and timber. Phosphate mining in Mt. Holly and nearby was a profitable business until the discovery of more easily mined deposits in Florida. Phosphate beds were bountiful in the Goose Creek, Back River and Foster Creek areas. Phosphate of lime was a valuable agricultural fertilizer but needed large amounts of manual labor to extract it.[12] The Mt. Holly Clay Products Co. produced brick. This and the North Eastern Railroad Company were essential businesses in Mt. Holly.

Other Goose Creek inhabitants made a livelihood at numerous tasks. Mr. C.J. Bryant, Sr., made caskets and tombstones. He was also a balcksmith who shod horses, made wagon wheels and fashioned metal into hinges and hardware.[13] Like most, he farmed a small plot of land. Joseph Bryant was the "week-end butcher." He delivered meat on the weekends, travelling from home to home.[14]

A large labor force was also needed to dig a tunnel more than two miles long from Back River to Goose Creek to supply water to the Goose Creek reservoir. One Mt. Holly man was employed as an oxen driver to move tons of marl and clay from the tunnel. Making corn whiskey was also a lucrative business in Goose Creek.[15]

Black Goose Creekers relied on each other and the products of the land for substenance. Neighbors, family and hard work were the most important ingredients to community life. Three gun shots in the air meant "emergency" and all the residents would do their part of fighting a fire or assisting an injured neighbor. The Goose Creekers relied on their own resources for medical care, but when absolutely necessary they would travel the 20 miles to Charleston or 15 miles to Moncks Corner for medical assistance.

Despite the lack of medical facilities, and despite the claim that health was considerably better during those days, people did get sick, and were forced to rely on natural medicines. What resulted was a considerable repertoire of homemade cures. For sore throats, the swamp spanish oak was a sure cure. "My grandmother would chop it off, steep it with alum. It was a good gargle for sore throats," recalls one Goose Creeker. "It was good for you, but I hated the stuff

THE 20TH CENTURY

because it would tie up your mouth."[16]

For stomach aches and pains and bad colds, the plant called "rabbit tobacco" or blackroot was a common cure. It would be dug up, washed and then boiled. The boiled mash was allowed to steep and settle. A tea from the juice was sipped until it brought relief.

One of the most common trees in Goose Creek was the swamp willow or Coastal Plain willow. Most Goose Creek homes kept one planted at the chimney corner of the home. It was steeped to make a "stump drink" and used as a common remedy from fever and dysentery. Dysentery was also relieved by sipping blackberry juice, a tea made of strawberry leaves or a tea made from the bark of a persimmon tree. Willow tree tea was the most common cure. "It cures the dysentery nine times out of ten," it was said.[17]

For babies with hives or colic, catnip tea was prescribed. Catnip grew in small bunches in many yards, and a tea was made from it by boiling the leaves, which induced sleep. The heartleaf or snakeroot grew with a long winding root, which was coiled and placed into a jar with whiskey. After sitting for a time the brew could be sipped for backache, aches and pain from colds or rheumatism. For vomiting, high blood pressure or gas pains, garlic, commonly called "wild leek," was helpful. The bulb was cut up and placed in a jar with red vinegar, lemon juice and epsom salts. It was also used for cooking. Medicinal treatment was a seasonal practice. Every change of season the children (and consenting adults) received a fair amount of homemade medicine to prepare them for the new season. Home remedies provided for "clean stomachs, clean bowels and clean blood."[18]

In addition to the medicinal qualities of the natural products of the woods and marsh, many cooking uses were found for them. Herbs, roots and leaves of the Goose Creek countryside added spice to the local dinner table. Sassafras tea was kept handy in a bag in most kitchens. No stew or soup was complete without a bit of "pot magic." This small brown root was cooked with other foods to enhance the flavor. Poke weed or poke salad was an herb with palatable leaves, and was cooked while tender and young. Wild asparagus or smilox can still be found along the sides of the old Moncks Corner Road and elsewhere in Goose Creek. This climbing vine was eaten cooked as a vegetable or made into soup. Wild asparagus and "pot magic" can still be purchased from the roadside vegetable vendors in Charleston.

Goose Creek supported several general stores during this period. Cannon's store was the only store in Goose Creek proper,[19] and was located near the entrance to the Oaks Plantation. Although no longer in use, it still stands today (1981) as a reminder to passing motorists. At Mt. Holly was the Morning Star Grocery and Kodoma's Store. George and Eloise Gowder purchased the grocery from Tom Addison in 1946. They owned and managed the store for ten years.[20] Tokyo Kodoma and his family lived on the second floor over their store located near the Morning Star Grocery. This same Japanese family lived on Marrington Plantation for many years before it became part of the Naval Weapons Station.[21] Another store was located at the Mt. Holly Post Office under the management of Mrs. Hilma Watkins. Mrs. C.B. Linder managed the post office and also the store for many years. Orven and Anne Thomason operated Thomason's Store from 1946 to 1971. It is located on the corner of Highway 176 and Thomason Boulevard.

The general stores of Goose Creek were multi-purpose establishments. Besides providing the various groceries and hardwares, the stores marketed much of the locally-grown produce. The owners were also sought to provide legal and medical advice and family counselling.[22] Often the store's owner had the only means of motorized transportation. The vehicle served as an ambulance in case of emergencies and carried many mothers to the hospital when childbirth was too difficult for the "grannys" or midwives.

A small collection of white families made up the Mt. Holly subsection of Goose Creek. James A. Hargroves, Sr., resided at the Mt. Holly plantation house owned by Smith Richardson.[23] Walter Dangerfield lived and worked at Mt. Holly as the section railroad foreman. The Wade family resided at the Montague plantation house. The remains of this house can still be found under large oaks east of the Boulder Bluff subdivision. The house burned in 1977. Although the white community was well entrenched, their numbers were too small to support churches or schools. The families travelled to Summerville, Moncks Corner, Deer Park or the north area of Charleston for religious services. White children attended school in Moncks Corner.

THE 20TH CENTURY

The ladies of Mt. Holly organized the Mt. Holly Home Demonstration Club that was well and frequently attended for many years. The clubhouse remained until it was demolished for its lumber in 1979. The club members participated in arts and crafts, chair caning, rug making, exchanging recipes and preserving techniques. The ladies had similar activities through the Mt. Holly 4-H organization. Mrs. Elizabeth Boykin coordinated the Home Demonstration Club for many years. Some of the more active members were Mrs. C.B. Linder, Mrs. D.T. Rhoad, Mrs. W.B. Nix, Mrs. G.W. Dangerfield, Mrs. Scarborough, and Mrs. Alma Brown.[24]

The white families of Mt. Holly were few in number but represented the most significant white community in Goose Creek. Some of the families were Mr. and Mrs. C.B. Linder, Mr. and Mrs. J.R. Cannon, Mr. and Mrs. J.A. Hoyle, Mr. and Mrs. J.H. Dangerfield, Mr. and Mrs. G.W. Dangerfield, Mr. and Mrs. W.E. McKenzie, Mr. and Mrs. Waring Bunch, Mr. and Mrs. G.B. Cannon, and Mr. and Mrs. B.W. Mixon.[25]

A reminder of the small white community is the private burial site at Droze cemetery, located on Highway 176 about one half mile from Foxborough subdivision. The markers here are of Goose Creekers of the post-Civil War and 20th century. The cemetery is protected by a fence and is approached by a dirt road that leads to two brick pillars and an iron gate. The right brick pillar has a slab with the inscription: "The Droze Cemetery, 1861." The left is inscribed, "Memorial of W.J. Brown, 1913." Many of the Brown family are interred here.

On November 5, 1941, just more than a month prior to the Japanese attack on Pearl Harbor, the United States Ammunition Depot was established. Throughout World War II, the depot was engaged in receiving ammunition from assembly plants, storing, performing maintenance on and issuing it. After the war, the depot handled fleet returns from ships being deactivated. In February 1950, the depot was placed in a "partial maintenance" status, but due to the Korean conflict, it changed to active and full operations resumed. The activities of the depot continued to expand during the 1950's and the civilian community increased nearby. "Liberty Hall Annex" was acquired from the U.S. Army in 1954. This area contained 5,219 acres and later became the Naval Weapons Annex.

HISTORIC GOOSE CREEK

In 1956, U.S. Naval Guided Missile Service Unit 213 was established for the support of Fleet and Marine Corps requirements for the Terrier missile. The Marine Barracks was later established, and in April of 1959 the Naval Weapons Annex was established in support of the Polaris Fleet Ballistic Missile Weapons System.

In addition to playing a vital role in nation defense, the expansion of the federal installation caused an influx of civilian and military personnel. This was the beginning of a new Goose Creek. In the early 1960's the farm lands began to be subdivided to provide housing for the new arrivals.

The population increased quickly during the 1960's. In 1969, Goose Creek was the fastest-growing area in the United States according to a survey.[26] That year Goose Creek experienced a 58% population increase.[27] During the 1960's, millions of investment dollars flowed to the new industrial complex at Bushy Park near Goose Creek, bringing subsequent secondary commercial and residential demands.

During this decade of transition, Goose Creek showed a need for community leadership. Its new residents were in no position to take charge of the decision-making for the community to which they had so recently arrived. The officials in the county seat were more than 15 miles from the area and seemed to give little attention to the haphazard development of their neighbor community. The few established residents of Goose Creek appeared to have been overwhelmed by the magnitude of it all. As a consequence of the lack of planning and leadership, a very poor foundation of public service was provided.

A substandard water and wastewater system was installed. The road-sides began to be cluttered by unsightly household trash and debris due to the lack of sanitation services. The county roads were overcrowded with new traffic and the newly arrived populace found fire and police service inadequate. Even electrical and phone service had trouble keeping pace.

Some much needed leaderhsip began to surface from the "Old Goose Creek" faction. Men like Waring Bunch, Jack Etling, J.B. Brown, Jr., Lonnie B. Holland, Edgar Neis, Edgar Anderson and Edgar Binnar started pulling local talents together to explore solutions to the problems at hand. Through their efforts a section of the greater Goose Creek

THE 20TH CENTURY

area incorporated on March 22, 1961.[28] The first mayor was Hilton W. Bunch.

From a modest beginning evolved a city which was to become the population center of Berkeley County. Within ten years after the incorporation, the population numbered more than 6,000. From 1958 to 1968, an average of ten families a week moved into Goose Creek. A special census in 1968 revealed that the city's population had tripled in ten years.[29] The Naval Weapons Station was annexed in 1978. The city became the largest and most populated municipality in Berkeley County, with nearly 17,000 residents.[30] The problems confronted by the young city in the 1960's were monumental to the city fathers of that time. It seems that from the onset the city had a disproportionate share of problems and a considerable amount of publicity.

The lack of public services and facilities presented formidable obstacles to the young city, and the shortage of operating revenue compounded matters. The first city revenue came from fines collected for charges of disturbing the peace. An auto accident at the intersection of Highways 52 and 176 resulted in one injured party and ambulances from two different private ambulance companies. The Goose Creek Police Department fined the ambulance drivers for arguing and fighting over the right to transport the injured motorist.[32]

The city had only one policeman during the early years. He had no radio in his cruiser and relied on his wife to relay messages. She would take police calls at her home and tie a white cloth on the front door knob to signal the passing cruiser.[33] Such communication problems resulted in some alarming events. On New Year's Eve, 1964, a very serious auto accident resulted in a number of dead and injured being thrown onto the highway. The unlit road and an unusually dark night made it difficult for oncoming traffic to avoid hitting the victims as they lay in the road. This incredible problem persisted until the South Carolina State Highway Patrol was summoned from a private phone.[33]

The young city was confronted with problems unheard of today, but the early city fathers held the city together, often acting above and beyond the call of duty. City leaders personally co-signed a loan to purchase the first police cruiser and signed again to bond some city employees and to purchase a fire truck.[35] With few financial resources, progress was slow, but the city was to endure.

Compounding the city's problems was bad publicity. Goose Creek was singled out by the American Automobile Association as one of the 38 places in the United States where members were warned to "exercise extreme caution."[36] A heated verbal battle ensued between Goose Creek and the American Automobile Association when the organization's report claimed that motorists had a likely chance of getting a traffic ticket. The controversy was given considerable publicity, and the city's only policeman, Weyman Turner, resigned as a result.

A controversy which centered around poor water and wastewater service resulted in a number of local meetings of disgruntled water customers. It was from these meetings that the leadership of Malvin Mann evolved. He arrived in Goose Creek from John's Island in 1963, served as mayor of the city for four terms and came to be known by some as Goose Creek's "controversial mayor."[37]

Malvin Mann was born in Independence, Missouri in 1927. After serving in the Air Force he settled in South Carolina, selling office furniture and supplies. He became interested in Goose Creek politics shortly after his arrival, because in his words "I was alarmed over some political figures I believed were harmful to Goose Creek."[38]
Mann worked as campaign manager for Goose Creek's second mayor, Smith Hinnant. He also served as president of the Goose Creek Civic Club and was an active participant in the American Legion. The Civic Club bought the first radio system for the Goose Creek Police Department and played an important role in coordinating the young city.[39]

Mann's first bid for political office was unsuccessful. He was defeated by Hattie Turner in the race to fill the vacated council seat of Kelly Curtis. Mr. Curtis had resigned for reasons of health.[40] This was the last time Mann would see defeat until his bid for his fifth mayoral term in 1978.

Malvin Mann rose to political leadership during the years of turmoil. He recalled when the early Council meetings were quite disruptive or, in his words, "rousing."[41] He said the city officials would have "fist fights and would slap each other around pretty good."[42] The minutes of the meetings record none of these disruptions, but time and time again

THE 20TH CENTURY

controversy would cloud the business at hand.

Although Malvin Mann supported Smith Hinnant in his successful bid for mayor in 1964, Mann later opposed him. When Hinnant ran for mayor in 1966, Mann lost faith in him and refused to offer support.[43] Malvin Mann entered the mayoral race in 1968 against Smith Hinnant and Oliver Yon, and won easily.

He remembers his first term as mayor as being a difficult one. He was faced with a city that was badly in debt, had made little progress toward solving the water and sewer problems and had already begun to receive bad publicity. In 1968 the police department consisted of two men, two badly worn cruisers and a police headquarters that was little more than a shanty.

A new police cruiser had been ordered, but the city had no money or credit to pay for it. Mayor Mann and Councilman Earl Bounds co-signed a bank loan to make the purchase.[44] Additional revenue was found when Mayor Mann ordered a special census in 1968 which increased city revenue from the state's wine and liquor rebates.

Mayor Mann provided strong and dynamic leadership for the troubled city, but his methods were often questioned, and time and time again controversy arose in regard to his office. No doubt many rebuked the mayor's efforts to lead the development of the city, and on more than one occasion the city council called for Mann's resignation. Despite the differing opinions relative to the "controversial Mayor," the City of Goose Creek continued to improve its municipal services. Few can deny the sincerity of Malvin Mann and his good intentions to improve the living conditions in Goose Creek. He admitted his personal attraction for trouble but claimed that it "rolled off my back like water off a drake."[45]

From his earliest days as mayor, Mann confronted a well known Goose Creek developer, S.E. "Speedy" Felkel. As mayor, Mann became a vocal protestor of the severe water and wastewater problems. He began meeting with Senator Rembert C. Dennis to explore ways of improving the system. Mayor Mann investigated ways for the city to purchase the private water company, and also considered purchasing water from Charleston instead of relying on the Goose Creek wells. This immediately put Malvin Mann and Speedy Felkel at odds. Felkel would not support Mann in his race for mayor and saw the mayor's opposition as being politically motivated. This was only one of Malvin Mann's controversial confrontations. He had some bad luck prior to the 1972 election which made the Charleston papers.[46] The paper reported: "Mann's inordinate ability to land on his feet in the wake of ominous controversy didn't work so well last year during an incident at the American Legion Post in Goose Creek!! The city's mayor said or did something that caused the Air Force sergeant to strike the mayor with considerable force .... A lot of people say I was involved in a barroom brawl," the mayor said, "It was over in less than five seconds and brawls usually last much longer." The incident resulted in the mayor being injured and losing sight in one eye.

There was also controversy involving Mann's influence in the operation of the police department. An investigation by the South Carolina Law Enforcement Division was requested by Charleston attorney J. Lawrence Duffy. In his letter to Governor John West, Duffy sited a "grave and serious problem in the Goose Creek area" involving the "mayor and the law enforcement of that city."[47] The S.L.E.D. investigation found no evidence of wrongdoing, and Governor West terminated the investigation after a short time.

What resulted from the investigation was the resignation of the city's police chief, James L. Hood. He blamed the mayor's order to cease issuing citations for driving under the influence of intoxicants.[48] Mayor Mann fired police captain Marion Wilson at the same time as the Chief's resignation for, in the mayor's words, "keeping the police department in a constant state of confusion and discontent."[49]

A request for another investigation was made in 1972 by Mrs. Margaret Herring, City Clerk-Treasurer. She was fired by Mayor Mann and, upon termination, made a number of public accusations. Mrs. Herring accused the mayor of favoritism in levying sanitation charges, mismanagement of the city's police retirement fund and unethical land transactions between the city and private citizens.[50] This 1972 controversy resulted in a petition signed by 250 citizens calling for the removal of Mayor Mann from office for "conduct generally unbecoming to a Mayor."[51] The city recorder, Carl Barrs, defended the mayor, refusing to acknowledge the validity of the impeachment petition.

THE 20TH CENTURY

This controversy was followed in 1973 with a request from City Council for the voluntary resignation of the Mayor. Councilmen William E. Infinger and Thomas G. Poor asked the mayor to resign during an executive session of Council. Infinger alleged that the mayor had reneged on an unwritten agreement with Council to refrain from interfering with police and court activities.[52] Mann refused to resign but Council did not act further on the matter. Malvin Mann did not run for office in 1974 but was returned by an overwhelming victory in 1976 for another two-year term. He was elected mayor four times and served during some of the most troubled years of municipal development.

Malvin Mann was instrumental in the expansion of the municipal boundaries. In 1970, Foxborough subdivision was annexed to the city and Boulder Bluff was annexed in June of 1971. Boulder Bluff added 2,000 to the municipality, but only temporarily. The Boulder Bluff annexation was opposed from the onset by Mr. Loring E. Van Kleek, who worked for the establishment of a Public Service District in lieu of annexation.[53] Harold L. Elrod brought a successful suit against the annexation, claiming that the annexed territory was greater than 25% of the municipal territory and was thus in violation of the state annexation laws.[54] Boulder Bluff was successfully annexed in 1977 in a second election.

Perhaps the most controversial issue in 20th century Goose Creek was the problems resulting from poor water and wastewater services. These problems surfaced time and time again as major political issues and were unquestionably a constant worry to the city officials. The beginning of this problem can be traced to the construction of Forest Lawn subdivision. In 1958, Forest Lawn was the only residential area in Goose Creek except for a few homes at Maple Ridge. Forest Lawn was a necessary addition to rural Goose Creek. Homes were much in demand for the military and civil servants arriving daily. Forest Lawn residents began to experience problems that were to reappear as subdivisions inched across the sleepy rural Goose Creek community. The crux of the problem is found approximately 20 feet below the soil surface, where there is a heavy stratum of marl. The Goose Creek marl is a firm but porous yellow substance containing a high percentage of carbonate of lime.[55] The marl strata are the same phosphate beds which provided a livelihood for many Goose Creekers during the 1930's and 1940's. The new residents found it extremely difficult to dig good wells or provide septic disposal of wastewater in the clay and marl soils of Goose Creek. Thus, from the onset there was a need for a water and wastewater disposal system.

It was S.E. "Speedy" Felkel who took the lead in the water and wastewater business in Goose Creek. Felkel embarked upon his Goose Creek development venture on August 13, 1956 when he purchased 126 acres of land.[56] He went into lot promotion and sales with Forest Lawn as his first project. With help from the Farmers Home Administration, he designed a water system in 1959, which he named Coastal Water Company.[57] That was the same year the state's General Assembly passed legislation permitting the operation of private wastewater companies. "Speedy" Felkel built the first private system in South Carolina.[58]

Demand for service was high. Felkel extended his services to accommodate the new Boulder Bluff subdivision and soon extended his service lines into the incorporated limits of the City of Goose Creek. The city explored the possibilities of starting a publicly owned system, but lacked sufficient assessed valuation to borrow the money. Thus, the new Camelot subdivision relied on Felkel's company for service. Similar needs caused Felkel's system to extend into other parts of the city.

The first of a number of serious problems for Mr. Felkel resulted when a Small Business Administration loan was disapproved. The extended lines were already in the ground, short term notes were coming due and new construction had already begun to be dependent of Felkel's lines.[59] The system's problems were compounded when city residents were not required to tap on to the private system. Many did not and continued to rely on numerous substandard wells and septic tanks. Mr. Felkel was not able to amortize the loans to the company.[60] As the Goose Creek area developed, the private water and wastewater system became unable to accommodate the number of users, and the fees paid by the customers were inadequate to provide needed maintenance.

Despite the increasing inadequacy of the private system, Mr. Felkel received considerable praise from the Goose Creek City officials and residents during the first eight years of the

THE 20TH CENTURY

1960's. The phenomenal growth which so characterized Goose Creek during the 1960's would have been unlikely without Felkel's services. But this rapid suburbanization, coupled with the lack of sufficient revenues, soon overburdened the system to the point that customer complaints became commonplace.

Water and sewer problems became a central political issue in the 1968 general election, and Goose Creek was the scene of heated local battles.[61] Republican Lloyd E. Sineath, Democrat Rembert C. Dennis and Independent W.A. Barnette were all senatorial candidates in 1968. The Republicans had the majority of the low country senate seats and feared that if Rembert Dennis was re-elected, the Republicans would lose their dominance in the Charleston area. Goose Creek was ready-made for the Republican purpose, and Lloyd Sineath entered the race with great vigor. The water and wastewater issue became volatile and mobilized the local residents.

Senator Rembert Dennis gave Goose Creek its first statewide coverage when he called for an investigation by the South Carolina Public Service Commission.[62] Lloyd Sineath appeared before numerous civic clubs in Goose Creek and blamed Senator Dennis for the belated call to the Public Service Commission for assistance. Sineath also verbally attacked Senator Ernest F. Hollings for his inattentive service to troubled Goose Creek. Senator Dennis was re-elected. The controversy continued.

The Goose Creek citizenry was quite vocal in the months following the election. In the Charleston *News and Courier* of May 27, 1969, Mr. Ed Caffrey aptly expressed the frustrations of many local residents when he wrote:

> In reply to Mrs. Taylor of Goose Creek, I would like to inform her that she is mistaken about the cost of water in our area. It isn't, "all the water you can use for $3.00 per month." It is really, "all the water you can get for $3.00, and in our area that isn't much."

Community groups assembled to seek solutions and to voice complaints, many of which were aimed at Mr. Felkel. Mayor Malvin Mann used the community forums to unify the citizenry with a common concern. Mann reported the presence of raw sewage in ditches, and of low water pressure. Mr. Felkel blamed Malvin Mann's political motivations for the perpetuation of the inflamed controversy. He stated "if it weren't for Coastal Water Company, Goose Creek still would be a country cross roads."[63] Felkel repeatedly contended that he was "primarily interested in the betterment of Goose Creek and the continued further development of the area."[64] The political motivation, he contended, was due to his refusal to support Malvin Mann in his bid for mayor, and Mann in turn had inflamed the citizenry against him.

Despite the controversy associated with Mr. Felkel, there were many in Goose Creek who greatly respected him and admired his acts of generosity. Felkel Field is a large playground named after him, and a popular gathering place for hundreds of baseball and softball enthusiasts. He gave six acres of property to the Greater Goose Creek Parks and Playground Commission and two acres to the Beverly Hills Civic Club.

In 1969 the people of Goose Creek received some assistance from the South Carolina Public Service Commission, which began imposing a $100 a day fine on the company for failing to comply with the Commission's orders.[65] In August, 1969, a $1,000 fine was imposed on the company for being late with a promised engineering study, yet most remained displeased with the P.S.C. direction. On October 17, 1969 the Charleston *News and Courier* reported that many Goose Creekers were enraged at the "inactivity and partiality" of the South Carolina Public Service Commission in its handling of the water company.

Representatives from four housing subdivisions near Goose Creek mailed letters to Governor Robert E. McNair requesting an audience with him to discuss an acute shortage of potable water. One letter stated that they had "lost faith in the South Carolina Public Service Commission." The same letter also stated that "during the past year, the residents have sought help from state and local health authorities, local politicians and the South Carolina Public Service Commission."[66] The subdivision representatives were concerned with the possibility that the Veterans Administration and Farmers Home Administration might resume granting loans. New construction meant additional water service burdens, and was dreaded by many Goose Creekers. In response to requests, Governor McNair met with Goose Creek residents and promised to take action to relieve the water

THE 20TH CENTURY

problems. Two weeks later, on July 14, 1969, the Carolina Water Company was called before the P.S.C. to show cause why its certificates to do business in Goose Creek should not be revoked.

The community began to organize its protest. A three man committee was formed to answer complaints and to enforce health standards. Only about half of the faulty water and wastewater system was in the incorporated city limits. Mr. C.W. Whatley, member of City Council, represented the city on the committee. Mr. R. Harold Tyner represented the area builders and Don Walling represented Coastal Water Company.[67] The committee called for a federal investigation in addition to the probing work of the State Public Service Commission.

A federal report from the Federal Housing Authority cited "certain deficiencies" in the Coastal Water Company's water and sewer system and required that no F.H.A. or V.A. loans for new construction be allowed in the Goose Creek area until health authorities certified the presence of adequate water and wastewater service.

Dr. Cecil Jacobs, district health director, declared four subdivisions in Goose Creek "a public health hazard and a public health nuisance."[68] He said, "I saw homes with yards four to six inches deep in sewerage, children's tricycles, trucks and other toys were floating in or covered by raw sewerage." He continued, "the potential for transmission of disease to children and adults is as great as any situation I have witnessed in this country." Speedy Felkel stated, "With all the publicity, you get a lot of hot-heads and it's hard to control them." Felkel cited system sabotage as a cause for some of the problems. He also cited political complexities for the exaggeration of the crisis. He continued, "another problem we have is a bunch of publicity-crazed town councilmen." "I think we just supported the wrong man for mayor."[69] Coastal Water Company attempted to remedy the water problem by connecting the Goose Creek system to a twelve inch water main of the Charleston Commission of Public Works for an "emergency supply" of water to insure uninterrupted service.

Charleston lawmakers became involved with the Goose Creek problem when it became obvious that the Public Service Commission had not been successful in preventing the flow of wastewater into the Goose Creek water reservoir. The Charleston delegation was successful in having the Coastal Water Company put into receivership. Bartley J. Riddock became the receiver for the company and immediately surveyed the conditions of the system. Bartley J. Riddock reported that "he could not overemphasize the emergency of the situation that exists here." A report written for the water company by an engineering firm reported to Riddock that "Frankly, the things I have seen are almost unbelieveable. There is almost no way to describe the condition of the system as it now exists. The health hazard is so acute that I cannot understand why there is not an epidemic . . . ."[70] Some improvements were made with the company while it was in receivership, but it was soon returned to the private stockholders. The water and wastewater company was reorganized under the name of Southeastern Water Corporation. The reorganization included severing company ties with Felkel, and a strict reporting system to the Public Service Commission was established.[71]

Mayor Mann filed a petition with Berkeley County which called for a special election to give city authorities permission to own a water and sewer system. The town Council passed a resolution nullifying the proceeding of the town's prior administrations which gave Coastal Water Company an exclusive five year contract to operate within the town's boundary. The company's franchise was disaffirmed by Council's action. During this same period Foxborough subdivision had protested the annexation of their 74 acre subdivision tract. The protest was withdrawn, however, when the City of Goose Creek agreed to allow the subdivision to provide its own sewer system and purchase water from Charleston Commission of Public Works.

Under the leadership of Mayor Malvin Mann and the City Council the city continued to work for a municipally-owned water and sewer system. The Mayor hoped to issue $800,000 in municipal general obligation bonds to purchase the private system. The bond issue was approved by a referendum but was contested in court. Mayor Mann was not successful in seeing the purchase of the system through during his 1972-74 term. He did outline what he believed to be a workable plan and stressed the need for the city to purchase the private system. He did not wish for the Goose

THE 20TH CENTURY

Creek system to be absorbed by the Charleston Commission of Public Works, but he did believe that the system should be tied into the Commission-owned mains and that the city pay for the main extension over a period of time.

Malvin Mann did not seek the Mayor's office in the spring of 1974. James M. Richards was elected, and served only one two-year term as Mayor. He brought a great deal of personal energy and farsightedness to city hall. His contributions, however, were overshadowed by a heated controversy over the city's purchase of the troubled water system. This controversy had waned for many years and the city's political struggles had hampered any consistent improvements in the situation. Richards, upon taking office stated that the "time had come to inject some method into the madness."[72] His method involved a frontal assault upon the most pressing municipal problem, and the new mayor went to work to carry through the purchase of the beleaguered water system.

The new city-owned system was eligible for federal assistance through various environmental and community development grants, but the Mayor received mixed support from the general public. The city was little prepared to expertly manage or finance an area-wide water and wastewater system. Municipal bonds were sold to purchase the system, but little financial support was immediately available for day-to-day system operations. Consequently, problems began to arise regarding maintenance of the system. The long-awaited improvements did not come the first year and the understandably impatient customers shifted their complaints from the private to the public officials in charge. In addition, the city-owned system had to be paid for with higher user rates. Customer frustration became more severe as the 1976 election approached.

Again, Malvin Mann returned to office in the wake of controversy surrounding the water system. The veteran mayor began his fourth term with what he said was "an inexperienced City Council."[73] It was another controversial term of office for Mann. In 1977 the mayor was released on a $2,000 bond after being served with a warrant charging him with harrassment. The charges were later dropped when a jury of the General Sessions Court could not reach an agreement.[74] The next year the mayor threatened to resign be-

cause of a police department dispute. Later his efforts to terminate the police chief were rebuked by Council.[75]
Despite the controversy which found its way to the newspapers, the city prospered and began attracting new residents and businesses.

In October, 1976, the South Carolina Department of Health and Environmental Control (DHEC) declared Goose Creek a "severe and urgent health hazard" because of its substandard and inadequate water and sewerage systems. As a result, the DHEC imposed a moratorium on new water and sewer taps onto the city-owned system. The 1976 moratorium was the accumulation of more than a dozen years of problems.

Several actions have been taken since 1976 to address the problem. The DHEC declared Goose Creek the number one priority statewide for EPA 201 Phase I wastewater facilities construction grants. The city borrowed its 25% share of the $1.3 million total Phase I construction package and rehabilitation began. Today, Goose Creek remains the only city in South Carolina that has to gain prior approval by the DHEC before accepting new water customers.

The election of Mayor Michael J. Heitzler and his six city council running-mates in May of 1978 brought what many thought was a sense of stability to the turbulent political arena. The city government which for many years had been divided on many issues was now represented by seven city officials who professed a unity of philosophy and purpose. In addition, the new Mayor was elected for a four year term for the first time in the city's history, and the six council members were elected for two and four year terms depending on the number of votes received. The longer term of office contributed to the stability of the local government.

The City of Goose Creek began reorganizing in 1978 in preparation for the demands of the 1980's. The mission of the city officials was to provide efficient municipal service in a most cost effective manner. They recognize the need to consolidate the greater Goose Creek area through annexation of the unincorporated areas. There was a conspicuous need for public service in the unincorporated areas. As ur-

THE 20TH CENTURY

banization continued, the need of adequate public safety, planning and zoning and public health becomes of paramount importance. Consolidation is needed to insure planned and orderly growth.

Consolidation through annexation remained the central theme of the Heitzler administration. The Naval Weapons Station, the Polaris Missile Facility and the Woodlawn Heights subdivision were annexed in December of 1978. The consolidation efforts were slowed in the Fall of 1979 when the city's efforts to annex the Holly Court subdivision and the Bushy Park Industrial Park were thwarted by a lawsuit by the Bushy Park industrialists.

Consolidation is one way to improve the cost effectiveness of the municipal service and a method to counteract the efforts of inflation on municipal budgets. If consolidation is accomplished, Goose Creek may emerge as one of the larger and more prosperous municipalities in the state. This success depends, in a large measure, on the willingness of the Goose Creek people to unify their resources and to recognize and meet their communal responsibilities in the 1980's.

The history of the Goose Creek community in the 20th century is one of striking contrasts. Goose Creek during the first 50 years of this century was a poorly-defined collection of small, black, rural settlements. The same community experienced dramatic changes during the 1950's, 1960's and 1970's. The economic boom following World War II and the installation of military bases on the worn plantation lands brought new residents, new money, and new business. A small section of the greater Goose Creek area incorporated into a municipality in 1961 to become the political focal point of the area. The new municipality provided the forum through which residents dealt with local issues and began to develop adequate public service facilities such as water, sewer, sanitation and public safety service.

Goose Creek withstood the problems of rapid change on repeated occasions. Especially during the two decades from 1960-1980, the problems caused by the sheer numbers of expanding population have resulted in political battles which brought the townspeople to the polls. Yet it wasn't just numbers that complicated politics. Most of the residents of Goose Creek were from outside of the community. The population is composed of a great variety of residents with varied backgrounds, cultures, educations and ethnic origins. Diverse backgrounds made it difficult for the electorate to reach concensus on many issues.

It is not only the people who are responsible for the development of a community. Natural forces have had, and are still having impact on local development. The creek from which the community derives its name and the surrounding river system has been the single most important influence on the development of the area. The same waters which led the earliest colonists to settle and prosper are, in the latter half of the 20th century, the primary attractions to modern industry. Through the careful planning on the county and state levels, modern industry began to find its way to Goose Creek and its proximity during the 1970's. The problems confronted by local leaders are to bring prosperity with dignity, prosperity with planned development and prosperity with pride.

Pride is an integral part of a wholesome and viable community. The "Goose Creek Men" and women are in many ways the products of the water near which they live and of the political environment which was born of the proud independence which has pervaded Goose Creek for more than 300 years.

APPENDIX A

GOOSE CREEK CITY OFFICIALS, 1961 - 1978

April 6, 1961 to April 5, 1962
Mayor H.W. Bunch
Edgar Binnar, Council
E.W. Etling, Council
E.Q. Neis, Jr., Council
Roger Anderson, Council
Clancy Walker, Clerk Treasurer
L.C. Turner, City Recorder
J.B. Brown, Town Marshall

April 5, 1962 to May 21, 1964
Mayor H.W. Bunch
E.W. Etling, Council
E.M. Griffin, Council
E.B. Binnar, Council
Gary Elsey (Resigned February 12, 1963) Council
Smith E. Hinnant (Sworn July 9, 1963 for unexpired term) Council
Marion W. Hatchell, Clerk Treasurer
Weyman Turner, Police Chief

May 21, 1964 to May 17, 1966
Mayor Smith E. Hinnant
Oliver Sona, Council
Charles E. Caldwell, Council
Oliver Yon, Council
Kelley Curtis (Resigned because of health reasons) Council
Hattie V. Turner (Elected to replace Kelley Curtis) Council
Hattie Mae Barrs, Clerk Treasurer
Sheldon E. Hopson, Chief of Police
Jetter Cain, Recorder

May 17, 1966 to May 14, 1968

> Mayor Smith E. Hinnant
> Oliver Yon, Council
> Oliver Sona, Council
> Charles Caldwell, Council
> W.R. Wren, Council
> Nora Gonda, Clerk Treasurer
> Faye McKinley, Clerk Treasurer (March 25, 1968 to June 10, 1968)

May 14, 1968 to May 20, 1970

> Mayor Malvin Mann
> Carl V. Barrs, Sr., Council
> Charles Caldwell, Council
> Adam R. Hernandez (Resigned Feb. 20, 1969) Council
> Earl H. Bounds, Council
> Michael H. Bowick (Appears July 8, 1969) Council
> Vivian A. Woods, Clerk Treasurer

May 28, 1970 to May 25, 1972

> Mayor Malvin Mann
> Carl V. Barrs, Sr., Council
> E.G. Wright, Council
> Michael H. Bowick, Council
> Earl H. Bounds, Council
> Charles C. Caldwell, Council
> Orris F. Caldwell, Council

May 25, 1972 to May 22, 1974

> Mayor Malvin Mann
> Carl V. Barrs, Sr., Council
> Michael Bowick, Council
> Louis Hatchell, Council
> William Infinger, Council
> Thomas Poor, Council
> Earl Bounds, Council

APPENDIX

May 22, 1974 to June 15, 1976

Mayor James M. Richards
Thomas G. Poor, Sr., Council
Orris E. Caldwell, Council
Uldis Jaunzemiz (Resigned Aug. 31, 1974) Council
Sidney A. Eadie, Council
Otis Crawford (Resigned Sept. 9, 1975) Council
Shirley Johnson (Sworn Oct. 31, 1974 for unexpired term) Council
Marguerite Brown (Sworn Dec. 9, 1975 for unexpired term) Council
Phil Hurt, Police Chief; Solon Lewis, Police Chief
Steven Best, Recorder
Janice Hulbert, City Administrator

June 15, 1976 to May 15, 1978

Mayor Malvin Mann
Shirley Johnson, Council
Marguerite Brown, Council
Michael J. Heitzler, Council
Nancy Lawson, Council
John Barnette, Council
William S. Gibson, Council
Lois Hodges, Clerk Treasurer
Carl Barrs, Sr., Recorder
Solon Lewis, Police Chief

May 15, 1978 to

Mayor Michael Heitzler
Shirley Johnson, Council
Marguerite Brown, Council
Joseph S. Daning, Council
E. Calvin Woods, Council
William E. Gibson, Council
Philip E. Hurt (May 1978-Sept. 1979) Council
John G. Barnette (January 22, 1980 to May 1980) Council
Doreen Davis (May 1980) Council
Lagette Shiver (May 1980) Council
Gail McNaughton, Clerk Treasurer
Dennis Harmon, City Administrator
Solon Lewis, Police Chief, Richard Ruonala, Police Chief

APPENDIX B

Memorials to Col. John Gibbes, Jane Gibbes, Ralph Izard and Peter Taylor on the interior walls of the St. James' Church.

Underneath this lyes the late Col. John / Gibbes who deceased on the 7th August / 1711 Age 40.

Near this place / Lyes the body of Jane Gibbes / Late wife of Mr. Benjamin Gibbes / Who departed this life ye 19th of / August 1717 / Aged 35 years.

Under the window, on the outside of this / wall lies the remains of the Honourable / Ralph Izard of the Parish of St. James / Goose Creek. /
    He was born on the 23rd Jany 1742 and / departed this life on the 30th of May 1804. / He was eminently adorned by the virtues of / public and private life. /
    The good of his country / which his accurate judgement enabled him to / promptly discover He pursued with the most / undeviating integrity and the most ardent zeal. / His private life was marked by a high / spirit of honour and justice / His dignified manners, his cultivated and / polished mind, his ready wit, / Commanded respect and admiration from all; / While the sincerity of his friendship, / his conjugal and parental virtues. / The melting tenderness of his manly and / noble heart secured their esteem, their / veneration, and their love / His whole life was a poetical lesson of active and useful virtues / and his death of resignation and fortitude. / *Hoc Ago.*

To the Memory of / Peter Taylor Esq. / Who lies interred near this Place / He adorned the several Relations / And Stations of Life he passed through / With a Conduct / Worthy the Christian and Gentleman. / He departed this life / Oct. 1st 1765. / Aged 67 years. / And by him lies his first wife / Mrs. Amerentia Taylor / and their son Joseph.

APPENDIX C

Testimonial presented to Rev. Timothy Millechampe upon his departure from Goose Creek.

SOUTH CAROLINA

We, the Churchwardens and Vestry of the Parish of St. James, Goose Creek, do Certify whom it may concern, that the Rev. Timothy Millechampe, Missionary for the Venerable and Honorary Society for the Propagation of the Gospel in Foreign parts to this Parish, has behaved as a worthy Clergyman of the Church of England among us, nigh the space of fourteen years, and whom we believe well affected to the present Constitution, both in Church and State: and in all things, whether respecting his Life or Doctrine, acquitted himself as a good Pastor, and Discharged the Duties of his Holy function with all Deligence and Fidelity, to the Advancement of the good work the Society are engaged in, and to our Benefit and Approbation. Given under Hands at the Parish Church in the Province aforesaid the 25th day of June 1746.

BENJ. MAZYCK
GIDEON DUPONT
Churchwardens.

WILLIAM MIDDLETON
PETER TAYLOR
ZACK. VILLEPONTOUX
RICH. SINGLETON
HENRY IZARD
THOMAS MIDDLETON
Vestrymen.

APPENDIX D

Thomas Bromley's memorial inscription from St. James' Church, copied by Samuel G. Stoney and translated by Norman A. Chamberlain.

Vere suo dum Vivens sub hoc Menore nunc mortuus / Requiescit / THOMAS BROMLEY generosus / Ex antiquo Stirpe in agro Castrensi oriundus / LONDINI natus / Banco regio apud Anglos rerum forensium / PROCURATOR / Curiae magnae Cancellariae ibidem / ADVOCATUS / Concionibusque Plebis in Provincia Carolinae Australia / AMANUENSIS / Et quod maximum / Viris bene potantibus quadquaversum / A CALVULIS / Et festivis undicumque omni genere Facetiae / EXPEDITISSUMUS / Morbo obiit Bilioso / Vigesimo Secumco die Augusti / ANNO SALUTIS / 1765 / Etatis / 35 / Where be your Gibes now? your Gambols? / your Song? your Flashes of Merriment / that were wont to set the Table / in a Roar?

Translation:

In the flower of his years, beneath this grave where in life he was wont to rest, now in death rests Thomas Bromley, Gentleman, of an old family in the county of Chester, and born in London. He was an attorney in the Court of King's Bench and barrister of the High Court of Chancery in England, and clerk to the Commons House of Assembly in the Province of South Carolina; but above all, wherever good fellows met and the cup went merrily round, foremost in quip and crank. He died of bilious fever in the year of Grace August 22nd. 1765, at the age of 35.

APPENDIX E

Gravestone Inscriptions from St. James' Church.

Sacred / To The Memory of / Archibald McKewn Esq. / Who died on the 14th / of October 1829 aged / 63 Years. / Husband Affectionate / Father Indulgent / Master Human / The Perfect Man and / Son and behold the / upright the end of / that man is Peace / Jesus can make a dying bed / soft as downey pillows and / white as his breast near my / heart.

Sacred / To the Memory of / Mrs. Mary McKewn / Who was born 30th / May 1801 / The 6th February / 1847 aged 46 years, / 9 months and 24 days. / Mother rest from sin and sorrow / Death is over and life is won, / Thy slumbers dawn no morrow.

Sacred / To The Memory of / Henry Middleton / Parker Who died / Nov. 17th 1844 / Aged 60 Years / and 6 months.

This Monument and / the one beside it / were moved in 1952 / For preservation / From The Parker / Burial Ground At / Hayes Plantation / in this Parish / *Verus Fidea* /, on the same stone with:

John Parker / Born October 31, 1787 / Died September 3, 1849 / His wife Emily S. Rutledge / Born June 2, 1797 / Died October 10, 1827 / Honor Thy Father and thy Mother / John Parker /, on the same stone with:

To / Emily Rutledge / Our Mother / We render this Tribute of reverence and love for her memory. Her children rise up and call her blessed / *Bonae Omnibus Probatus* /, on the same stone with:

John Parker / Born June 24, 1759 / Died April 20, 1832 / His wife Susannah Middleton / Born January 1760 / Died August 20, 1834 / The Path of the just is as the Shining light / John Parker appointed a Member of the Old Congress that Met From 1774 to 1789.

HISTORIC GOOSE CREEK

In Memory of M. Ann Mazyck / wife of Lieut. Stephen Mazyck / and Daughter of Mr. Walter Easton / Newport Rhode Island / Who departed this life / June 27, AD 1785 / Aged 23 Years / And here rests her infant male child / The Righteous Shall be had in / Everlasting Remembrance.

Sacred To The Memory of / Mrs. Mary Mazyck / Wife of Stephen Mazyck / Deceased / Who Departed this life on the 29th of May 1845 / Aged 82 Years. Lord let me die the death of the righteous / And let my last be like hers.

Mary Jane Elfe / Wife of George Elfe / and daughter of Stephen and Mary Mazyck / who departed this life on the 16th day of December A.D. 1839 / Aged forty years 3 months and ten days.

Sacred To The Memory of / Margaret M. Hopkins / Wife of James Hopkins / who departed this life February 2nd, 1825 / Aged 27 Years and 8 months / Also of James Hopkins / who departed this life February 4th 1826 / Aged 41 Years 11 months and 15 days / Erected by James Albert Hopkins / Also tribute to the Memory of his father and stepmother.

Sacred To the Memory of / Charles L. Desel / Born in Charleston July 13th 1795 / Died July 1st 1855 / Aged 59 years 11 months and 18 days / By his habits of industry he was enabled to support and educate a large family of children. His unbending integrity and purity of character won the confidence and esteem of his fellow men. The love and gratitude he cherished by his mourning widow and fatherless children are memories of his devotion as a husband and affection as a father. His house was the seat of hospitality and his heart ever faithful to his friends. He was a professor of his Savior and contributed liberally to its support. A kind Master, he promoted religious training among his servants the purity and piety of his life have left on the hearts of his family The community(s) the assurances that Blessed _____ dead who died in _____ Loved _____ _____

APPENDIX

In Memory of / William Stitt / Son of William and Elizabeth Stitt / Who died February 1801 / Age 24 Years / 11 months / and 8 days.
(Family Coat of Arms)
(British Coat of Arms)
Sacred to the Memory of / Tobias Cambridge / Who departed this life on Friday the 25th day of September / Anno Dominus 1808 / Aged 34 Years and 27 days / Words could not express too much in favor of this man. He has left an affectionate wife and eight children to lament the loss of an affectionate Husband and fond father. Near him lies six of his children / He lived, loved and died lamented.

Nearby there is an unmarked grave with no stone or inscription. The site is indicated by a mound of bricks. Near the unmarked site is the grave of Ann Glover and others as follows:

Sacred to the Memory of / Ann Glover / Amiable Consort of / Charles Glover / Who departed this life on the 28 of October 1791 / in the 25th year of her age / and of Sarah / their daughter / who died the 1st of August 1791 being in her third year.

In Memory of / Mrs. Francis Withers / wife of John Withers Sen. / who departed this life September 29th 1805 / Aged 49 Years.

Sacred to the Memories of / Benjamin Coachman Esquire / and Rebecca Smith / his consort / who departed this life on the 7th January 1814 / Aged 62 Years and 1 month / also their son Benjamin / Not last blessed thought but only one gone before.

Margaret McBride / departed this life / December 13, 1791 / Aged 69 Years.

Memory of / Jane Pennington / who departed this life / 28th December 1815 / aged 52 years.

Sacred to the Memory of John Hesley / Aged 33 Years / and also of his son / John Hesley / who departed this life the 5th September 1850 / Age 5 years and 15 days.

Sacred to the Memory of Ms. Ann Collins / who departed this life / 15th March 1827 / in the 64th year of her age / also To the Memory of her son / William John Collins / who departed this life / on the 15 January 1828 / in the 32nd year of his age.

APPENDIX F

Grave Stone Inscriptions of Moultrie family from St. James' Church.

Sacred to the Memory of / Major William Moultrie / who departed this life December 12th 1796 / He was a man of intrinsic worth and whose urbanity of manners and uniform rectitude throughout life secured to him the esteem and admiration of all who knew him.

Other members of the Moultrie family moved from the Windsor Hill burial grounds are also at the Goose Creek church. William Ainslie Moultrie was the son of William Moultrie and grandson of the famous general.

Underneath are deposited the remains of / William Ainslie Moultrie Esq. / who departed this life in the 29th of August 1811 / in the 33 year of his age. He lived in the anxious pursuit of Truth and Justice and in the constant observance of the Social and Manly Virtues / He died (alas how soon) with piety resignation of a christian / His inconsolable sister and affected friends erected this tablet to his worth and their affection. He was of soul sincere / In action faithful and in honor clear.

Sacred to the Memory of / Edw. D. Ainslie Brailsford / Obed Oct. 12th 1805 / Age 4 months and 3 days / Rest Lovely Babe / Wait the Almighty will then rise unchanged and be an angel still.

APPENDIX G

Grave Stone Inscriptions from Goose Creek Chapel of Ease.

In Memory of / Dr. Robert Broun / who departed this life / 25th Nov. 1757 / Aged 43 years.

Long may this marble remain to testify to the filial affection of Mrs. Mary Loocock who caused it to be erected / Sacred to the Memory of her beloved Brother Robert Broun, M.D. / who departed this life / 6th June 1766 / Aged 44.

Long may this marble as a testimony of filial affection of Robert Broun / who caused to be erected / Sacred to the Memory of / his beloved Brother / Archibald Brown / who departed this life the 1st day of Dec. 1797 / Aged 16 years.

Sacred to the Memory of Aaron Loocock Esq. / who departed this Life 10th Feby. 1794 / Aged 61 years.

Sacred to the Memory of / Mrs. Carolina Deas / who departed this Life / on the Evening of 21st Dec. 1816 / Aged 35 years 7 mns 3 days.

Sacred to the Memory of / Richard Couch Esq. / who died 2nd Feby 1786 / Aged 45 years.

Mr. John Reidheimer / who departed this Life on May 10th, 1826 / Aged 72 years / Actively patriotic in the War of the Revolution, he sustained the character / of firm love for his Country. As a Christian he was devout / As a man honest / As a friend sincere. And he now reaps the reward, of his toils in the Bosom of his God.

Sacred to the Memory of / Peter Reidheimer / who departed this Life / July 17th, 1812 / Aged 57 years / "Come hither mortal cast an eye / Then go thy way prepared to die. Here read thy doom for die thou must Some day like me be turned to dust."

APPENDIX H

Goose Creek Water Tunnels

There are many great engineering accomplishments in the Charleston area, some of which are the magnificent churches and the Cooper River Bridge, but there is another that goes unnoticed by most. One of the unique engineering attainments in the world is the Edisto River tunnel, 25 miles long, excavated in 1927 and 1937, which carries millions of gallons of fresh water directly to the Goose Creek water plant and from there to Charleston. This tunnel was dug laboriously by hand, yet it could be left without supports or liner pipes because it runs through Cooper River marl, the deposits of rock lying 20 to 40 feet below the surface of the low country.

In 1903 the city fathers of Charleston contracted with the Charleston Light and Water Company to build a dam across Goose Creek. The reservoir created by the dam was used as a source of drinking water to replace the shallow wells in Charleston.

The Goose Creek reservoir water came from swampy sources, and because the plant's treatment of it did not always meet standards, Charleston bought the water company in 1917 and renamed it the Commission of Public Works.

Under the direction of James E. Gibson, the water system was continually improved by the use of water tunnels. A five mile tunnel through the marl from the Ashley River to the Goose Creek water plant was begun in 1927 and completed in a year. This provided an aditional source of water. As new industries and new residents began to move into the area the water supply had to be improved. In 1938 a 19 mile long tunnel, seven feet in height, was dug from the Edisto River to the Goose Creek treatment plant. Later, to accommodate the Bushy Park Industrial complex, a two mile tunnel from Cooper River to Goose Creek was completed.

Today the Goose Creek plant has a 45 million gallon capacity and is presently being expanded to accommodate 80 million. The Cooper River marl and good engineering combined to provide an abundant source of potable water to 55,000 homes and businesses in 1980.

REFERENCES

CHAPTER ONE

1 Interview with Mr. A.L. Collier in the *Charleston Evening Post*, North Metro edition, June 30, 1977.

2 Stephen Carter & Associates, *Land Use Study*, prepared for the City of Goose Creek, 1976. Hereafter cited as *Land Use Study*.

3 U.S. Postal Service, 1977.

4 John K. Wright, "The Study of Place Names: Recent Work and Some Possibilities," in *Geographical Review*, 1929, 149-154.

5 Eleanor T. McColl, "Place Names in Marlboro County," in *Names in South Carolina*, 16:15.

6 Claude Henry Neuffer, "Notes on Names," in *Names in South Carolina*, 13:6.

7 Elias B. Bull, "Community and Neighborhood Names in Berkeley County," in *Names in South Carolina*, 13:37.

8 *Ibid.*, 37, 38.

9 *Ibid.*, 38.

10 *Ibid.*

11 W.P.A. Federal Writer's Project. *Palmetto Place Names* (Columbia, S.C., 1941), 147.

12 *Ibid.*, 146.

13 *Ibid.*, 120.

14 *Ibid.*

15 Henry A.M. Smith, "Goose Creek," in the *South Carolina Historical and Genealogical Magazine*, 29:20, 21. Hereafter cited as Smith, *Goose Creek*.

16 *Ibid.*, 20.

17 Henry A.M. Smith, "An Historical Sketch of St. James, Goose Creek," in the Charleston *News & Courier*, April 23, 1906; also Minutes of the Vestry of St. James Parish, Goose Creek, 1872-1876 and 1882-1925, on deposit with the South Carolina Historical Society, Charleston. Hereafter cited as Vestry Minutes.

18 A.S. Salley, ed., *Warrants for Land in South Carolina* (Columbia, S.C., 1973), 590. Hereafter cited as *Warrants*.

19 *Ibid.*, 173.

20 Smith, *Goose Creek*, 21.

21 *Ibid.*

22 Oscar M. Lieber, "Vocabulary of the Catawba Language, with Some Remarks on its Grammar, Construction

and Pronunciation," in *Collections of the South Carolina Historical Society*, 2:327-342. Hereafter cited as Lieber.

23 *Ibid.*, 333.

24 *Warrants*, 82.

25 John B. Irving, *A Day on Cooper River* (Charleston, 1869), 99. Hereafter cited as Irving, *Cooper River*.

26 Mrs. St. Julien Ravenel, *Charleston, The Place and the People* (New York, 1922), 8. Hereafter cited as Ravenel.

27 Frederick Dalcho, *An Historical Account of the Protestant Episcopal Church in South Carolina* . . . . (Charleston, 1820), 324. Hereafter cited as Dalcho.

28 Henry Ravenel Dwight, *Some Historic Spots in Berkeley [County]* (Pinopolis, S.C., 1921), 21. Hereafter cited as Dwight.

29 Thomas Cooper, *et al.*, eds., *Statutes of South Carolina* (Columbia, S.C., 1836), II:328. Hereafter cited as *Statutes*. Also Maxwell Clayton Orvin, *Historic Berkeley County, South Carolina, 1671-1900* (Charleston, 1973), 4. Hereafter cited as Orvin, *Historic Berkeley*.

30 *Statutes*, 8:199.

31 Orvin, *Historic Berkeley*, 6.

32 *Ibid.*

33 *Statutes*, 22:309.

34 *Ibid.*, 22:595.

35 *Ibid.*, 33:184.

36 *Land Use Study*.

37 U.S. Census Bureau. Special Census for the City of Goose Creek, April, 1979.

CHAPTER TWO

1 Frank J. Klingberg, ed., *The Carolina Chronicle of Dr. Francis LeJau, 1706-1717* (Berkeley & Los Angeles, 1956), 205. Hereafter cited as Klingberg, *LeJau*.

2 Max Savelle, *A History of Colonial America* (New York, 1966), 57.

3 *Ibid.*

4 *Ibid.*

5 *Ibid.*

6 Converse D. Clowse, *Economic Beginnings in South Carolina* (Columbia, S.C., 1971), 4. Hereafter cited as Clowse.

7 *Ibid.*, 5.

REFERENCES

8 Ravenel, 15, 16.
9 Orvin, *Historic Berkeley*, 17.
10 *Ibid.*, 15; also J.P. Thomas, Jr., "The Barbadians in Early South Carolina," in *SCHGM* 31:75-80, hereafter cited as Thomas, *Barbadians*.
11 Ravenel, 8.
12 Clowse, 54; also Langdon Cheves, ed., "The Shaftesbury Papers and Other Records Relating to South Carolina and the First Settlement on Ashley River Prior to the Year 1676," containing a letter from Joseph West to Lord Ashley dated March 21, 1671. In *Collections of the South Carolina Historical Society*, 5:298. Hereafter cited as *Shaftesbury Papers*.
13 *Shaftesbury Papers*, 360.
14 Clowse, 54.
15 *Ibid.*
16 *Ibid.*
17 Ravenel, 9.
18 Henry A.M. Smith, "The Orange Quarter and the First French Settlers in South Carolina," in *SCHGM* 18:105.
19 Orvin, *Historic Berkeley*, 15.
20 Dwight, 21.
21 *Warrants*, i.
22 *Ibid.*, 82.
23 *Ibid.*, 112.
24 Joseph S. Ames, "Cantey Family," in *SCHGM* 11:205, 210, 211.
25 *Warrants*, 206.
26 *Ibid.*, 485.
27 Smith, *Goose Creek*, 11.
28 *Warrants*, 623.
29 Smith, *Goose Creek*, 11.
30 *Warrants*, 173.
31 *Ibid.*, 486.
32 Smith, *Goose Creek*, 34.
33 *Warrants*, 107.
34 Smith, *Goose Creek*, 273.
35 *Ibid.*
36 *Warrants*, 317-318.
37 *Ibid.*, 299.
38 *Ibid., passim.*
39 *Ibid.*, 434.

40 Caroline T. Moore, ed., *Abstracts of the Wills of the State of South Carolina* (Columbia, S.C., 1960-74, 4 vol.), I & II. Hereafter cited as Moore, *Wills*.

41 William J. Rivers, *A Sketch of the History of South Carolina* (Spartanburg, S.C., 1972), 172. Hereafter cited as Rivers.

42 *Ibid.*, 173.

43 Arthur Henry Hirsch, *The Huguenots of Colonial South Carolina* (London, 1962), 21. Hereafter cited as Hirsch.

44 "Letters of Rev. Mr. Thomas to the Society for the Propagation of the Gospel in Foreign Parts," in *SCHGM* 5:21-55.

45 Smith, *Goose Creek*, 11.

46 Henry A.M. Smith, "The French Huguenot Church of the Parish of St. James, Goose Creek," in *Transactions of the Huguenot Society of South Carolina*, 16:43. Hereafter cited as Smith, *French Huguenot Church*.

47 *Ibid.*

48 *Ibid.*, 43-44.

49 *Ibid.*

50 *Ibid.*

51 Mrs. E.A. Poyas, *The Olden Time of South Carolina* (Charleston, S.C., 1855), 36-37. Hereafter cited as Poyas. Also Hirsch, 21.

52 Chapman J. Milling, *Red Carolinians* (Chapel Hill, N.C., 1940), 61. Hereafter cited as Milling.

53 Allan Nevins, *Slave Trading in the Old South* (N.Y., 1959), 4.

54 Frank J. Klingberg, *An Appraisal of the Negro in Colonial South Carolina* (Washington, 1941), 50. Hereafter cited as Klingberg, *An Appraisal*.

55 *Ibid.*, 2.

CHAPTER THREE

1 David Duncan Wallace, *South Carolina: A Short History* (Columbia, 1951), 5. Hereafter cited as Wallace. See also Orvin, 14.

2 Milling, 34-35.

3 *Ibid.*

4 Douglas Summers Brown, *The Catawba Indians, the People of the River* (Columbia, 1966), 60. Hereafter cited as Brown. Also John Reed Swanton, *Indians of the Southeastern United States* (Washington, 1946), 120, 183. Hereafter cited as Swanton.

REFERENCES

5 Lieber, 327-342.
6 Swanton, 632.
7 *Ibid.*
8 Klingberg, *LeJau*, 105.
9 Milling, 12.
10 *Ibid.*, 16.
11 *Ibid.*
12 Milling, 30.
13 *Ibid.*, 31.
14 *Ibid.*
15 Clowse, 29.
16 Wallace, 39-44.
17 Clowse, 40.
18 *Ibid.*, 37; Milling, 17.
19 Clowse, 40.
20 Milling, 60.
21 Brown, 147.
22 Klingberg, *LeJau*, 105.
23 *Ibid.*
24 *Ibid.*, 68; Milling, 20.
25 Milling, 47.
26 Brown, 61.
27 Verner W. Crane, *The Southern Frontier, 1670-1762* (Durham, N.C. 1928), 153. Hereafter cited as Crane.
28 *Ibid.*; also Milling, 59.
29 Klingberg, *LeJau*, 78.
30 Milling, 208.
31 Brown, 137.
32 Crane, 44.
33 Milling, 63.

CHAPTER FOUR

1 Clowse, 79; also Henriette Kershaw Leiding, *Historic Houses of South Carolina* (Philadelphia, 1921), 22. Hereafter cited as Leiding.
2 Richard Hofstadter, *The American Republic* (Englewood Cliffs, N.J., 1959), 2:301. Hereafter cited as Hofstadter.
3 *Ibid.*
4 *Ibid.*, 302.
5 *Warrants*, ix.
6 Thomas Newe, "Letters from South Carolina in 1682," in A.S. Salley, ed., *Narratives of Early Carolina* (New York, 1911), 480.

7 Crane, 110; also Clowse, 86.
8 *Ibid.*
9 Klingberg, *LeJau*, 104.
10 Joseph Ioor Waring, *St. James' Church, Goose Creek, S.C., A Sketch of the Parish from 1706 to 1909* (Charleston, 1911), 16. Hereafter cited as Waring, *St. James'*.
11 Wallace, 190.
12 Clowse, 34.
13 *Ibid.*, 35.
14 *Ibid.*, 34.
15 Klingberg, *LeJau*, 104.
16 *Ibid.*, 100.
17 *Ibid.*
18 St. Julien Ravenel Childs, *Malaria and Colonization in the Carolina Low Country, 1526-1696* (Baltimore, 1940), 255. Hereafter cited as Childs. See also Joseph Ioor Waring, *A History of Medicine in South Carolina, 1670-1825* (Charleston, 1964-67), 1:13. Hereafter cited as Waring, *Medicine*.
19 Childs, 255.
20 Waring, *Medicine*, I:15.
21 *Ibid.*, 385.
22 *Ibid.*
23 *Ibid.*
24. Klingberg, *LeJau*, 53.
25 *Ibid.*, 81.
26 *Ibid.*, 113.
27 *Ibid.*, 23.
28 *Ibid.*, 27.
29 Wallace, 73.
30 Klingberg, *LeJau*, 73n. For more information about Atkin Williamson, see Frank J. Klingberg, *Carolina Chronicle: The Papers of Commissary Gideon Johnson, 1707-1716* (Berkeley, California, 1946), 47.
31 Klingberg, 80.
32 *Ibid.*, 68.
33 Ravenel, 17.
34 Dalcho, 245.
35 Asa H. Gordon, *Sketches of Negro Life and History in South Carolina* (Columbia, S.C.: 1971), 82.
36 Klingberg, *LeJau*, 60.
37 *Ibid.*, 137.
38 *Ibid.*, 55, 78.

REFERENCES

39 Wallace, 186.
40 Klingberg, *LeJau*, 108.
41 *Ibid.*
42 *Ibid.*, 129.
43 *Ibid.*, 60.
44 Crane, 109.
45 *Ibid.*, 44.
46 Brown, 60.
47 Clowse, 40.
48 *Ibid.*, 65.
49 Crane, 113.
50 Milling, 57.
51 *Ibid.*, 55.
52 *Ibid.*
53 Shaftesbury Papers, 474.
54 Milling, 57.
55 *Ibid.*, 56.
56 *Ibid.*
57 *Ibid.*, 55.
58 *Ibid.*, 56.
59 *Ibid.*
60 *Statutes*, 2:108-110.
61 *Ibid.*
62 *Ibid.*
63 *Ibid.*
64 Milling, 59.
65 Brown, 137.
66 *Ibid.*, 134.
67 Wallace, 87.
68 Klingberg, *LeJau*, 152.
69 Brown, 134.
70 William L. McDowell, ed., *Documents Relating to Indian Affairs, 1754-1765* (Columbia, S.C., 1970), 96. Hereafter cited as *Indian Affairs*.
71 *Ibid.*, 87.
72 Brown, 134.
73 Klingberg, *LeJau*, 39.
74 *Ibid.*, 94.
75 *Ibid.*, 109.
76 Brown, 135.
77 *Ibid.*
78 *Ibid.*

79 Poyas, 110.
80 Smith, *Goose Creek*, 72.
81 *Ibid.*, 18.
82 Milling, 143.
83 *Ibid.*
84 Poyas, 111.
85 Milling, 144.
86 *Ibid.*
87 Crane, 172.
88 *Ibid.*, 169.
89 Milling, 145.
90 Brown, 139.
91 Milling, 61.
92 Orvin, *Historic Berkeley*, 42.
93 *Ibid.*
94 *Ibid.*, also Poyas, 111-112.

CHAPTER FIVE

1 Klingberg, *LeJau*, 29.
2 M. Eugene Sirmans, *Colonial South Carolina: A Political History*, 1663-1763 (Williamsburg, Va.: 1966), 24. Hereafter cited as Sirmans.
3 Wallace, 36, 38, 48; also Orvin, 28.
4 Hofstadter, 53; also Cooper & McCord, *Statutes* I:43-56.
5 Savelle, 190.
6 Sirmans, 29-41; Wallace, 37-38.
7 Sirmans, 30.
8 *Ibid.*, 34.
9 *Ibid.*, 38.
10 Orvin, *Historic Berkeley*, 28-29; Wallace, 46.
11 Clowse, 46.
12 Orvin, *Historic Berkeley*, 28-29.
13 *Ibid.*, 29; Clowse, 78.
14 Sirmans, 41.
15 Edward McCrady, *History of South Carolina under the Proprietary Government, 1670-1719* (New York, 1897), 367. Hereafter cited as McCrady, *1670-1719*.
16 Poyas, 36; McCrady, *1670-1719*, 238-239; Ravenel, 37.
17 Orvin, *Historic Berkeley*, 15.

REFERENCES

18 *Ibid.*, 29; Sirmans, 43; Crane, 119.
19 Shirley C. Hughson, *The Carolina Pirates and Colonial Commerce* (Baltimore, 1894), 10-16. Hereafter cited as Hughson. See also Clowse, 88.
20 Sirmans, 43.
21 Ravenel, 42; Rivers, 169.
22 Eugenia Burney, *Colonial South Carolina* (Camden, N.J., 1970), 62-63. Hereafter cited as Burney.
23 Sirmans, 46.
24 *Ibid.*, 48.
25 *Ibid.*, 50.
26 Orvin, *Historic Berkeley*, 29; McCrady, *1670-1719*, 689.
27 McCrady, *1670-1719*, 237; Rivers, 160.
28 Orvin, *Historic Berkeley*, 30.
29 McCrady, *1670-1719*, 238; Wallace, 50; Rivers, 176.
30 Orvin, *Historic Berkeley*, 33.
31 Sirmans, 57; Crane, 129-136; Swanton, 110-154.
32 Orvin, *Historic Berkeley*, 32.
33 Sirmans, 70.
34 Orvin, *Historic Berkeley*, 32; Wallace, 53.
35 Orvin, *Historic Berkeley*, 33.
36 Hughson, 37; Sirmans, 74.
37 McCrady, *1670-1719*, 563-564; Sirmans, 79.
38 Ravenel, 42-44; Wallace, 72.
39 Klingberg, *LeJau*, 29.
40 Sirmans, 89-90.
41 Milling, 144.
42 Wallace, 95.
43 William A. Schaper, *Sectionalism and Representation in South Carolina* (New York, 1968), 108. Hereafter cited as Schaper.
44 Orvin, *Historic Berkeley*, 43.

CHAPTER SIX

1 Ravenel, 8-9.
2 Leiding, 22.
3 Irving, *Cooper River*, xi.
4 Savelle, 191; Orvin, 12, 25.
5 Leila Sellers, *Charleston Business on the Eve of the American Revolution* (New York, 1970), 5. Hereafter cited as Sellers.

6 Wallace, 188, 362. For a detailed description of rice production, see David Doar, *Rice and Rice Planting in the South Carolina Low Country* (Charleston, 1936).

7 Orvin, *Historic Berkeley*, 21.

8 Herbert Ravenel Sass, *The Story of the South Carolina Low Country* (West Columbia, S.C., 1956), 183. Hereafter cited as Sass.

9 John B. Irving, *The South Carolina Jockey Club* (Charleston, 1857), 183.

10 Joseph Johnson, *Traditions and Reminiscences, Chiefly of the American Revolution in the South* (Charleston, 1851), 235, 238. Hereafter cited as Johnson.

11 J.H. Easterby, ed., *The Journal of the Commons House of Assembly, 1741-1742* (Columbia, S.C., 1953), 396. Hereafter cited as *Commons House Journal*.

12 Waring, *Medicine*, I:385-386; Johnson, 194.

13 Waring, *Medicine*, I:386.

14 U.S. Census, Seventh Census, 1850. St. James' Parish, Goose Creek. Hereafter cited as Census.

15 1860 Census.

16 Edmund Berkeley and Dorothy Smith Berkeley, *Dr. Alexander Garden of Charles Town* (Chapel Hill, 1969), 326-327. Hereafter cited as Berkeley.

17 Frederick P. Bowes, *The Culture of Early Charleston* (Chapel Hill, 1942), 20. Hereafter cited as Bowes.

18 *Ibid.*, 71.

19 *Ibid.*

20 Klingberg, *LeJau*, 50; also LeJau to the Secretary, St. James', Goose Creek, dated February 18, 1709; typed manuscript at the South Carolina Historical Society, Charleston.

21 Wallace, 183.

22 Orvin, *Historic Berkeley*, 148.

23 1790 Census; also Sellers, 26.

24 Sellers, 27.

25 Klingberg, *An Appraisal*, 48.

26 *Ibid.*, 47.

27 John Hope Franklin, *From Slavery to Freedom: A History of Negro Americans* (New York, 1969), 78. Hereafter cited as Franklin.

28 Clayton Maxwell Orvin, *A History of Moncks Corner,*

REFERENCES

Berkeley County, South Carolina (Charleston, 1950), 6. Hereafter cited as Orvin, *Monck's Corner*.
    29 *Ibid.*, 7.
    30 *Ibid.*
    31 Orvin, *Historic Berkeley*, 69.
    32 Irving, *Cooper River*, xi.
    33 *Ibid.*, 101.
    34 Klingberg, *An Appraisal*, 37-38.
    35 *Ibid.*, 39.
    36 Klingberg, *LeJau*, 16; also Francis LeJau to John Chamberlayne, February 1, 1709/10 in SCHS.
    37 M. Alston Read, "The Original Members of the Goose Creek Friendly Society or River Club," *SCHGM* 27:188
    38 Joe M. King, *A History of South Carolina Baptists* (Columbia, 1964), 135. Hereafter cited as King.
    39 Leah Townsend, *South Carolina Baptists, 1607-1805* (Florence, S.C., 1935), 107.
    40 Klingberg, *LeJau*, 92.
    41 *Ibid.*, 93.
    42 1790 Census.
    43 1850 Census.
    44 *Ibid.*
    45 1870 Census.
    46 1880 Census.
    47 Dwight, 21.

CHAPTER SEVEN

    1 Klingberg, *An Appraisal*, 48.
    2 Irving, *Cooper River*; also Smith, *Goose Creek*.
    3 Irving, *Cooper River*, 66; Dwight, 26.
    4 Alexander S. Salley, "The House at Medway," in *SCHGM* 33:245-246. Hereafter cited as Salley, *Medway*.
    5 *Ibid.*, 245.
    6 Leiding, 22.
    7 Poyas, 32.
    8 Leiding, 30.
    9 Salley, *Medway*, 246; Poyas, 32.
    10 *Ibid.*
    11 Henry A.M. Smith, "The Baronies of South Carolina," *SCHGM* 13:16.
    12 Irving, *Cooper River*, 68.
    13 *Ibid.*

14 *Ibid.*; also Samuel Gaillard Stoney, *Plantations of the Carolina Low Country* (Charleston, 1964), 48. Hereafter cited as Stoney.
15 Irving, *Cooper River*, 69.
16 *Ibid.*
17 *Ibid.*, 70.
18 *Ibid.*
19 *Ibid.*
20 *Ibid.*, 71.
21 *Ibid.*
22 *Ibid.*, 18.
23 Leiding, 29.
24 *Warrants, 1672-1711*, 278.
25 Anna Wells Rutledge, *Artists in the Life of Charleston* (Philadelphia, 1949), 178. Hereafter cited as Rutledge.
26 Johnson, 381.
27 Henry A.M. Smith, "Charleston and Charleston Neck," in *SCHGM* 19:69.
28 *Ibid.*
29 *Ibid.*
30 Poyas, 52.
31 *Ibid.*, 70.
32 Irving, *Cooper River*, 107.
33 McCrady, *1670-1719*, 705.
34 Irving, *Cooper River*, 108. The inscriptions from the family burying ground were copied by Anne King Gregorie and Flora Belle Surles on September 1, 1935 and were published in *SCHGM*, 36.
35 Smith, *Goose Creek*, 273.
36 *Ibid.*
37 *Ibid.*
38 Waring, *St. James'*, 15.
39 Smith, *Goose Creek*, 276.
40 *Ibid.*, 277.
41 *Ibid.*
42 *Ibid.*
43 *Ibid.*, 8.
44 *Ibid.*, 9.
45 *Ibid.*; also *Proceedings of the American Philosophical Society* XXVI, No. 129.
46 Smith, *Goose Creek*, 10.
47 *Ibid.*

REFERENCES

48 *Ibid.*, 11.
49 *Ibid.*, 12.
50 *Ibid.*
51 *Ibid.*, 13.
52 *Ibid.*
53 Charles Fraser, *A Charleston Sketchbook, 1796-1806* (Charleston, 1959), 21. Hereafter cited as Fraser.
54 *Ibid.*
55 Smith, *Goose Creek*, 20.
56 *Ibid.*, 167; Stoney, 79.
57 Smith, *Goose Creek*, 168.
58 *Ibid.*, 170.
59 *Correspondence of Mr. Ralph Izard of South Carolina From the Year 1774 to 1804 with a Short Memoir* (New York, 1844), XI; also Johnson, 88.
60 Dwight, 24.
61 *Ibid.*, 25.
62 *Ibid.*; also Stoney, 79.
63 Leiding, 28.
64 Smith, *Goose Creek*, 172.
65 *Ibid.*, 173.
66 *Ibid.*
67 *Ibid.*
68 *Ibid.*
69 Leiding, 28.
70 Smith, *Goose Creek*, 172.
71 Leiding, 29.
72 *Ibid.*, also Rutledge, 173.
73 Smith, *Goose Creek*, 15.
74 *Ibid*, 14.
75 *Ibid.*, 15.
76 Fraser, 20.
77 Rutledge, 172-173.
78 *Ibid.*, 20.
79 *Ibid.*, 21.
80 *Ibid.*
81 Edward McCrady, *South Carolina Under the Royal Government, 1719-1776* (New York, 1899), 416. Hereafter cited as McCrady, *1719-1776*.
82 Smith, *Goose Creek*, 23; Waring, *St. James'*, 232-233.
83 Johnson, 238.

84 Waring, *St. James'*, 227, 228, 230, 233; Bowes, 90; Berkeley, 29.
85 Waring, *St. James'*, 229.
86 Bowes, 90.
87 *Ibid.*
88 Berkeley, 58-59.
89 Smith, *Goose Creek*, 23.
90 *Ibid.*; Stoney, 71.
91 *Ibid.*, 24.
92 Leiding, 27.
93 *Ibid.*
94 *Ibid.*
95 Smith, *Goose Creek*, 25.
96 Leiding, 26.
97 Smith, *Goose Creek*, 25.
98 Stoney, 71.
99 *Ibid.*
100 Leiding, 28.
101 Debbie Walker, "Past Lives at Otranto," in *Low Country News and Review*, Charleston, S.C., May 3, 1977.
102 Leiding, 28.
103 Smith, *Goose Creek*, 174.
104 *Ibid.*
105 *Ibid.*, 180.
106 *Ibid.*
107 Smith, *French Huguenot Church*, 40-41.
108 Smith, *Goose Creek*, 71. The town in France is spelled "Fontainbleau."
109 *Ibid.*, 71.
110 *Ibid.*, 74.
111 *Ibid.*, 75.
112 *Ibid.*, 76.
113 *Ibid.*
114 *Ibid.*, 80; Leiding, 198, 200.
115 Smith, *Goose Creek*, 80; Leiding, 199.
116 Leiding, 199.
117 *Ibid.*, 200.
118 Johnson, 397.
119 Smith, *Goose Creek*, 81.
120 *Ibid.*, 266.
121 *Ibid.*
122 *Ibid.*

REFERENCES

123 *Ibid.*, 267; Waring, *St. James'*, 21.
124 Dwight, 23; Leiding, 24-25; Stoney, 56.
125 Smith, *Goose Creek*, 269.
126 Dwight, 23-24.
127 Smith, *Goose Creek*, 271.
128 Leiding, 25.
129 *Life in Carolina and New England During the Nineteenth Century, As Illustrated by Reminiscenses and Letters of the DeWolf Family of Bristol, Rhode Island* (Bristol, R.I., 1929), 64. Hereafter cited as *Life in Carolina*.
130 Leiding, 23.
131 *Life in Carolina*, 65; Johnson, 197.
132 Dwight, 21.
133 Leiding, 23.
134 Smith, *Goose Creek*, 2.
135 *Ibid.*, 4.
136 *Ibid.*, 84.
137 *Ibid.*, 87.
138 Waring, *St. James'*, 65.

CHAPTER EIGHT

1 George C. Rogers, Jr., *Charleston in the Age of the Pinckneys* (Norman, Okla., 1969), 15. Hereafter cited as Rogers.
2 Schaper, 112.
3 *Ibid.*, 114-115.
4 Orvin, *Historic Berkeley*, 48; also W. Roy Smith, *South Carolina as a Royal Province, 1719-1776* (New York, 1903), 145-146. Hereafter cited as Smith, *South Carolina*.
5 Schaper, 108.
6 Sirmans, 151.
7 Wallace, 138.
8 Orvin, *Historic Berkeley*, 53.
9 Wallace, 138.
10 Orvin, *Historic Berkeley*, 54; Wallace, 138.
11 Orvin, *Historic Berkeley*, 54; Smith, 248.
12 Smith, 249-250.
13 Orvin, *Historic Berkeley*, 54.
14 Smith, *South Carolina*, 256.
15 Richard Maxwell Brown, *The South Carolina Regulators* (Cambridge, Mass., 1963), 62-63. Hereafter cited as Brown, *Regulators*.

16 *Ibid.*, 38.
17 *Ibid.*, 52.
18 *Ibid.*, 62.
19 *Ibid.*
20 *Ibid.*, 217.
21 Schaper, 109.
22 Orvin, *Historic Berkeley*, 63.
23 Wallace, 231.
24 *Ibid.*, 282.
25 Berkeley, 268; Johnson, 383.
26 Rogers, 343.
27 McCrady, *1719-1776*, 805.
28 Rogers, 49.
29 *South Carolina Gazette*, January 30, 1775.
30 *Ibid.*, September 7, 1775.
31 Orvin, *Historic Berkeley*, 77.
32 *Ibid.*, 78.
33 *Ibid.*, 280-281.
34 Orvin, *Historic Berkeley*, 79.
35 *South Carolina Gazette*, December 8, 1779.
36 Edward McCrady, *South Carolina in the Revolution, 1775-1780* (New York, 1901), 739. Hereafter cited as McCrady, *1775-1780*.
37 Orvin, *Historic Berkeley*, 112.
38 *Ibid.*, 65; Johnson, 397-398.
39 Johnson, 381-382.
40 Rogers, 49.
41 George Smith McCowen, Jr., *The British Occupation of Charleston, 1780-1782* (Columbia, S.C., 1972), 77. Hereafter cited as McCowen.
42 J. Harold Easterby *et al.*, eds., *The State Records of South Carolina: Journals of the House of Representatives* (hereafter, *House Journals*), for January 6, 1783 to March 17, 1783, 60.
43 McCowen, 77.
44 *House Journals*, 1783-1784, 229, 640.
45 *Ibid.*, 144.
46 McCowen, 139.
47 *Ibid.*, 139.
48 *Ibid.*, 153.
49 *Ibid.*, 129-130.

REFERENCES

CHAPTER NINE

1 Orvin, 148.
2 Wallace, 188, 362.
3 *Ibid.*, 190.
4 Rogers, 117.
5 *State Gazette of South Carolina*, June 2, 1788; Orvin, 155.
6 *City Gazette*, April 25, 1790; Orvin, 156.
7 Thomas A. Bailey, *The American Pageant, A History of the Republic* (Lexington, Mass., 1971), 262.
8 *Ibid.*
9 Charleston *Mercury*, October 15, 1828.
10 *Ibid.*, December 10, 1841.
11 Schaper, 208.
12 Charleston *Mercury*, December 10, 1841.
13 David D. Wallace, *History of South Carolina*, II:143-144.
14 Bailey, 391.
15 Charleston *Mercury*, August 24, 1835.
16 *Ibid.*, Sept. 18, 1835.
17 Orvin, 171.
18 Charleston *Courier*, September 10, 1851.
19 *Ibid.*, March 9, 1855.
20 *Ibid.*, August 18, 1851.
21 *Ibid.*
22 Orvin, 173.
23 E. Milby Burton, *The Siege of Charleston, 1861-1865* (Columbia, S.C., 1970), 1. Hereafter cited as Burton.
24 *Ibid.*
25 *Ibid.*, 4.
26 Charleston *News and Courier*, August 17, 1877.
27 Burton, 263.
28 *Ibid.*
29 Charleston *Courier*, July 14, 1863.
30 Interview with Mrs. R.A. Dordal of Goose Creek on October 5, 1978, and copy of an unpublished family history compiled by Mrs. Evelyn Rees Burt in the possession of Mrs. Dordal.
31 *Ibid.*
32 *Ibid.*
33 *Ibid.*
34 *Ibid.*

35 Burton, 99.
36 *Ibid.*, 312.
37 *Ibid.*, 316.
38 1870 Census, St. James' Parish, Goose Creek.
39 Orvin, *Historic Berkeley*, 178.
40 *Ibid.*
41 Charleston *News and Courier*, September 1, 1876.
42 *Ibid.*, August 28, 1876.
43 Orvin, *Historic Berkeley*, 180.
44 Charleston *News and Courier*, June 11, 1877.
45 *Ibid.*, October 4, 1879.
46 *Ibid.*, January 9, 1882.
47 *Ibid.*, July 20, 1882.
48 *Ibid.*
49 *Ibid.*, July 9, September 6 and November 25, 1882.
50 *Ibid.*, November 10 and 14, 1886.
51 Orvin, *Historic Berkeley*, 195.
52 *Ibid.*, 204.

CHAPTER TEN

1 Bernard Bailyn, *Education in the Forming of American Society* (New York, 1960), 22.
2 *Ibid.*, 15.
3 Bowes, 40.
4 *Ibid.*
5 Edgar W. Knight, *Public Education in the South* (Boston, 1922), 26.
6 Dalcho, 244-263.
7 Newton Edwards and Herman G. Richey, *The School in the American Social Order* (Boston, 1911), 3. Hereafter cited as Edwards and Richey.
8 Klingberg, *An Appraisal*, 4-5.
9 Waring, *St. James'*, 6.
10 Klingberg, *An Appraisal*, 8-9.
11 *Ibid.*, 12.
12 *Ibid.*, 18.
13 *Ibid.*, 20.
14 *Ibid.*
15 Klingberg, *An Appraisal*, 95n.
16 Klingberg, *LeJau*, 95n, 123.
17 Klingberg, *An Appraisal*, 26.

REFERENCES

18 *Ibid.*
19 Waring, *St. James'*, 8; Poyas, 189.
20 J.G. Dunlop, ed., "Letters from John Stewart to William Dunlop," *SCHGM* 32:25.
21 Bowes, 35.
22 Wallace, 81; also "An Act for the Founding and Erecting of a Free School, For the use of the Inhabitants of South Carolina, 1710. No. 290," *Statutes* 2:342-346. See also Poyas, 189.
23 Edwards and Richey, 134.
24 *Statutes*, 2:342-46.
25 "An Act for Founding and Erecting of a Free School in Charleston for the Use of the Inhabitants of this Province, of South Carolina, 1712. No. 319," *Statutes*, 2:389-395.
26 *Ibid.*
27 *Ibid.*
28 *Ibid.*
29 "An Act for the Better Relief of the Poor of this Province, 1712. No. 325," *Statutes*, 2:593-98.
30 Edwards and Richey, 136.
31 Klingberg, *LeJau*, 50.
32 *Ibid.*, 70n.
33 Wallace, 82.
34 *Ibid.*
35 *Ibid.*
36 *Ibid.*, 12.
37 *Ibid.*, 13.
38 *Ibid.*, 15.
39 *Ibid.*
40 *Ibid.*
41 *Ibid.*, 16.
42 *Ibid.*
43 *Ibid.*, 23.
44 *Ibid.*
45 *Ibid.*
46 *Ibid.*, 17.
47 Smith, *French Huguenot Church*, 15.
48 Bowes, 41.
49 *Acts . . . of the General Assembly*, 1858, Report of the Committee on Education (Columbia, 1858).
50 Waring, *St. James'*, 19.
51 *Ibid.*

52 *Ibid.*
53 Vestry Minutes, 1872-1876.
54 *Ibid.*, 1882-1925.
55 *Ibid.*
56 *Ibid.*
57 *Ibid.*
58 *Ibid.*
59 *Statutes*, 1811, No. 1980, 5:639-641.
60 *Ibid.*
61 *Ibid.*
62 "Repŏrt of the Free School Commissioners to the State Legislature," 1830 to 1860, at the South Carolina Department of Archives and History, Columbia. Hereafter cited as Commissioner's Reports.
63 Censuses of 1830, 1840, 1850 and 1860, St. James' Parish, S.C.
64 1860 Census.
65 Commissioner's Reports, 1830-1860.
66 *Ibid.*
67 *Ibid.*
68 *Ibid.*, 1836.
69 *Ibid.*, 1856.
70 *Ibid.*, 1854.
71 *Ibid.*, 1859; also Waring, *St. James'*, 19.
72 Commissioner's Reports, 1859; also Charleston *Royal Gazette*, April 7-11, 1781.
73 McCowen, 121.

CHAPTER ELEVEN

1 Poyas, 176.
2 McCrady, *1690-1719*, 707; Waring, *St. James'*, 24; and Vestry Minutes 1872-1876 and 1882-1925.
3 Waring, *St. James'*, 24; Poyas, 177.
4 Waring, *St. James'*, 24.
5 *Ibid.*, 25.
6 Dalcho, 244-245.
7 Hirsch, 68.
8 Waring, *St. James'*, 5; Dalcho, 245.
9 Vestry Minutes, 1882-1925, p. 51, in an article from *The Mission Field*, November, 1908, found in the minutes.
10 *Ibid.* Some of the correspondence of the Rev. Thomas is in *SCHGM*, 4 and 5.

REFERENCES

11 *Ibid.*
12 *Ibid.*
13 Dalcho, 51.
14 Letters of the Society for the Propagation of the Gospel in Foreign Parts to the Ministers of St. James' Church, Goose Creek, 1702 to 1765. Copies at the South Carolina Historical Society, Charleston. Hereafter cited as S.P.G. Letters.
15 S.P.G. Letters, 1705; Dalcho, 244-245.
16 Waring, *St. James'*, 6.
17 Dalcho, 244; Orvin, 4.
18 Hirsch, 68.
19 Smith, *French Huguenot Church*, 45; Hirsch, 67; McCrady, *1690-1719*, 324; and deed in Charleston County R.M.C. Office, book G, No. 6 and 95.
20 Smith, *Goose Creek*, 265; McCrady, *1670-1719*, 337.
21 Hirsch, 67.
22 Smith, *Goose Creek*, 266.
23 Hirsch, 68.
24 Waring, *St. James'*, 7.
25 *Ibid.*
26 *Ibid.*
27 Dalcho, 245; Poyas, 187.
28 Waring, *St. James'*, 7; Dalcho, 247.
29 *Ibid.*; Poyas, 188.
30 Klingberg, *An Appraisal*, 22.
31 *Ibid.*, 23-24.
32 Poyas, 189; Hirsch, 69-70.
33 Waring, *St. James'*, 9.
34 Dalcho, 248; Poyas, 189.
35 Waring, *St. James'*, 9; Poyas, 190.
36 *Ibid.*
37 *Ibid.*
38 Hirsch, 71; McCrady, *1719-1776*, 435.
39 Klingberg, *LeJau*, 50.
40 Parish Register for St. Andrew's Parish, 1728-, at the South Carolina Historical Society, Charleston.
41 Waring, *St. James'*, 11.
42 *Ibid.*, 12.
43 Dalcho, 258.
44 Klingberg, *LeJau*, 92.

45 *Ibid.*, 93.
46 *Ibid.*, 93-94.
47 Waring, *St. James'*, 14; Klingberg, *LeJau*, 96.
48 Waring, *St. James'*, 16.
49 Klingberg, *LeJau*, 96.
50 *Ibid.*
51 *Ibid.*
52 *Ibid.*
53 *Ibid.*, 16; Poyas, 192.
54 Waring, *St. James'*, 16.
55 *Ibid.*, 15.
56 *Ibid.*
57 *Ibid.*
58 Ravenel, 299; Poyas, 186; and Johnson, 382.
59 Poyas, 178.
60 Johnson, 382.
61 *Ibid.*, 384.
62 Waring, *St. James'*, 17.
63 Leiding, 26.
64 Fraser, 17.
65 Waring, *St. James'*, 17.
66 *Ibid.*
67 *Ibid.*
68 *Ibid.*
69 Charleston *News and Courier*, April 22, 1900.
70 *Ibid.*, April 23, 1906.
71 *Ibid.*
72 Waring, *St. James'*, 22.
73 Vestry Minutes, September 22, 1886.
74 McCrady, 707; also Hazel Crowson Sellers, *Old South Carolina Churches* (Columbia, S.C., 1941), 30.
75 Charleston *News and Courier*, April 20, 1925.
76 Poyas, 144.
77 McCrady, *1719-1776*, 707n.
78 Poyas, 186.
79 *Ibid.*, 178.
80 Waring, *St. James'*, 23.
81 Fraser, 10.
82 Joseph I. Waring, comp., "Inscriptions from the 'Chapel of Ease' of St. James Church, Goose Creek," *SCHGM*, 13:67-69.

REFERENCES

83 Poyas, 192.
84 Klingberg, *LeJau*, 141.

CHAPTER TWELVE

1 Margaret Rhett Martin, *Charleston Ghosts* (Columbia, S.C., 1963), 67. Hereafter cited as Martin. Also Irving, *Cooper River*, 103-105.
2 Poyas, 95; Martin, 68.
3 Martin, 68.
4 *Ibid.*
5 *Ibid.*, 69.
6 Poyas, 83.
7 Irving, *Cooper River*, 108.
8 *The Goose Creek Church, A Morbid Tale* (New York, 1901), 7.
9 *Ibid.*, 9.
10 *Ibid.*, 16.
11 *Ibid.*, 17-18.
12 *Ibid.*, 20.
13 *Ibid.*, 21.
14 McCrady, *1719-1776*, 196-197.
15 *Ibid*, 197.
16 Irving, 73.
17 McCrady, *1719-1776*, 197.
18 Martin, 89.
19 Johnson, 67-68; Rogers, 298.
20 Martin, 90.
21 Martin, 83; Johnson, 68.
22 John Bennett, *The Treasure of Peyre Gaillard* (New York, 1906), 3, 5, and 9.
23 Martin, 85.
24 *Ibid.*
25 Irving, 69.
26 *Ibid.*, 21.

CHAPTER THIRTEEN

1 "Map of Small Farms, Situate Berkeley Co., S.C. Near Otranto on A.C.L. Rwy. April, 1916. Richard C. Rhett, Surveyor." Original in the possession of Jack Etling, Goose Creek.

2 I.A. Newby, *Black Carolinians* . . . *1895-1968* (Columbia, S.C., 1973), 253.

3 Personal interview with Mrs. Bertha Middleton, resident of Casey, January 21, 1979.

4 Personal interview with Mrs. Loretta Parson, resident of Casey, April 4, 1978.

5 *Ibid.*

6 *Ibid.*

7 Personal interview with Mrs. Jennie Mae Jefferson, resident of Casey, March 17, 1978.

8 *Ibid.*

9 Personal interview with Mrs. Gertrude Trescott, April 15, 1979.

10 Orvin, *Monck's Corner*, 64.

11 Personal interview with Mrs. Trescott.

12 Earle Sloan, *Mineral Localities of South Carolina* (Columbia, S.C., 1908).

13 Personal interview with Mr. C.J. Bryant, Sr., August 8, 1976, at Mt. Holly.

14 Personal interview with Mrs. Parsons.

15 Personal interview with Fred Moseley, October 15, 1978, at his residence on Liberty Hall Road, Goose Creek.

16 Personal interview with Mrs. Parsons.

17 *Ibid.*

18 *Ibid.*

19 Personal interview with Mr. M.C. Cannon, June 8, 1979 at the Phillipine Hut Restaurant, Goose Creek.

20 Personal interview with Mrs. Eloise Gowder, May 1, 1979.

21 *Ibid.*

22 *Ibid.*

23 *Ibid.*

24 *Berkeley Democrat*, February 18, 1973.

25 *Ibid.*, September 7, 1939, February 2, 1939, February 6, 1936, and May 6, 1937.

26 *Berkeley Democrat*, August 18, 1971.

27 *Ibid.*

28 Certificate of Incorporation, January 11, 1961. Copy in Goose Creek City Hall.

29 *Berkeley Democrat*, April 11, 1979.

30 *Berkeley Democrat*, April 11, 1979.

REFERENCES

31 Minutes of City Council, City of Goose Creek, at Goose Creek City Hall.
32 Personal interview with Mayor Malvin Mann, January 20, 1978. Hereafter cited as Mann interview.
33 *Ibid.*
34 *Ibid.*
35 Personal interview with Mr. Jack Etling, Pineview Development Company, February 4, 1979.
36 Charleston *News and Courier*, February 20, 1964.
37 *Ibid.*, April 29, 1973.
38 Mann interview.
39 *Ibid.*
40 *Ibid.*
41 *Ibid.*
42 *Ibid.*
43 *Ibid.*
44 *Ibid.*
45 Charleston *News and Courier*, April 29, 1973.
46 *Ibid.*
47 *Berkeley Democrat*, February 9, 1972.
48 Charleston *News and Courier*, February 4, 1972.
49 *Berkeley Democrat*, February 2, 1972.
50 Charleston *News and Courier*, October 20, 1972.
51 *Berkeley Democrat*, October 11, 1972.
52 *Hanahan News*, 1973, *passim*.
53 Charleston *News and Courier*, March 27, 1971.
54 *Ibid.*, May 10, 1973.
55 *Ibid.*, May 30, 1970.
56 Personal interview with S.E. "Speedy" Felkel, August 4, 1978. Hereafter cited as Felkel interview.
57 *Ibid.*
58 *Ibid.*
59 *Ibid.*; Charleston *News and Courier*, August 6, 1968.
60 Charleston *News and Courier*, August 6, 1968.
61 *Ibid.*, August 11, 1968.
62 *Ibid.*, May 15, 1969.
63 *Ibid.*, August 6, 1968 and Felkel interview.
64 Felkel interview.
65 Charleston *News and Courier*, August 22, 1969.
66 *Ibid.*, June 11, 1969.
67 *Ibid.*, July 14, 1968.
68 *Ibid.*, January 16, 1969.

69. *Ibid.*
70 *Ibid.*, July 6, 1970.
71 *Ibid.*, August 30, 1973.
72 Charleston *Evening Post*, February 7, 1975.
73 Mann interview.
74 Charleston *News and Courier*, May 18, 1977.
75 Charleston *Evening Post*, June 10, 1977.

BIBLIOGRAPHY

1. Primary Sources

Letters of the Society for the Propagation of the Gospel in Foreign Parts to the ministers of St. James' Church, Goose Creek, 1702 - 1765. At the South Carolina Historical Society, Charleston. Typescript.

St. Andrew's Parish. Parish register of St. Andrew's Parish, 1728 -. Copy at the South Carolina Historical Society.

St. James' Church, Goose Creek. Minutes of the Vestry, 1872 - 1925. On deposit at the South Carolina Historical Society.

Minutes of the City Council of the City of Goose Creek, S.C.

2. Journals and Periodicals

Berkeley Democrat
Charleston *Courier*
Charleston *Evening Post*
Charleston *Mercury*
Charleston *News and Courier*
Charleston *Royal Gazette*
Hanahan News
Names in South Carolina, edited by Claude Neuffer. Columbia: Department of English, University of South Carolina. Volume XVI.
Proceedings of the American Philosophical Society, XXVI, No. 129.
South Carolina Gazette
South Carolina Historical and Genealogical Magazine. Charleston: South Carolina Historical Society, 1900 -.
State Gazette of South Carolina
Transactions of the Huguenot Society of South Carolina 1886 -. Charleston: Huguenot Society of South Carolina.

3. Interviews

Mr. A. L. Collier, in the *Charleston Evening Post*, North Metro edition, June 30, 1977.

Mayor Malvin Mann, January 20, 1978 at Goose Creek City Hall.

Mr. Jack Etling, Pineview Development Co., February 4, 1979.

Mrs. Bertha Middleton, resident of Casey, January 21, 1979 at Westview Elementary School, Goose Creek.

Mrs. Loretta Parsons, resident of Casey, April 4, 1978 at Westview Elementary School, Goose Creek.

Mrs. Gertrude Trescott, April 15, 1979 at Westview Elementary School, Goose Creek.

Mrs. Jennie Mae Jefferson, resident of Casey, March 17, 1978 at Boulder Bluff Elementary School, Goose Creek.

Mr. M. C. Cannon, June 8, 1979 at the Phillipine Hut Restaurant, Goose Creek.

Mr. Fred Moseley, October 15, 1968 at his residence on Liberty Hall Road, Goose Creek.

Mr. C. J. Bryant, Sr., August 8, 1976 at his residence at Mt. Holly.

Mrs. Eloise Gowder, May 1, 1979 at the Berkeley County Library, Monck's Corner.

Mr. S. E. "Speedy" Felkel, August 4, 1978 at the Goose Ceeek City Hall.

Mrs. R. A. Dordal, October 5, 1978.

4. Published Sources

Act for the better relief of the poor of this Province, 1712. No. 325.

Act for the founding and erecting of a free school in Charleston . . . 1712. No. 319.

Act for the founding and erection of a free school . . . 1710. No. 290.

Baily, Thomas A. *The American Pageant: A History of the Republic.* Lexington, Massachusetts: D.C. Health & Co., 1971.

Bailyn, Bernard. *Education in the Forming of American Society.* New York: Vantage Press, 1960.

Bennett, John. *The Treasure of Peyre Gaillard.* New York, 1906.

Berkeley, Edmund and Dorothy Smith Berkeley. *Dr. Alexander Garden of Charles Town.* Chapel Hill, N.C.: University of North Carolina Press, 1969.

Bowes, Frederick P. *The Culture of Early Charleston.* Chapel Hill, N.C.: University of North Carolina Press, 1942.

BIBLIOGRAPHY

Brown, Douglas Summers. *The Catawba Indians: The People of the River.* Columbia, S.C.: University of South Carolina Press, 1966.

Brown, Richard Maxwell. *The South Carolina Regulators.* Cambridge, Massachusetts: Belknap Press of Harvard University, 1963.

Burney, Eugenia. *Colonial South Carolina.* Camden, N.J.: Thomas Nelson, Inc., 1970.

Burton, E. Milby. *The Siege of Charleston, 1861-1865.* Columbia, S.C.: University of South Carolina Press, 1970.

Carter, Stephen & Associates. *Land Use Study.* Prepared for the City of Goose Creek, 1976.

Cheves, Langdon, ed. "The Shaftesbury Papers and other records relating to Carolina and the first settlement on Ashley River prior to the year 1676," in *Collections of the South Carolina Historical Society,* V (1897).

Childs, St. Julien Ravenel. *Malaria and Colonization in the Carolina Low Country, 1526-1969.* Baltimore, Md.: John Hopkins Press, 1940.

Clowse, Converse D. *Economic Beginnings in South Carolina.* Columbia, S.C.: University of South Carolina Press, 1971.

Correspondence of Mr. Ralph Izard of South Carolina for the Years 1774 to 1804, with a short memoir. New York: Charles Francis & Co., 1844. 2 vol.

Crane, Verner W. *The Southern Frontier, 1670-1752.* Durham, N.C.: Duke University Press, 1928.

Dalcho, Frederick. *An Historical Account of the Protestant Episcopal Church in South Carolina.* Charleston, S.C.: A.E. Miller, 1820; reprinted 1969.

Doar, David. *Rice and Rice Planting in the South Carolina Low Country.* Charleston, S.C.: Charleston Museum, 1936.

Dwight, Henry Ravenel. *Some Historic Spots in Berkeley.* Pinopolis, S.C.: Women's Auxiliary of Trinity Church, 1921; reprinted 1944.

Easterby, J.H., ed. *Journal of the Commons House of Assembly, May 18, 1741 - July 10, 1742.* Columbia, S.C.: Historical Commission of South Carolina, 1953.

Edwards, Newton and Herman G. Richey. *The School in the American Social Order.* Boston: Houghton-Mifflin Co., 1911.

Franklin, John Hope. *From Slavery to Freedom: A History of Negro Americans.* New York: Vantage Books, 1969.

Fraser, Charles. *A Charleston Sketchbook, 1796-1806.* Rutland, Vt.: Charles E. Tuttle Co.

The Goose Creek Church, A Morbid Tale. New York: Printed at the Sign of the Eagle, 1901.

Gordon, Asa H. *Sketches of Negro Life and History in South Carolina.* 1929, reprinted Columbia, S.C.: University of South Carolina Press, 1971.

Hirsch, Arthur Henry. *The Huguenots of Colonial South Carolina.* London: Archon Books, 1962.

Hofstadter, Richard. *The American Republic.* Englewood Cliffs, N.J.: Prentice-Hall, 1959. 2 vol.

Hughson, Shirley C. *The Carolina Pirates and Colonial Commerce, 1670 - 1740.* Baltimore: John Hopkins Press, 1894.

Irving, John B. *A Day on Cooper River.* Charleston, S.C.: A.E. Miller, 1869.

Irving, John B. *The South Carolina Jockey Club.* 1857, reprinted Spartanburg, S.C.: The Reprint Co., 1975.

Johnson, Joseph. *Traditions and Reminiscenses, Chiefly of the American Revolution in the South.* Charleston, S.C.: Walker & James, 1851.

King, Joe M. *A History of South Carolina Baptists.* Columbia, S.C.: R.L. Bryan, 1964.

Klingberg, Frank J. *An Appraisal of the Negro in Colonial South Carolina.* Washington: Associated Publishers, 1941.

Klingberg, Frank J. *The Carolina Chronicle of Dr. Francis LeJau, 1706-1717.* Berkeley & Los Angeles: University of California Press, 1956.

Klingberg, Frank J. Carolina Chronicle: *The Papers of Commissary Gideon Johnson, 1707-1716.* Berkeley & Los Angeles: University of California Press, 1946.

Knight, Edgar W. *Public Education in the South.* Boston: Ginn & Co., 1922.

Leiding, Henriette Kershaw. *Historic Houses of South Carolina.* Philadelphia: J.B. Lippincott, 1921.

BIBLIOGRAPHY

Lieber, Oscar M. "Vocabulary of the Catawba Language, with some Remarks on its Grammar, Construction and Pronunciation," in *Collections of the South Carolina Historical Society*, II: 327-342.

Life in Carolina and New England during the Nineteenth Century, as Illustrated by Reminiscences and Letters of the DeWolf Family of Bristol, Rhode Island. Bristol, R.I.: privately printed, 1929.

Lind, Ivan. "Geography and Place Names," in Philip Wagner and Marvin Mikesell, eds., *Readings in Cultural Geography*. Chicago: University of Chicago Press, 1962.

McCowen, George Smith, Jr. *The British Occupation of Charleston, 1780-1782.* Columbia, S.C.: University of South Carolina Press, 1972.

McCrady, Edward. *History of South Carolina* . . . New York: McMillan, 1897-1801. 4 vol.

McDowell, William L., ed. *Documents Relating to Indian Affairs, 1754-1765.* Columbia, S.C.: University of South Carolina Press, 1970.

Map of Small Farms, Situate Berkeley County, S.C., near Otranto on A.C.L. Railway. April, 1916.

Martin, Margaret Rhett. *Charleston Ghosts.* Columbia, S.C.: University of South Carolina Press, 1963.

Milling, Chapman J. *Red Carolinians.* Chapel Hill, N.C.: University of North Carolina Press, 1940.

Moore, Caroline T., ed. *Abstracts of the Wills of South Carolina.* Columbia, S.C.: R.L. Bryan, 1960-1974. 4 vol.

Nevins, Allan. *Slave Trading in the Old South.* New York: Frederick Ungar Publ. Co., 1959.

Orvin, Maxwell Clayton. *Historic Berkeley County, S.C., 1671-1900.* Charleston, S.C.: Comprint, 1973.

Orvin, Maxwell Clayton. *A History of Monck's Corner, Berkeley County, South Carolina.* Charleston, S.C.: author, 1961.

Poyas, Mrs. E.A. *The Olden Times of South Carolina.* Charleston, S.C.: S.G. Courtenay & Co., 1855.

Ravenel, Mrs. St. Julien. *Charleston, the Place and the People.* New York: McMillan, 1912.

"Report of the Committee on Education," in *Acts, Reports and Regulations of the General Assembly of South Carolina.* Columbia, S.C.: R.W. Gibbes, 1858.

Reports of the Free School Commissioners to the State Legislature, 1830-1860.

Rivers, William J. *A Sketch of the History of South Carolina.* 1856, reprinted Spartanburg, S.C.: The Reprint Co., 1972.

Rogers, George C., Jr. *Charleston in the Age of the Pinckneys.* Norman, Oklahoma: University of Oklahoma Press, 1969.

Rutledge, Anna Wells. *Artists in the Life of Charleston.* Philadelphia: American Philosophical Society, 1949.

Salley, Alexander S., Jr. *Narratives of Early Carolina.* 1911, reprinted New York: Barnes & Noble, 1967.

Salley, Alexander S., Jr. *Warrants for Land in South Carolina, 1672-1711.* Columbia, S.C.: Historical Commission of South Carolina, 1910-1915. 3 vol.

Sass, Herbert Ravenel. *The Story of the South Carolina Low Country.* West Columbia, S.C.: J.F. Hyer Publishing Co., 1956. 3 vol.

Savell, Max. *A History of Colonial America.* New York: Holt, Rinehart & Winston, 1966.

Schaper, William A. *Sectionalism and Representation in South Carolina.* New York: DaCapo Press, 1968.

Sellers, Hazel Crowson. *Old South Carolina Churches.* Columbia, S.C.: Crowson Printing Co., 1941.

Sellers, Leila. *Charleston Business on the Eve of the American Revolution.* Chapel Hill, N.C.: University of North Carolina Press, 1934.

Sirmans, M. Eugene. *Colonial South Carolina: A Political History.* Chapel Hill, N.C.: University of North Carolina Press, 1966.

Sloan, Earle. *Mineral Localities of South Carolina.* Columbia, S.C.: State Co., 1908.

Smith, W. Roy. *South Carolina as a Royal Province, 1719-1776.* New York: MacMillan, 1903.

Stoney, Samuel Gaillard. *Plantations of the South Carolina Low Country.* Charleston, S.C.: Carolina Art Association, 1964.

Swanton, John Reed. *Indians of the Southeastern United States.* Washington: Government Printing Office, 1946.

BIBLIOGRAPHY

Thompson, Theodora J., ed. *Journals of the South Carolina House of Representatives, 1783-1784.* Columbia, S.C.: University of South Carolina Press, 1977.

Townsend, Leah. *South Carolina Baptists, 1607-1805.* Florence, S.C.: Florence Printing Co., 1935.

U.S. Census Bureau. Federal Population Censuses, 1790-1880. National Archives microfilm.

U.S. Census Bureau. Special Census for the City of Goose Creek, April, 1979.

Walker, Debbie. "Past Lives at Otranto," in *Low Country News and Views in Review,* Charleston, S.C., May 3, 1977.

Wallace, David Duncan. *The History of South Carolina.* New York: American Historical Society, 1934. 4 vol.

Wallace, David Duncan. *South Carolina: A Short History.* Columbia, S.C.: University of South Carolina Press, 1951.

Waring, Joseph Ioor. *A History of Medicine in South Carolina.* Charleston, S.C.: S.C. Medical Association, 1964-67. 3 vol.

Waring, Joseph Ioor. *St. James' Church, Goose Creek, South Carolina: A Sketch of the Parish from 1706-1909.* Charleston: Daggett Printing Co., 1911.

W.P.A. Federal Writer's Project. *Palmetto Place Names.* 1941, reprinted Spartanburg, S.C.: The Reprint Co., 1975.

Wright, John K. "The Study of Place Names: Recent Work and some Possibilities," in *Geographical Review,* 1929, 149-154.

INDEX

- A -

Abbott, Dr. H.J., 73
Abolitionists, 147
Adams, Robert, 34, 169
Addison, Tom, 222
"Adsham," Indian term, 6
Adthan Creek, 4,16,94
Agassiz, Prof., 110
Agrarian Laws, 53
Agricultural Soc. of S.C., 94
Ainslie, Hannah, 198
Alex, a slave, 153
Alford, James, 46
Alhambra Hall, Mt. Pleasant, 158
Allen, J. Beard Madera, 20
Allen, Jacob, 103
Allen, William, 17,79,168
Allen's Plantation, 20
American Automobile Assn., 226
American Philosophical Soc., 91,96
Amory, Jonathon, 59
Anabaptists (see also Baptists), 14,36,79
"Anchaw," Indian term, 94
"Ancient Lady," pen name for Mrs. Elizabeth Poyas, 92
Ancrum, William Washington, 108
Anderson, Edgar, 224
Anderson, Elizabeth, 162
Anderson, Roger, 239
Andrews, Rev. William, 45
Anglican Church (see also Church of England, Episcopal Church, S.P.G.) 13,49,162
Anglicans, 61,79
Animals & Livestock mentioned: Cattle, 32,71,74; Hogs, 32,71; (Race) Horses, 71,88,106
Appalachicola Indians, 46
Appeebee Creek, 4
Apprentices, 166
Ararat Plantation, 84
Archdale, Gov. John, 42, 43,60,61,87
Ashe, Mr., 20
Ashley, Lord, 12,40
Ashley River, 5,12,14,111, 113,117,155
Atlantic Coast Line RR, 2, 9,193
Avenue of the Oaks, 116
Azaleas, 118

- B -

Bachman, Dr., 84
Back River, 3,7,8,14,16,19, 29,85,86,89,212,213,215, 220
Back River Lower Road, 84
Back River Upper Road, 84
Bacon's Bridge, 133
Bacot, _____, 108
Bacot, Peter, 18,133
Bagbee, John, 17
Baker, James, 19
Baker, Richard, 19
Baker, Thomas Jr., 19
Baker, Thomas, Sr., 19
Ball, Catherine, 197

Ball, Mrs. Elias, 19
Baptists, (see also Anabaptists), 14,79,166,199
Barbadians, 21,29,31,49, 50,51,54,175,179
Barbados Party, organized, 50
Barbados, W.I., emigrants from, 10,11,12,14,30,67, 97,112,121,160
Barker, Charles, 120
Barker, Jacob, 145
Barker, John, 83
Barker, Maj., 156
Barker, Sarah, 20
Barker, Mrs. Sarah, 78
Barker, Thomas, 15,16,17, 20
Barker, Capt. Thomas, 46
Barley, 99
Barnett, William, 119
Barnett, John, 241
Barnett, John G., 241
Barnett, W.A. 231
Barnwell, Col. John, 64
Baronies, established, 51
Barrett, Jacob, 99
Barrie, James, 76
Barrs, Carl, 228
Barrs, Carl, Sr., 241
Barrs, Carl V., Sr., 240
Barrs, Hattie Mae, 239
Bartlett, Mrs., 113
Bartram, John, 91,104
Battle of Videau's Bridge, 212
Bauyly, John, 17
Bayley, James, 168
Beaird, Matthew, 17
Beauregard, Gen., 154
Bee, Gen. Bernard, 171
Bee, Bernard E., 120
Bee, Thomas, 120
Bella, a Negro servant, 91
Bellinger, Edmund, 61
Bennett, John, 212
Bennett, Nicholas, 19
Bernard, James, 19
Berringer, John, 112
Berringer, Margaret, 92
Berringer, Mary, 112
Berringer Plantation, 16
Berkeley County, 1,2; present Co. formed, 8; 22,59,81,129,134,143, 149,151,158,176
Berkeley, Dorothy Smith, 91
Berkeley, Edmund, 91
Berkeley, Regiment of Militia, 123,136
Berkeley Training High School, 219
Best, Steven, 241
Beverly Hills subdivision, 3
Bigelow (e), Cyprian, 83,97
Bigelowe's grant, 15; plantation, 97,101,103
Binah, a free Negro, 81
Binnar, E.B., 239
Bisco, Samuel, 19
Bishop of London, 184,186
Bishop Robert, 112
Blackbeard, a pirate, 64
Blackman, Thomas, 145
Blake, Gov. Joseph, 59,61, 62
Blake, Mr., 86

Blake, W., 168
Blockade of Charleston Harbor, 151
Bloomfield Plantation, 16, 95
Bloomville Plantation, 95
Board of Trade, 61
Bob, a Negro slave, 77
Boddely, Col. John, 135
Boddin, Dr. Richard, 73
Boddin, Robert, 79
Bodett, Peter, 34
Boggs, Mrs. F.G., 196
Boisseau, John, 18
Boisseau, Mary, 19
Bonneau, Anthony, 18
Bonneau,S.C., 157
Bonnet, Stede, a pirate, 55,64
"Boo-Chaw-A," Indian term, 16
Booshooe Plantation, 5
Boone, Gov., 129,130
Boone, John, 41
Boone, Mr., 86
Boulder Bluff subdivision, 3,91,137,159,219,222, 229
Bounds, Earl, 227,240
Bounds, Earl H., 240
Bowens Corner, S.C., 215, 216,219
Bowick, Michael H., 240
Boykin, Mrs. Elizabeth, 223
Boyle, Charles, 158
Braddeley, John, 139
Bradley, John, 134
Bradwell, Sr., 148
Bradwell, Isaac, 145,148
Bradwell, Isaac Jr., 147, 148
Brailsford, Edward D., 248
Breaker's Tavern, 85
Brick, manufactured, 88
Brick Hope Plantation, 84, 88
Brick House Plantation, 15, 119
Brickman, Mrs., 152
Brisbane, John Stanyarne, 106
Broad Path (see also New Broad Path), 67,83
Bromley, Thomas, 196,244
Broom Hall Plantation, 16, 94,95
Broomfield Plantation, 94
Broomville Plantation, 94
Broughton, Alexander, 134
Broughton, Andrew, 79
Broughton, Anne, 112
Broughton, family, 199
Broughton, Lt. Gov., 74
Broughton, Nathaniel, 79, 200
Broughton, Thomas, 112
Broun family, 199
Broun, Dr. A., 73
Broun, Dr. Robert, 249
Brower, Pieter, 11
Brown, Dr. A., 73
Brown, Mrs. Alma, 223
Brown, Archibald, 249
Brown, C.P., 150
Brown, family, 223
Brown, J.B., 239
Brown, J.B., Jr., 224
Brown, James, 19

Brown, John, 20,137
Brown, Keith, 151
Brown, Marguerite, 241
Brown, Mrs., 92
Brown, Richard M., 126
Brown, Robert, 169
Brown, Dr. Robert, 73,196, 197
Brown, W.J., 223
Browning, H.T., 149
Browning, L.S., 158
Browning, T.S., 156,158
Brownlee, John, 148
Bruck, John Jacob, 17
Bruneau, Henry, 18
Bryant, C.J., 218
Bryant, C.J., Sr., 220
Bryant, Joseph, 220
Bubose, Peter, 137
Bull, Lt. Gov., 197
Bull, Stephen, 168
Bull, William, 46
Bull, Gov. William, 129
Bulline, John, 120
Bullins, ____, 20
Bunch, H.W., 239
Bunch, Hilton W., 225
Bunch, Waring, 223,224
Bunch, Mrs. Waring, 223
Burbridge, John, 137
Burke, Edmund, 98
Bushy Park Ind. Park,237
Bushy Park, 224,250
Butler, Gen. M.C., 150
Byrd family, 68

- C -

Caciques, established, 51; titles sold, 61
Caffrey, Ed., 231
Cain, Jetter, 239
Caldwell, Charles, 240
Caldwell, Charles E., 239
Caldwell, Orris E., 241
Caldwell, Orris F., 240
Cambridge, Tobias, 247
Camelot Village subdivision, 4,230
Campbell, Capt. Archibald, 210,211
Campbell, Gov., 101
Cane Grinding Day, 158
Cannon, G.B., 223
Cannon, Mrs. G.B., 223
Cannon, George, 137
Cannon, J.R., 223
Cannon, Mrs. J.R., 223
Cannon, Lewis, 100
Cannon's Store, 222
Cantey, Capt. 45
Cantey, George, 14,15,182
Cantey, Capt. John, 107, 182
Cantey, Tiege, 14
Capers, Rt. Rev. Ellison, 193
Caree Indians, 45
Carlisle, Earl of,11
Carne, Samuel, 114
Carolina Water Co., 232
Carrington, Charles, 206, 209
Carroll family, 68
Carter family, 68
Carwile, John, 97
Casey Cemetery, 217
Casey Church, 3,159,217
Casey Assembly Hall, 3
Casey Fellowship Hall, 217
Casey Friendship Hall, 218
Casey Hill, 3

Casey M.E. Church, 218
Casey, Mr., a Freedman, 216
Casey School, 217,219
Casey,S.C., 3,215,216,217 219
Catawba Indians, 5,6,45,47
Cates, Rev., 186
Catholics of France, 17
Centennial Dem. Club of St. James', Goose Creek, 156
Charles I, King of England, 86
Charles IV, King of England, 17
Charleston Comm. of Pub. Wks., 101,233,234
Charleston Co., divided 1882,158
Charleston High School, 153
Charleston Light Dragoons, 88
Charleston Light Infantry, 102
Charleston Museum, 107,110
Charleston Neck, 8,83,119, 133,151,155
Charleston,S.C., colony of, est., 12;
Charleston, schools of, 160;capture by British, 133,175
Chamberlain, Gov., 157
Chamberlain, Norman A., 244
Chambers, Robert, 20
Channing, John, 169
Cherokee Indian War, 187
Cherokee Indians, 45,46, 57,60,80
Cherry Hill Estate, 108
Chickasaw Indians, 60
Chicken, Capt. George, 3, 15,19,46,47,54,64
Chicken Creek, 3
Children's Day, 218
Childs, Isaac, 79
Chinnus, R. 148
Chisholm, Mrs. Nathalie, 219
Choctaw Indians, 60
Chunkey, an Indian game, 23
Church Act of 1706, 7,121
Church of England, (see also Anglican Church, Episcopal Church, S.P.G.) 49;established as State Church, 63,179,180)
Civil War, inflation from, 151; end of, 154
Clark, Albert, 149
Clinton, Sir Henry, 133
Coachman, Benjamin, 132 169,188,189,247
Coachman, James, 169
Coastal Water Co., 230, 232,233,234
Cockfield, John, 148
Cockran, John, 148
Cocrane Art Gallery, 118
Cohens, Frank, 218
Cohens, Willie Mae, 218
Coleman, Edith, 206,207
Coleman, James, 208
College of Charleston, 110
Colleton, Gov., 56,57,58, 86
Colleton, Gov. James, 56
Collier, A.L., 1
Collins, Ms. Ann, 248
Collins, William John, 248
Colored Orphan Aid Soc., 109

Commissioners of Indian Trade, 41,45
Committee of Safety & Corres., 149
Confederate Honor College, 172
Confederate Nitre & Mining Bureau, 110
Confederate States of America, 150
Confiscation Act., 139
Congaree Indians, 48
Conner, George, 158
Connor, T.T., 158
Continental Association, 132
Cooper, Lord Anthony, 50
Cooper, Dr. Bernard Christian, 34
Cooper, Dr. Christian, 20
Cooper, John, 137
Cooper, Lucretia, 97
Cooper River, 6,8,12,13,29, 30,38,67,69,70,83,84, 88,94,112,142,156,173, 180
Copley, Mrs., 99,101
Corben, Rev. William, 179
Cordensville,S.C., 154
Corn, 24,32,35,69,75,91, 99,113,142,151
Cornwallis, General, 134
Cotebas Plantation, 85
Cottage Plantation, 84,90
Cotton, 70,130,142,144,158
Cotton Gin, introduced, 142
Couch, Richard, 249
Council of Safety, 131,132, 138
Craven, Gov., 46
Cravon, Mrs. Ann, 19
Crawford, George, 145,149
Crawford, J.T., 149
Crawford, Otis, 241
Creek Indians, 46,60,125
Cripp, John Splatt, 119
Cripp's Plantation, 97,119
Cromartie, Earl of, 116
Crops and plants,(see separate listings for azaleas, barley, corn, cotton, grapes, hickory, indigo, laurel, olive oil, pink root, rice, silk, sugar, & tobacco)
Crovat, Theodore F., 106
Crovatt's Plantation, 106
Crowfield Estate, Beaufort Co., 114
Crowfield Hall, England, 113
Crowfield Plantation, 17, 111,115,129
Crowley, an Etiwan Indian, 20,47
Cudja, a runaway slave, 76
Culpepper map of Charleston, 1672, 107
Currency, shortage of, 55
Curtis, Kelly, 226,239
Cusabo Indians, 22,24,41-43
Cypress Camp Ground, 148
Cypress Swamp, 19,85

- D -

Daisey Swamp, S.C., 2
Dalcho, Rev. Frederick, 199,200
Dangerfield, G.W., 223
Dangerfield, Mrs. G.W., 223

Dangerfield, J.H., 223
Dangerfield, Mrs. J.H., 223
Dangerfield, Walter, 222
Daniel, Robert, 62
Daniel, Maj. Robert, 54,61
Daning, Joseph S., 241
D'Arssens, Jean, 87
(de Arssens), John, 16,86
Dasseu, Pierre, 18
Davies, John, 132
Davis, Mrs. Anne, 185
Davis, David, 17
Davis, Capt. David, 19
Davis, Doreen, 241
Davis, John N., 145,146
Dealton, James, 20
Dean, Capt., 150
Dean, Daniel, 19
Deas, Mrs. Carolina, 249
Deas, David, 20
Deas, Capt. David, 78,182
Davis, family, 2,199
Davis, John, 91,118,133, 136,137,144,169
Davis, John Jr., 74,144
Davis, Mrs. John, 110
Davis, Mr., 91,92
Davis, William Allen, 144
Deer Park,S.C., 222
DeFrance, Isaac, 18
DeHay, Andrew, 137
de Lancey, Anne, 99
Delancey family, 143
De La Plaine, Abraham, 18, 20
De La Plaine, Marianne, 18
De La Plaine's Plantation, 108
Democratic Party, 156,158
Dennis, Benjamin, 19,165, 166
Dennis, Sen. Rembert C., 227,231
Desel, Charles L., 84,246
deVignou, Sabina, 86,213
Dickson, John, 46
Dillwyn, William, 114
Dingle, Alexander, 168
Diseases mentioned: diptheria, 34; dysentary, 34; malaria, 33,74,143; measles, 34,74; scarlet fever, 34; smallpox, 34, 74,90,104; yellow fever, 74
Dissenters, 12,36,49,52, 54-57,62,63,165
Dobbins, Joseph, 169
Dorchester County, S.C., 8; established, 158
Dorchester Road, 83,85
Dorchester, S.C., 108, 114, 132,133,148
Douglas, Alexander, 137
Douglas, Jones, 137
Downing, John, 137
Drayton, Dr. Charles, 97
Drayton, Thomas, 87
Drayton, William, 196
Droze Cemetery, 223
Dry, Capt. William, 76, 125,126
Dubose, Theodore Samuel, 87
Duffy, J. Lawrence, 228
Dugue, J., 18
Dunlopp, William, 86
Dupont, Abraham, 18
Dupont, G., 168
Dupont, Gideon, 141,243
Dupont, Gideon Jr., 69
Dupre, Cornelius, 168
Durand, Rev., 186

Dutarque, Mr., 199,200

- E -

Eadie, Sidney A., 241
Earle, Capt., 150
Earnest, Col. J.B., 149
Earnest, Col. T.B., 149
Earnist, B., 148
Easton, Walter, 246
Eckles, William, 133
Edgehill, Richard, 20
Edict of Nantes, 17,18
Edisto River Water Tunnel, 250
Edwards, Gen. E.H., 191
Edwards, Maj. Edward H., 191
Eighteen Mile House, 152
Eighteen Mile House Tavern, 85
18th Regiment, 152
Eldress, J., 19
Election Act of 1721, 122
Elfe, George, 246
Elfe, Mary Jane, 246
Ellington, Rev. Edward, 37, 130,188-190,193,211
Elliott, Rev. C.P., 191
Elliott, Jane, 94
Elliott, Thomas, 134
Ellis, John, 104
Elms Plantation, 16,20,82, 98,99,108,130,135,139
Elrod, Harold L., 229
Elsey, Gary, 239
Emperor, Madame, 19
Emperor, John 17
England, 19,35,94,113,179, 185,186,244
Episcopal Church (see also Anglican Church, Church of England, S.P.G.), 106
Etiwan Indians, 4,6,20,22; festivals of, 23;crops of, 24; women's roles of, 24,25,26; ceremonies of, 27,36,37,40,43; population of 1715, 44,47
Etling, E.W., 239
Etling, Jack, 224
Evans, Rev. William, 217
Exeter Plantation, 212

- F -

Fairlawn Barony, 8
Faucheraud, Charles, 20
Faucheraud, Gideon, 18,20
Fauling, Thomas, 145
Faurcheraud, C., 169
Feare, John, 20
Felkel Field, 232
Felkel, S.E.("Speedy"), 227,230-234
Feltham, Joseph, 162
Ferguson, Maj., 133
Ferguson, Thomas, 119
Fibbin, John, 169
Filbien, John, 20
Fining, Maj. Charles, 109
Fishbourne, Senator, 157
Fisher, John, 97
Fisherau, Gideon, 20
Fitch, Jonathon, 41
Fitz, Jonathon, 20
Fitzsimmons, Dr. L., 73
Flagg, Ernest, 117
Flagg, George, 134
Flagg, Ralph, 139
Fleury, Abraham, 108

Fleury, Abraham de la Plaine, 18
Fleury, Isaac, 18
Fleury, Marianne de la Plaine, 18
Fleury Plantation, 181
Flood, Capt., a pirate,55
Floree, Mr., 20
Flud, Thomas, 19
Fontainbleu Plantation, 83,103,109,110,119
Ford, Arthur Peronneau, 106
Ford, Timothy, 75
Forest Lawn subdivision, 3,229
Fort Dorchester, 84
Fort Moultrie, 151,198
Fort Sumter, 88
Fortescue, Charles Walker, 162
Foster, John, 4,17
Foster's Creek, 4,7,14,84, 220
Four Hole Swamp, 85
Fourcherad, Gideon, 168
Fowler, Rev. Andrew, 192
Foxborough sibdivision, 217,223,229,234
France, 17,89,181
Franchomme, Charles, 18
Franklin, Benjamin, 91,99
Franklin, Mrs. Sadie, 219
Fraser, Alexander, 98
Fraser, Lt. Alexander, 135
Fraser, Charles, 191,195
Fraser, John, 46,98
Frederick's Plantation, 16, 95
French Garden Plantation, 83,95,96
French Protestants: see Huguenots
French Revolution, 57
Friendly Club, 79
Frost, Eugenia C., 91
Frost, Dr. Henry R., 171
Frost, Mrs., 20
Fuller, William, 41
Fundamental Constitutions of Carolina, 49-53,57, 60,68,75,128
Furman, Richard, 79

- G -

Gadsden, Bishop, 192
Gadsden, Christopher, 129, 131,135
Gadsden, Col., 136
Gadsden, John, 175
Gadsden, Rev. Philip, 192
Gadsden, Thomas, 106
Gaillard, Tacitus, 127
Galloway, David, 20
Galloway, family, 68
Garden, Dr. Alexander, 73, 83,91,103
Garden, Maj. Alexander, 105,135
Garden, Alexander Jr., 138
Gardenias, 103
Garrat, Joseph, 19
Garrison, William Lloyd, 147
Gasquette Meeting House, 173
Geddings, Dr., 20
Geddings, Dr. Eli, 101
Dendron, Mary Magdolen, 89
Genillat, Jean Francois de, 120

George, King of England, 130
German Lutheran Church of Charleston, 153
Germany, 152
Gibbes, Arthur S., 95
Gibbes, Benjamin, 19,94, 185,242
Gibbes, Jane, 178,242
Gibbes, John, 185
Gibbes, Col. John, 95,112, 178,242
Gibbes, Mary Anna, 105
Gibbes, Robert, 17,54
Gibbes, Col. Robert, 4
Gibbes, Robert Reeve, 105
Gibson, James E., 250
Gibson, Moses, 152
Gibson, William E., 241
Gibson, William S., 241
Gickie, William, 97
Gignilliat, James, 19,182
Gignilliat, Jean Francois de, 120
Gignilliat, John Francis, 98
Giles, Julia, 119
Gill, Mr., 20
Gillard, Madame Elizabeth, 19
Gillon, Capt. A., 145
Gilmore, Dr. L.B., 73
Gilson, Thomas L., 75
Gilson, Dr. Thomas L., 73
Girard, Peter, 13,181
Gish, Dorothy, 118
Glaves, C.W., 151
Glaze's Plantation, 120
Glen, Gov., 69
Glen, James, 44
Glen, John, 119
Glen's Plantation, 119
Glover, Ann 247
Glover, Charles, 247
Glover, Joseph, 74
Glover, Sarah, 247
Goble, John, 18
Godfrey, Benjamin, 149
Godin, Benjamin, 17,18,20, 54,83,103,109,182,185
Godin, David, 103
Godin, Isaac, 101
Goffe, Roger, 19
Gonda, Nora, 240
Goodbee, James, 17
Goodby, John, 17
Goodby, Jonathon Sr., 19
Goose Creek American Legion Post, 228
Goose Creek Baptist Church, 80
Goose Creek Bridge, 84,105, 108,190
The Goose Creek Church, a Morbid Tale, a novel, 206
Goose Creek City Council, 226
Goose Creek, City of, chartered, 9
Goose Creek Civic Club, 226
Goose Creek Council of Safety, 119
Goose Creek Friendly Soc., 79
Goose Creek Neck, 92,118, 136
Goose Creek Parks & Playground Commission, 232
Goose Creek Party, 52
Goose Creek Planation, (see Yeamans Hall)
Goose Creek Police Dept.,
225, 226
Goose Creek Reservoir, 220
Goose Creek Road, 92
Goose Creek, S.C., origin of name, 1; settlement of, of, 10; population in 1709, 35; population in 1720, 21; population in 1790, 81; population in 18th century, 166; population in 1850, 81; population in 1860, 81; population in 1870, 81, 155; population in 1875, 155; population in 1880, 81; Indians of, 22; starvation at, 29,32,33; crops of, 32; livestock of, 32; diseases of, 35; 1715 evacuation of, 47; women of, 49,79; land of, 68,80; physicians of, 71; slave population in 1790, 74; roads of, 76; water system of, 224
Goose Creek Tavern, 84,177
Goslington Plantation, 105
Gouden, George, 18
Gough, John, 79
Gough, Richard, 79
Gourdin, George, 18
Gourdine, Pauline, 218
Gowder, Eloise, 222
Gowder, George, 222
Graham, Capt. James, 135
Grange, Col., 19
Grange, Hugh, 17
Grange, Capt. Jehu, 76
Grant, Calin McKay, 84
Grapes, 91
Gravely, Cowlan, 195
Gray, Peter, 135,144
Great Britain, arms of, 178,189
Greene, Gen. Nathaniel, 105,133-135
Greenview Acres subdivision, 3
Griffin, E.M., 239
Grimball, Paul, 53,58
Grooms family, 2
Groomsville Road, 2
Groomsville School, 170
Groomsville,S.C., 2,46
Grove Hall, 159,215,216,219
Grove Hall School, 219
Groves, Charles, 84
Guerard, Gov. Benjamin, 109
Guerin, Francis, 18,20
Guerin, Peter, 20
Guerry, Rev. Canon Edward B. 198
Guy, Rev. William, 184,186

- H -

Haggatt, William, 114
Hall, George Abbott, 106
Hall, Maris, 106
Hamilton, Tamil, 175
Hamilton, Dr. Tamil H., 73
Hampton, Col, 133
Hampton, Capt. Frank, 150
Hampton Social Mounted Club, 156
Hampton, Gen. Wade, 155,157
Hanahan,S.C., 8
Hargroves, James A Sr., 222
Harmon, Dennis, 241
Harris, Rev. James, 219
Harrison, Rev. James, 80, 85,169,170,187,188,193
Hart, Hamilton, 149
Hartley, Samuel, 15,97
Hasell, Rev., 184
Hasford, John, 20
Hasfort, Joseph, 168
Hastings, Charles, 46
Hatchell, Louis, 240
Hatchell, Marion W., 239
Hawkins, Humphrey, 19
Hayes Plantation, 15,16,83, 98,108,110,119,136,137, 139,174,245
Hayne, Robert Y., 98
Hayward, Rev., 218
Heitzler, Michael J., 236, 237,241
Henri, Pierre, 91
Herbert, John, 20,46
Herbert, Capt. John, 48
Herbert, Col. John, 17
Herbert, Philip, 17
Hernandez, Adam R., 240
Herne, John, 46
Herring, Mrs. Margaret, 228
Hesley, John, 248
Hext, Mary, 162
Hickory, 101
Himley, J.J., 97
Hinnant, Smith E., 226,227, 239,240
His Majesty's Horse Guards, 90
Hodges, Lois, 241
Holland, 16,17
Holland, Lonnie B., 224
Holleck, Gen., 154
Hollings, Sen. Ernest F., 231
Holly Court subdivision, 237
Holly Hill,S.C., 85,173
Holmes, Francis L., 194
Holmes, Francis S., 110
Holmes, Francis Simmons, 110
Holmes, Francis Williams, 193
Holmes, Frank, 116
Holmes, John Bee, 87
Holmes, Prof., 111
Home Medicine, 220
Honour, Mrs. Lee, 178
Hood, James L., 228
Hopkins, James, 246
Hopkins, James Albert, 246
Hopkins, Margaret M., 246
Hopson, Sheldon E., 239
Horne, Robert, 188
Horry, Col., 133
Horry, Elie, 18
Horry, Mrs., 84
Howe Hall Plantation, 16, 84,215,216,219
Howe Hall Road, 219
Howe Hall School, 219
Howe, Job, 16,56,57,60,84
Howe, Robert, 19
Hoyle, J.A., 223
Hoyle, Mrs. J.A., 223
Huger, Gen. Isaac, 133,135
Hughes, J.P., 175
Hughes, James P., 173
Huguenin, Maj., 156
Huguenot Church of Goose Creek, 19,108,181
Huguenot Soc. of S.C., 109, 181,198
Huguenots, (French Protestants), 13,17,18,21,29, 34,56; disenfranchised, 58,59,62,79,87,89,108, 175,179,180,181
Hulbert, Janice, 241

Hume, Mr., 67
Hume, Peter, 79
Hume, Robert, 71,169
Hurne, Peter, 17
Hurne, Dr. Peter, 73
Hurt, Phil, 241
Hurt, Philip E., 241
Hutson, Richard, 134
Hyrene, Edward, 19
Hyrne, Edward, 54
Hyrne, Capt. Edward, 76
Hyrne, Col. Edward, 205
Hyrne, Mary, 203-206
Hyrne, Dr. Peter, 73

- I -

Inabnit, John, 148
Inabnit, Joseph, 148
Indian Slaves & Slavery, 27,37; price of, 41,42, 49,52,55,56,60,61
Indian Town, 40
Indian Trade & Traders, 25, 28,29,34,40; abuses of, 43,44-46,57,58,60-63,71, 121,164
Indian Tribes: (see listings for the Appalachicola, Caree, Catawba, Cherokee, Choctaw, Congaree, Creek, Cusabo, Etiwan, Mohawk, Notchee, Santee, Sorrow, Sewee, Tuscarora, Wando, Wateree, Westo, Winyaw and Yemassee tribes.)
Indians, Crops of, 25; effects of disease on, 26; 1715 census of, 26; settlements of, 31; education and Christianization of, 35,78,164, 165; uprisings of, (see also Yemassee War), 36; tribute required of, 43, 160
Indigo, 34,68,70,74-76; bounty on, ended, 80,91; vats for making, 107, 113,130,141
Infinger, Carl, 229
Infinger, William, 240
Inglesby, William, 97
Inglesby's Plantation, 97
Ingelside Plantation, 111, 194
Inglish, Henroyda, 20,54,
Ireland, 17,173
Irish Rebellion of 1641, 54
Irving, Dr. John B., 85, 90
Ittiwan (Itawan) River, 6, 14,92
Izard family, 16,98; hatchment of, 179; Charleston residence of, 101
Izard, George, 99
Izard, Gen. George, 100
Izard, Henry, 98-100,168, 243
Izard, John, 131
Izard, Lt. John, 135
Izard, Mag. Elizabeth, 168
Izard, Martha, 168
Izard, Mary, 168
Izard, Ralph, 16,54,56,57, 59,60,62,74,83,98,99,101, 103,108,130,135,139,143, 144,178,182,242

Izard, Mrs. Ralph, 101
Izard, Ralph Jr., 105
Izard, Ralph Sr., 139

- J -

Jacksonboro Assembly, 138, 139
Jacksonboro, S.C., 134
Jacobs, Dr. Cecil, 233
Jamaica, West Indies, 15
Jaunzemiz, Uldis, 241
Jefferson, Mrs. Earlene, 219
Jefferson, Janie Mae Bryant, 218
Jefferson, Thomas, 99,140-142
Johnson, Charles, 137
Johnson, Dr., 103
Johnson, Joseph, 118
Johnson, Dr. Joseph, 71,91, 135,189
Johnson, Gov., 64
Johnson, Gov. (Sir) Nathaniel, 56,59,62,180,200
Johnson, Gov. Robert, 26, 65
Johnson, Shirley, 241
Johnson, William, 118,129, 134,139,210
Johnson, Lt. William, 135
Johnson, Wooford, 218
Joiner, Nelson, 175
Jones, Lewis, a Pee Dee Indian, 44
Jones, Rev. Lewis, 185
Jones, Dr. R.H., 148
June, John, 19
June, William, 46

- K -

Keating, Edward, 17,79
Keating, Maurice, 17,168
Keckley's Plantation, 120
Kidd, Captain, a pirate, 55
King, Robin, an Etiwan Indian, 20,47
Kinlock, James, 79,168
Kirk, Francis, 17
Kirkland, Moses, 127
Kittleby, Abel, 184
Kodoma, Tokyo, 222
Kodoma's Store, 22
Korean War, 223
Kyrle, Gov. Sir Richard, 56

- L -

Ladson, John, 59
Ladson, S.C., 9
Lafayette, General, 99
Lafayette Lodge, 99
Lamb, Peter, 17,19
Landgraves, extablished, 51; titles sold, 61
Langley, Miss M. Elise, 89
Langstaffe's Plantation, 97,119
Lansac, Lewis, 15,101
Lansac, Susanna, 168
Latham, Mrs., 203-205
Laurel, 113
Laurens, Henry, 131,132
Lawrence, John, 149
Lawrence, Nathaniel, 146
Lawrence, Capt. Nathaniel, 145

Lawson, James, 19
Lawson, Nancy, 241
LeBrasseur, Ann, 18
Lee, Arthur, 99
Lee family, 68
Lee, General, 135
Lee's Legion, 105,115,133
Legendre, Sidney Hennings, 88,89
Legendre, Mrs. Sidney Hennings, 89
LeJau, Lt. Col. Francis, 209
LeJau, Rev. Francis, 36, 38,40,44,45,47,63,78, 164,166,181-184,193,196
Lewis, Sedgwick, 169
Lewis, Solon, 241
The Liberator, abolitionist newspaper, 147
Liberty Hall Annex, 223
Liberty Hall Plantation, 84,88,215,219
Liberty Tree Men, 118
Lieber, Oscar, 5
Linder, C.B., 223
Linder, Mrs. C.B., 222,223
Linnaeus, a botanist, 103, 104
Liquor (see also rum), 56
"Little Miss Rebellion," a movie, 118
Live Oak Hill Plantation, 96,119
Lloyd, John, 67
Locke, John, 49,50,68,75
Lockwood, Eliza F., 94
Lockwood, Leize F.B., 6,94
Logan, William, 134,137, 141
Loocock, Aaron, 127,133, 143,144,249
Loocock, Mrs. Mary, 249
Lords Proprietors of Carolina, 13,14,30; land grant policies of, 31, 41,42,48-64; overthrow of, 65,70,86,87,119,128
Louis XIV, King of France, 17
Lousi, Mr., 90
Lowndes, Rawlins, 114,129
Lowndes, Ruth, 162
Loyalists (Tories), 105, 130,131,137-139
Lucas, Eliza, 113,130
Lucas, James, 17
Lucas, John, 191
Lucy, a Negro servant, 104
Ludlam Fund, 167,169,171, 188,194
Ludlam, Mrs., 185
Ludlam, Rev. Richard, 75, 167,170,185,188,193
Ludwell, Gov. Philip, 58, 59
Lynch, Mrs. Hannah, 197
Lynch, James, 169

- M -

M.S. Allison, a steamship, 156
Mack, Rev. C.J., 218
Mackdaniel, Daniel, 17
Mackenzie, J., 129
Mackenzie, John, 169
Mackey, Lt. Col. Alex, 64
Macky, Col., 46
Mahoney, Mr. L.C., 219
Mallard, Col. William, 136
Mallock Plantation, 16

Mallock, Robert, 94
Manigault, Mrs. Anne, 102
Manigault, Charles, 196
Manigault, Gabriel, 101, 139,144
Manigault, Peter, 83,101, 102,196
Mann, Malvin, 226-234,240, 241
Maple Ridge, 229
Marion, Benjamin, 17-20,98
Marion, Francis, 19,84
Marion, Capt. Francis, 132
Marion, Gen. Francis, 87, 111,134,136,137
Marion, James, 168
Marion, Job, 87
Marion, Samuel, 214
Marion, Theodore Samuel, 87
Marion's Oak, 111
Marrington Plantation, 84, 222
Marritt, Rev. Thomas, 185
Martin, Robert, 137
Martin, William Sr., 149
Martindale('s) Plantation, 15,83,119
Martini, Dr. John, 73
Mason, William, 162
Mathewes, Elizabeth, 97
Mathew(e)s, Maurice, 29, 40,41,50,54-48
Mathews, John, 134
Mathews, Lois, 106
May, John, 137
Mazyck, Alexander, 132
Mazyck, Benjamin, 54,74, 79,132,168,189,243
Mazyck family (Negro), 82
Mazyck, M. Ann, 246
Mazyck, Mary, 246
Mazyck, Mrs. Mary, 196, 246
Mazyck, Mr., 20
Mazyck, Paul, 18,168
Mazyck, Stephen, 246
Mazyck, Lt. Stephen, 136, 246
McAllsers, Rev. Mathew, 80
McBride, Margaret, 247
McCants, J.J., 148,149
McCants, Nathaniel, 144
McCants, Robert, 137
McCrady, Edward, 93
McCrady, John, 195
McKay, John, 17
McKelphin, James, 79
McKenzie, W.E., 223
McKenzie, Mrs. W.E., 223
McKewn, Archibald, 245
McKewn, Capt. J.C., 150
McKewn, Mrs. Mary, 245
McKinley, Faye, 240
McNair, Gov. Robert E.,232
McNaughton, Gail, 241
McWilliams, William, 149
Mead, Joseph, 20
Medina, Moses, 94
Medway Plantation, 16,86, 88,89,174,202,212
Mell, Thomas, 16,17,83
Mellard, Col. Thomas, 149
Mellard, Col. William, 145
Menriv Park, 3
Mereau, Moses, 19
Merry, Rev. Francis, 185
Michaer, William, 137
Michaux, Andre', 83,96, 100,101
Michaux, F. Andre', 96
Middle Temple, London, 184
Middleton, Arthur, 5,15,54,

Middleton, Arthur (cont'd) 58,102,103,106,107,112, 113,115,117,123,124,125, 182,184
Middleton, Capt. Arthur,19
Middleton, Commodore, 115
Middleton, Edward, 4,5,6, 15,16,17,94,102,103,116, 117
Middleton family (Negro), 82
Middleton, Henry, 115-117, 132,188
Middleton, Gov. Henry, 115
Middleton, Henry A., 115
Middleton, John, 115
Middleton, Mary, 95
Middleton, Lady Mary, 116
Middleton, Mrs. Mary, 103
Middleton, S., 168
Middleton, Sarah, 116
Middleton, Susannah, 110 245
Middleton, Thomas, 79,114 116,117,132,139,168,243
Middleton, William, 79 113-115,168,178,187,243
Middleton Place, 111,113, 116
Mikell, Rev. Henry J., 193
Mill, Thomas, 119
Millechampe, Rev. Timothy, 85,168,186,193,243
Miller, Mr. C., 191
Mill's Plantation, 119
Mims, C., 148
Mims, Coswell, 145
Mims, Thomas, 149,175
Mims, Capt. Thomas, 148
Minus, Richard, 148
Missionairies (see also Society for the Propagation of the Gospel in Foreign Parts), 18,23, 35,45,77
Mitchell, Capt. James, 136
Mixon, B.W., 223
Mixon, Mrs. B.W., 223
Mohawk Indians, 45
Monck, Stephen, 19
Monck, Thomas, 76
Moncks Corner Road, 91, 136
Moncks Corner, S.C., 85, 133,172,222
Montague Plantation, 222
Moore, Col., 15
Moore, Gov., 62
Moore, James, 54-56,60,62, 91,92,185
Moore, Capt. James, 16, 182
Moore, Col. James, 19,58, 59,62,64,112,185
Moore, Gov. James, 54
Moore, James, II, 65
Moore, John, 46,120
Moore, Lady, 78
Moore, Lt. Gen., 165
Moore, Maurice, 46
Moore, Madam Maurice, 19
Moore, Roger, 54
Moore, Capt. Roger, 76
Moore, Thomas, 16
Morgan, Henry, a pirate, 55
Morning Star Grocery, 222
Morris, George, 137
Morris, Jane, 168
Morris, Mr., 70
Morton, John, 79,168
Morton, Gov. Joseph 52,54, 56

Mottet, Dr. Lewis, 71,72, 103
Moultrie, Alexander, 97
Moultrie family, 83,97
Moultrie, James, 97
Moultrie, John, 97,103
Moultrie, Dr. John, 97,103, 197
Moultrie, John Jr., 169
Moultrie, Capt. Thomas, 97
Moultrie, William, 139,197, 198,248
Moultrie, Gen. William, 97, 132
Moultrie, William Jr., 198
Moultrie, William Ainslie, 248
Mt. Holly Clay Products Co., 220
Mt. Holly 4-H Club, 223
Mt. Holly Home Demonstration Club, 223
Mt. Holly Plantation, 3, 216,222
Mt. Holly Post Office, 222
Mt. Holly,S.C., 3,157,159, 215,218-220,222
Mount Parnassus Plantation, 90
Mt. Pleasant Mounted Club, 156
Mt. Pleasant Plantation, 84
Mt. Pleasant, S.C., 158
Mountain to the Sea Highway, 85
Mulberry Castle, 200
Mulberry Plantation, 112
Muller, Rev., 153
Murele, William, 15
Murray, H.H., 157
Murray, Isaac, 148
Murrell, William, 119
Muskhogean Language, 5
Myddagh, Anna Cornelie, 94

- N -

Nairne, Thomas, 46,163
Nathan, Mordica, 19
Navigation Acts, 12,128,129
Negro Churches, importance of, 216
Neis, E.Q.Jr., 239
Neis, Edgar, 224
New England Historical Society, 195
New York Tribune, 154
Newberry College, 153
Newe, John, 54
Newe, Capt. John, 20
Newe, Thomas, 31
Nichole, Henry, 175
Nicholson, Gov., 123
Nix, Mr., 223
Norman, Joseph, 168
Norman, William, 19
North Charleston,S.C., 8
Notchee Indians, 45
Nullification, Ordinance of, 146,147

- O -

Oakley,S.C., 2
Oaks Plantation, 17,68,84, 95,102,103,113,116,117, 222
Occupations mentioned: blacksmith, 19,20,68,81, 175; brickmaker, 81;

Occupations, (cont'd):
bricklayer, 68; butcher, 86; cabinetmaker, 97; capitalist, 175; cattle-driver, 152; carpenter, 20,68; coach maker, 81, 175; coal burner, 81; cooper, 19; hog drover, 152; laborer, 175; mariner, 97; mechanic, 175; midwife, 81,175; overseer, 19,81,1852; phosphate laborer, 176; physician, 33,34; pump mender, 81,175; railroad worker, 176; shoemaker, 68; slave trader, 54; surveyor, 81,175; tailor, 68; tanner, 68; toll-gate keeper, 81,175; watchmaker, 81,175; weaver, 19; wheelwright, 19,68,81,175; woodcutter, 81,175
Ogilby, James, 19
Oglethorpe, Gen., 209
Old Goose Creek Plantation, (See Yeamans Hall)
Old Monck's Corner Road, 217,128
Old Town Settlement, 22
Olive Oil, 17
Orangeburg Hunting Club, 84
Orvin, Maxwell Clayton, 135
Otranto Club, 106
Otranto Plantation, 5,15, 16,73,83,91,98,103,105, 106,107,109,135,177,178
Owen, John, 19

- P -

Palmettos Plantation, 83
Parishes, established 1706, 63; functions of, 122
Parker burial ground, 111, 245
Parker, Dr., 193
Parker family, 15,110
Parker, Dr. Francis LeJau, 193,194
Parker, George, 108
Parker, Henry Middleton, 245
Parker, Jr., 129
Parker, John, 15,20,76,83, 108,110,111,131,133,136, 137,144,169,174,188,245
Parker, Sarah, 110
Parker, Thomas, 144
Parker, William, 108,137, 139
Parker's Plantation, 108, 181
Parnassus Plantation, 3, 84,85,88,90,214
Parsons, Edward, 116
Parsons, Edwin, 117,193, 194
Parsons, Mrs. Loretta, 218
Pasquereau, Lovis, 20
Pepper Hill subdivision, 197
Pendarris, Joseph, 59
Pennington, Jane, 247
Percival, Andrew, 41
Peronneau, Isaac, 18
Peronneau, Elizabeth, 105
Perryman, William, 15,119
Petigru, James L., 106
Phillips, Rev. L., 192

Philps, Paulina, 210,211
Phosphate mining, 110,220
Pifer, Prof. Gus P., 153
Pight, John, 20
Pimlico S.C., 8
Pinckney, Col. Charles C., 131
Pine Grove Plantation, 88
Pineview Terrace subdivision, 3
Pineville,S.C., 81
Pink Root, 104
Pinopolis Academy, 172
Pinopolis,S.C., 81
Pirates and Pirate Trade, 49,54,55,56,58,60,63,64
Planters, Summer homes of, 81
Plat, John, 148
Pocotaglio,S.C., 46,64
Pogson, Rev. Milward, 79, 105,106,190,193
Pollock, Sir Henry, 115
Pompion Chapel, 3
Poor, overseers of, 116
Poor, Thomas, 240
Poor, Thomas G., 229,241
Poole, Mr., 20
Poppenheim, John F., 84
Porcher, Anna Maria, 88
Porcher, Isaac, 168
Porcher, Dr. Isaac, 18,19, 34
Porcher, Jane, 87
Porcher, Marion, 106
Porcher, Peter, 168
Porcher, Philip, 105
Porcher, Rachel, 169
Porter Academy, Charleston, 172
Portugal, 165
Postell, John, 18
Potatoes, 99
Potter, Gen. R.B., 106
Poutales, Count, 110
Powis, John, 59
Poyas, Dr., 73
Poyas, Mrs. E.A., 86,93, 197,199
Poyas, Mrs. Elizabeth, 6
Poyas, Mrs., 92
Price, William, 133
Prince, a free Indian, 44
Prince, Dr. George, 106
Pringle, Robert S., 158
Prioleau, Rev. Elias, 89
Prioleau family, 89
Prioleau, Samuel, 89
Prudhomme, Ant(h)oine, (Anthony), 7,17,18,181
Purcell, Joseph, 98,181
Pyatt, Rev., 218

- Q -

Quary, Gov. Robert, 56
Quit-rents, 53,55,57,60

- R -

Race horses & racing, 71, 88,106
Radical Republicans, 156
Ramsey, Allen, 102
Randolph family, 68
Rattone, John, 19
Ravenel, Capt., 136
Ravenel, Mrs. St. Julien, 6,67
Rawlins, Edward, 120
Read, Motte Alston, 79

Ready, Mr. R.E., 219
Realy, Bryan, 19
Reardon's Tavern, 85
Reardon's Twenty-five mile House, 85
Reconstruction, 156,157, 160
Red Bank, 92,136
Red Bank Landing, 84
Red Bank Plantation, 84, 118
Red Bank Road, 84
Red Shirts, 157
Redheimer, John, 249
Redheimer, Peter, 249
Redwood, John, 19
Regulators, 126-129
Republican Party, 156,158
Rhame, B., 151
Rhame, Dr. O.C., 73,157, 158
Rhett, William, 64
Rhoad, Mr. D.T., 223
Rice, 34,40,60,68,69,74-76,99,104,108,111,113, 120,130,141
Richards, James M., 241
Richardson, Smith, 222
Richmond ship, 13,17
Riddock, Bartley J., 234
Riggs, William, 148
River Club, 79
Rivers, L. Mendel, 3
Roberts, John, 19
Rochefoucault-Liancourt, Duke de la, 99
Rochford, James, 17
Rogers, Dr. George C. 121
Rose, Thomas, 35
Roupel, George, 102
Royal Government, established, 65
Royal Society of London, 104
Rum, addiction to, 12,43
Ruonala, Richard, 241
Rutledge, Edward, 139
Rutledge, Emily S., 245
Rutledge, Gov., 233,134
Rutledge, John, 114,129,132

- S -

Sabin, Charles, 117
Sage, Ann, 162
St. Augustine, Florida, 118
St. George's Church, Dorchester, 84
St. James' Academy, 171, 174
St. James' Episcopal Church, Goose Creek, vestry school of, 2,10,35-37, 63,75,79,84,163,166,168, 170; Chapel of Ease, Wassamassaw, 85,199,90, 111,114,130,134,143,159; vestry incorporated, 170; commissioners of, 182; repairs of, 191; consecration of, 192,226; tombstone inscriptions of, 245-248
St. James Parish, Goose Creek, boundaries of, 7, 65,67; representation of, 122,123,126; school commissioners of, 172; parish established, 181; 1707 population of, 182; 1741 population of, 186; 1758 population of, 187; schools of, 191

St. John, Dr. Stephen, 73
St. Julien, Elizabeth de, 197
St. Julien, Peter, 20,54
St. Luke's Episcopal Church, Charleston, 193
St. Michael's Episcopal Church, Charleston, 90
St. Paul's Cathedral, London, 181
St. Paul's Episcopal Church, Stono, 192
St. Paul's Episcopal Church, Summerville, 192
St. Stephen's Episcopal Church, Charleston, 192
Salley, Alexander S. Jr., 14,67
Salley, Elizabeth, 218
Salter, Mrs., 162
Sampson, a runaway slave, 67
Sanders, John, 15,17,182
Sanders, Capt. John, 98
Sanders, William, 109
Sanders, Wilson, 17
Santee Canal, 142
Santee Canal Company, 142
Santee Indians, 48
Santee Settlement, 34
Sanute, Indian chief, 46
Sarraw Indians, 47
Saso, Frank Sr., 218
Saunders, Capt. James, 20
Saunders, John, 20
Sayle, Gov., 50
Scarborough, Mrs., 223
Schencking(h), Benjamin, 19,54,76,182,185
Schools (see also St. James' Vestry School, Wassamassaw), 166
Scotland, 98
Scott, William, 46
Secession, 149
Secession Convention, 150
Secession, Ordinance of, 150
Second S.C. Regiment, C.S.A., 150
Sedgefield, 3
Seed, Polly, 214
Seigniories, established, 51
Senkler, Elizabeth, 197
Senkler, William, 197
Sequestered estates, 139
Sewee Indians, 4,22,24-28, 40,42,44
Shadow, a race horse, 71
Share-cropping, 155
Shay's Rebellion, 143
Shepard, ____, 20
Sherman, Gen., 154
Shingler, John N., 150
Shingler, S., 145
Shingleton, Richard, 79
Shipley, William, 104
Shiver, Lagette, 241
Shringler, G.W., 138
Shuler, John, 145
Silk, 17,68,70
Silk Hope Plantation, 180
Simma, William Gilmore, 118
Sims, Rev. A.G., 149
Sineath, Lloyd (E), 231
Singleberry, Richard, 19
Singleton, Benjamin, 169
Singleton, Capt. Benjamin, 136
Singleton, Col. Benjamin, 131

Singleton, Col., 71
Singleton family (Negro), 82
Singleton, James, 168
Singleton, Rebecca, 169
Singleton, Richard, 17, 168,243
Singleton, Lt. Richard, 136
Singleton, Thomas, 169
Siouen language, 5
Siri, Andrew, 162
Six Mile House, 155
Skene, Alexander, 125
Slave Traders, 54
Slaves, introduced, 13; education of, 20,35,163, 165,182,185; Slave Code, 39,75; torture of, 38-39; uprisings of, 37-39; polygamy among, 40; price of, 41,69,76-79; emancipation of, 82; 1722 population of, 124
Smith, Amarinthia, 95
Smith, Benjamin, 131,133, 139,144,169,205
Smith, Capt. Benjamin, 132, 197,209
Smith, Maj. Benjamin, 136
Smith, Bishop, 190
Smith, Elizabeth Ann, 197, 209
Smith, G., 148
Smith, G.C., 149
Smith, G.H., 147
Smith, George, 175
Smith, Dr. George, 73,93
Smith, George C., 149
Smith, George Henry, 6,93
Smith, Henry, 93,132,169
Smith, Mrs. Henry, 204
Smith, Henry A.M., 4-6, 85,93,95,100,108,109, 111,175,182,193,199
Smith, Henry Middleton, 95
Smith, J., 148
Smith, James, 144
Smith, Lt. James, 136
Smith, Jane, 20
Smith, John, 5,41
Smith, Mary, 5,197,209
Smith, Mrs., 138
Smith, Peter, 95,133,139, 144
Smith, Rebecca, 247
Smith, Mrs. Sabina, 87,89
Smith, T.H., 158
Smith, T. Henry, 158
Smith, Thomas, 19,46,76, 86,92,93,95,124
Smith, Col. Thomas, 87
Smith, (Gov.) Landgrave Thomas, 16,19,20,51,54, 60,87,89,93,94,124,125, 131,169,170,205,213
Smith, Thomas Jr., 54
Smith, Thomas Sr., 132
Smith, Thomas Henry, 93
Smith, William, 144
Smithfield tract, 88
Snow, Jacob, 19
Snow, James, 19
Snow, Nathaniel, 17
Snow, Dr. Nathaniel, 19,34
Society for the Propagation of the Gospel in Foreign Parts (S.P.G.) (See also Anglican Church, missionaries), 35,37,62, 75,77,80,162-170,175,178- 183,185-187,193,243
Sona, Oliver, 239,240
Sons of Liberty, 129

Sothel, Gov. Seth, 58
South Carolina Railway, 120
Southeastern Water Corp., 234
Southern Railway, 19
Spain, threat of invasion by, 29,55
Spring Grove, 120
Stamp Act, 129,131
Stanyarne, James, 56
State Road, 84,152
Steepbrook Plantation, 83, 101,102,196
Stephenson, R., 148
Stevens, Lamb, a free Negro, 108
Stevens, Mrs. Mary S., 90
Stevens, Norman Jr., 90
Stevens, Robert, 19,60,62, 182
Stevens, Rev. Robert, 163
Stevens Plantation, 16
Stevenson, Capt. James, 136,139
Stewart, John, 54
Stitt, Elizabeth, 247
Stitt, William, 247
Stock Law of 1881, 158
Stone fleet, 151
Stone, John, 20,76
Stone Landing,S.C., 71
Stone, Rev. Robert, 33,80, 142,186,193
Stoney, Arthur Jervey, 88
Stoney, Dwight, 193
Stoney, Isaac Dwight, 194
Stoney, Lt. Isaac Dwight, 88
Stoney, Louisa Cheves, 88
Stoney, P.G., 86
Stoney, Peter Gailliard, 88,90
Stoney, S. Porcher, 193
Stoney, Samuel G., 244
Stoney, Samuel Gaillard, 107,193
Stoney, T.S., 112
Stoney, Thomas Porcher, 88
Stoney, Capt. William Edmund, 88
Stowe, Harriet Beecher, Uncle Tom's Cabin, 149
Strawberry Democratic Club, 157
Strawberry Ferry, 154,199
Strawberry Landing, 156, 157
Strawberry Plantation, 2
Strawberry Station, 2
Streator, James, 132
Streator's Plantation, 119
Strohecker, J.L., 146
Sugar, planted on Barbados, 11; imported, 32,56,158
Sugar Act, 129
Sullivan's Island S.C., 132,198
Sully, Elizabeth, 95
Summerville,S.C., 7,12, 148,152,153,157,159,222
Sumter, Gen., 133,134
Swint, Dr. John Hendrick, 73

- T -

Tamplet, Peter, 169
Tares' estate, 85
Targate S.C., 173
Target S.C., 173
Tarhill,S.C., 173

Tariff of 1828 ("Tariff of Abominations"), 144,145
Tarkiln S.C., 173
Tarleton, Lt. Col. Banastre, 133
Tartar, a racehorse, 71
Taylor, Amerentia, 242
Taylor, Rev. J.W., 192
Raylor, Joseph, 242
Taylor, Peter, 17,79,129, 168,169,170,178,242,243
Taylor, Capt. Peter, 95
Taylor, Lt. Peter, 136
Taylor, Mrs., 231
Ten Mile House Tavern, 83
Tennent, Dr. Charles, 90
Tennent, Mrs., 90
30th Infantry Division, WWI, 88
Tile, manufactured, 84
Thomas, Col. John P., 193
Thomas, Rev. Samuel, 33, 37,79,163,179,180,185
Thomas, W.B., 149
Thomasen, Anne, 222
Thomason, Boulevard, 222
Thomason, Orven, 222
Thomason's Store, 222
Thomson, Rev. John, 193
Thorin, Capt. George M., 156
Thornley, Maj. Robert, 136
Thoroughgood Plantation, 16,91,118,136,137
Tobacco, 11,68
Tookerman, Richard, 168
Tories: see Loyalists
Townsend, Mrs. Hepzibah, 79
Townshend Act, 129
The Treasure of Pierre Gaillard, a novel, 212
Trinity College, Dublin, 184
Trouillort, Philip, 18
Turkish Spy, a novel, 204
Turner, Frederick Jackson, 30
Turner, Hattie, 226
Turner, Hattie V., 239
Turner, L.C., 239
Turner, Weyman, 239
Tuscarora Indians, 15
Tustian, Rev., 184
Twenty-three Mile House, 79
Tyner, R. Harold, 233

- U -

Union & States Rights Party, 146
Union College, Schenectady, N.Y., 172
Union Party, 147
U.S. Marine Barracks, 224
U.S. Military Academy, West Point, 115,120
U.S. Naval Academy, 118
U.S. Naval Guided Missile Service Unit, 213,224
U.S. Naval Weapons Annex, 222
U.S. Naval Weapons Station, 84,222,225,237
U.S. Navy, 151
U.S. Navy, Polaris Fleet Ballistic Missile Weapons System, 224
U.S. Navy, Polaris Missile Facility, 237

- V -

Van Arrsens, Jan, 16, 213
Vance, Maj. William, 137
Vanderdussen, Col. Alexander, 209
Vanderdussen, Mrs., 118
Vanderdussen's estate, 118
Van Kleek, Loring E., 229
Varner, Dr. I.B., 73
Varner, J., 148
Varner School, 219
Varnod, the widow, 162
Villeponteau, _____, 19
Villeponteaux Branch, 3
Villeponteaux, Zachariah, 3,18,79,90,168,214,243
Von Aarsens, Franciscus,86
Vose, Capt. Carston William, 152
Voters, qualifications of, 122

- W -

Wade family, 222
Wagner, Capt. 151
Walker, Clancy, 239
Walker, Richard, 67
Wallace, Rev. C., 171
Walling, Don, 233
Walpole, Horace, 106
Walter, Elizabeth, 114
Walter, Thomas, 132
Walter, William, 113
Wando Indians, 4,6
Wando River, 12,22
Wapensaw, an Indian term, 16
Waring, Benjamin, 56
Waring, Maj. Benjamin, 59
Waring, Dr. Joseph, Ioor, 2,100,106,177,193,194
Waring, Samuel Gaillard, 194
Waring, Thomas R., 106
Warner, Samuel, 45
Warnock, Capt. S.C., 149
Washington, President George, 134,141,143
Wassamassaw Baptist Church, 80
Wassamassaw Cavalry, 150, 151
Wassamassaw Causeway, 85
Wassamassaw Chapel of Ease, St. James' Church, 85, 145,149,171
Wassamassaw Mounted Club, 156
Wassamassaw Road, 85,133
Wassamassaw School, 170
Wassamassaw, S.C., 48,85, 122,136,137,173
Wassamassaw Swamp, 3,85, 170
Wateree Indians, 47
Waterland, William, 171
Watkins, Mrs. Hilma, 222
Watson, Dr. John, 73
Watson, Livinia, 119
Webb, Edward, 19
Webster, Daniel, 98
Webster, David, 19
Webster, Lt. Col. 133
Weekly, Edward, 20
West, Gov. Joseph, 12,41, 50-52,56,119
West Virginia Development Company, 115
Westfield, Capt. 150
Westo Indian War, 42
Westo Indians, 27

Weston, William, 19
Whaley, William, 149
Whatley, C.W., 233
White House Plantation, 92, 118,136
White, William, 20
Whitesville S.C., 170
Whitney, Eli, 142
Wiggins, Dr. J.B., 158
Wiggins, Dr. T., 158
Wiggins, T.W., 258
Wigton Plantation, 98
William, King of England, 102
Williams, Capt. 150
Williams, Jane, 162
Williams, Dr. John, 145
Williams, Rev. Stephen, 149
Williams, W., 148
Williams, West, 145
Williams, Rev. West, 149
Williams, William, 182
Williamson, Rev. Atkin, 36
Willoughby, Mrs., 19
Wilson, Dr. J., 148
Wilson, John, 101,149
Wilson, Marion, 228
Wilson, Moses, 17,101
Wilson, Rev. Robert, 7,193
Wilson's estate, 85
Windsor Hill Plantation, 83, 139,197,198
Wine, 17,32
Winlock, James, 19
Winter, Capt. Hugh Strain, 137
Winter, T.H., 150
Winyah Indian War, 42
Wither, William, 84
Withers, Mrs. Francis, 247
Withers, James, 17
Withers, John, 133
Withers, John Sr., 247
Withers, Richard, 139
Withers, Capt. Richard, 137
Withers, W., 169
Wolf's Castle Plantation, 120
Wood, Ben, 20
Wood, Robert, 96
Wood, William, 17,169
Woode, M.E., 175
Woodlawn Heights subdivision, 237
Woods, E. Calvin, 241
Woods, Vivian A., 240
Woodstock Plantation, 16, 83,98,108,119,120
Woorams, John, 46
Worley, Richard, a pirate, 55
Wragg, Henrietta, 190
Wren, W.R., 240
Wright, E.G., 240
Wright, John, 20,46,131
Wright, Capt. John, 137
Wright, T., 129
Wright, Thomas, 79

- Y -

Yeaman's Creek, 5,6,14,15, 18,92,102
Yeamans Hall Plantation, 6,46,77,83,92,93,96,118, 119,125,174,199,202
Yeamans, Sir John, 6,14,15, 50,54,92
Yeamans, Lady Margaret, 6, 14,92
Yemassee Indian War, 15,40, 44-48,63,64,165,184
Yemessee Indians, 35,46,68, 179
"Yeowee," Indian term, 6
Yeshoe Plantation, 5,15, 102,105
Yon, Oliver, 227,239,240